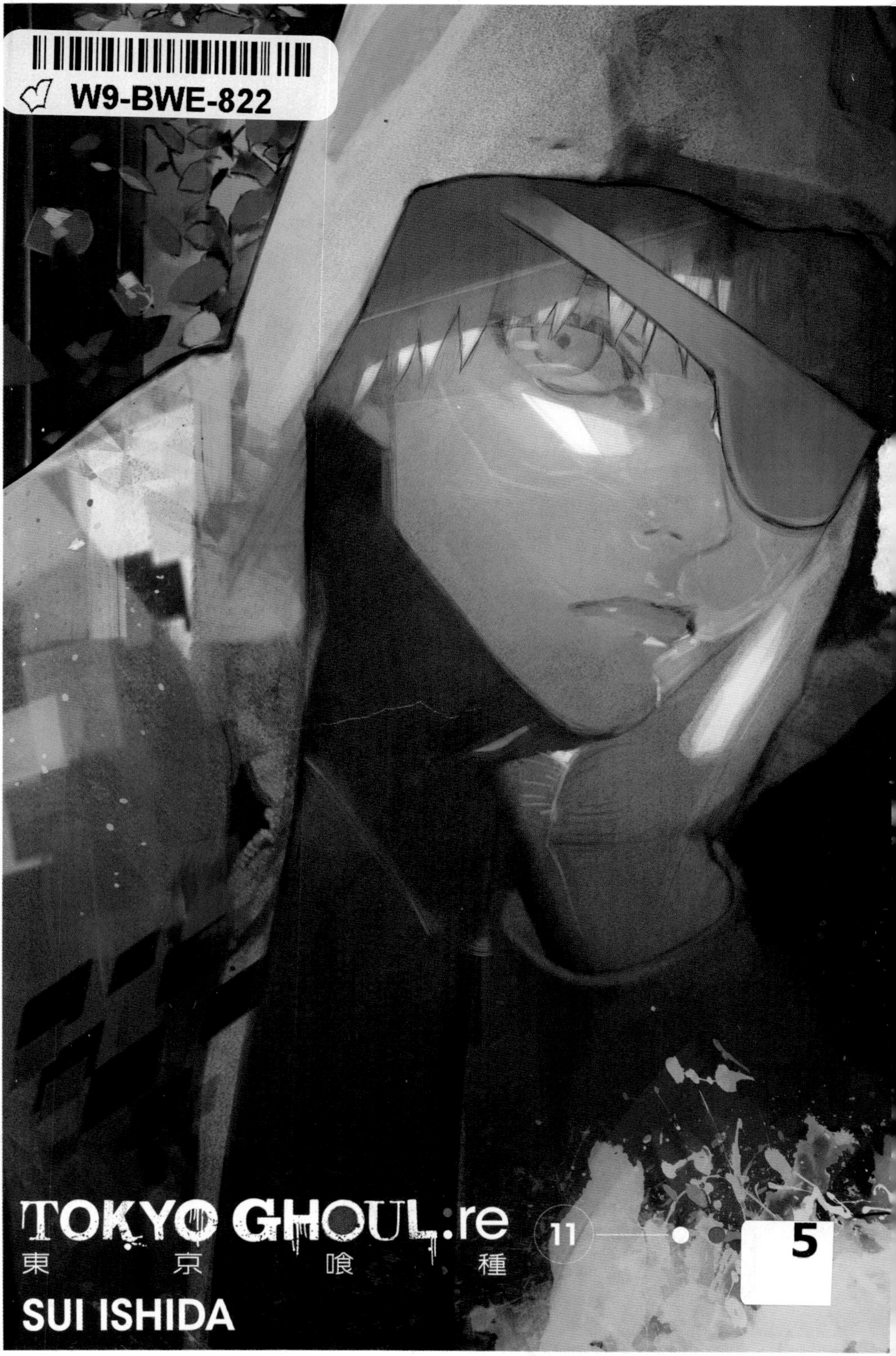

TOKYO GHOUL:re

11

東京喰種

SUI ISHIDA

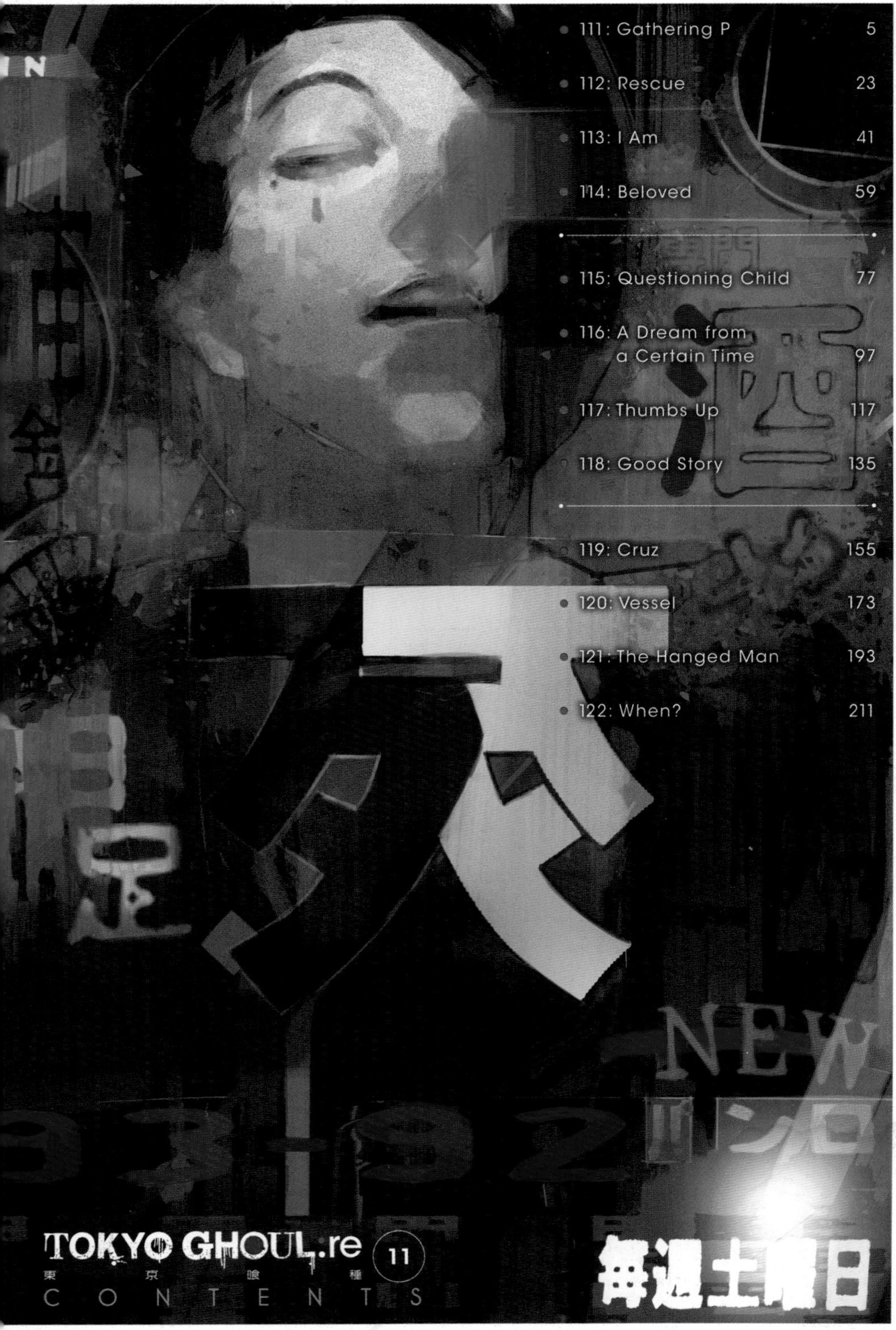
NEW

TOKYO GHOUL:re 11
東京喰種

CONTENTS

CCG Ghoul Investigators / Tokyo Ghoul : re

The CCG is the only organization in the world that investigates and solves Ghoul-related crimes. Founded by the Washu Family, the CCG developed and evolved Quinques, a type of weapon derived from Ghouls' Kagune. Quinx, an advanced, next-generation technology where humans are implanted with Quinques, is currently under development.

Mado Squad

Qs (Quinx)

- Investigators implanted with Quinques.
- They all live together in a house called the Chateau.

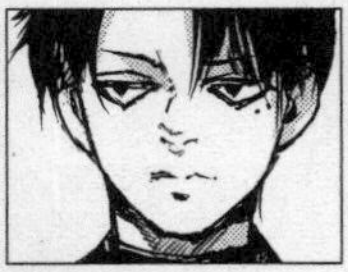

Kuki Urie
瓜江久生
Rank 1 Investigator
New Quinx Squad leader and most talented fighter in the squad. Demonstrating leadership after the death of Shirazu.

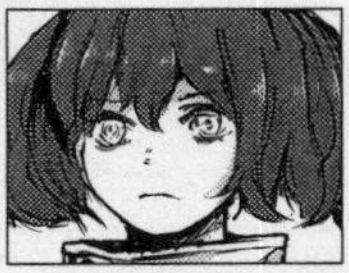

Saiko Yonebayashi
米林才子
Rank 2 Investigator
Supporting Urie as deputy squad leader while playing with her subordinates. Very bad at time management and a sucker for games and snacks.

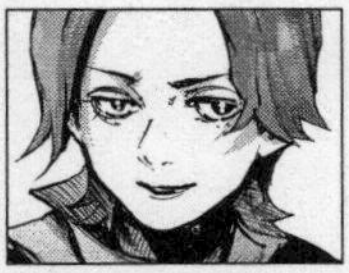

Toma Higemaru
米林才子
Rank 3 Investigator
Discovered his Quinx aptitude before enrolling in the academy. Looks up to Urie. Comes from a wealthy family.

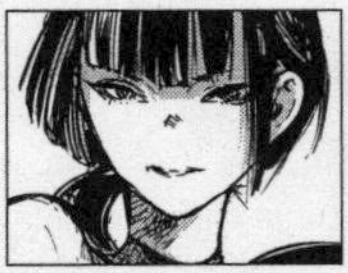

Ching-li Hsiao
小静麗
Rank 1 Investigator
From Hakubi Garden like Hairu Ihei. Skilled in hand-to-hand combat. Came to Japan from Taiwan as a child.

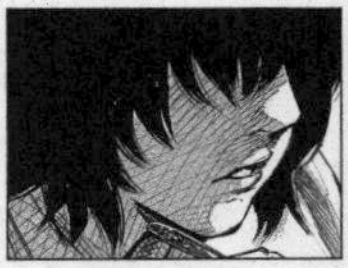

Shinsanpei Aura
安浦晋三平
Rank 2 Investigator
Nephew of Special Investigator Kiyoko Aura. Unlike his aunt, his grades were not that great.

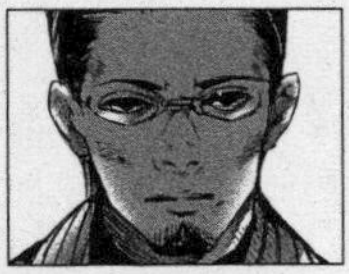

Matsuri Washu
和修 政
Special Investigator
Yoshitoki's son. A Washu Supremacist. Is skeptical of Quinxes. The only surviving member of the Washu family after the Rushima Operation.

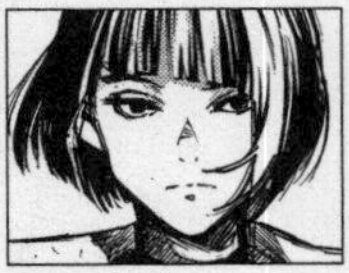

Kori Ui
宇井 郡
Special Investigator
Promising investigator formerly with Arima Squad. Became a speciali Investigator at a young age, but has a stubborn side.

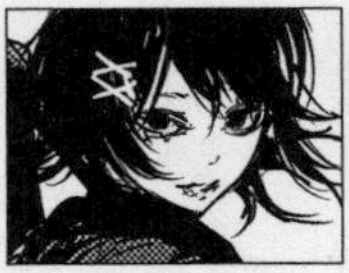

Juzo Suzuya
鈴屋什造
Special Investigator
Promoted to special investigator at 22, a feat previously only accomplished by Kisho Arima. A maverick who fights with knives hidden in his prosthetic leg.

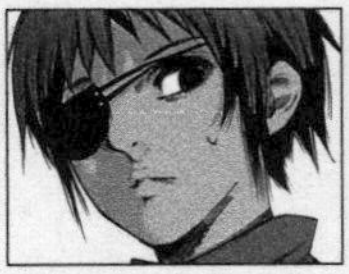

Toru Mutsuki
鈴屋什造
Rank 1 Investigator
Assigned female at birth, he transitioned after the Quinx procedure. Struggling with the lie he has been living with...

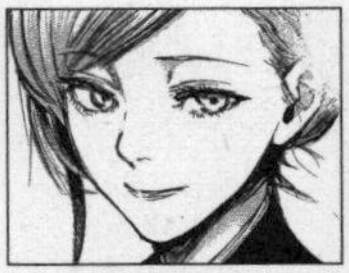

Akira Mado
真戸 暁
Assistant Special Investigator
Mentor to Haise. Wounded while aiding a Ghoul during the Rushima Operation. Currently in treatment.

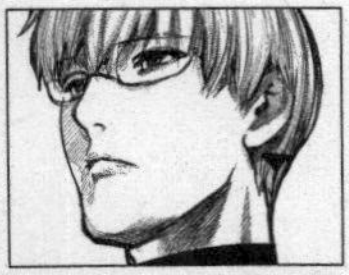

Kisho Arima
有馬貴将
Special Investigator
An undefeated investigator respected by many at the CCG. Killed at Cochlea by the One-Eyed King.

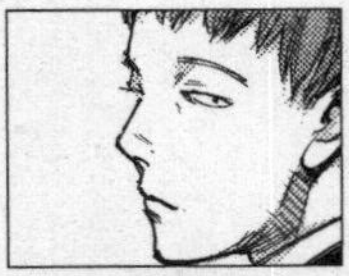

Take Hirako
平子 丈
Former Senior Investigator
Kisho Arima's former partner. Took over Squad Zero at Arima's request and aided the One-Eyed King's escape before leaving the CCG.

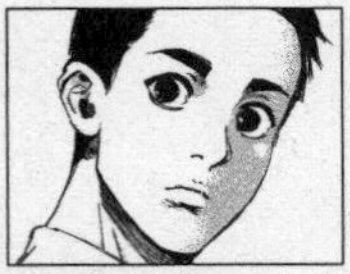

Takeomi Kuroiwa
黒磐武臣
Rank 1 Investigator
Son of Special Investigator Iwao Kuroiwa. Has a strong sense of justice and has restrained Ghouls with his bare hands.

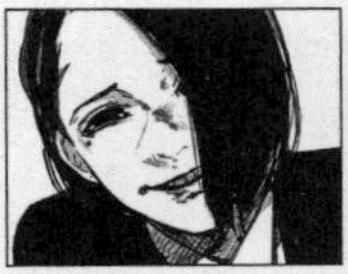

Nimura Furuta
旧多二福
Rank 1 Investigator
Former subordinate of the late Shiki Kijima. Has many secrets.

Special Operations:V Investigators

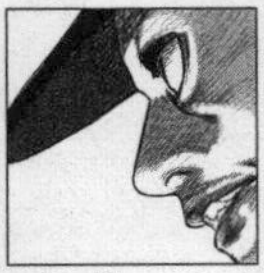

Kaiko
芥子
Mysterious armed group that appears when the CCG needs help. Covert Washu aides.

Tokyo Ghoul :re • Ghouls

They appear human, but have a unique predation organ called Kagune and can only survive by feeding on human flesh. They are the nemesis of humanity. Besides human flesh, the only other thing they can ingest is coffee. Ghouls can only be wounded by a Kagune or a Quinque made from a Kagune.

Goat

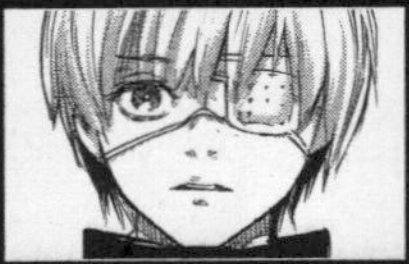

Ken Kaneki
金木 研

Served as the Qs Squad mentor as Haise Sasaki. A half-Ghoul who has succeeded Kisho Arima as the One-Eyed King. Living at Café:re and leading the anti-human group the Goat.

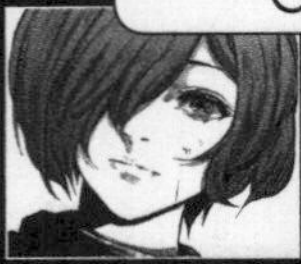

Touka Kirishima
霧嶋董香

Manager of Café:re. Wants to carry on the traditions of Anteiku.

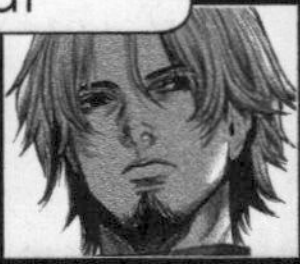

Renji Yomo
四方蓮示

:re barista. Touka and Ayato's uncle.

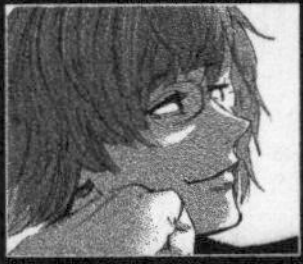

Nishiki Nishio
西尾 錦

The Ghoul known as Orochi. Tracking the Aogiri Tree.

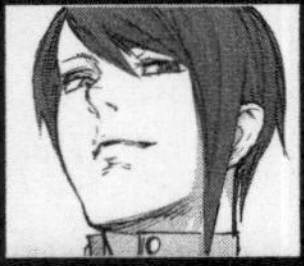

Shu Tsukiyama
月山 習

A gourmet Ghoul. Continues to pursue Ken Kaneki after the dissolution of his family's conglomerate.

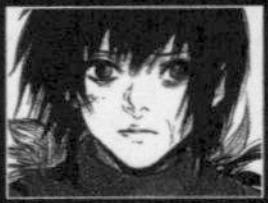

Ayato
アヤト

Touka's younger brother. A Rate SS Ghoul known as the Rabbit.

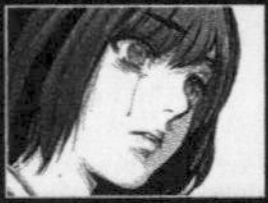

Hinami Fueguchi
フエグチ
ヒナミ

Freed from Cochlea by Kaneki.

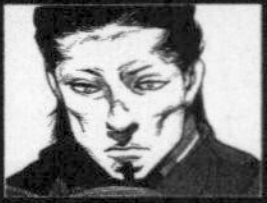

Banjo
バンジョー

Ayato's lieutenant. Treating Akira's wounds.

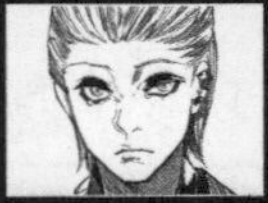

Naki
ナキ

Current leader of the White Suits. A Rate S, but frequently loses control.

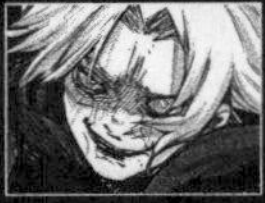

The Owl
オウル

Investigator Seido Takizawa's current form after Kano implanted him with a Kakuho. Overwhelmingly powerful.

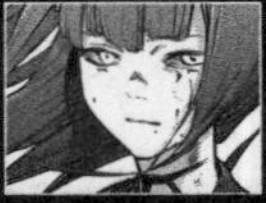

Kuro
クロ

Like Ken Kaneki, she underwent Kano's Ghoulification procedure. Absorbed her twin sister Shirona.

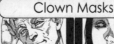

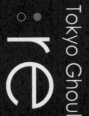

Tokyo Ghoul :re

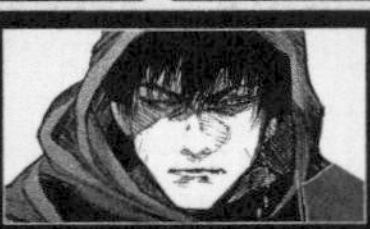

Kotaro Amon
亜門鋼太朗

Ex-CCG investigator. Failed subject of Kano's Ghoulification Procedure. Known as Floppy. A righteous glint still gleams in his eyes.

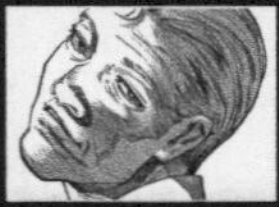

Akihiro Kano
嘉納明博

Medical examiner for the Aogiri Tree. Researching transplanting Kakuho into humans to create artificial half-Ghouls.

Clown Masks

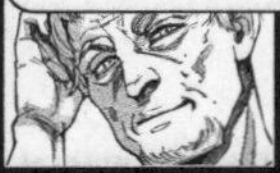

Donato Porpora
ドナート・
ポルポラ

Preyed on children as the priest of an orphanage. Kotaro Amon's adoptive father.

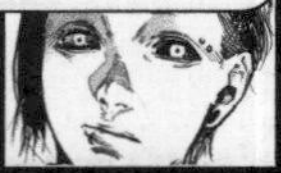

Uta
ウタ

Owner of HySy Artmask Studio. Made Kaneki and the Qs' masks.

So far in :re

The high-casualty Rushima Operation ends with Nimura Furuta wiping out the Washu family. Peace and quiet returns with the dissolution of the Aogiri Tree, but the CCG has begun to quietly collapse, revealing its dark secrets. Meanwhile, Ken Kaneki, who has regained his memory and succeeded Kisho Arima as the One-Eyed King, takes shelter at Café:re and forms the anti-human organization the Goat. Their goal is to create a world where humans and Ghouls can coexist, but then a group claiming to be led by the One-Eyed King begins to attack CCG offices...

Gathering P :111

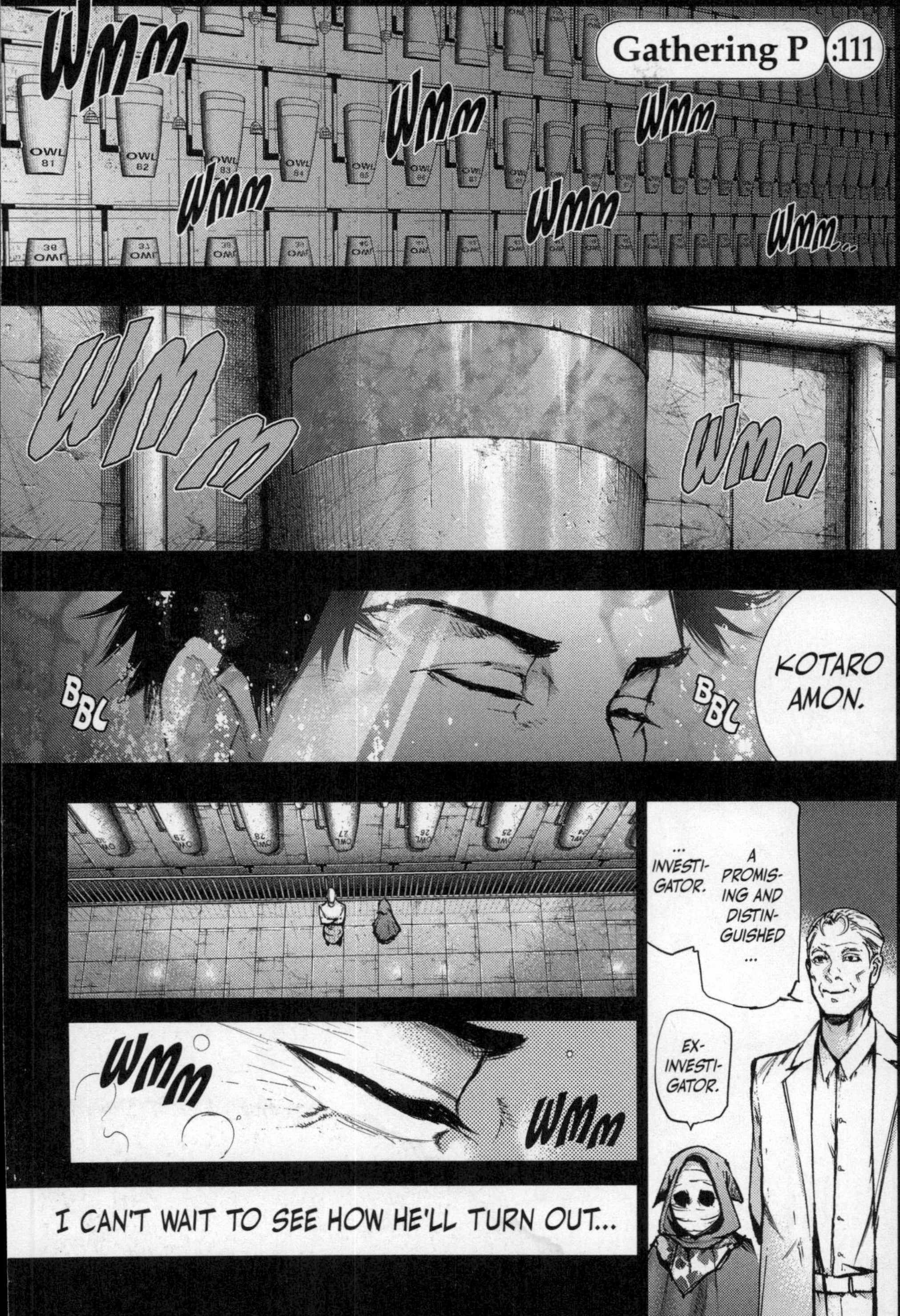

WMM...
WMM
WMM
WMM
WMM
WMM
WMM
WMM
KOTARO AMON.
BBL
BBL
A PROMISING AND DISTINGUISHED...
...INVESTIGATOR.
EX-INVESTIGATOR.
WMM
WMM
I CAN'T WAIT TO SEE HOW HE'LL TURN OUT...

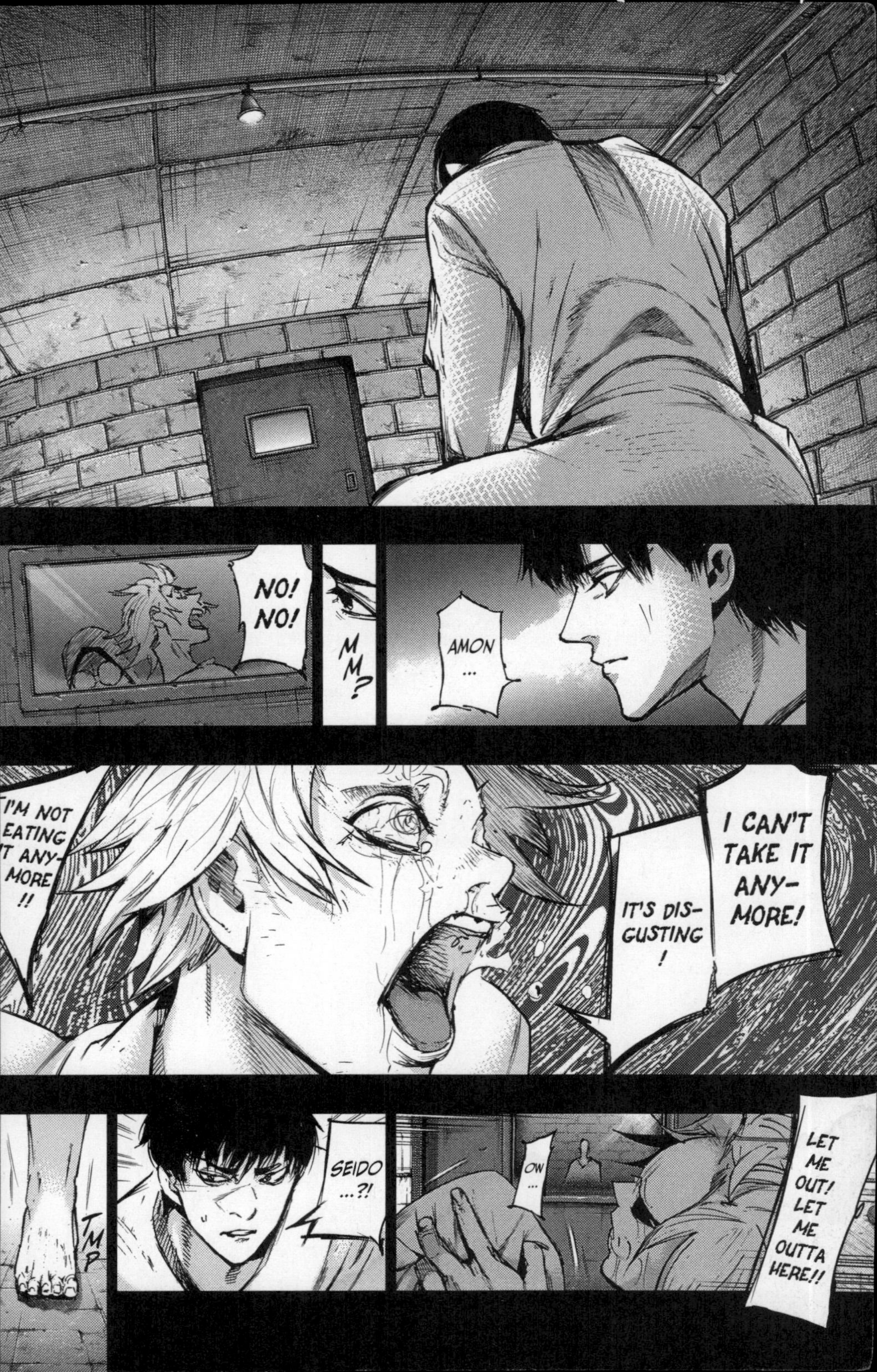
AMON ...
MM?
NO! NO!
I CAN'T TAKE IT ANY-MORE!
IT'S DIS-GUSTING!
I'M NOT EATING IT ANY-MORE!!
LET ME OUT! LET ME OUTTA HERE!!
OW ...
SEIDO ...?!
TMP

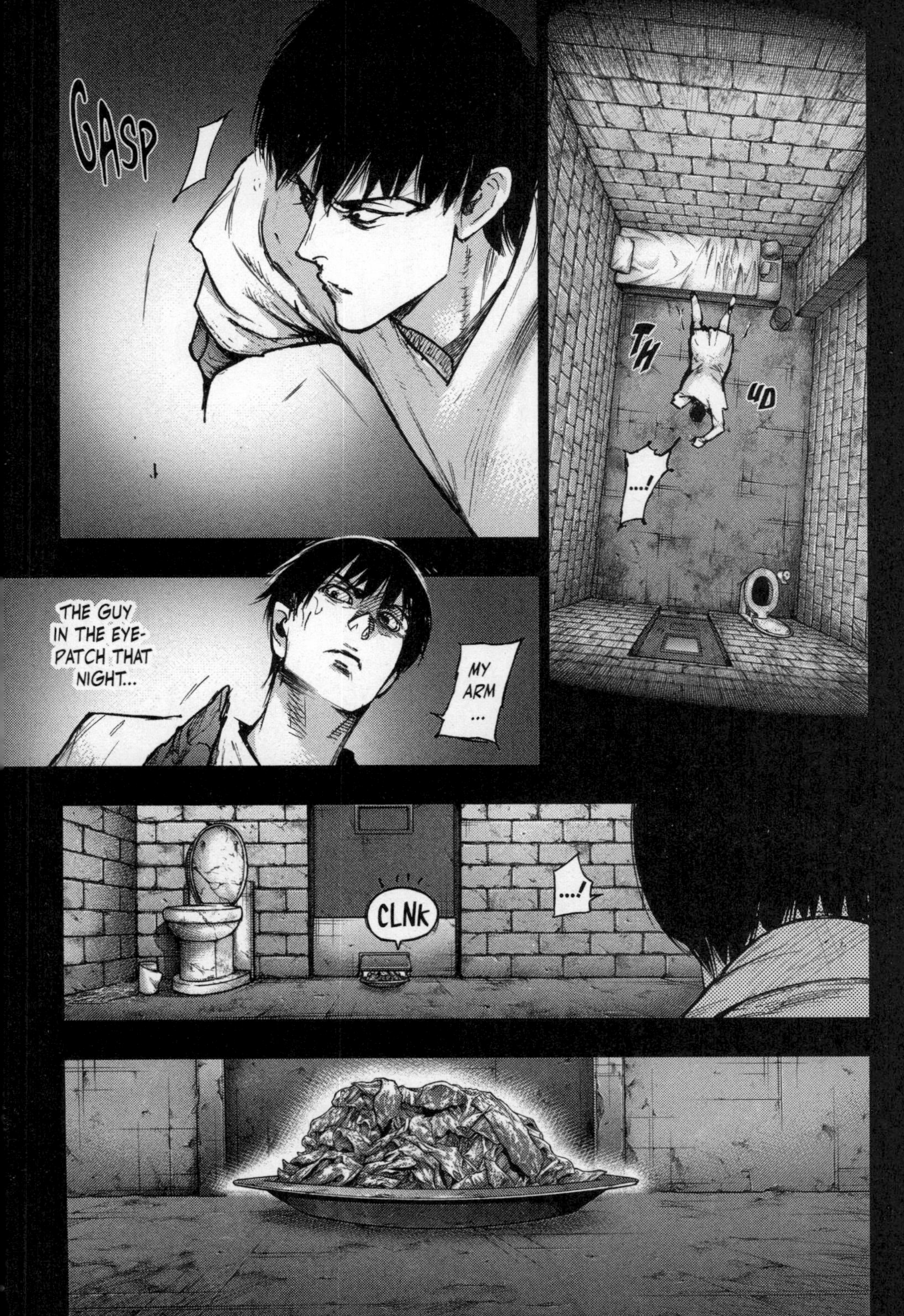
TH
UD
...!
GASP
MY ARM ...
THE GUY IN THE EYE-PATCH THAT NIGHT...
...!
CLNK

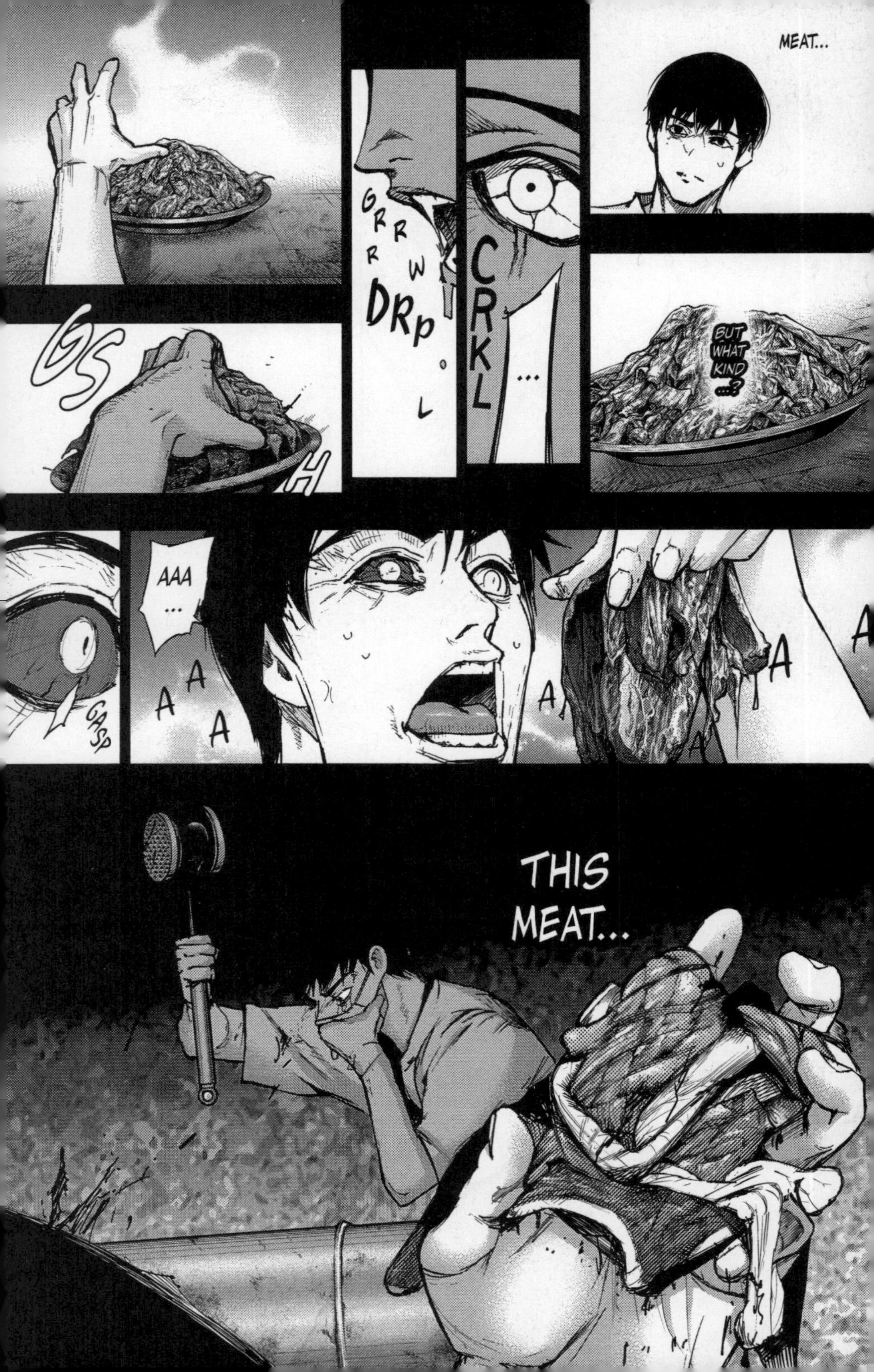

MEAT...
BUT WHAT KIND ...?
CRKL
...
GRRRWL
DRp
AAA ...
A A A A
GASP
THIS MEAT...

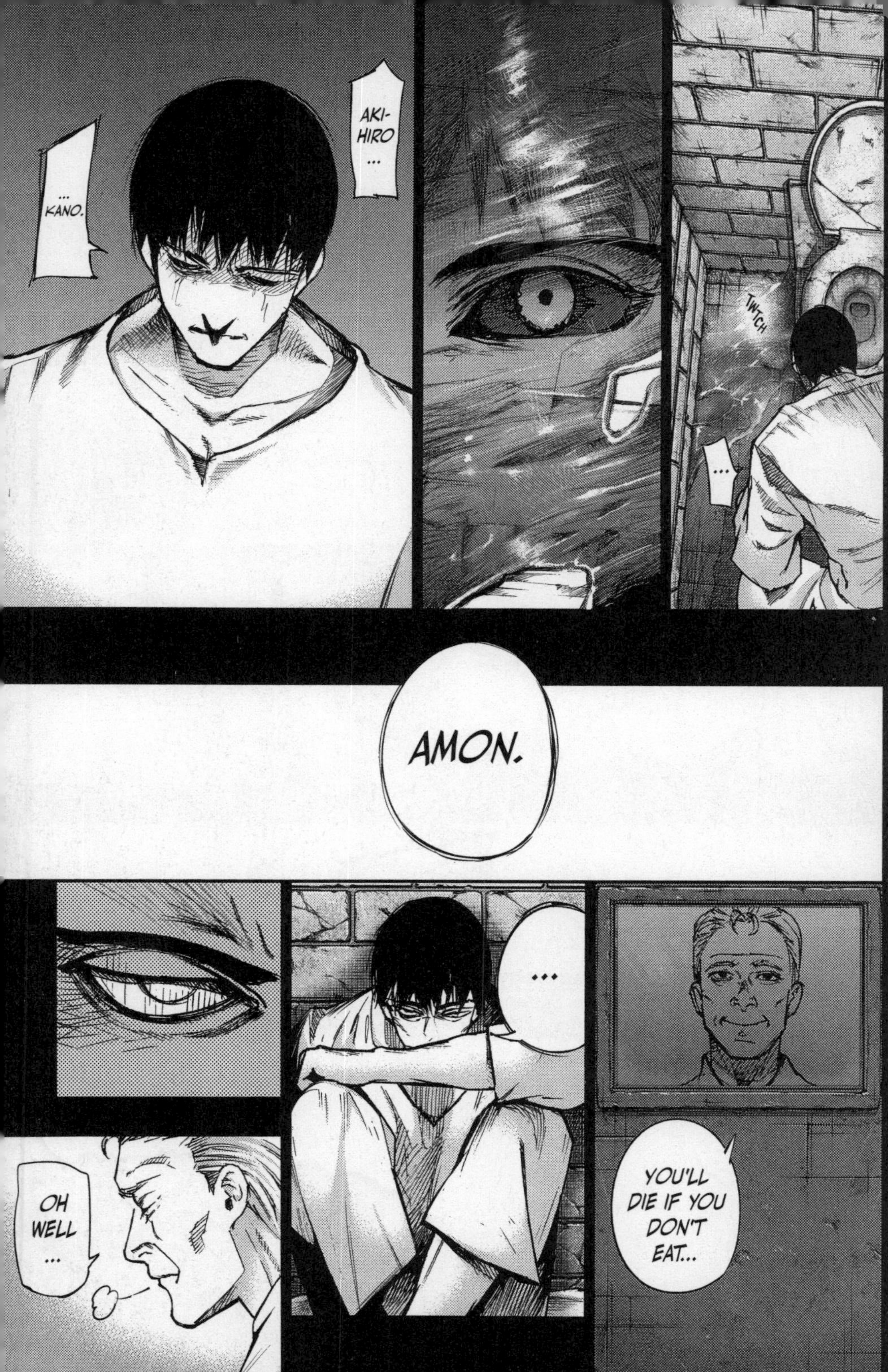
TWTCH
...
AKI-HIRO ...
... KANO.
AMON.
YOU'LL DIE IF YOU DON'T EAT...
...
OH WELL ...

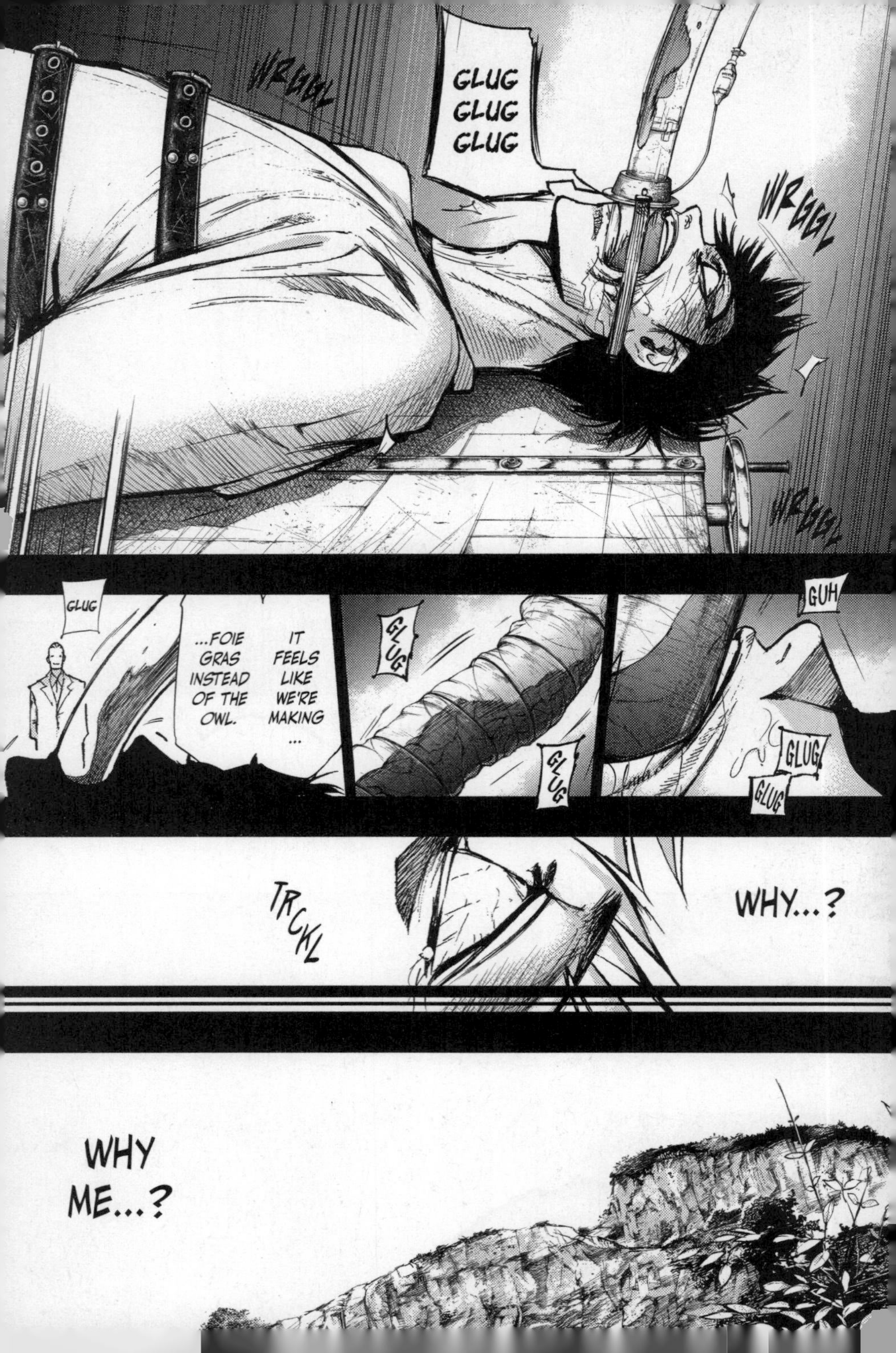
GLUG
GLUG
GLUG
GUH
GLUG
GLUG
GLUG
GLUG
IT FEELS LIKE WE'RE MAKING ...
...FOIE GRAS INSTEAD OF THE OWL.
GLUG
WHY...?
TRCKL
WHY ME...?

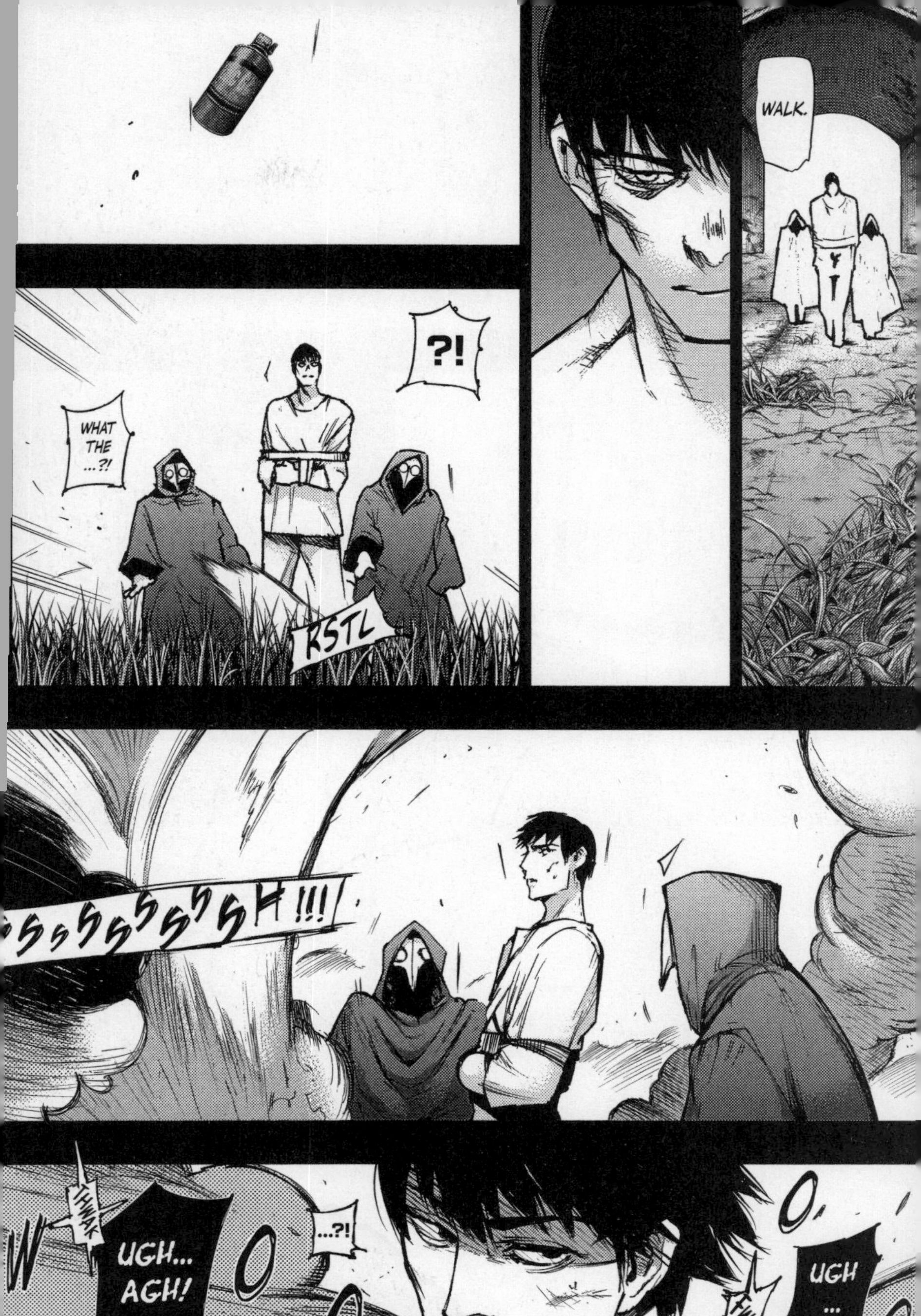
WALK.
?!
WHAT THE ...?!
RSTL
SSSSSSSSSH!!!
O
UGH ...
THWAK
...?!
O
UGH... AGH!
THWAK
W

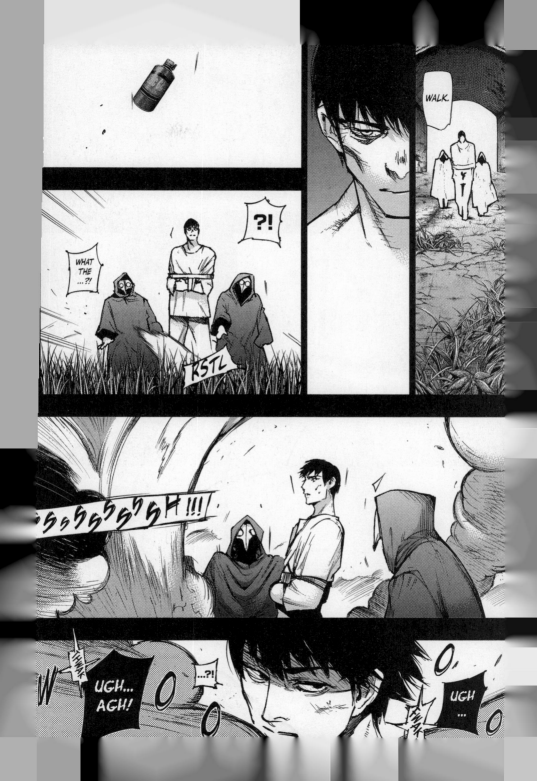

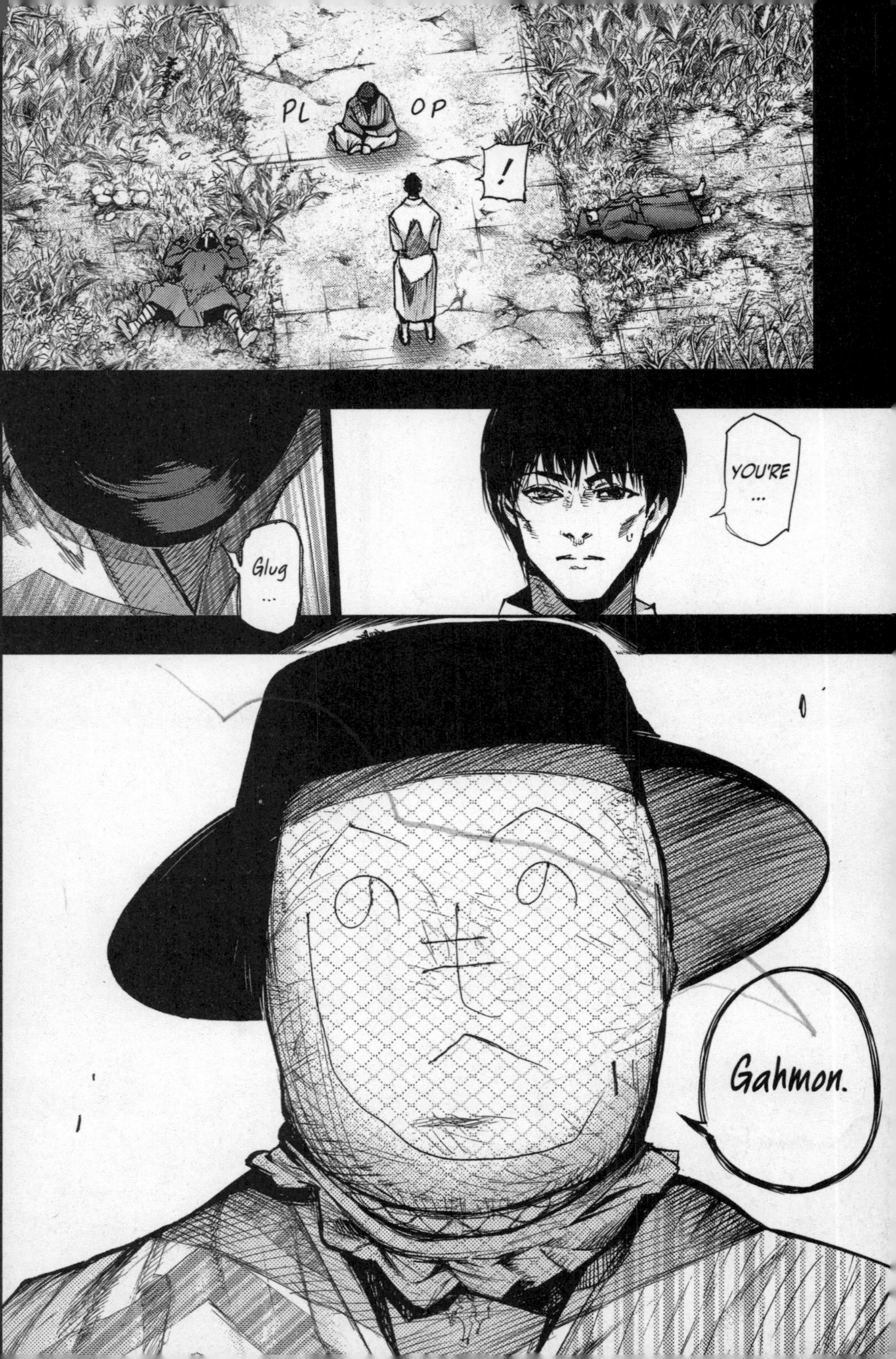
PL OP
!
YOU'RE ...
Glug ...
Gahmon.

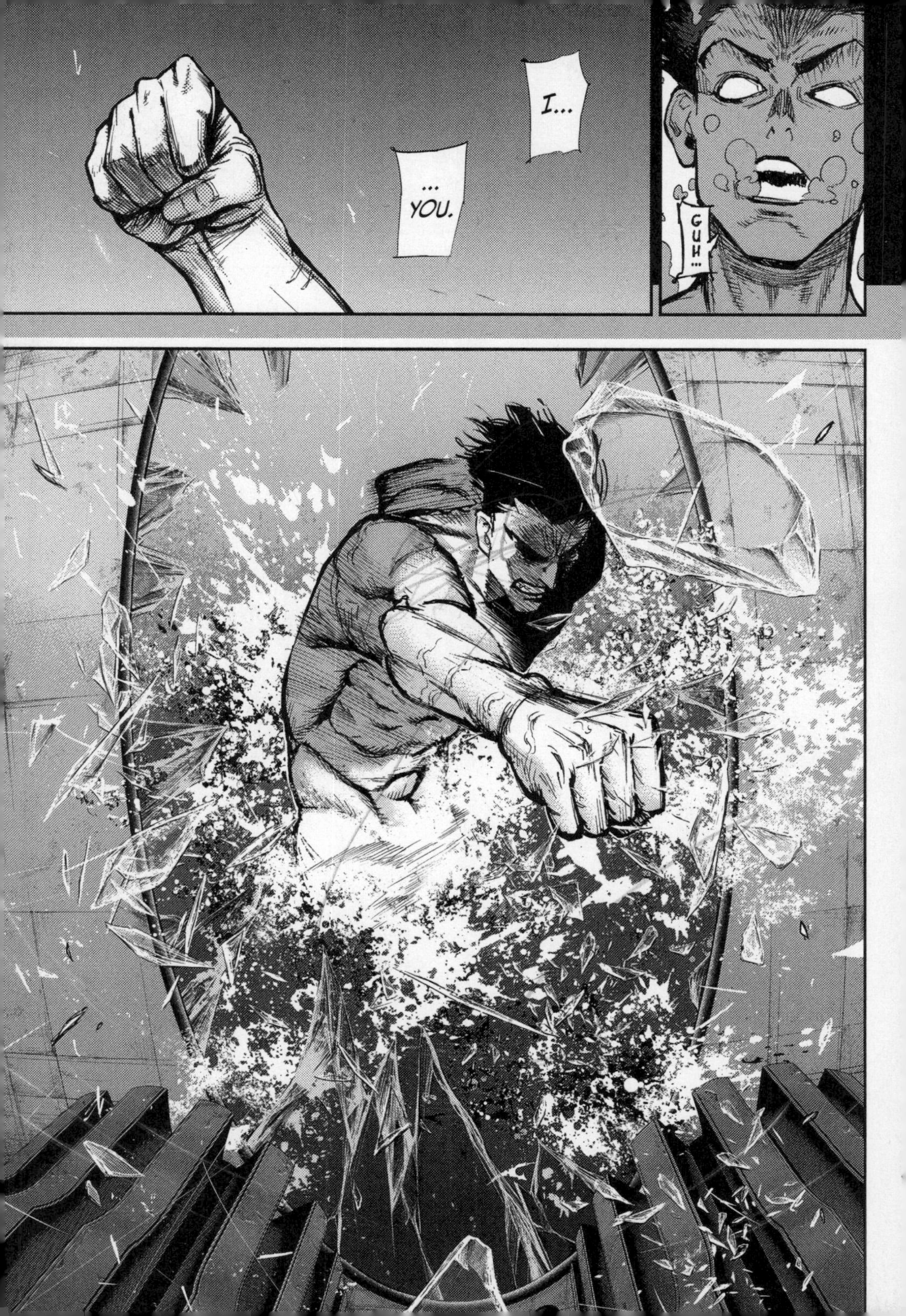
GUH...
I...
... YOU.

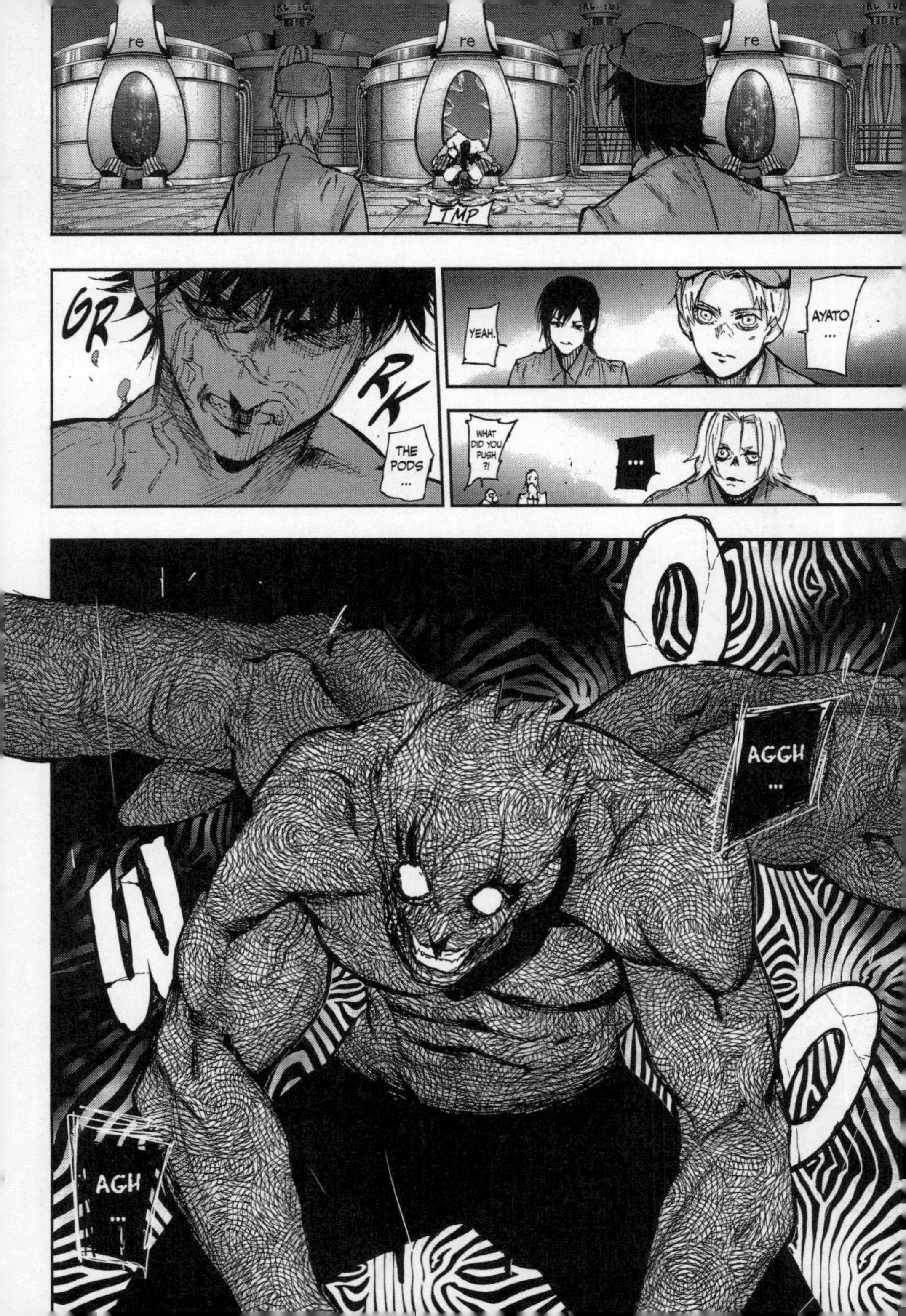
re
re
re
TMP
AYATO ...
YEAH.
...
WHAT DID YOU PUSH ?!
GR
RK
THE PODS ...
AGGH ...
AGH ...

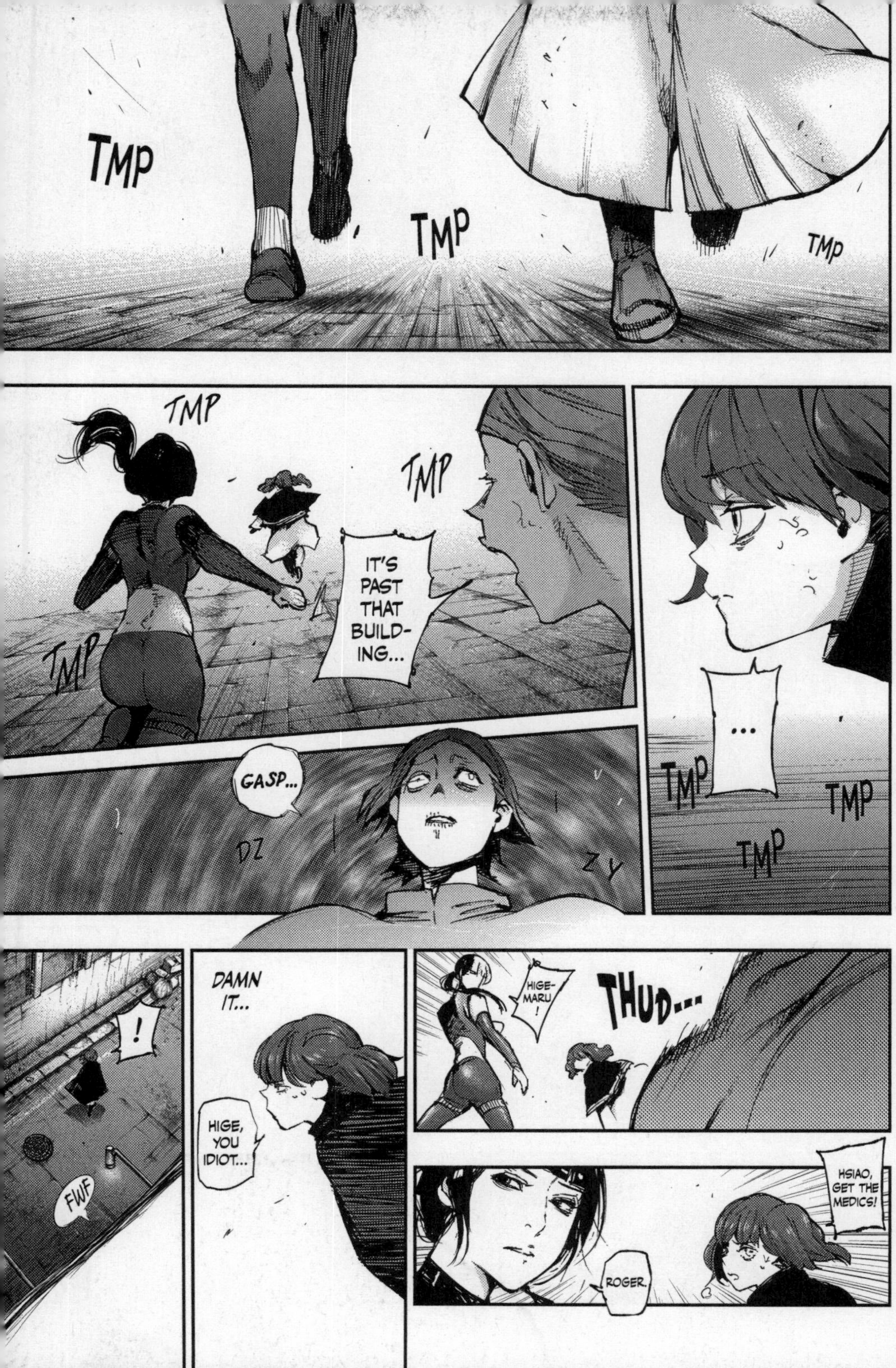
TMP
TMP
TMP
...
TMP
TMP
TMP
TMP
IT'S PAST THAT BUILDING...
TMP
TMP
GASP...
ZY
DZ
THUD...
HIGE-MARU!
HSIAO, GET THE MEDICS!
ROGER.
DAMN IT...
HIGE, YOU IDIOT...
!
FWF

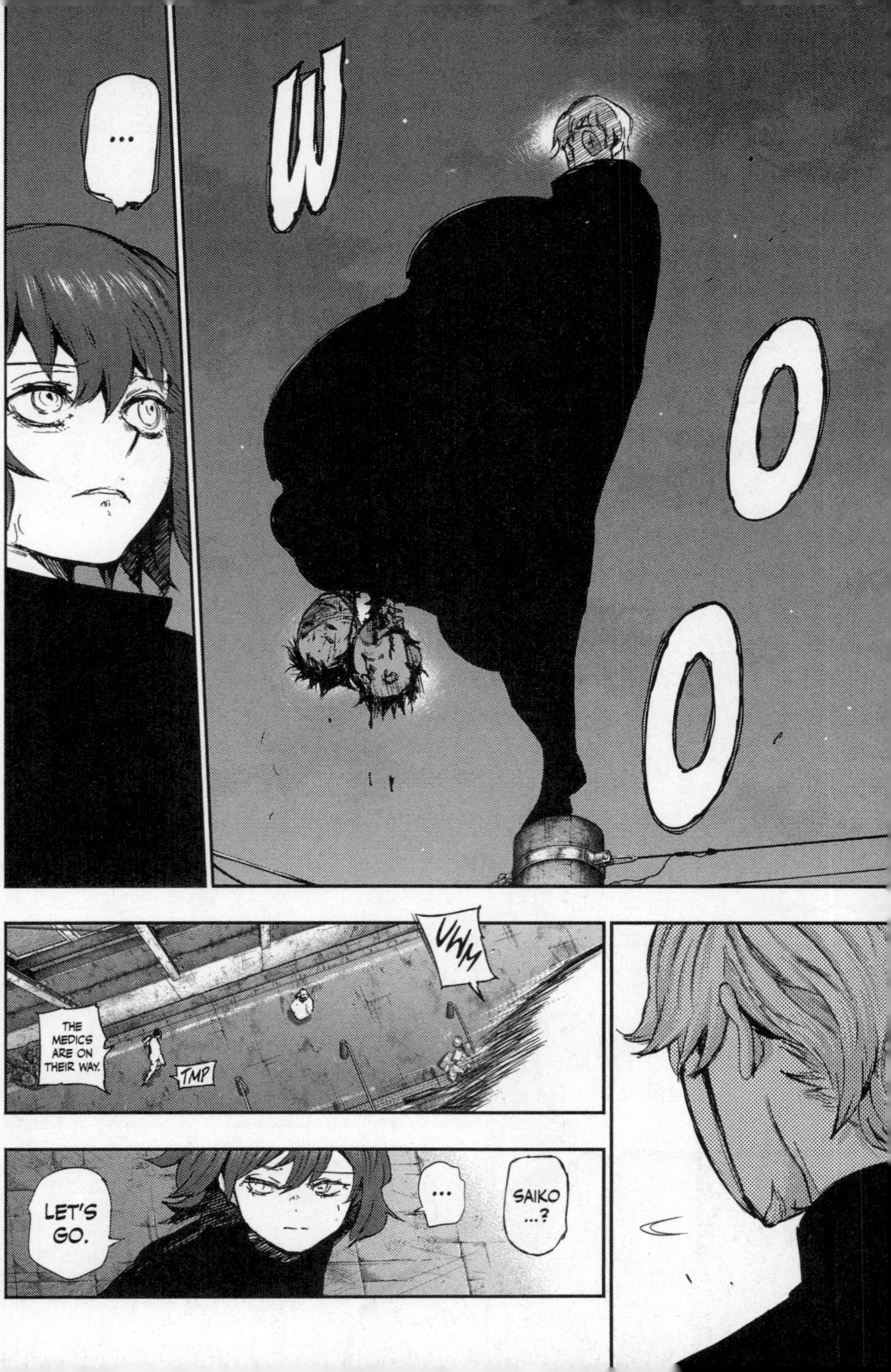
WOOO
...
UWM
THE MEDICS ARE ON THEIR WAY.
TMP
SAIKO ...?
...
LET'S GO.

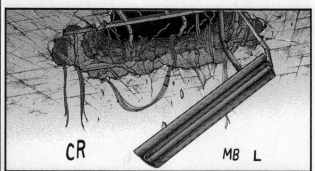

CR

MB L

THEY'RE ON THE ROOF...

SLA

M

!

SLAM

SLAM

SLAM

URI ...?

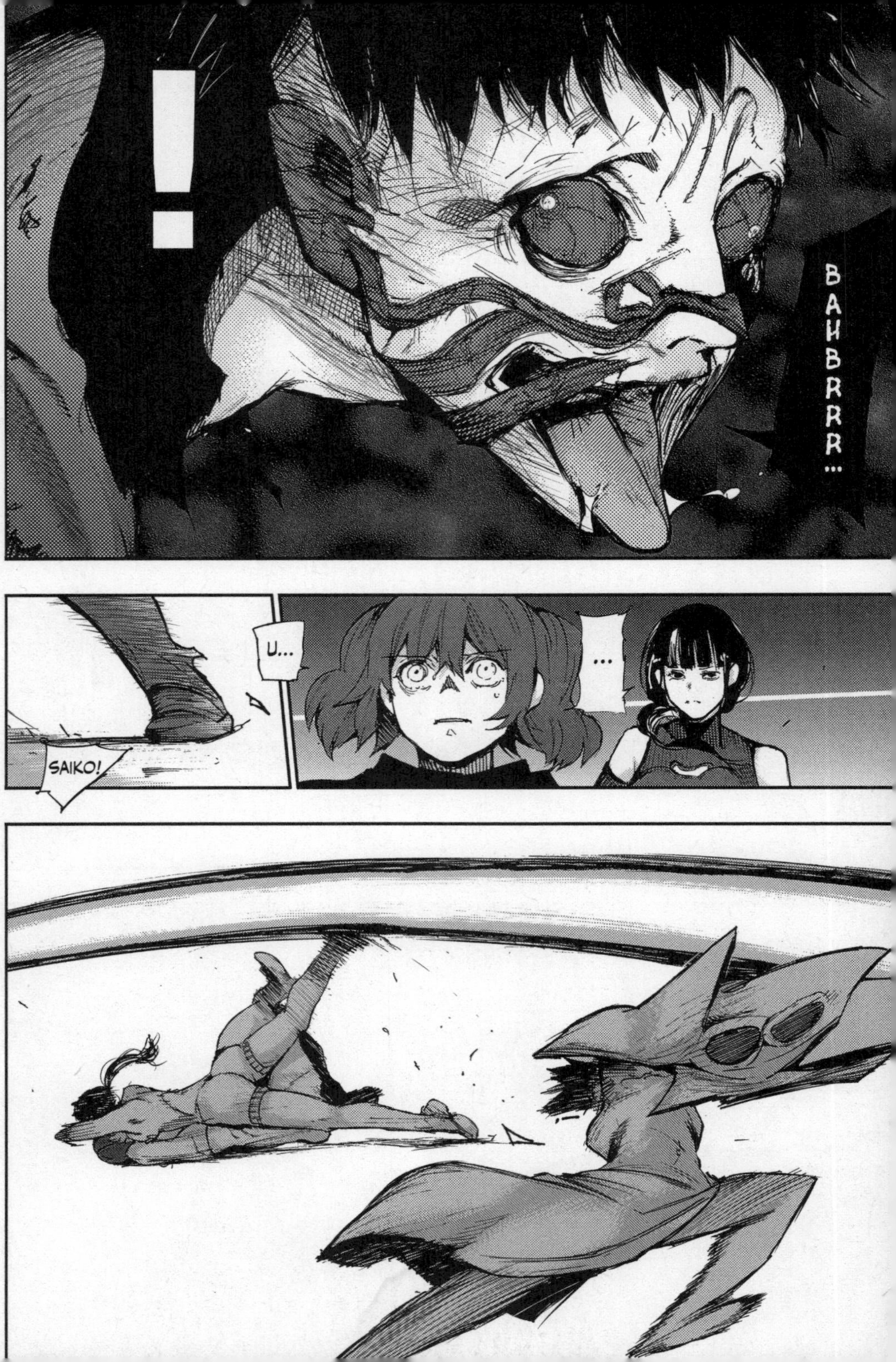
!
BAHBRRR...
...
U...
SAIKO!

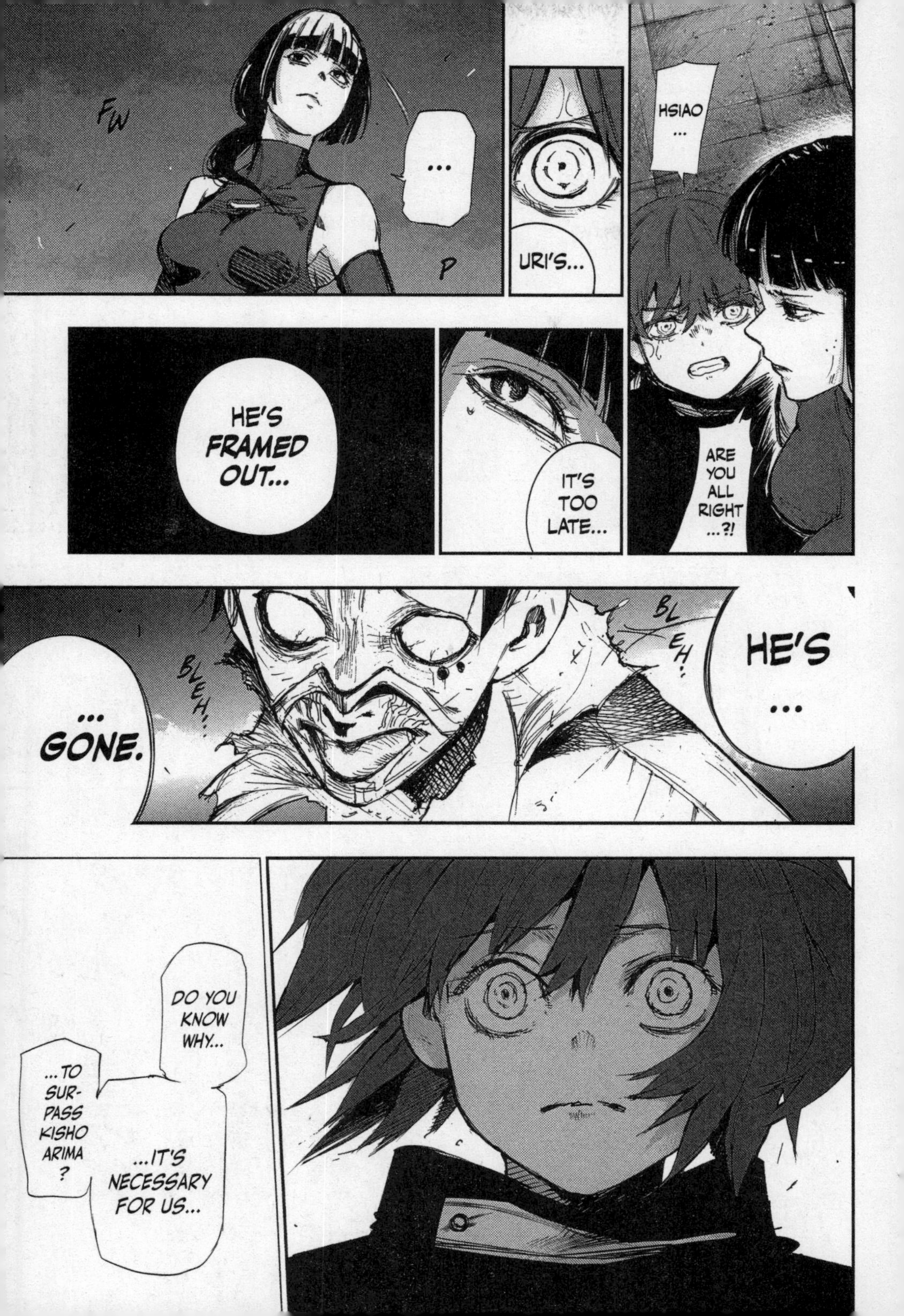
HSIAO ...
ARE YOU ALL RIGHT ...?!
URI'S...
FW
...
P
IT'S TOO LATE...
HE'S FRAMED OUT...
HE'S ...
BLEH!
BLEH!
... GONE.
DO YOU KNOW WHY...
...IT'S NECESSARY FOR US...
...TO SUR-PASS KISHO ARIMA ?

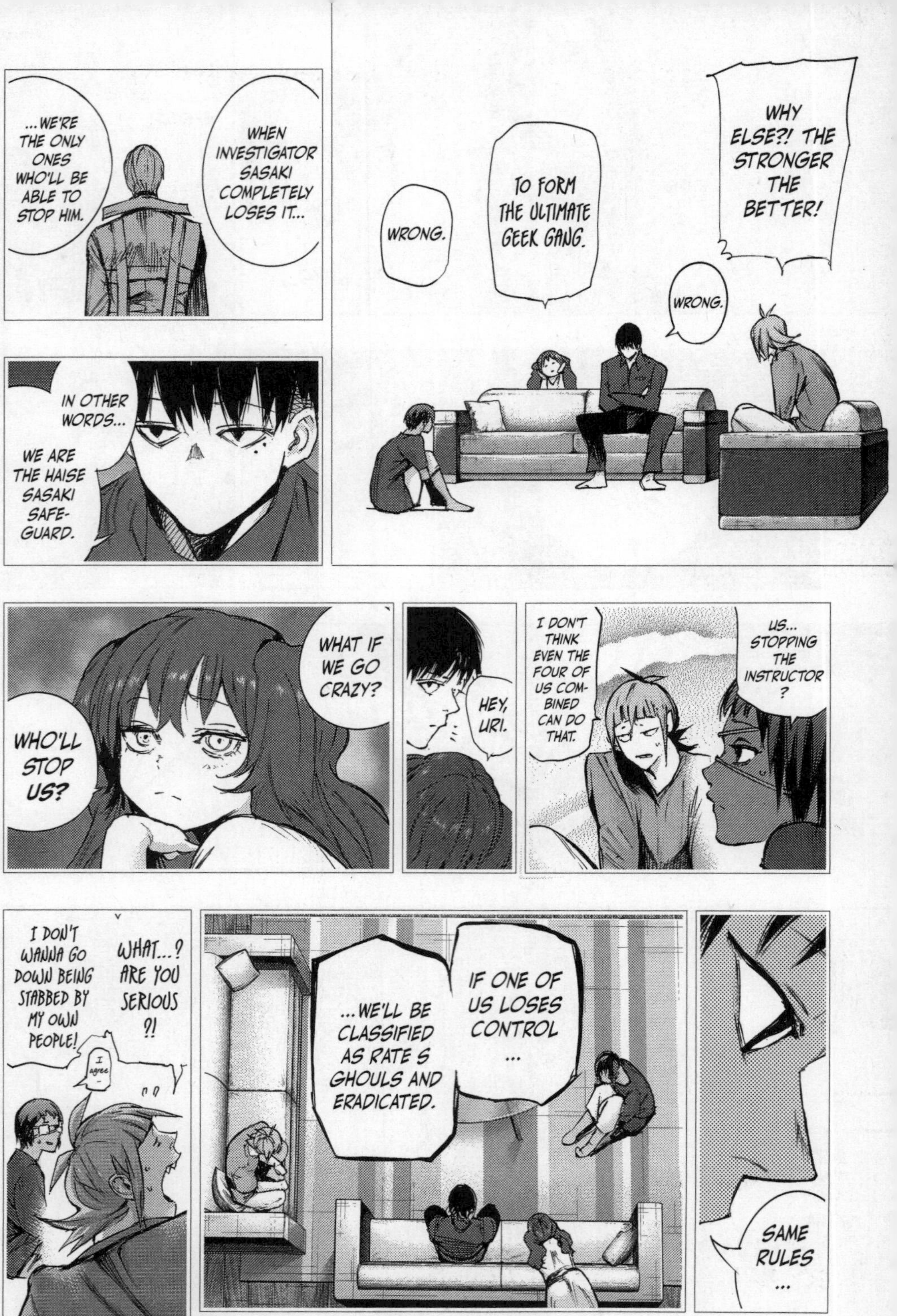
WHY ELSE?! THE STRONGER THE BETTER!
WRONG.
TO FORM THE ULTIMATE GEEK GANG.
WRONG.
WHEN INVESTIGATOR SASAKI COMPLETELY LOSES IT...
...WE'RE THE ONLY ONES WHO'LL BE ABLE TO STOP HIM.
IN OTHER WORDS...
WE ARE THE HAISE SASAKI SAFE-GUARD.
US... STOPPING THE INSTRUCTOR?
I DON'T THINK EVEN THE FOUR OF US COM-BINED CAN DO THAT.
HEY, URI.
WHAT IF WE GO CRAZY?
WHO'LL STOP US?
SAME RULES...
IF ONE OF US LOSES CONTROL...
...WE'LL BE CLASSIFIED AS RATE S GHOULS AND ERADICATED.
WHAT...? ARE YOU SERIOUS?!
I DON'T WANNA GO DOWN BEING STABBED BY MY OWN PEOPLE!
I agree

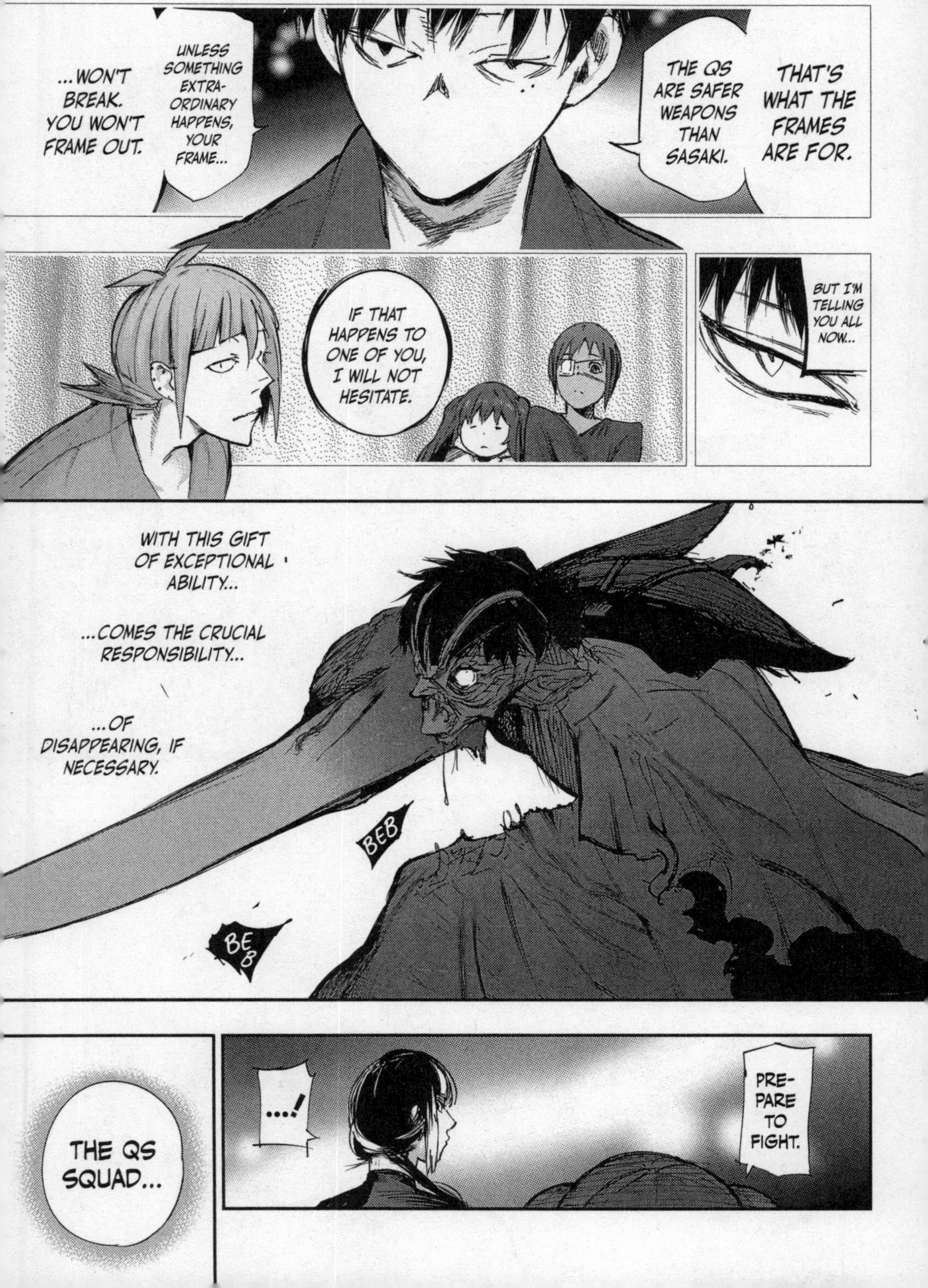
THAT'S WHAT THE FRAMES ARE FOR.
THE QS ARE SAFER WEAPONS THAN SASAKI.
UNLESS SOMETHING EXTRA-ORDINARY HAPPENS, YOUR FRAME...
...WON'T BREAK. YOU WON'T FRAME OUT.
BUT I'M TELLING YOU ALL NOW...
IF THAT HAPPENS TO ONE OF YOU, I WILL NOT HESITATE.
WITH THIS GIFT OF EXCEPTIONAL ABILITY...
...COMES THE CRUCIAL RESPONSIBILITY...
...OF DISAPPEARING, IF NECESSARY.
BEB
BEB
PRE-PARE TO FIGHT.
...!
THE QS SQUAD...

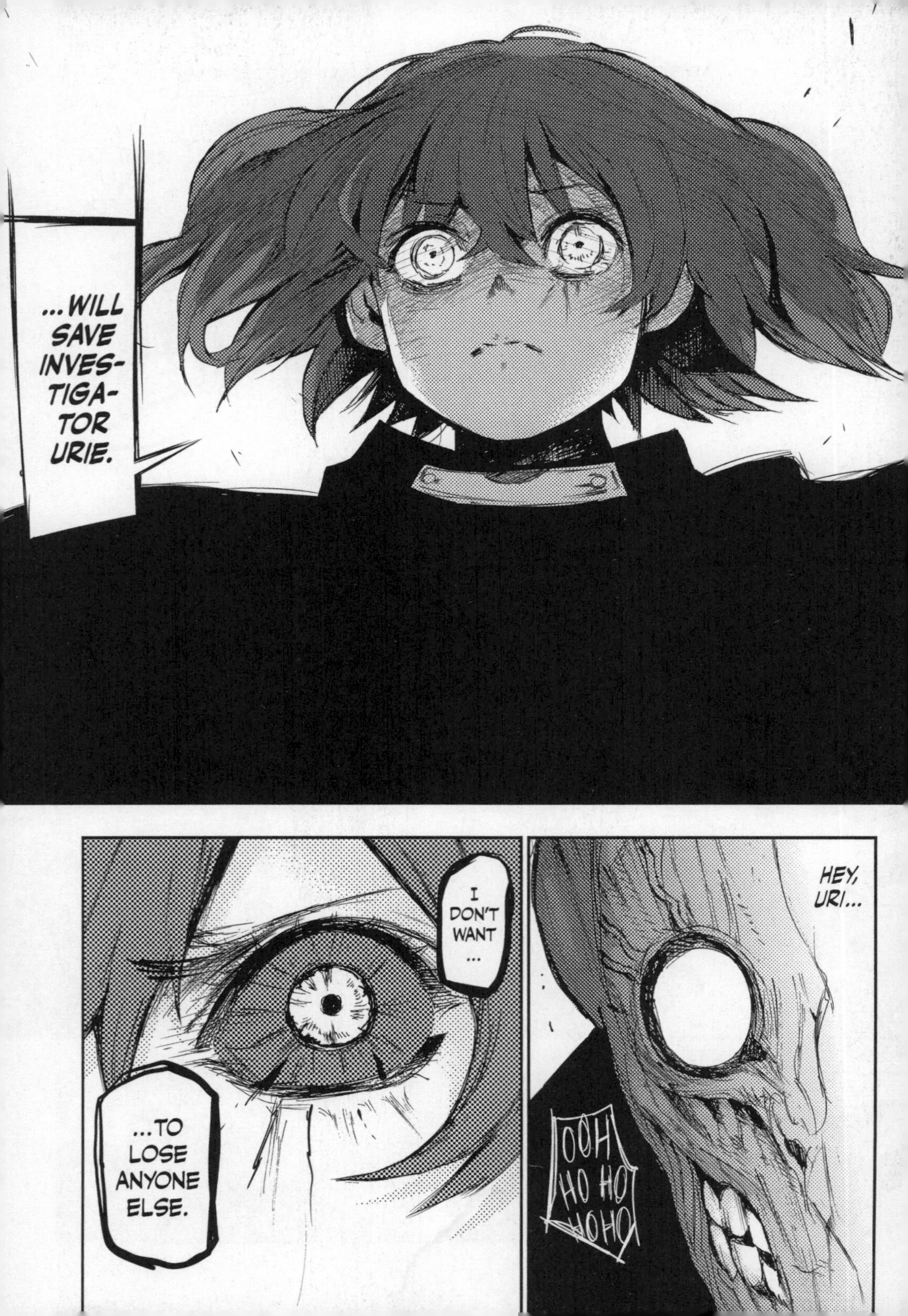
...WILL SAVE INVESTIGATOR URIE.
HEY, URI...
OOH HO HO HO HOHO
I DON'T WANT...
...TO LOSE ANYONE ELSE.

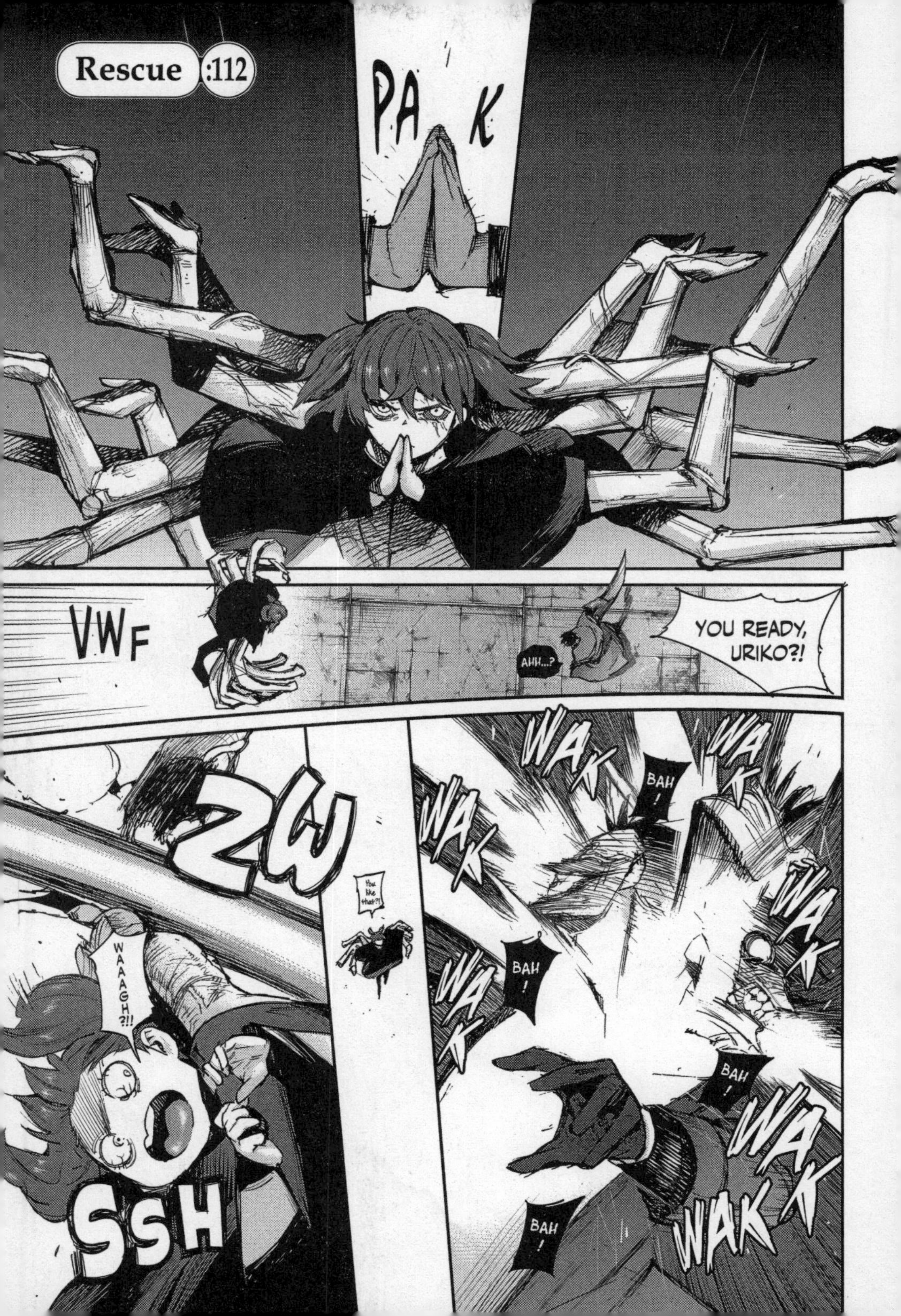
Rescue :112
PAK
YOU READY, URIKO?!
AHH...?
VWF
WAK
WAK
BAH!
WAK
WAK
BAH!
WAK
BAH!
WAK
WAK
BAH!
WAK
You like that?!
ZW
WAAAGH?!!
SSH

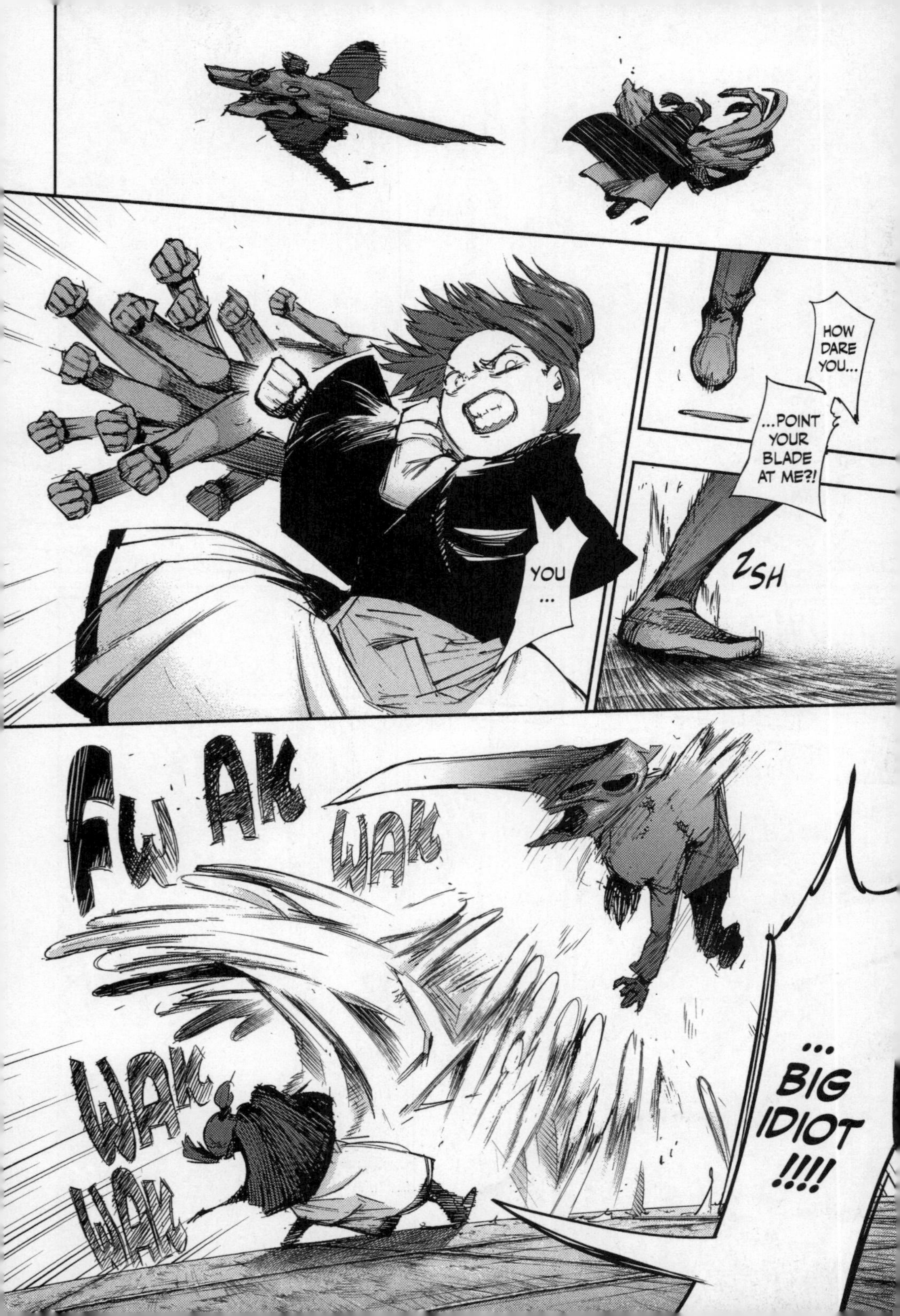
HOW DARE YOU...
...POINT YOUR BLADE AT ME?!
ZSH
YOU ...
FWAK
WAK
...BIG IDIOT!!!!
WAK
WAK

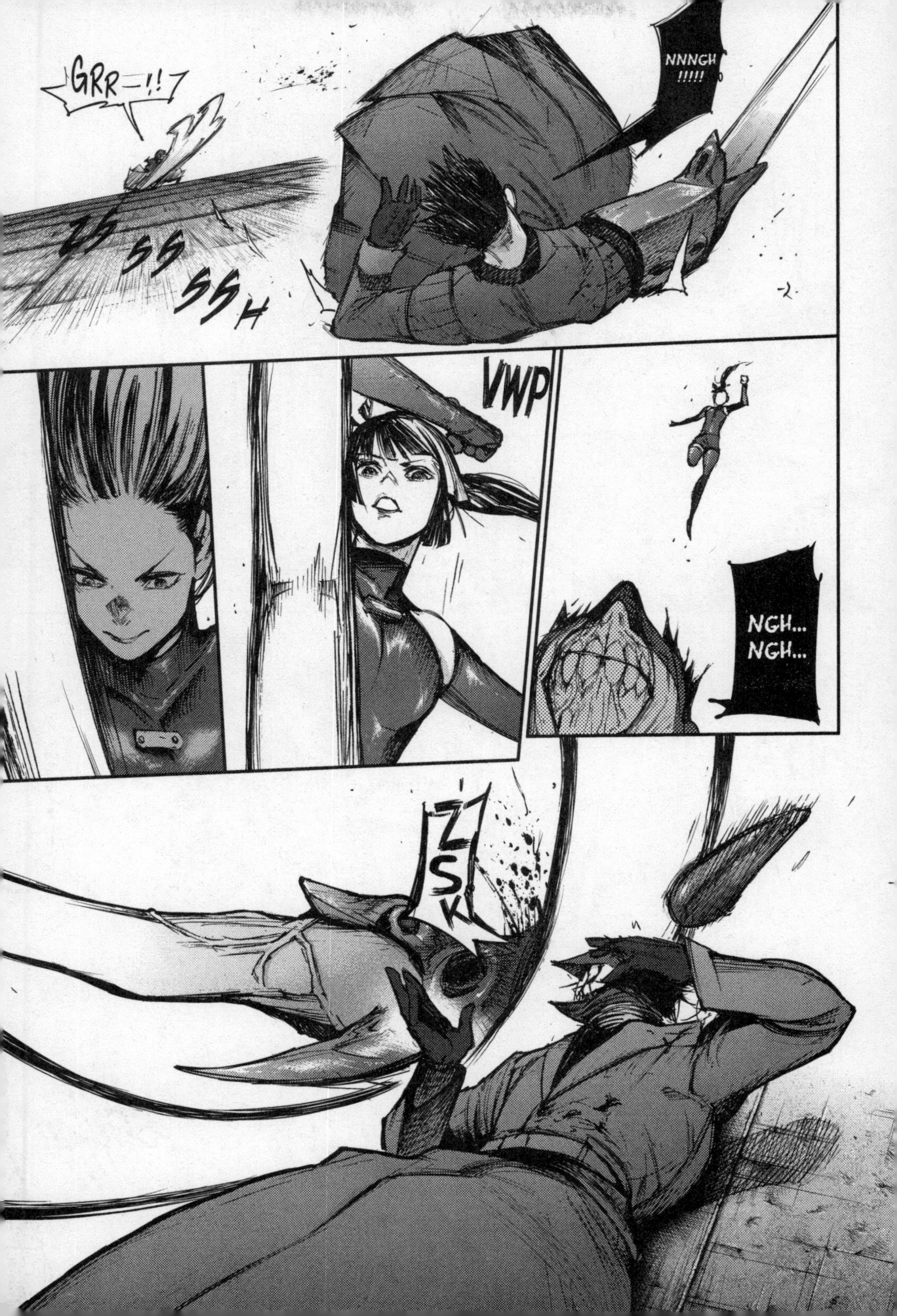
NNNGH !!!!!
GRR—!!
ZSSSSSH
NGH... NGH...
VWP
ZSK

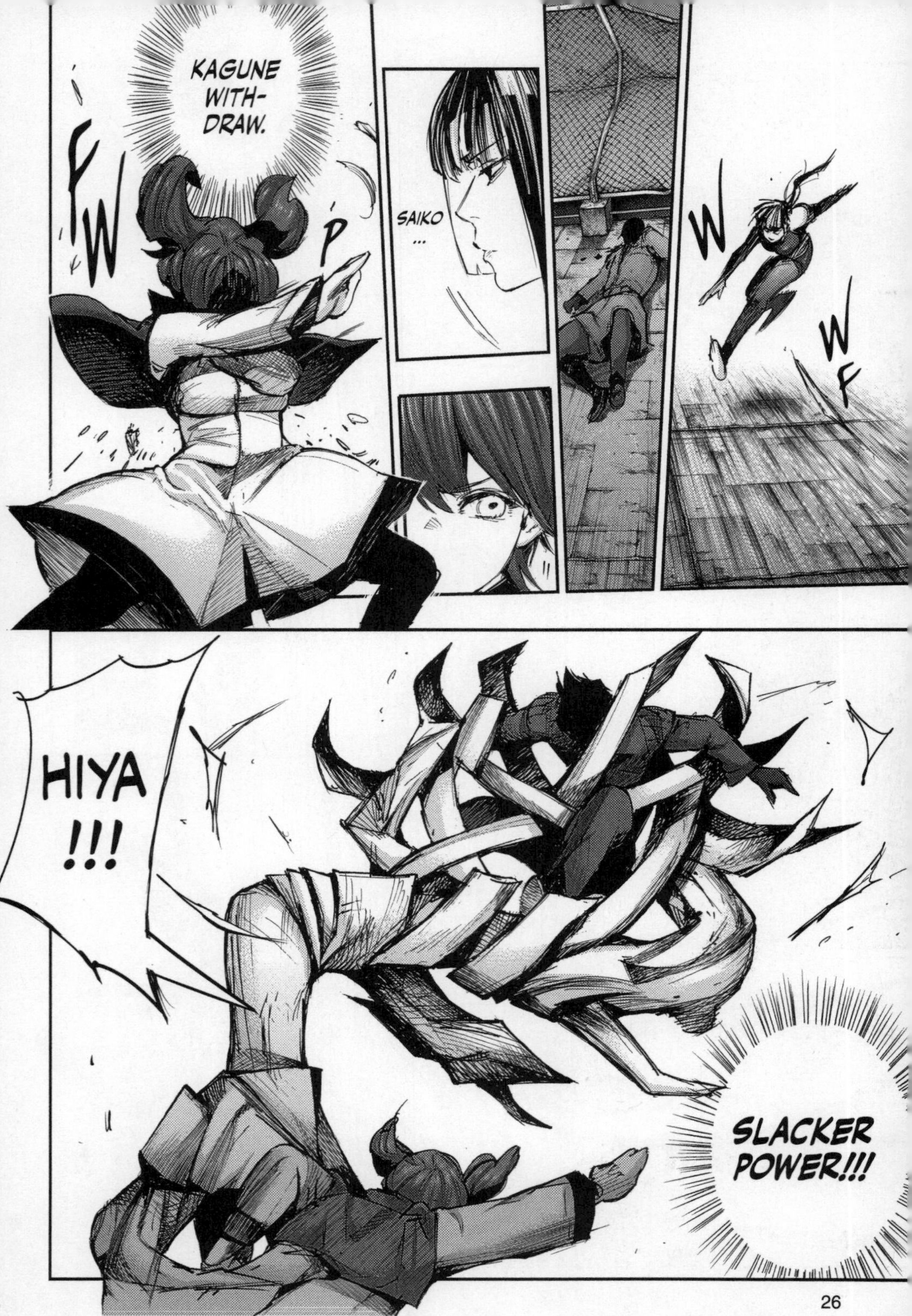
W
WF
SAIKO ...
KAGUNE WITH-DRAW.
FW
P
HIYA !!!
SLACKER POWER!!!

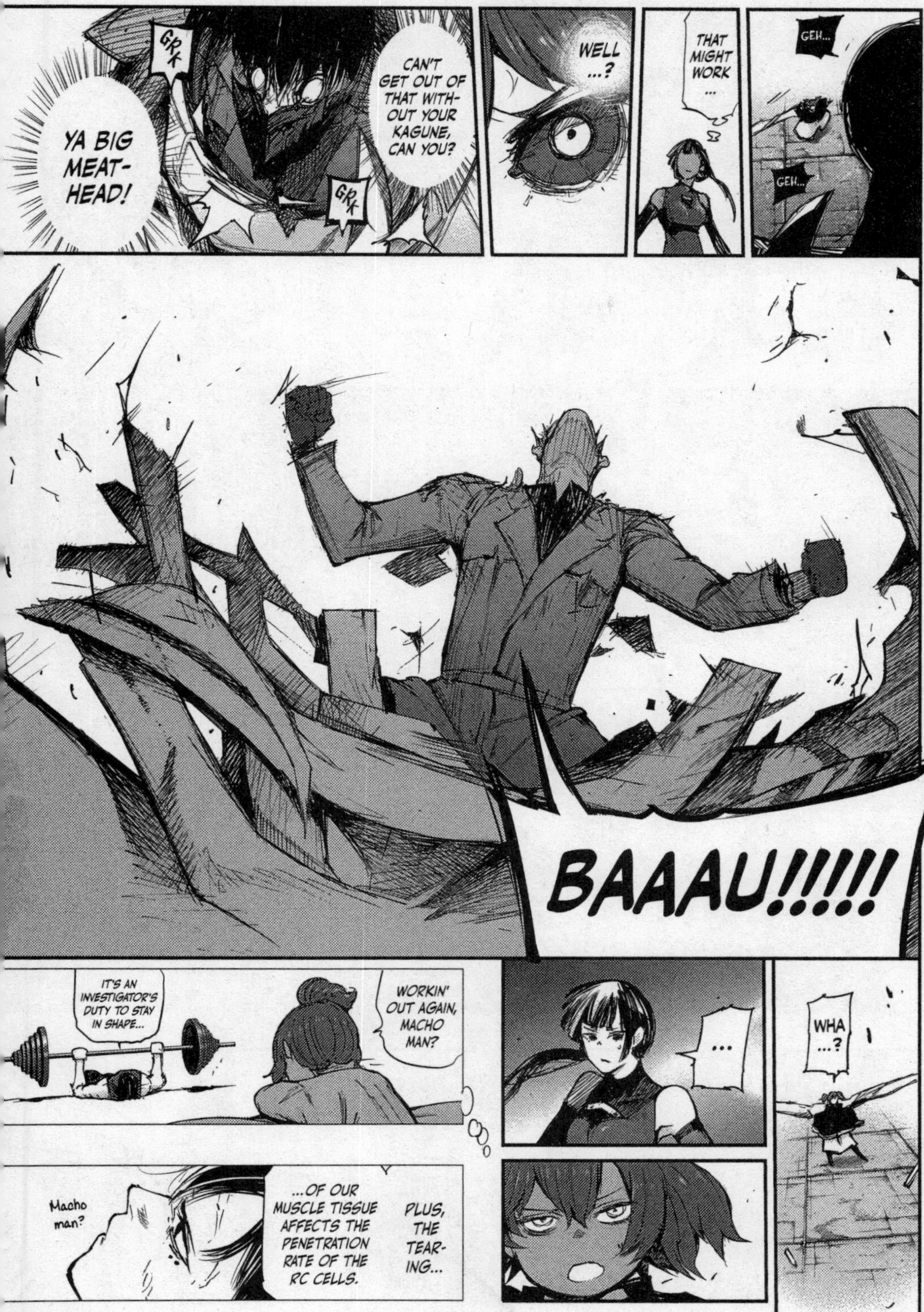
GEH...
GEH...
THAT MIGHT WORK...
WELL...?
CAN'T GET OUT OF THAT WITH-OUT YOUR KAGUNE, CAN YOU?
GRK
YA BIG MEAT-HEAD!
GRK
BAAAU!!!!!!
WHA...?
...
WORKIN' OUT AGAIN, MACHO MAN?
IT'S AN INVESTIGATOR'S DUTY TO STAY IN SHAPE...
PLUS, THE TEAR-ING...
...OF OUR MUSCLE TISSUE AFFECTS THE PENETRATION RATE OF THE RC CELLS.
Macho man?

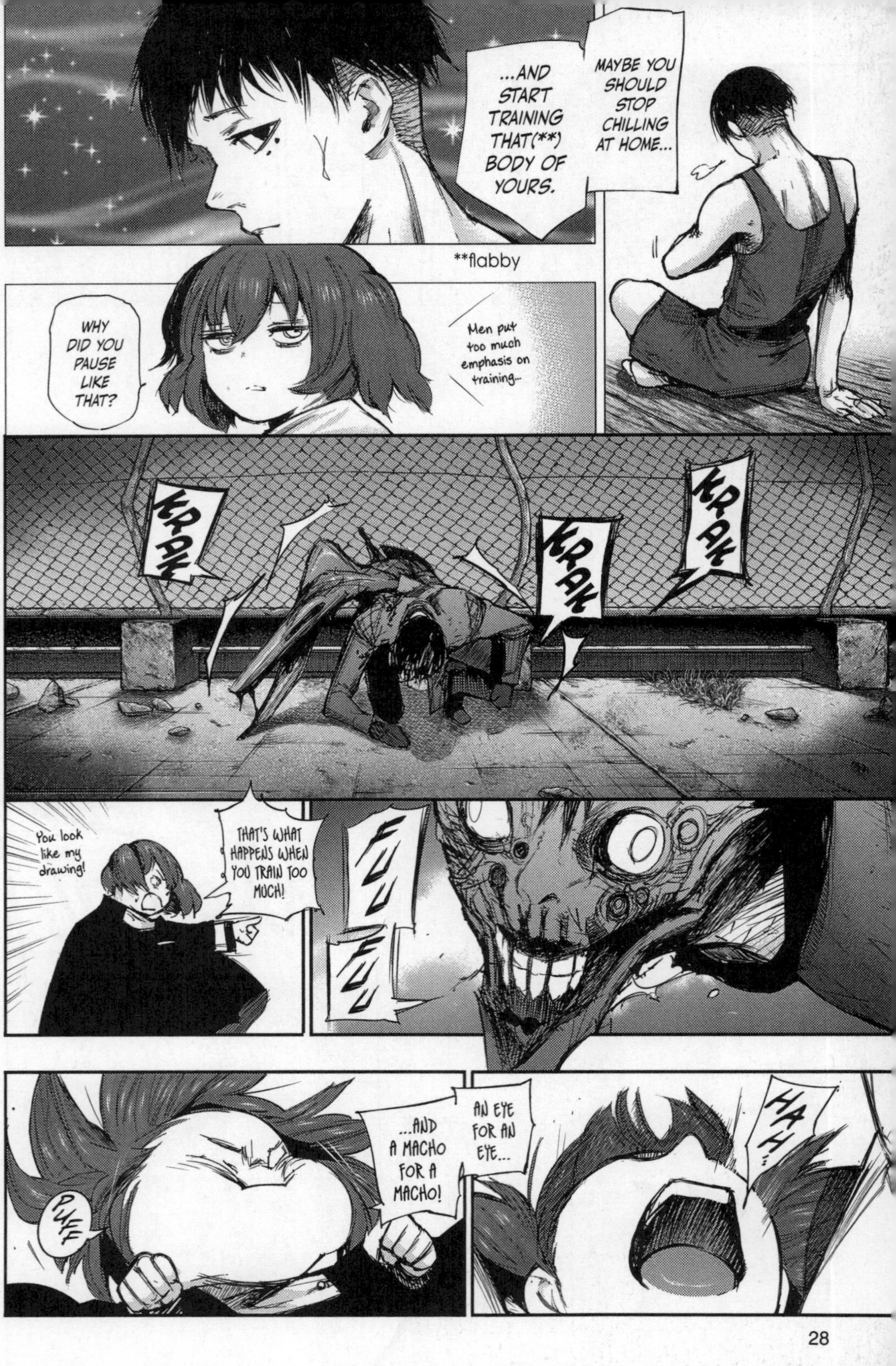

MAYBE YOU SHOULD STOP CHILLING AT HOME...
...AND START TRAINING THAT(**) BODY OF YOURS.
**flabby
Men put too much emphasis on training...
WHY DID YOU PAUSE LIKE THAT?
KRAK
KRAK
KRAK
FUU FUU
THAT'S WHAT HAPPENS WHEN YOU TRAIN TOO MUCH!
You look like my drawing!
HAH...!
AN EYE FOR AN EYE...
...AND A MACHO FOR A MACHO!
PUFF

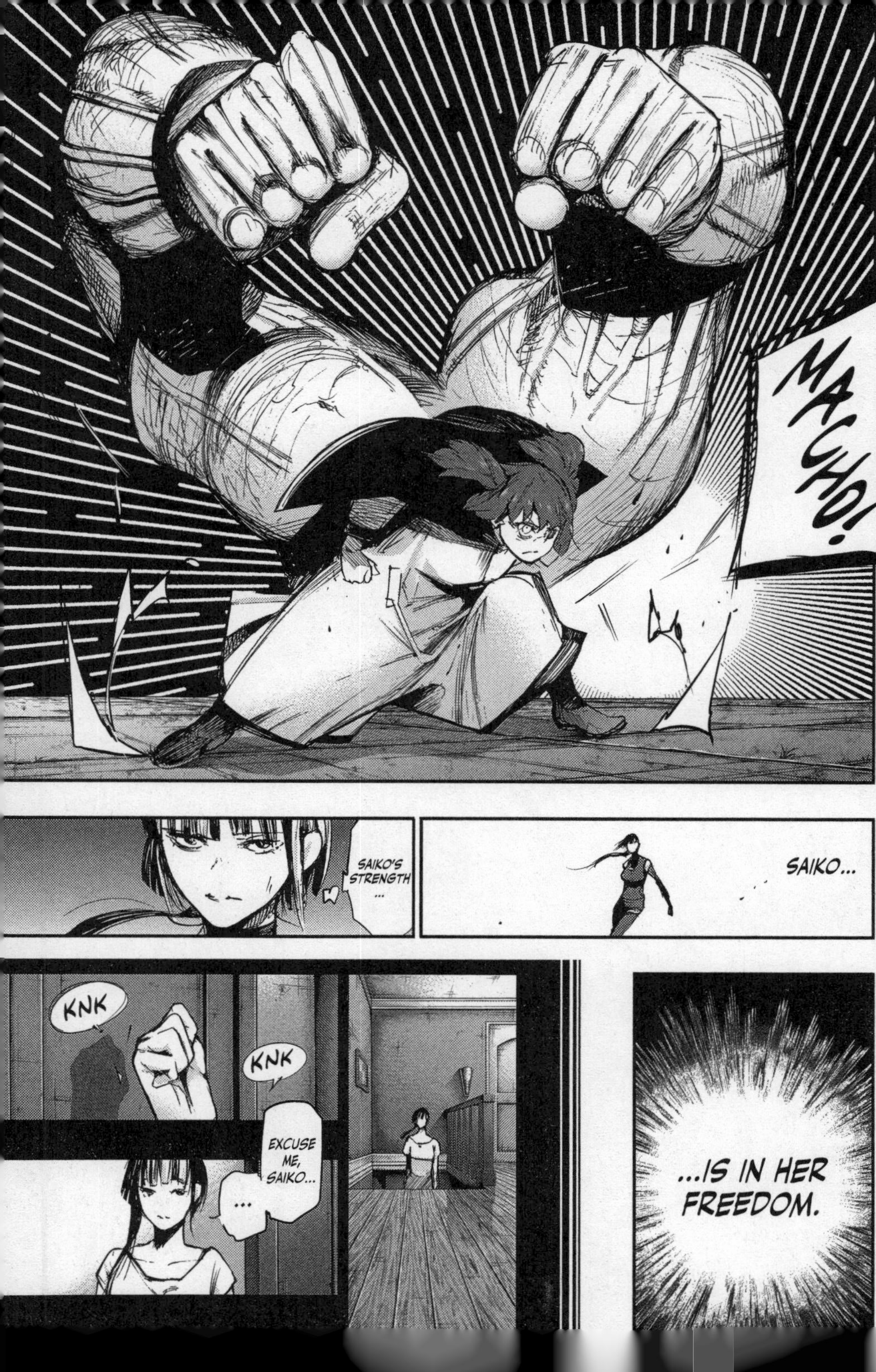
MACHO!
SAIKO...
SAIKO'S STRENGTH ...
...IS IN HER FREEDOM.
KNK
KNK
EXCUSE ME, SAIKO...
...

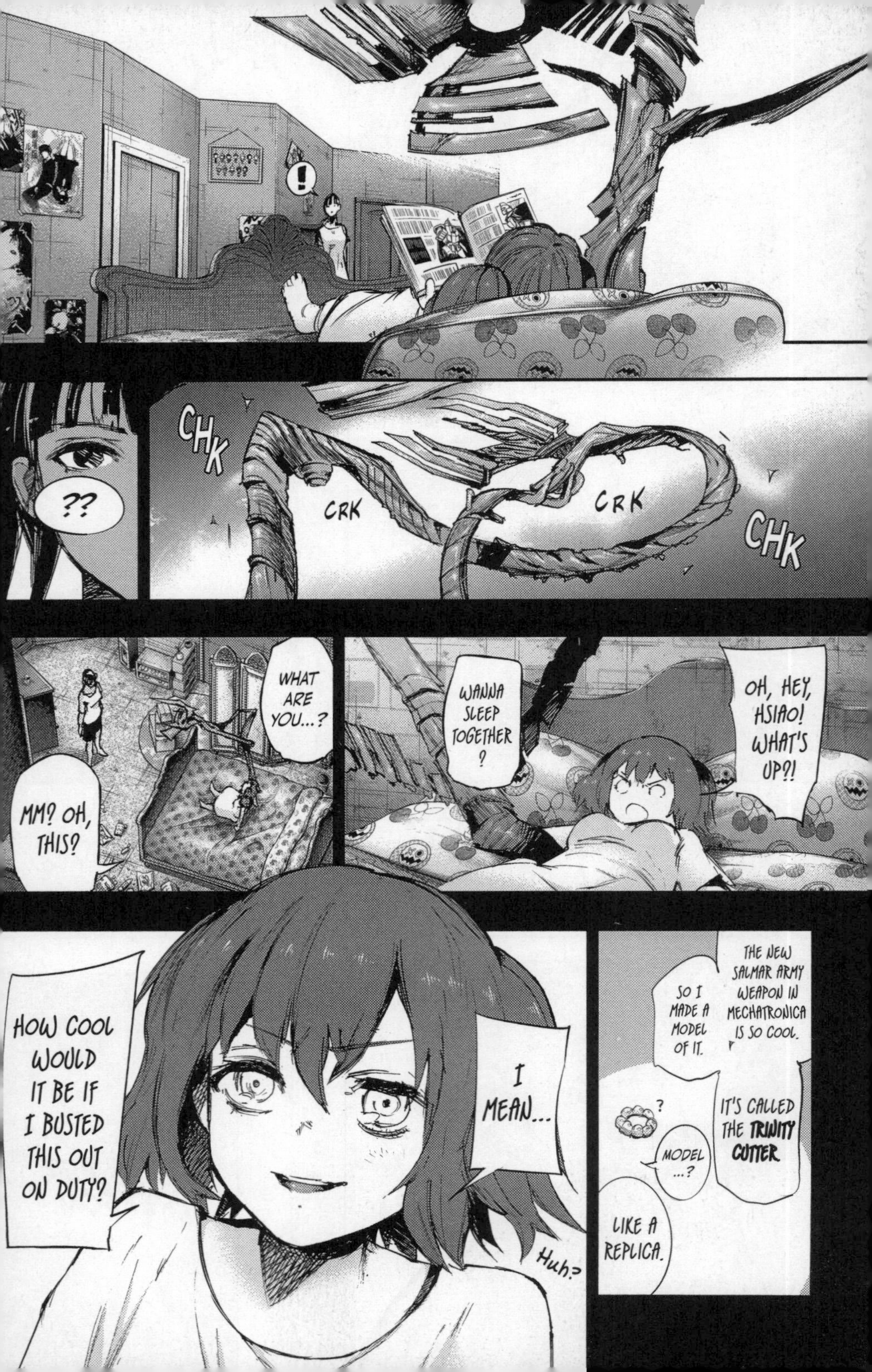
!
CHK
CRK
CRK
CHK
??
OH, HEY, HSIAO! WHAT'S UP?!
WANNA SLEEP TOGETHER?
WHAT ARE YOU...?
MM? OH, THIS?
THE NEW SALMAR ARMY WEAPON IN MECHATRONICA IS SO COOL.
SO I MADE A MODEL OF IT.
IT'S CALLED THE TRINITY CUTTER.
?
MODEL ...?
LIKE A REPLICA.
I MEAN...
HOW COOL WOULD IT BE IF I BUSTED THIS OUT ON DUTY?
Huh?

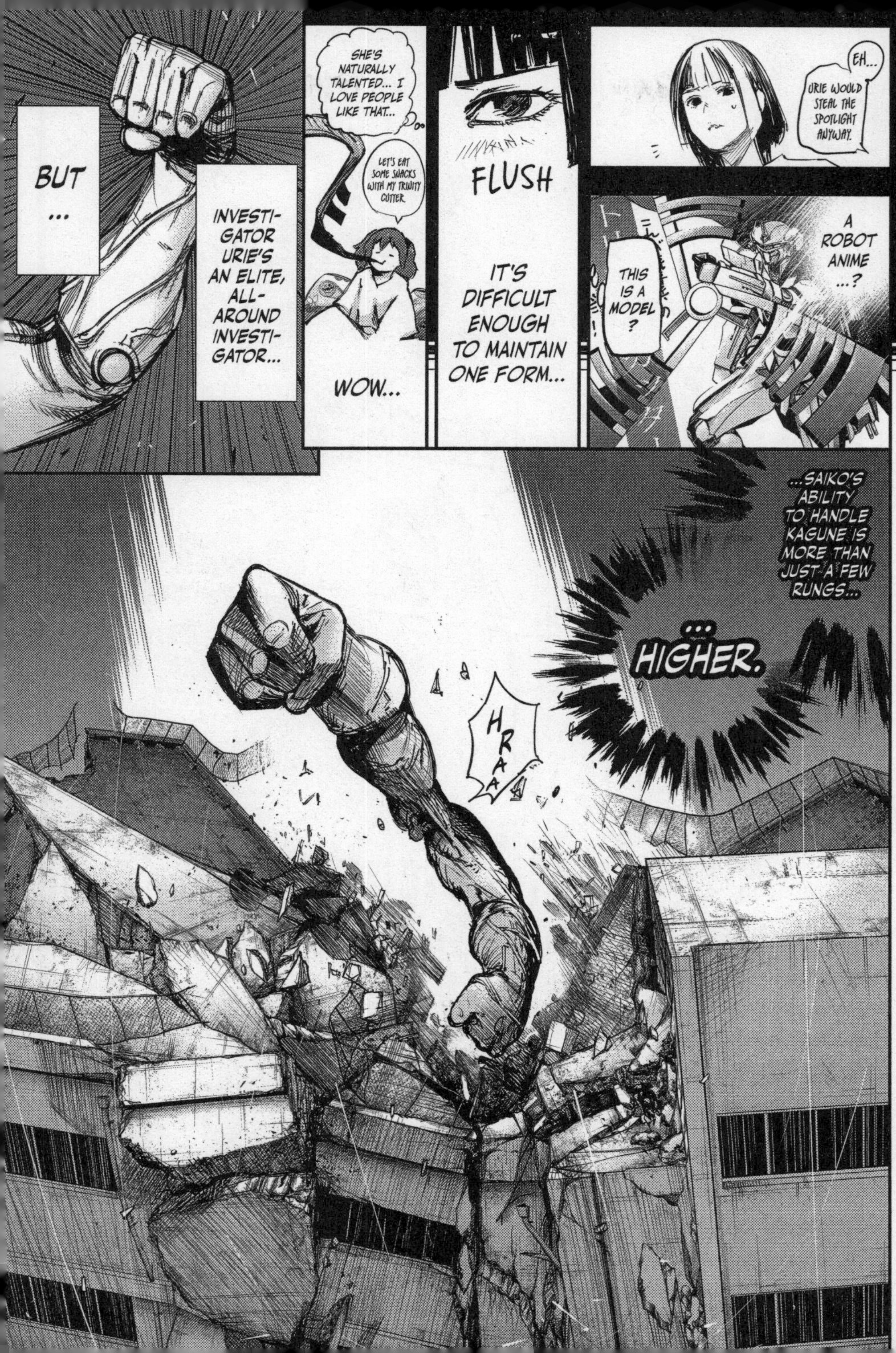
EH...
URIE WOULD STEAL THE SPOTLIGHT ANYWAY.
A ROBOT ANIME ...?
THIS IS A MODEL ?
FLUSH
IT'S DIFFICULT ENOUGH TO MAINTAIN ONE FORM...
SHE'S NATURALLY TALENTED... I LOVE PEOPLE LIKE THAT...
LET'S EAT SOME SNACKS WITH MY TRINITY CUTTER.
WOW...
INVESTIGATOR URIE'S AN ELITE, ALL-AROUND INVESTIGATOR...
BUT ...
...SAIKO'S ABILITY TO HANDLE KAGUNE IS MORE THAN JUST A FEW RUNGS...
... HIGHER.
HRAAA

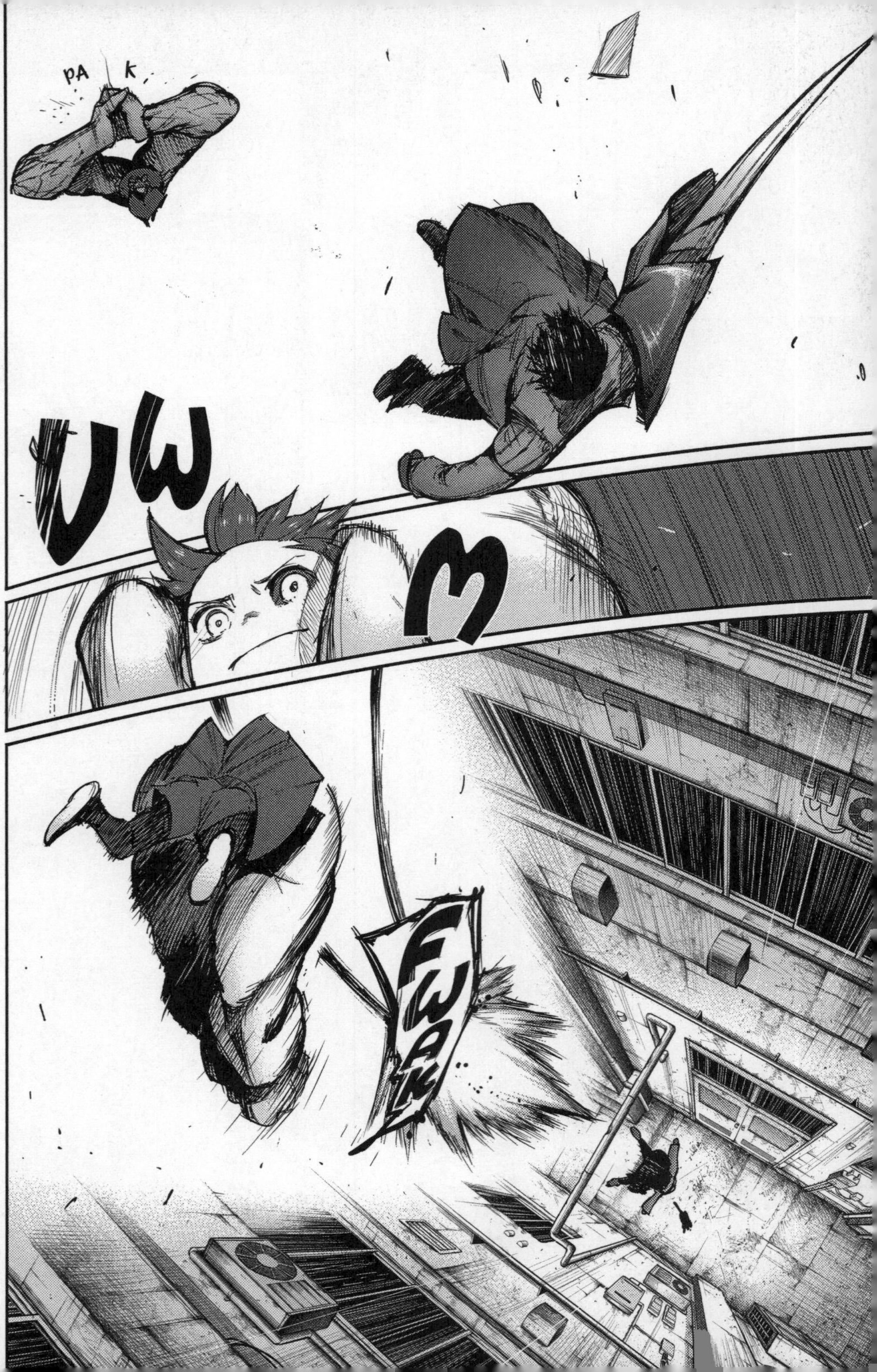
PAK
VWM
FWAM

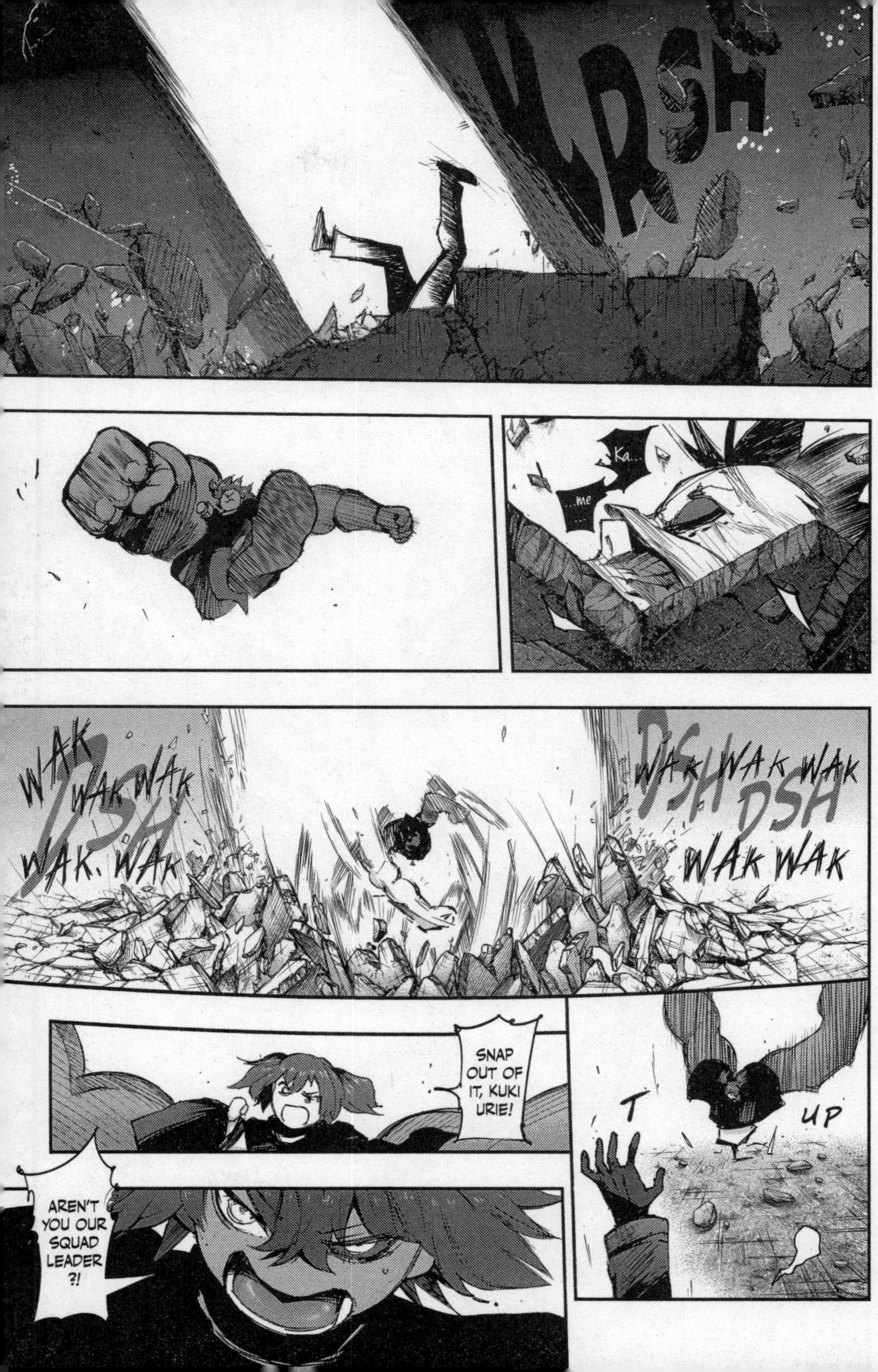
WRSH
...Ka...
...me...
WAK WAK WAK
DSH
DSH
WAK WAK
WAK
WAK WAK
DSH
WAK, WAK
T
UP
SNAP OUT OF IT, KUKI URIE!
AREN'T YOU OUR SQUAD LEADER ?!

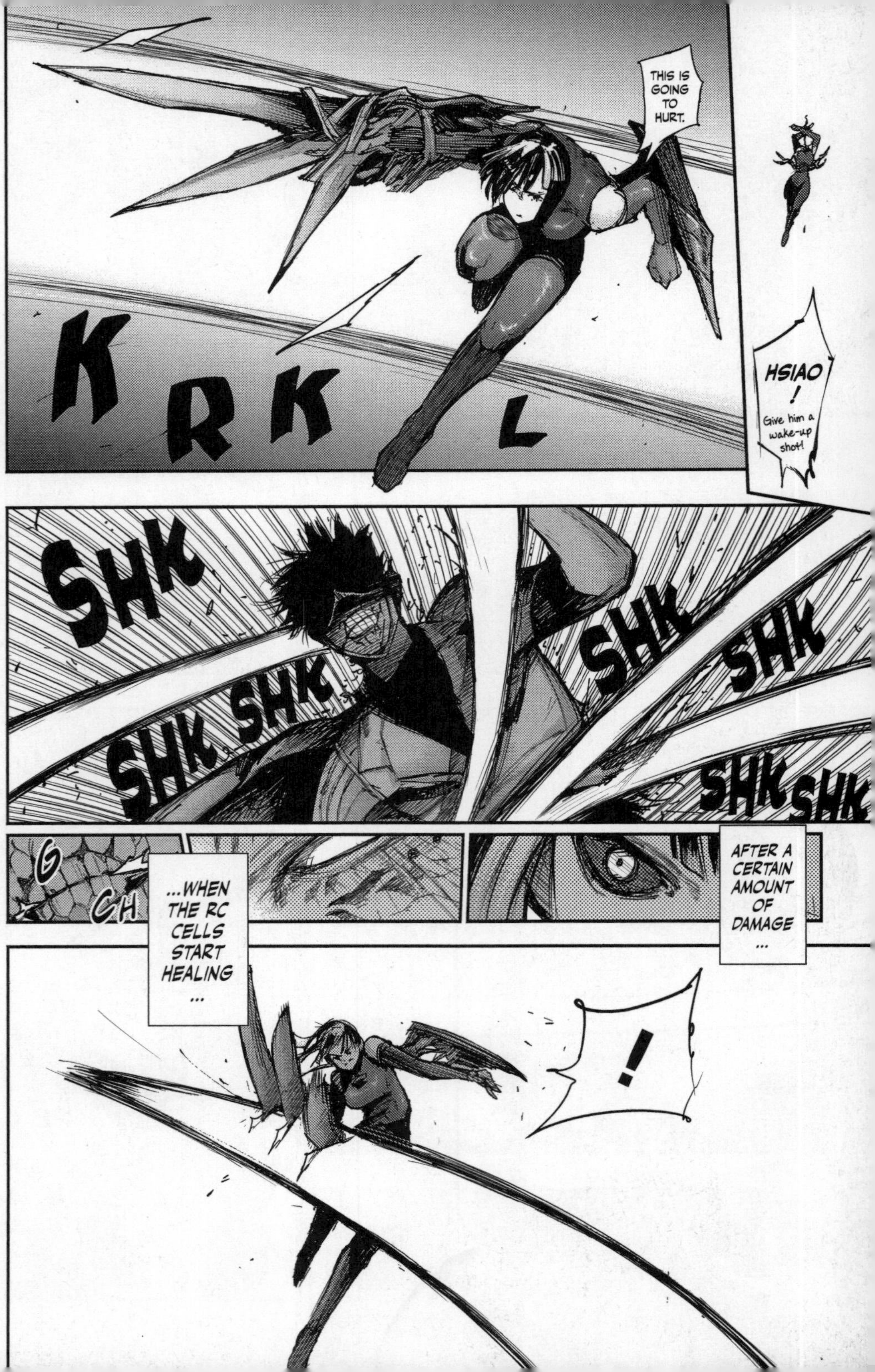
HSIAO!
Give him a wake-up shot!
THIS IS GOING TO HURT.
KRKL
SHK SHK SHK SHK SHK SHK SHK
AFTER A CERTAIN AMOUNT OF DAMAGE ...
...WHEN THE RC CELLS START HEALING ...
GCH
!

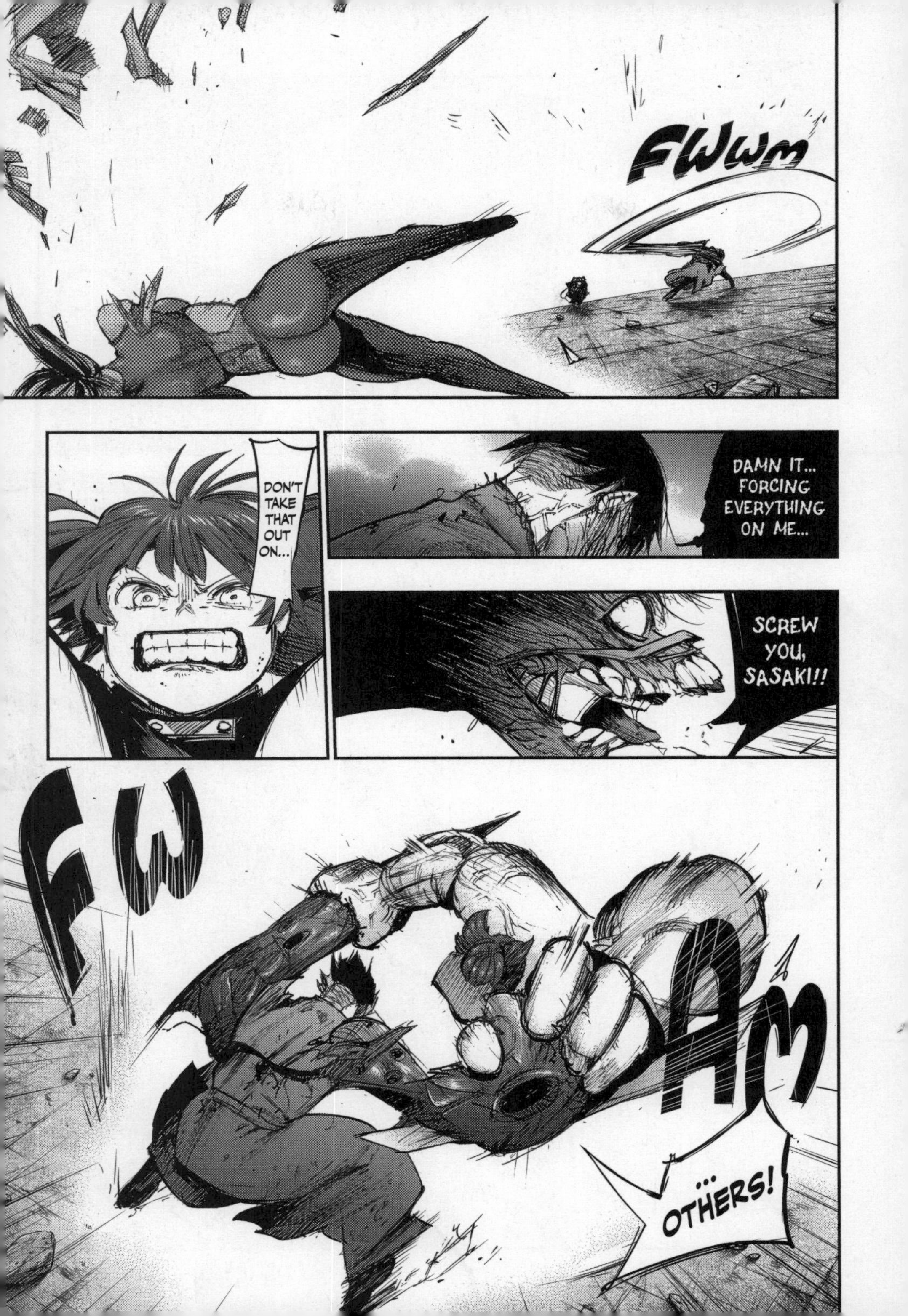
FWWM
DAMN IT... FORCING EVERYTHING ON ME...
SCREW YOU, SASAKI!!
DON'T TAKE THAT OUT ON...
FWAM
... OTHERS!

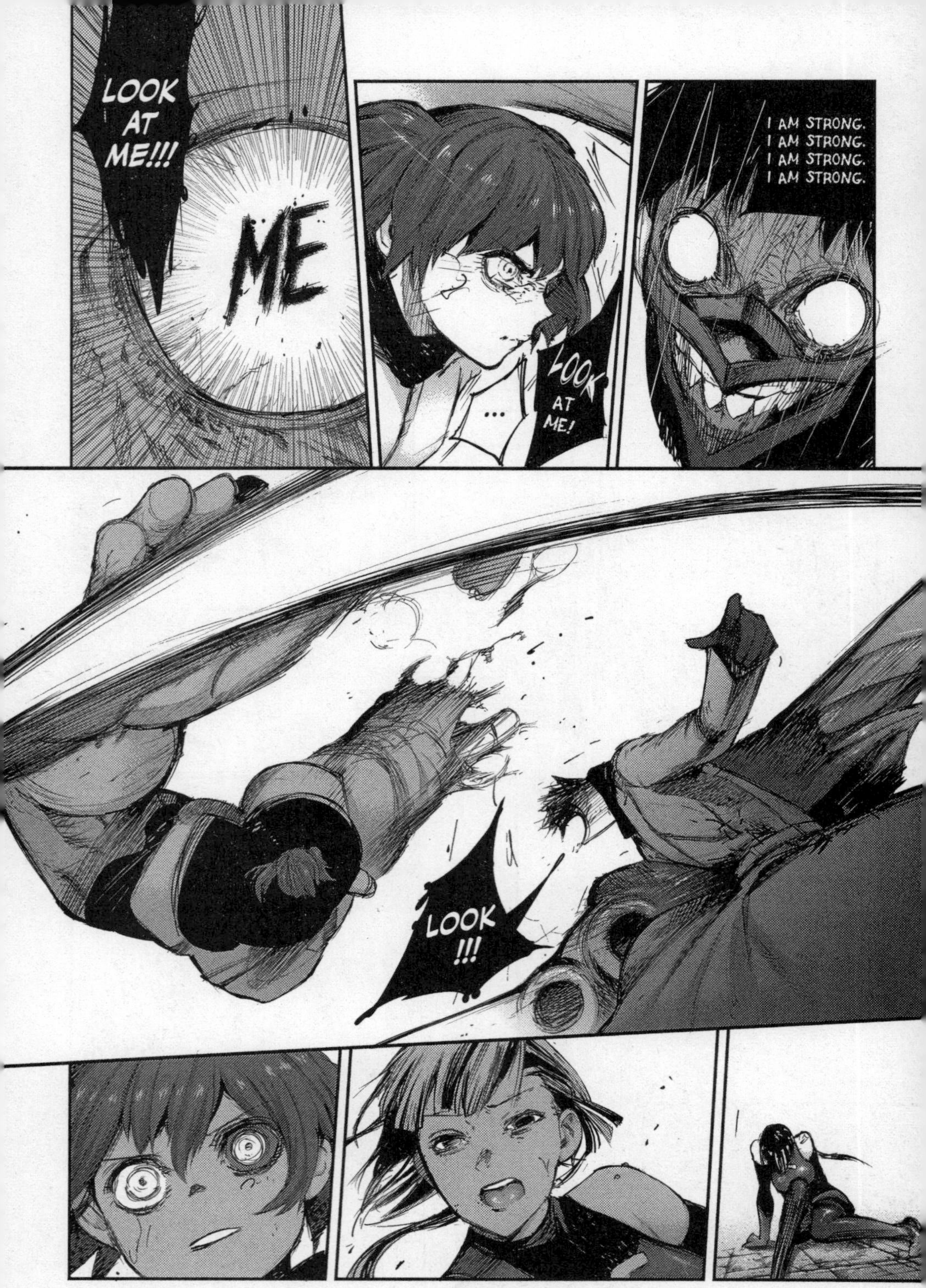
I AM STRONG.
I AM STRONG.
I AM STRONG.
I AM STRONG.
LOOK AT ME!
...
LOOK AT ME!!!
ME
LOOK !!!

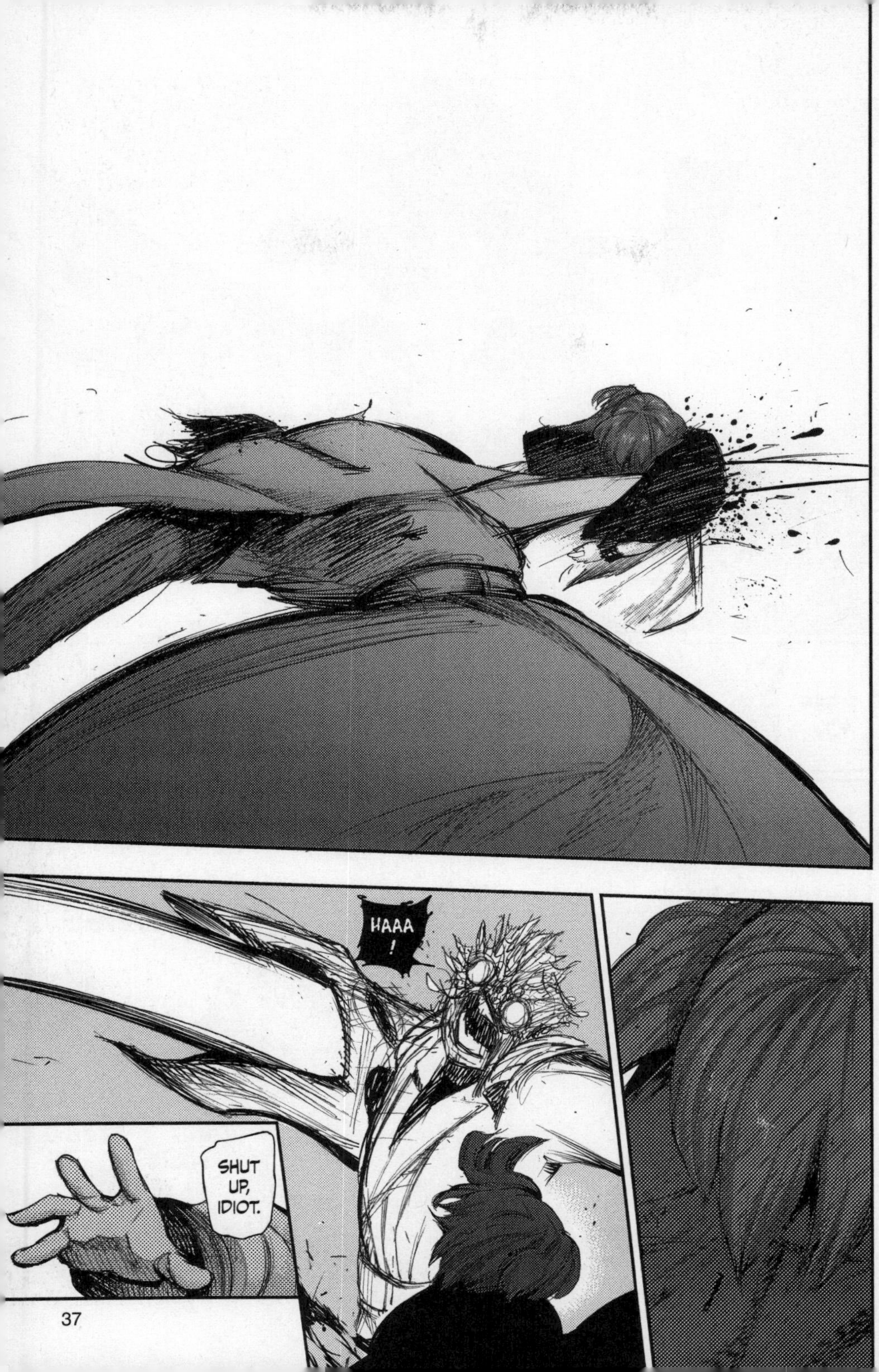
HAAA !
SHUT UP, IDIOT.

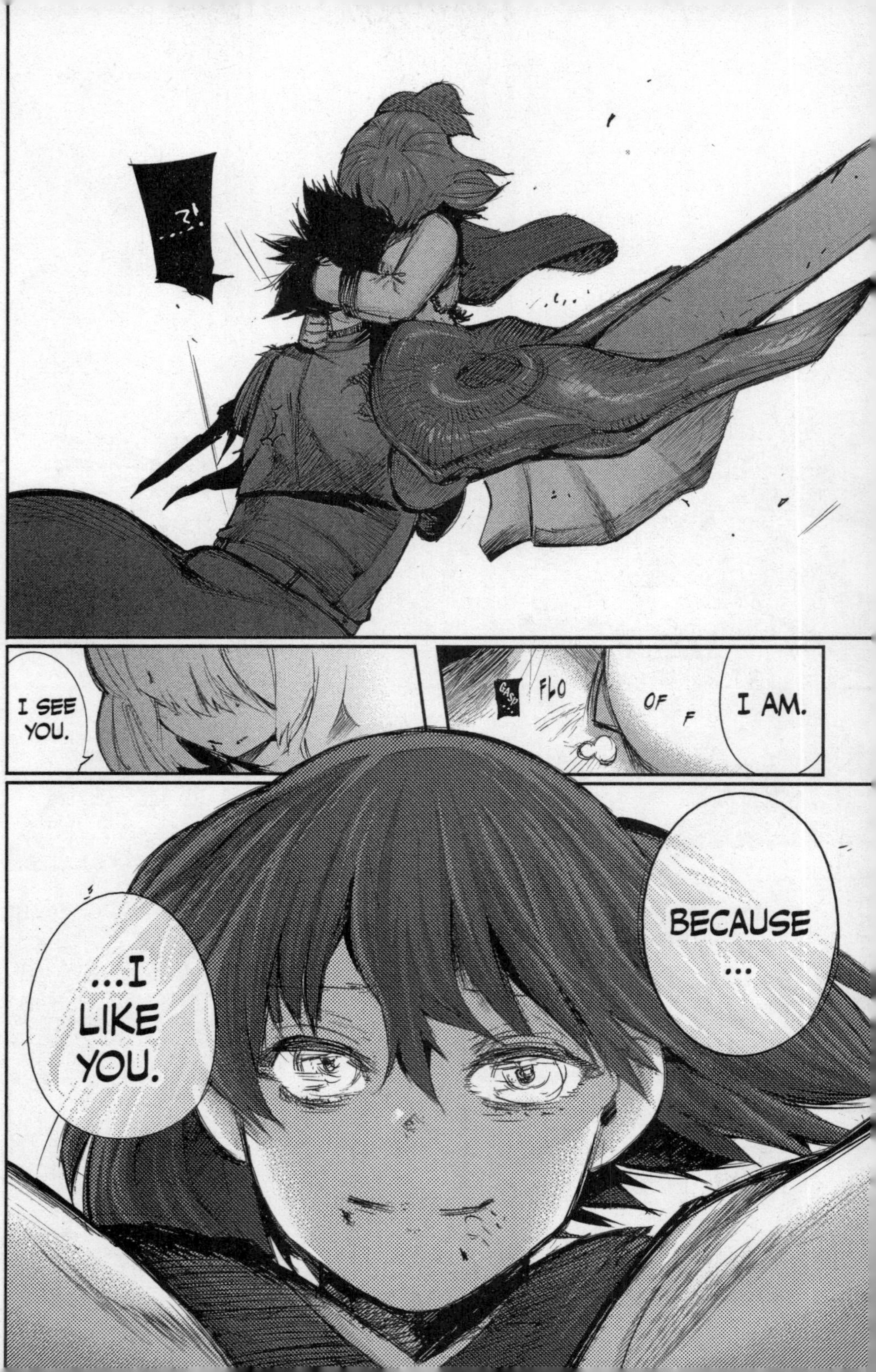
...?!
I AM.
FLO
OF
F
GASP
I SEE YOU.
BECAUSE ...
...I LIKE YOU.

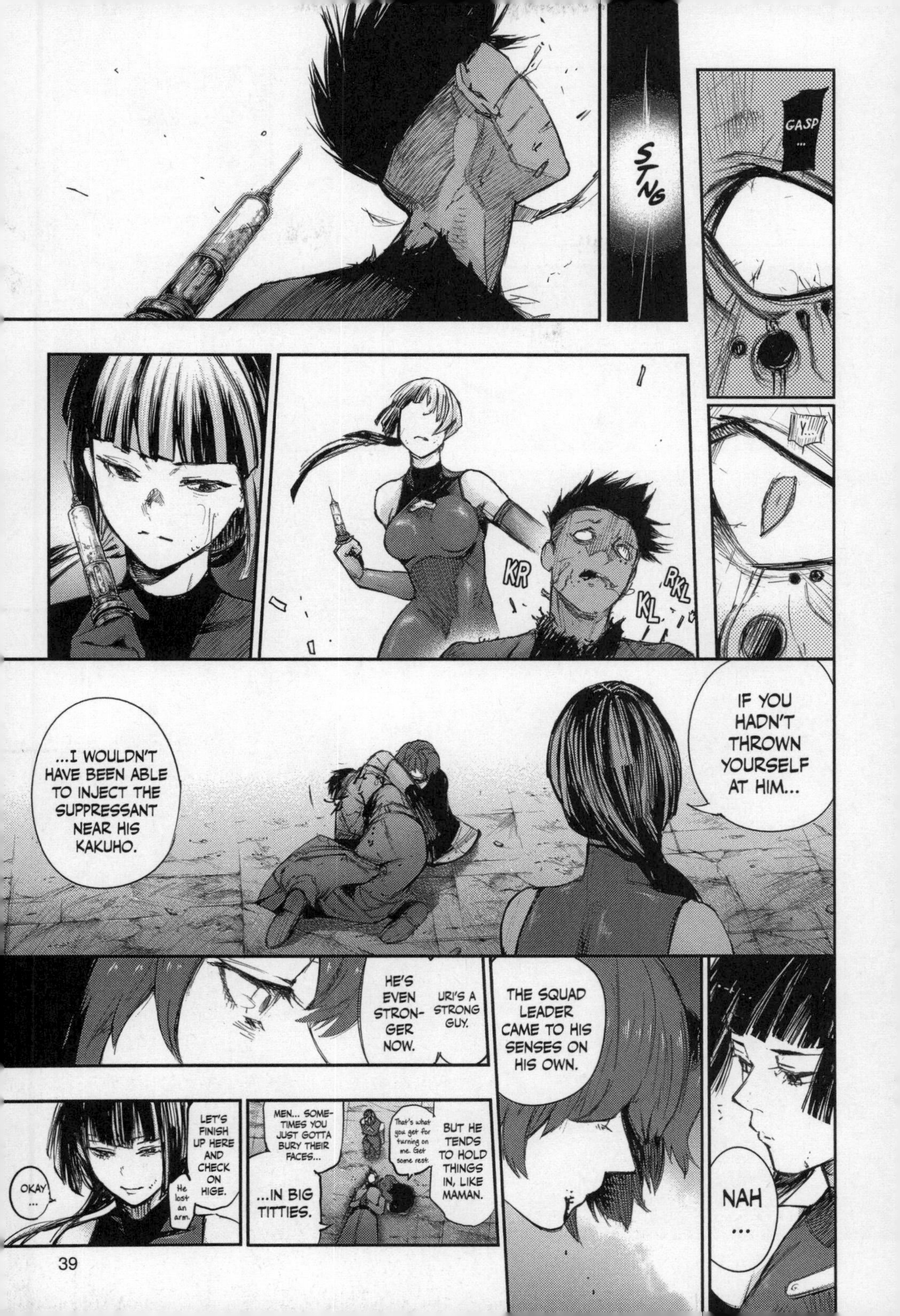
GASP ...
STNG
Y...
RKL
KL
KR
IF YOU HADN'T THROWN YOURSELF AT HIM...
...I WOULDN'T HAVE BEEN ABLE TO INJECT THE SUPPRESSANT NEAR HIS KAKUHO.
NAH ...
THE SQUAD LEADER CAME TO HIS SENSES ON HIS OWN.
URI'S A STRONG GUY.
HE'S EVEN STRONGER NOW.
BUT HE TENDS TO HOLD THINGS IN, LIKE MAMAN.
That's what you get for turning on me. Get some rest.
MEN... SOMETIMES YOU JUST GOTTA BURY THEIR FACES...
...IN BIG TITTIES.
LET'S FINISH UP HERE AND CHECK ON HIGE.
He lost an arm.
OKAY ...

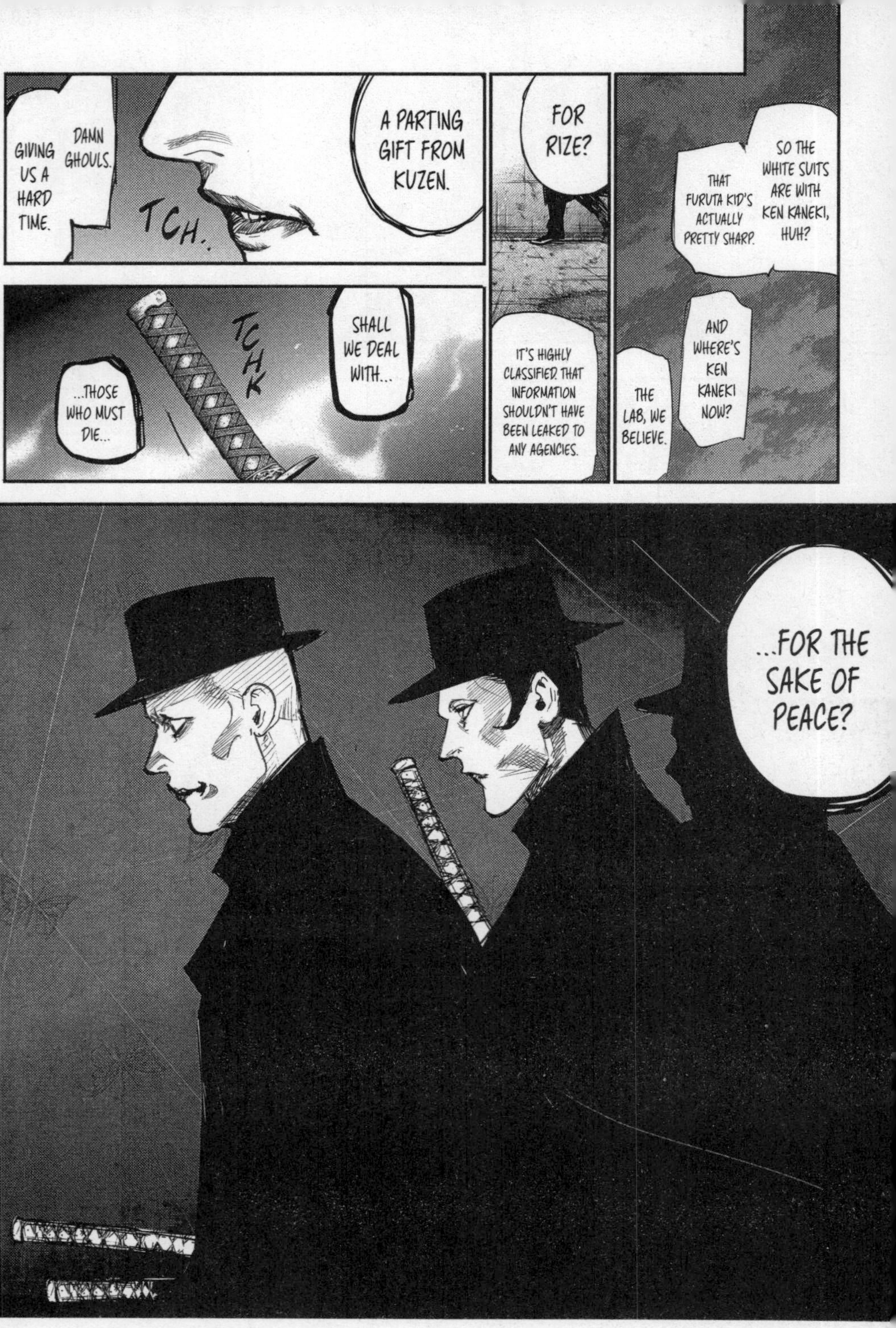
SO THE WHITE SUITS ARE WITH KEN KANEKI, HUH?
THAT FURUTA KID'S ACTUALLY PRETTY SHARP.
AND WHERE'S KEN KANEKI NOW?
THE LAB, WE BELIEVE.
FOR RIZE?
IT'S HIGHLY CLASSIFIED THAT INFORMATION SHOULDN'T HAVE BEEN LEAKED TO ANY AGENCIES.
A PARTING GIFT FROM KUZEN.
TCH..
DAMN GHOULS.
GIVING US A HARD TIME.
SHALL WE DEAL WITH...
TCHK
...THOSE WHO MUST DIE...
...FOR THE SAKE OF PEACE?

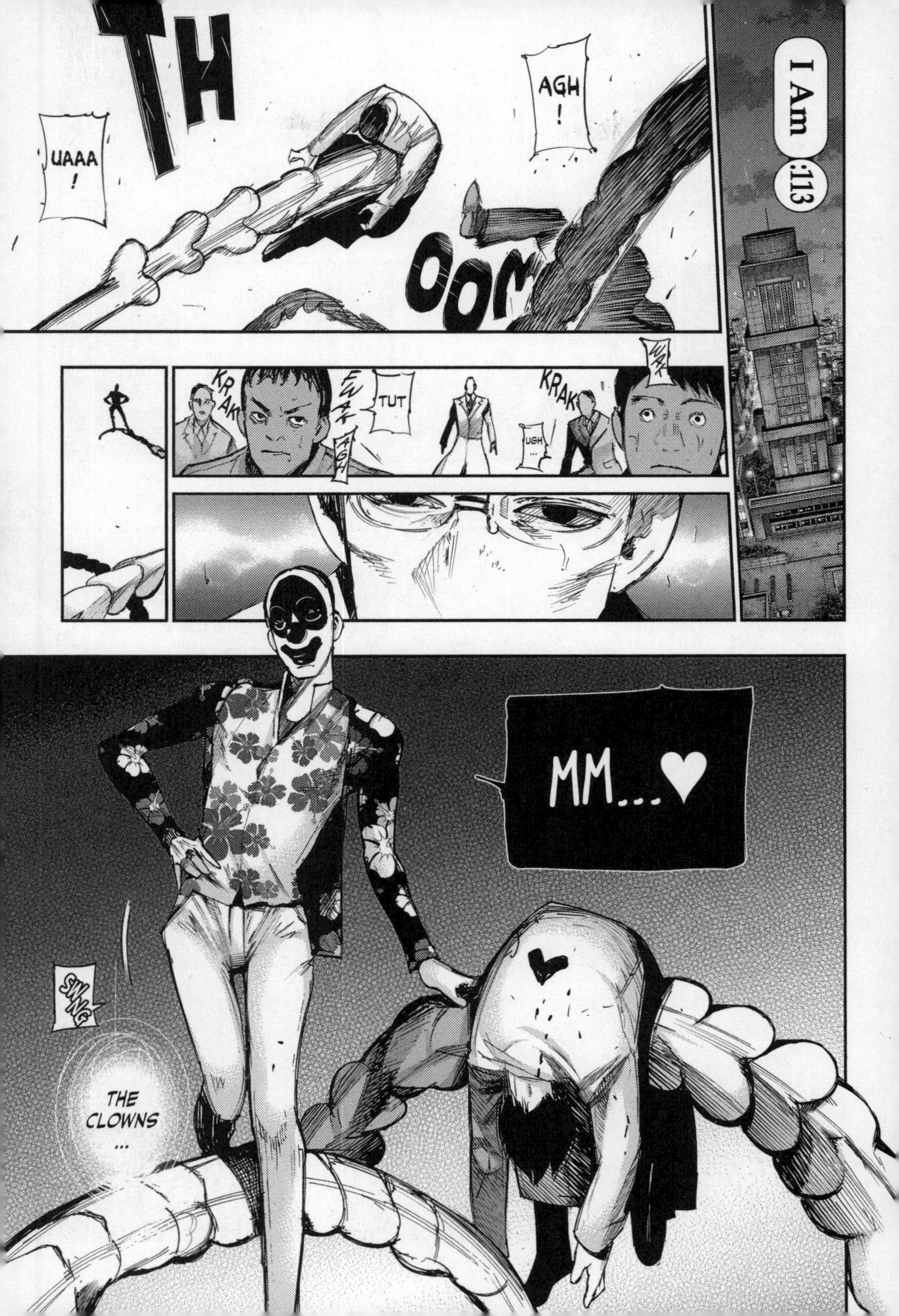
I Am :113
AGH !
TH
OOM
UAAA !
WAK
KRAK
UGH ...
TUT
FWAK
AGH
KRAK
MM...♥
SWNG
THE CLOWNS ...

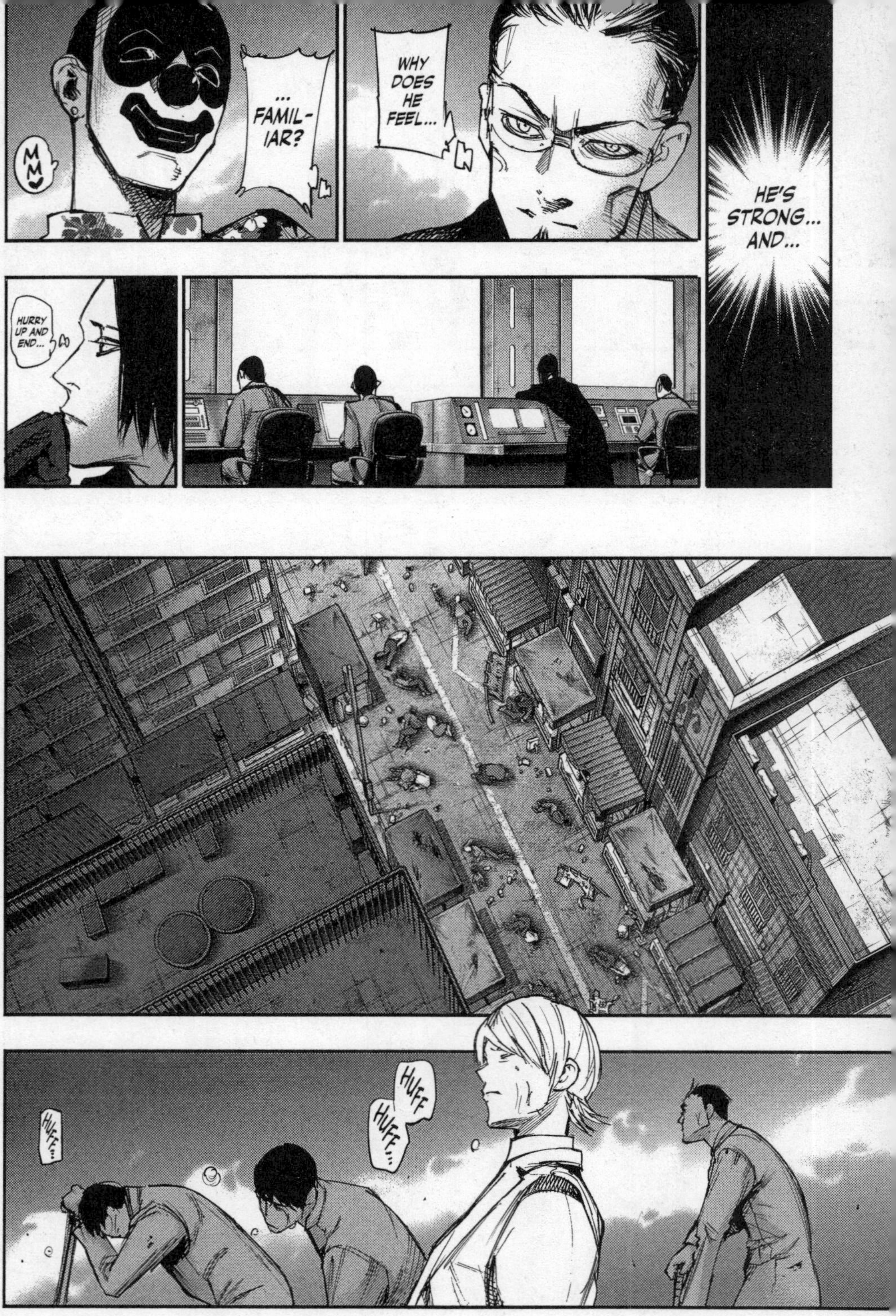
HE'S STRONG... AND...
WHY DOES HE FEEL...
... FAMIL-IAR?
MM
HURRY UP AND END...
HUFF HUFF...
HUFF...

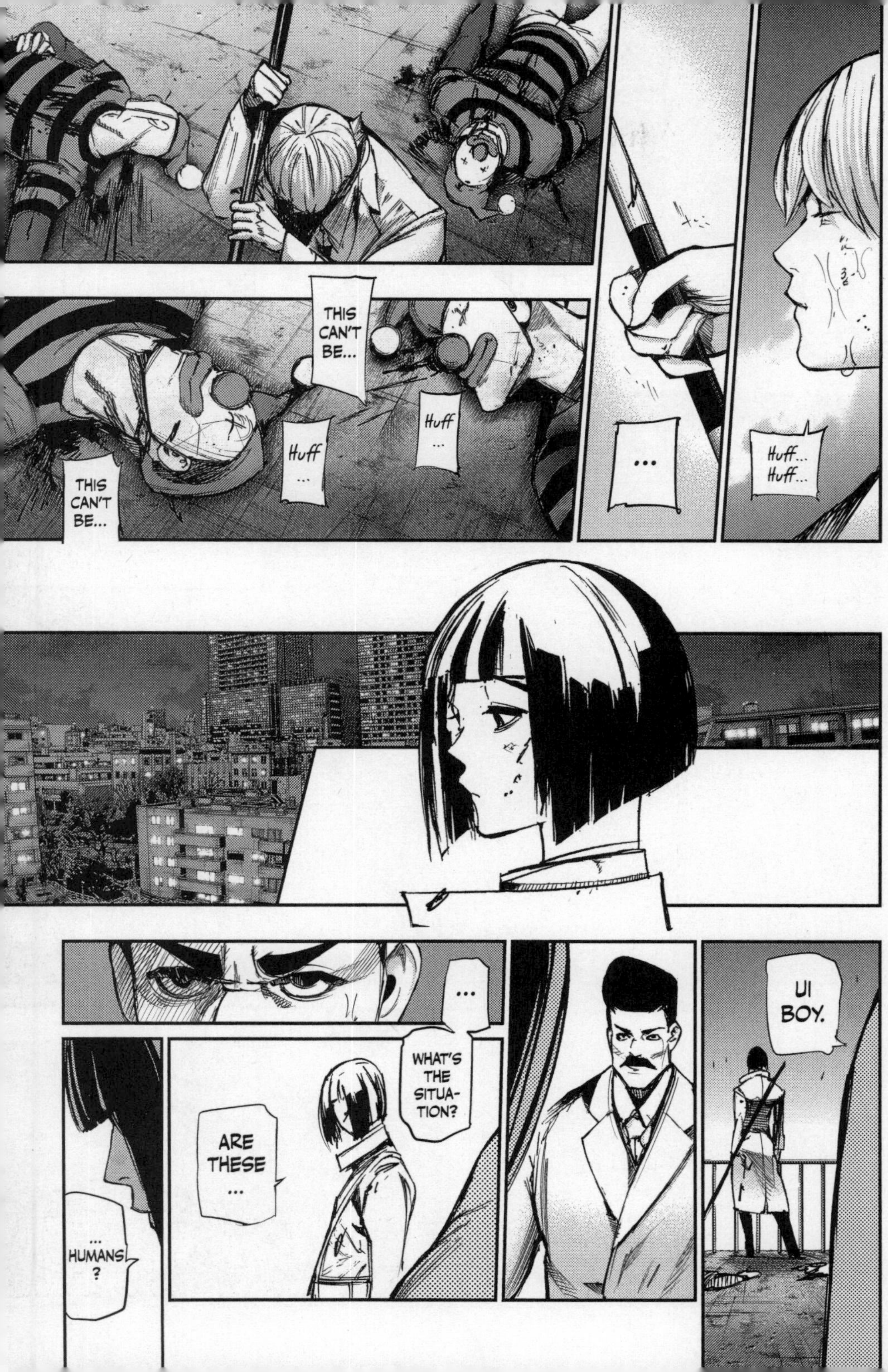
Huff... Huff...
...
Huff ...
THIS CAN'T BE...
Huff ...
THIS CAN'T BE...
UI BOY.
...
WHAT'S THE SITUATION?
ARE THESE ...
... HUMANS?

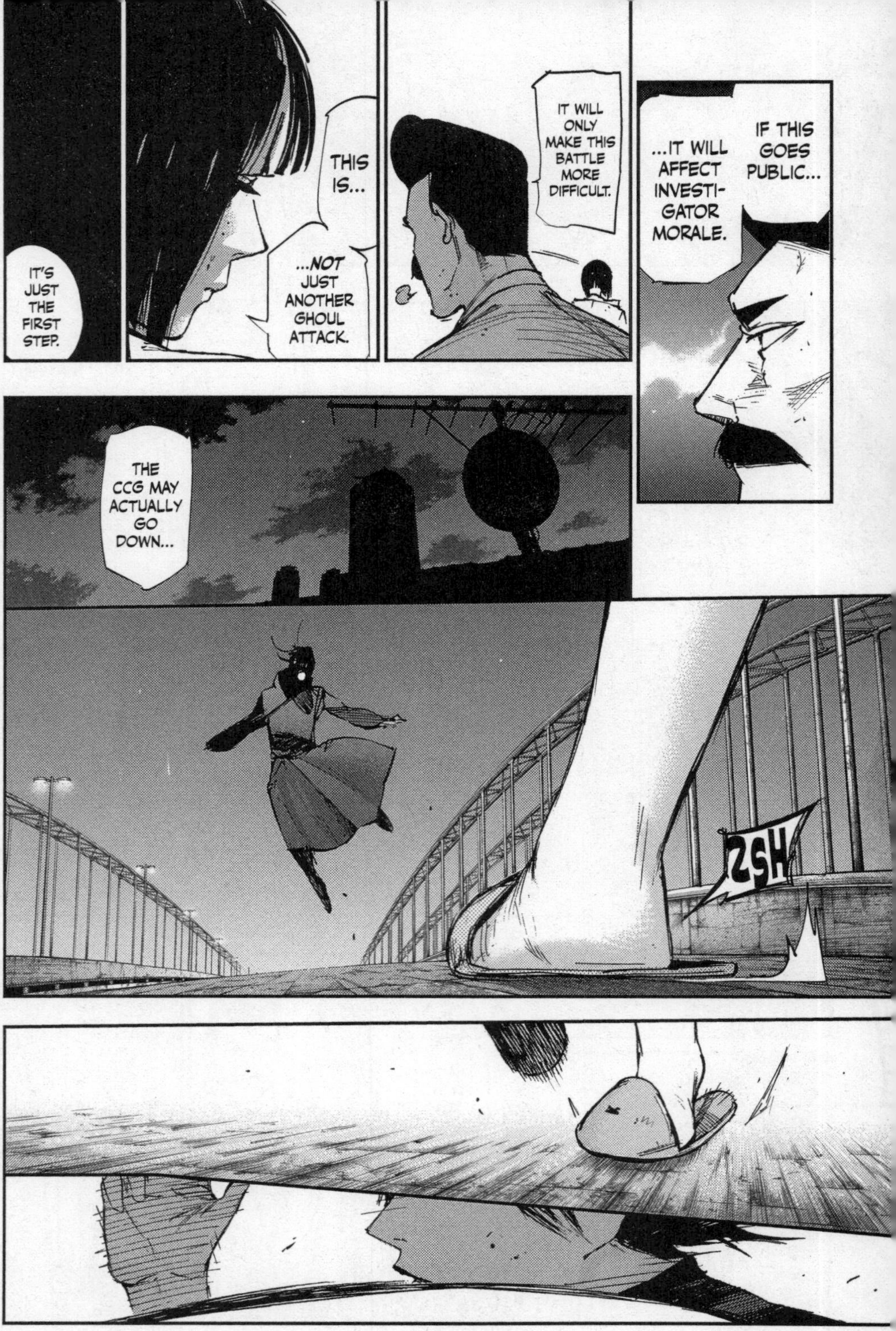
IF THIS GOES PUBLIC...
...IT WILL AFFECT INVESTIGATOR MORALE.
IT WILL ONLY MAKE THIS BATTLE MORE DIFFICULT.
THIS IS...
...*NOT* JUST ANOTHER GHOUL ATTACK.
IT'S JUST THE FIRST STEP.
THE CCG MAY ACTUALLY GO DOWN...

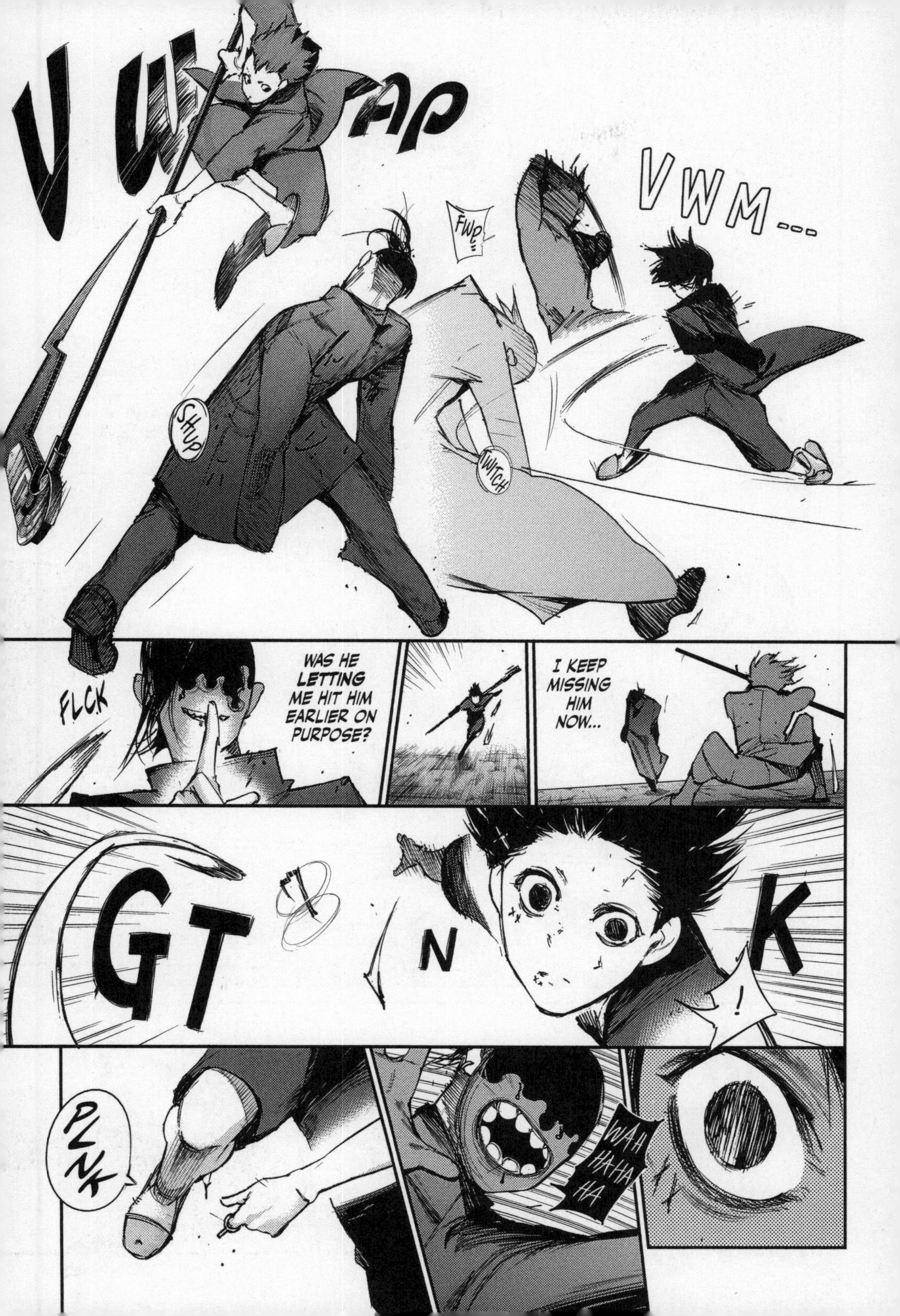
VWM...
FWP!
V W AP
TWITCH
SHUP
I KEEP MISSING HIM NOW...
WAS HE LETTING ME HIT HIM EARLIER ON PURPOSE?
FLCK
!
GT N K
WAHAHAHAHA
PLNK

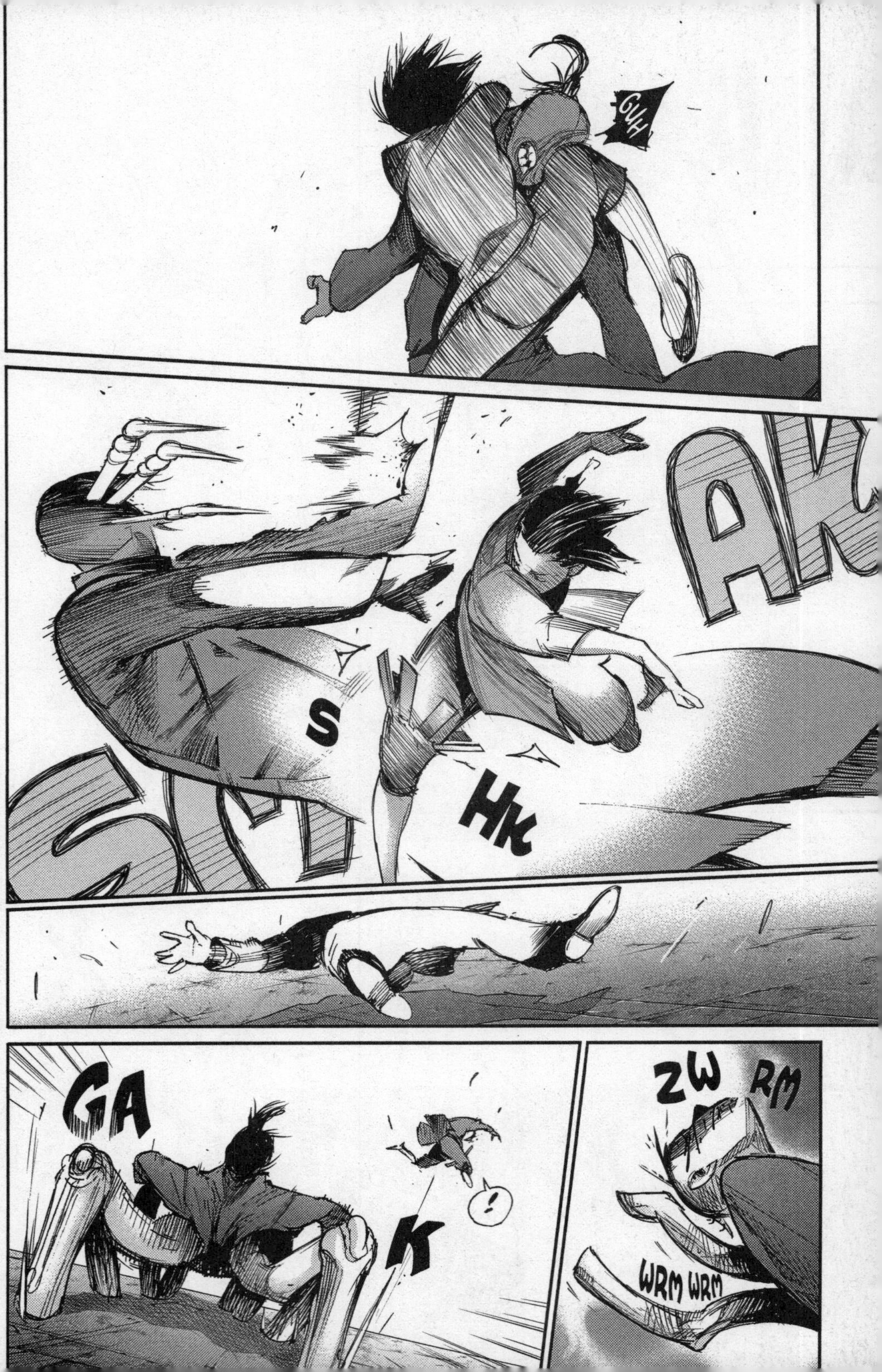
GUH
AK
S
Hk
ZW RM
WRM WRM
GA K
!

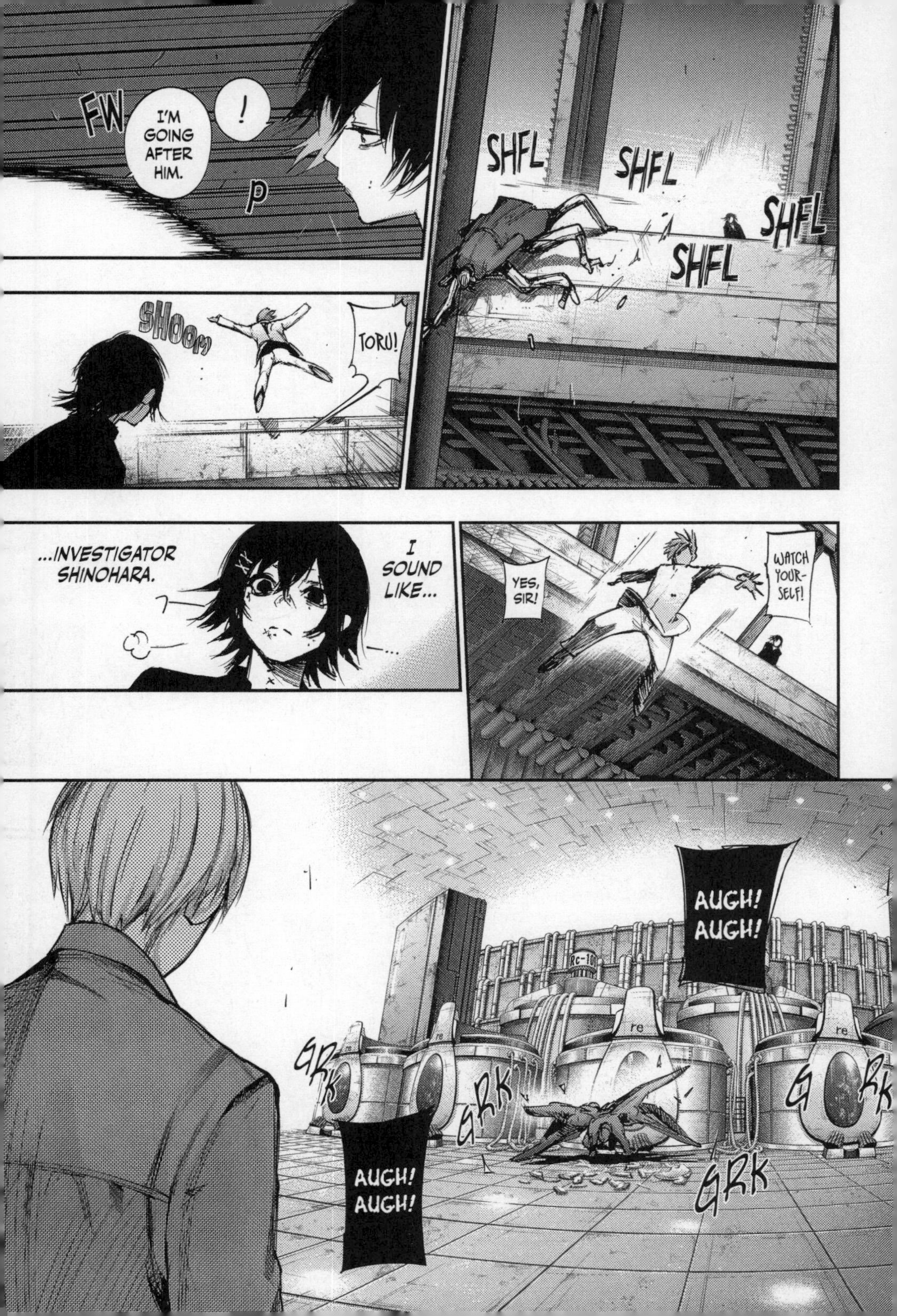
SHFL
SHFL
SHFL
SHFL
!
I'M GOING AFTER HIM.
FW
p
TORU!
SHOOM
WATCH YOURSELF!
YES, SIR!
I SOUND LIKE...
...INVESTIGATOR SHINOHARA.
AUGH! AUGH!
GRK
GRK
GRK
GRK
AUGH! AUGH!

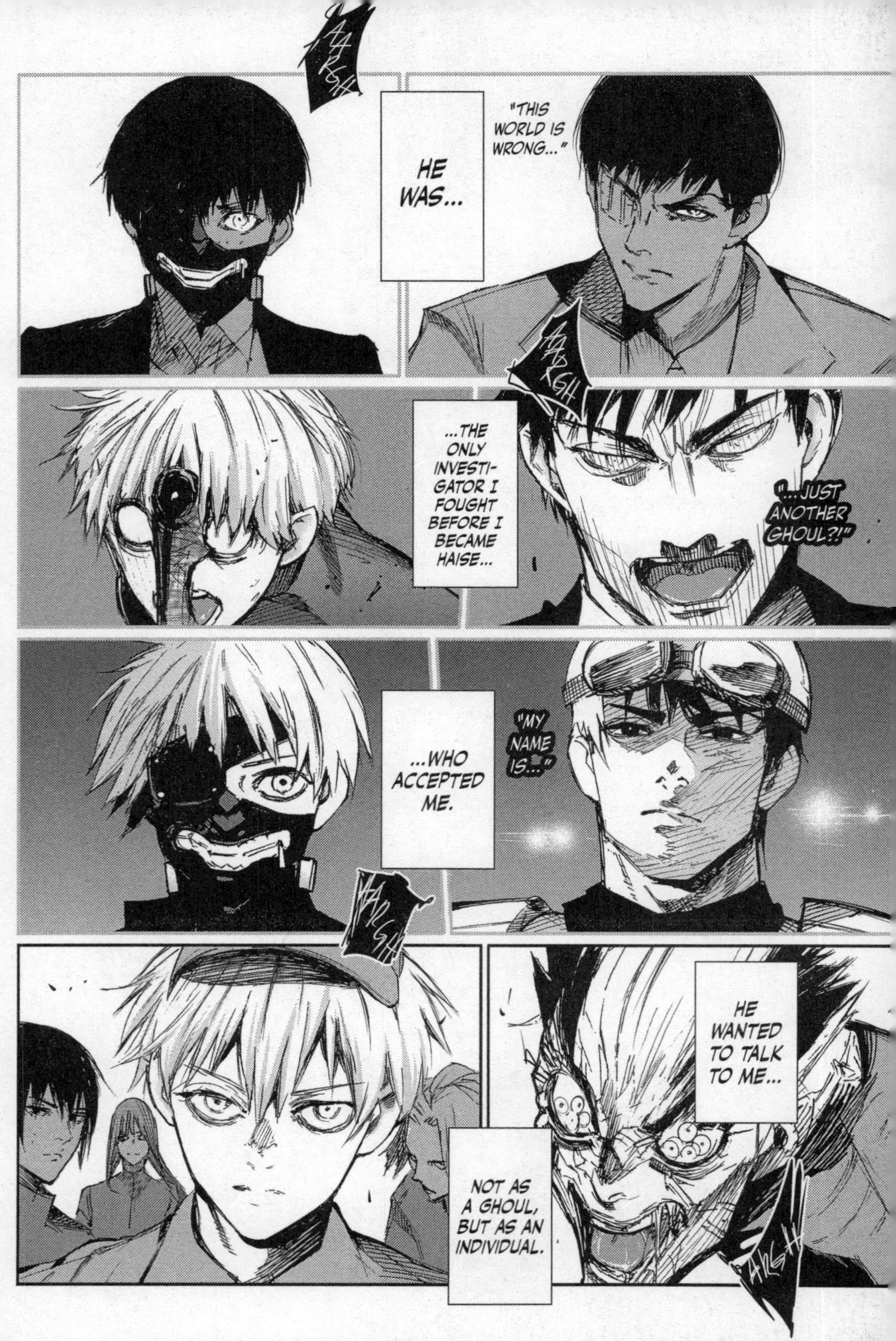
AARGH
"THIS WORLD IS WRONG..."
HE WAS...
AARGH
"...JUST ANOTHER GHOUL?!"
...THE ONLY INVESTI-GATOR I FOUGHT BEFORE I BECAME HAISE...
"MY NAME IS..."
...WHO ACCEPTED ME.
AARGH
HE WANTED TO TALK TO ME...
NOT AS A GHOUL, BUT AS AN INDIVIDUAL.
AARGH

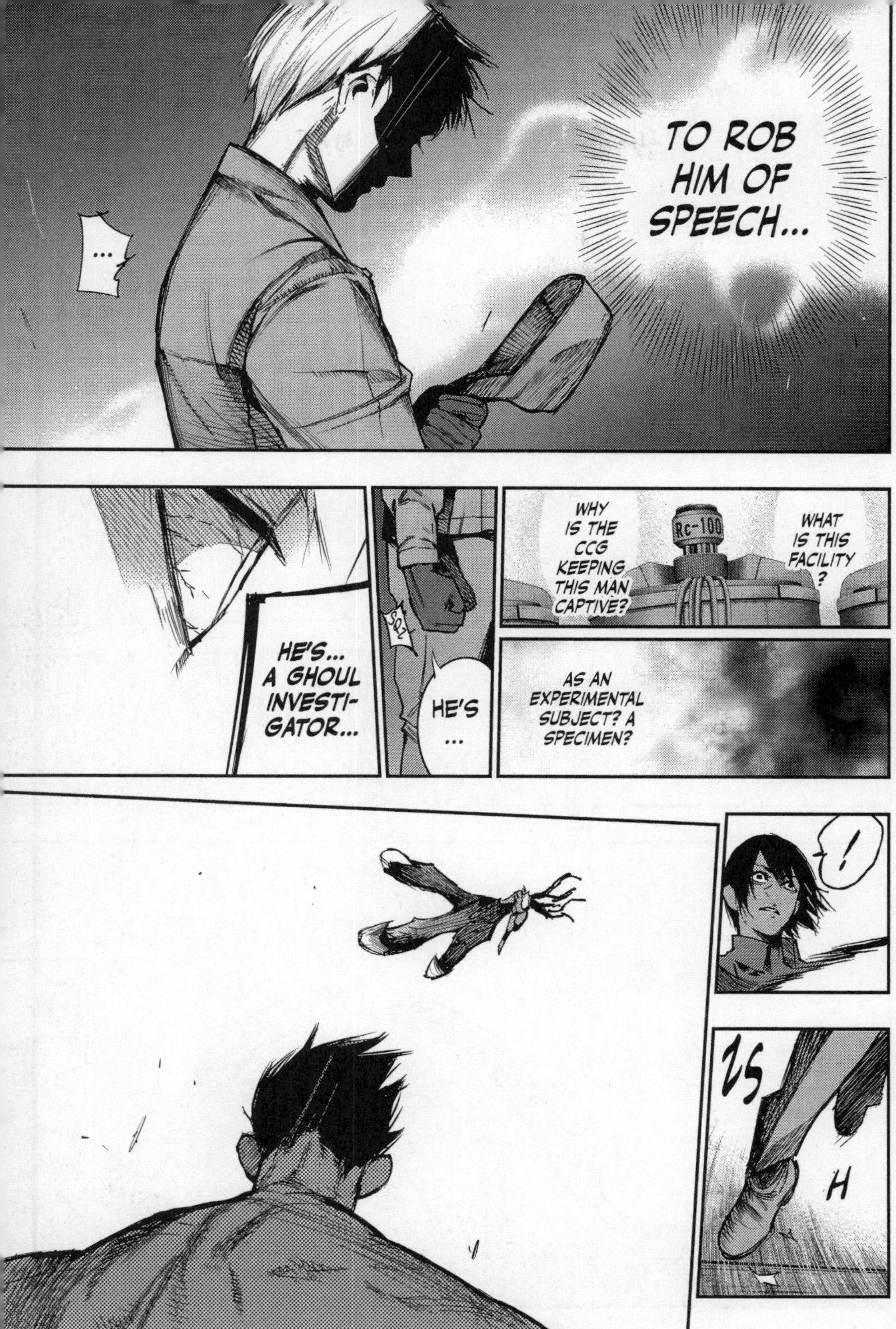

TO ROB HIM OF SPEECH...
...
WHAT IS THIS FACILITY?
WHY IS THE CCG KEEPING THIS MAN CAPTIVE?
Rc-100
AS AN EXPERIMENTAL SUBJECT? A SPECIMEN?
HE'S ...
HE'S... A GHOUL INVESTIGATOR...
!
ZS
H

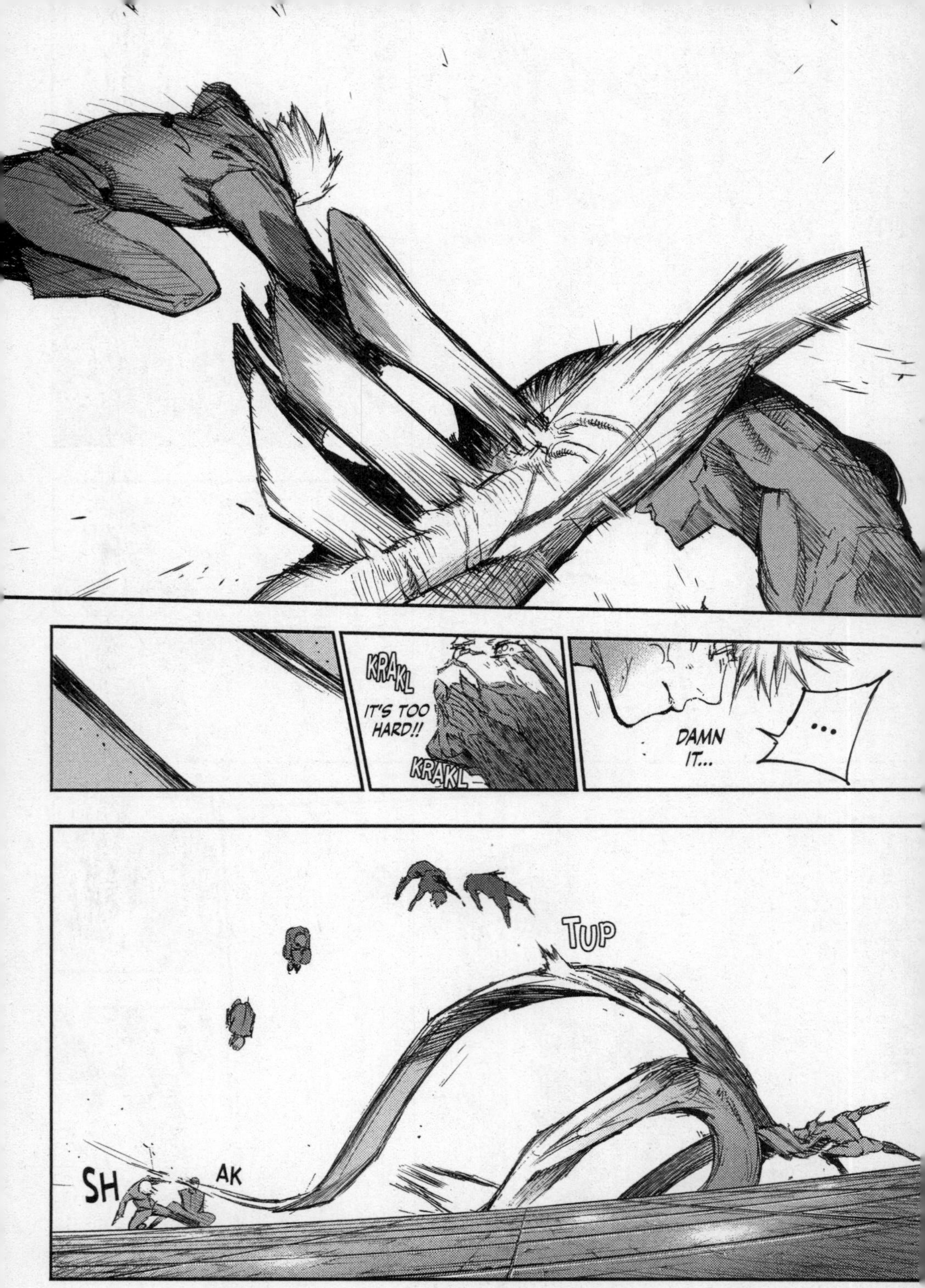
...
DAMN IT...
KRAKL
IT'S TOO HARD!!
KRAKL
TUP
SHAK

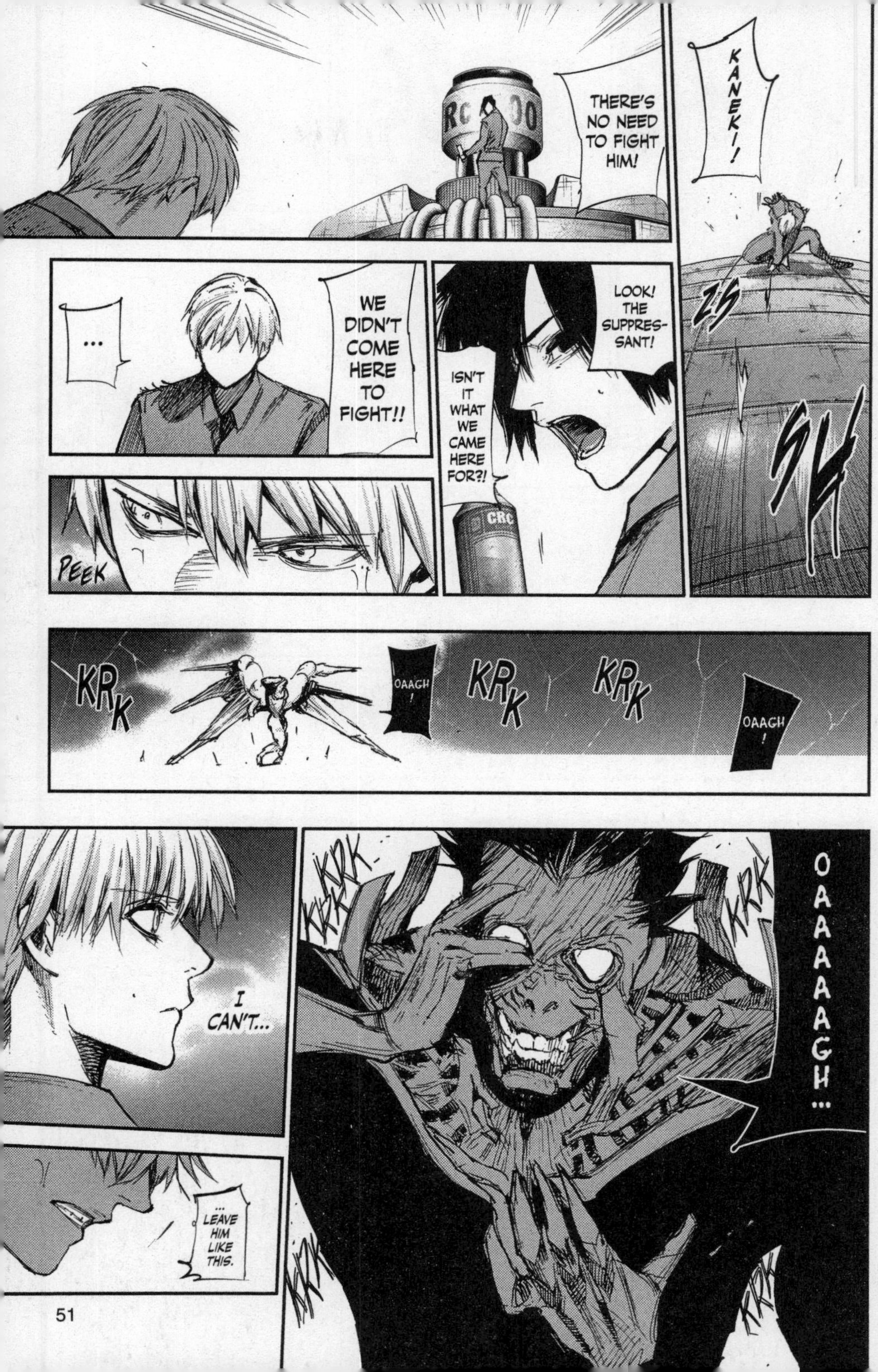
KANEKI!
ZS
SH
THERE'S NO NEED TO FIGHT HIM!
LOOK! THE SUPPRES-SANT!
ISN'T IT WHAT WE CAME HERE FOR?!
WE DIDN'T COME HERE TO FIGHT!!
...
PEEK
OAAGH!
KRK
KRK
OAAGH!
KRK
OAAAAAAAGH...
KRK
KRK KRK KRK
KRK
KRK
I CAN'T...
...LEAVE HIM LIKE THIS.

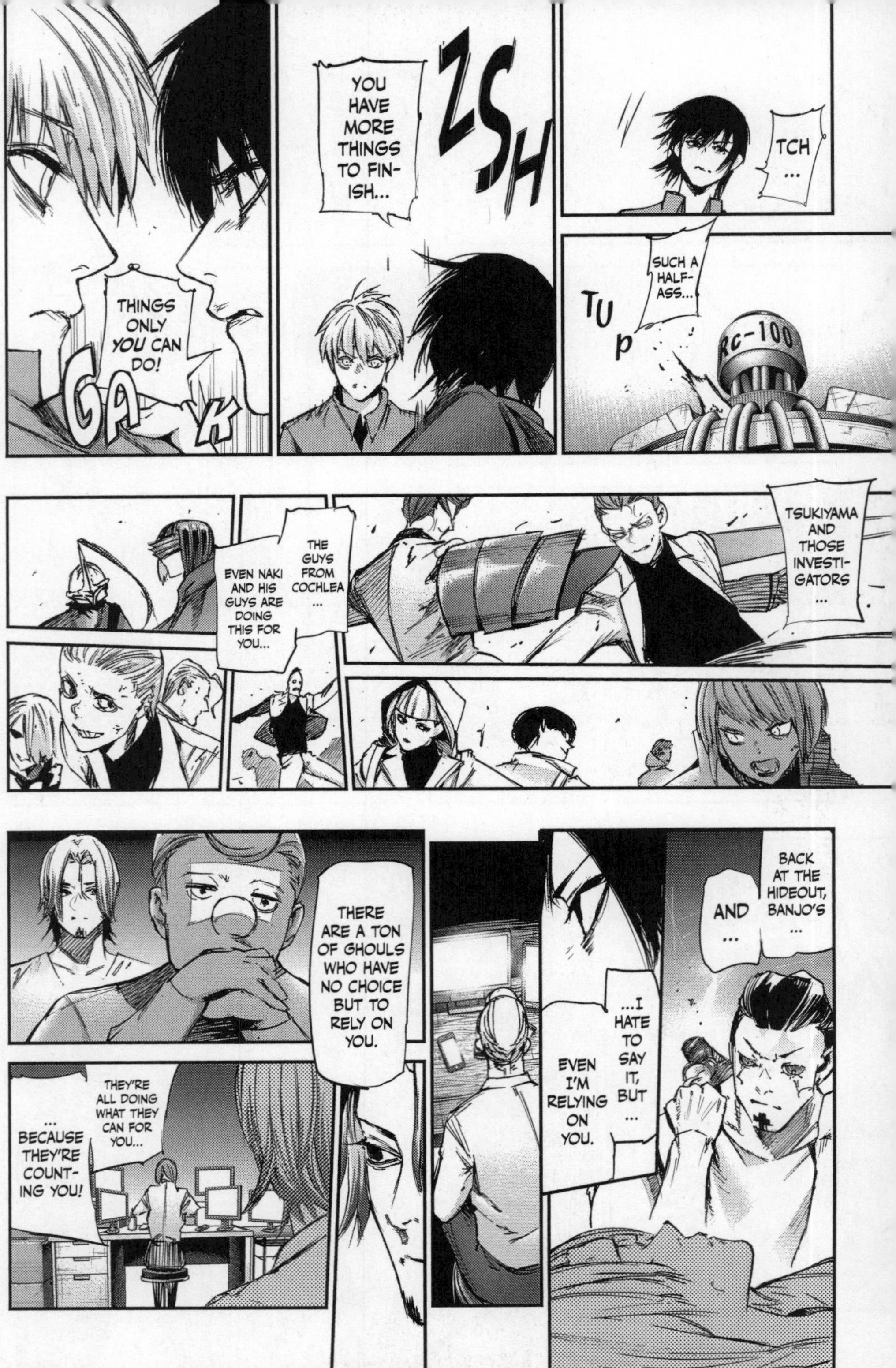
TCH ...
SUCH A HALF-ASS...
TUP
Rc-100
YOU HAVE MORE THINGS TO FIN-ISH...
ZSH
THINGS ONLY YOU CAN DO!
GAK
TSUKIYAMA AND THOSE INVESTI-GATORS ...
THE GUYS FROM COCHLEA ...
EVEN NAKI AND HIS GUYS ARE DOING THIS FOR YOU...
BACK AT THE HIDEOUT, BANJO'S ...
AND ...
...I HATE TO SAY IT, BUT ...
EVEN I'M RELYING ON YOU.
THERE ARE A TON OF GHOULS WHO HAVE NO CHOICE BUT TO RELY ON YOU.
THEY'RE ALL DOING WHAT THEY CAN FOR YOU...
... BECAUSE THEY'RE COUNT-ING YOU!

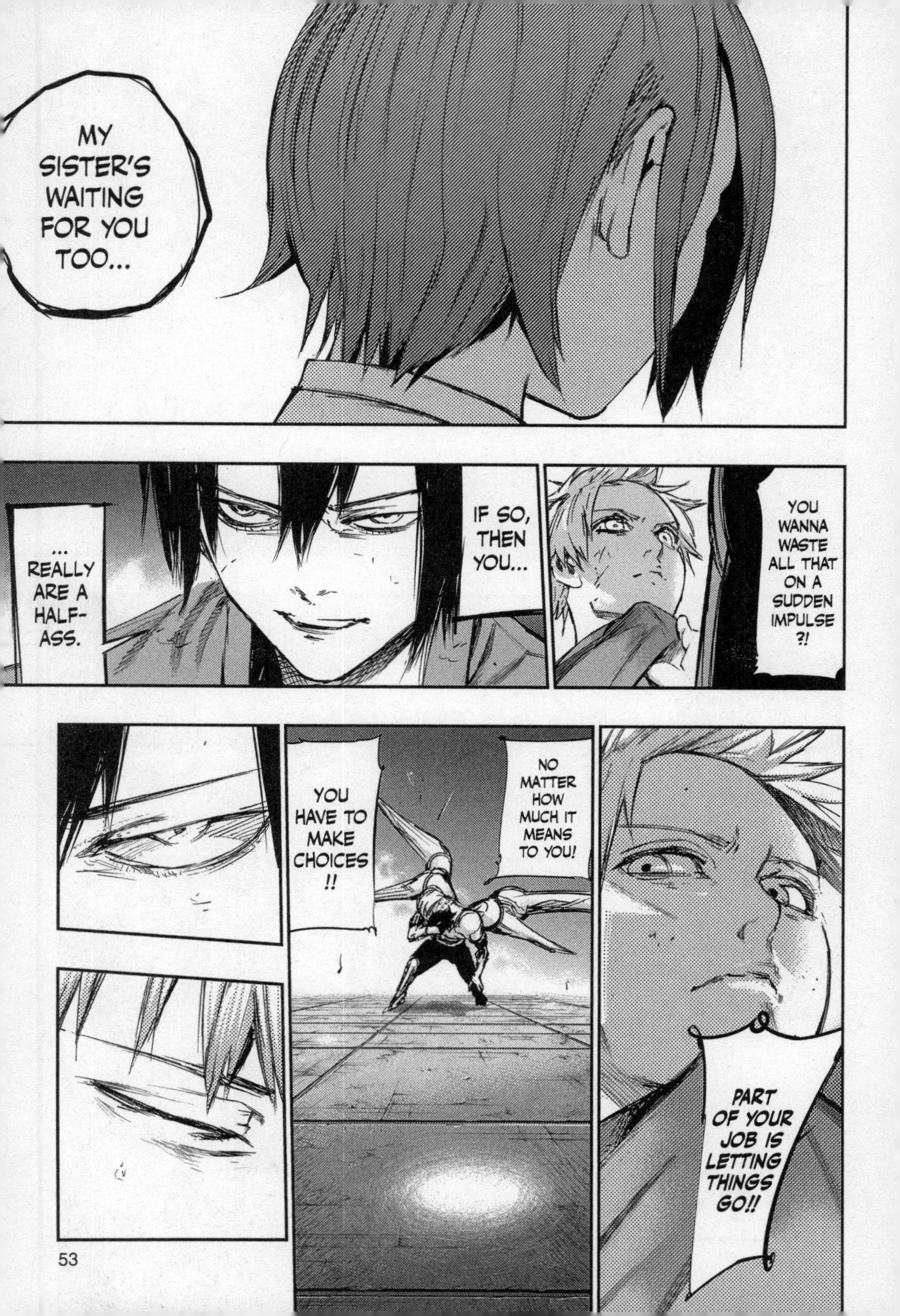
MY SISTER'S WAITING FOR YOU TOO...
YOU WANNA WASTE ALL THAT ON A SUDDEN IMPULSE ?!
IF SO, THEN YOU...
... REALLY ARE A HALF-ASS.
PART OF YOUR JOB IS LETTING THINGS GO!!
NO MATTER HOW MUCH IT MEANS TO YOU!
YOU HAVE TO MAKE CHOICES !!

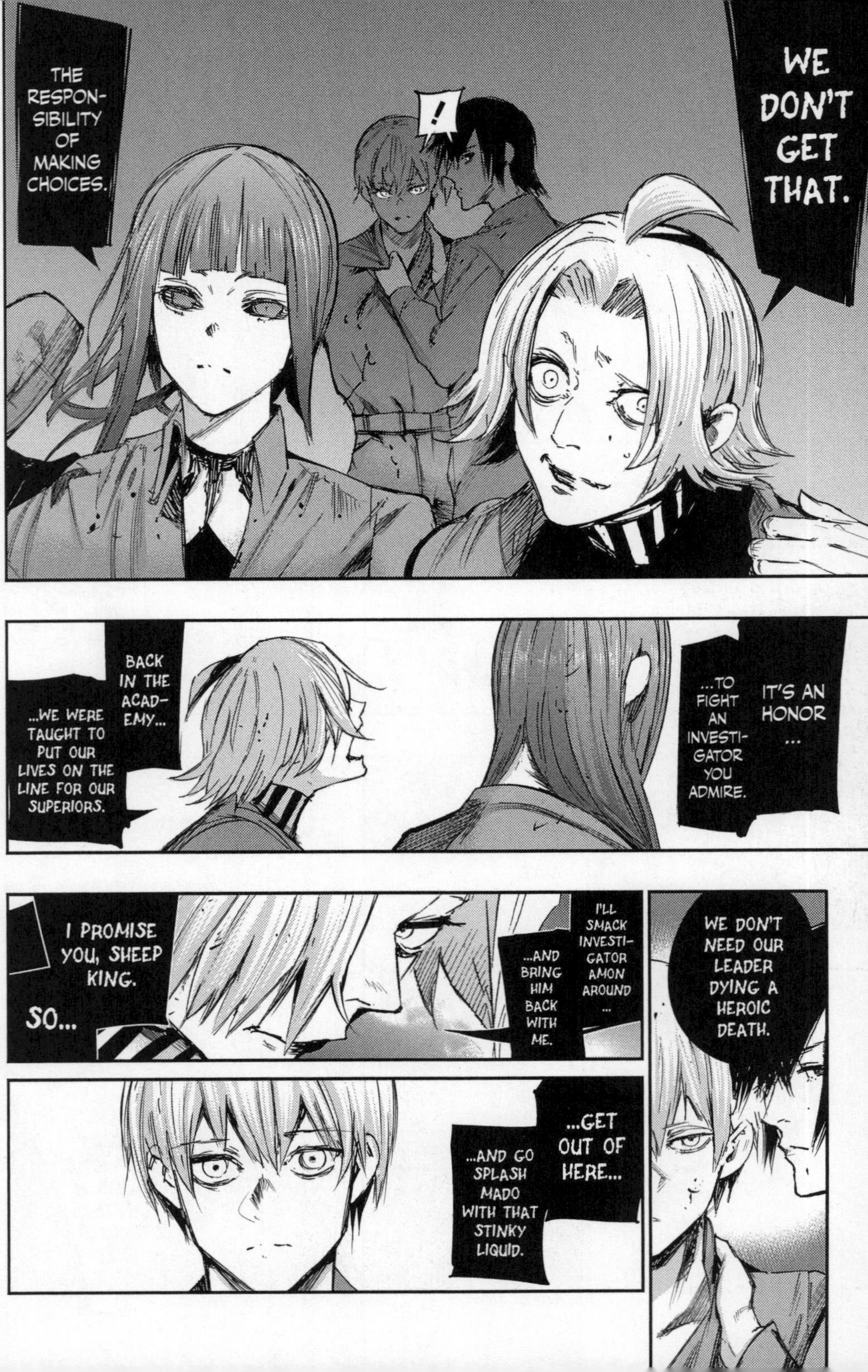
WE DON'T GET THAT.
!
THE RESPON-SIBILITY OF MAKING CHOICES.
IT'S AN HONOR ...
...TO FIGHT AN INVESTI-GATOR YOU ADMIRE.
BACK IN THE ACAD-EMY...
...WE WERE TAUGHT TO PUT OUR LIVES ON THE LINE FOR OUR SUPERIORS.
WE DON'T NEED OUR LEADER DYING A HEROIC DEATH.
I'LL SMACK INVESTI-GATOR AMON AROUND ...
...AND BRING HIM BACK WITH ME.
I PROMISE YOU, SHEEP KING.
SO...
...GET OUT OF HERE...
...AND GO SPLASH MADO WITH THAT STINKY LIQUID.

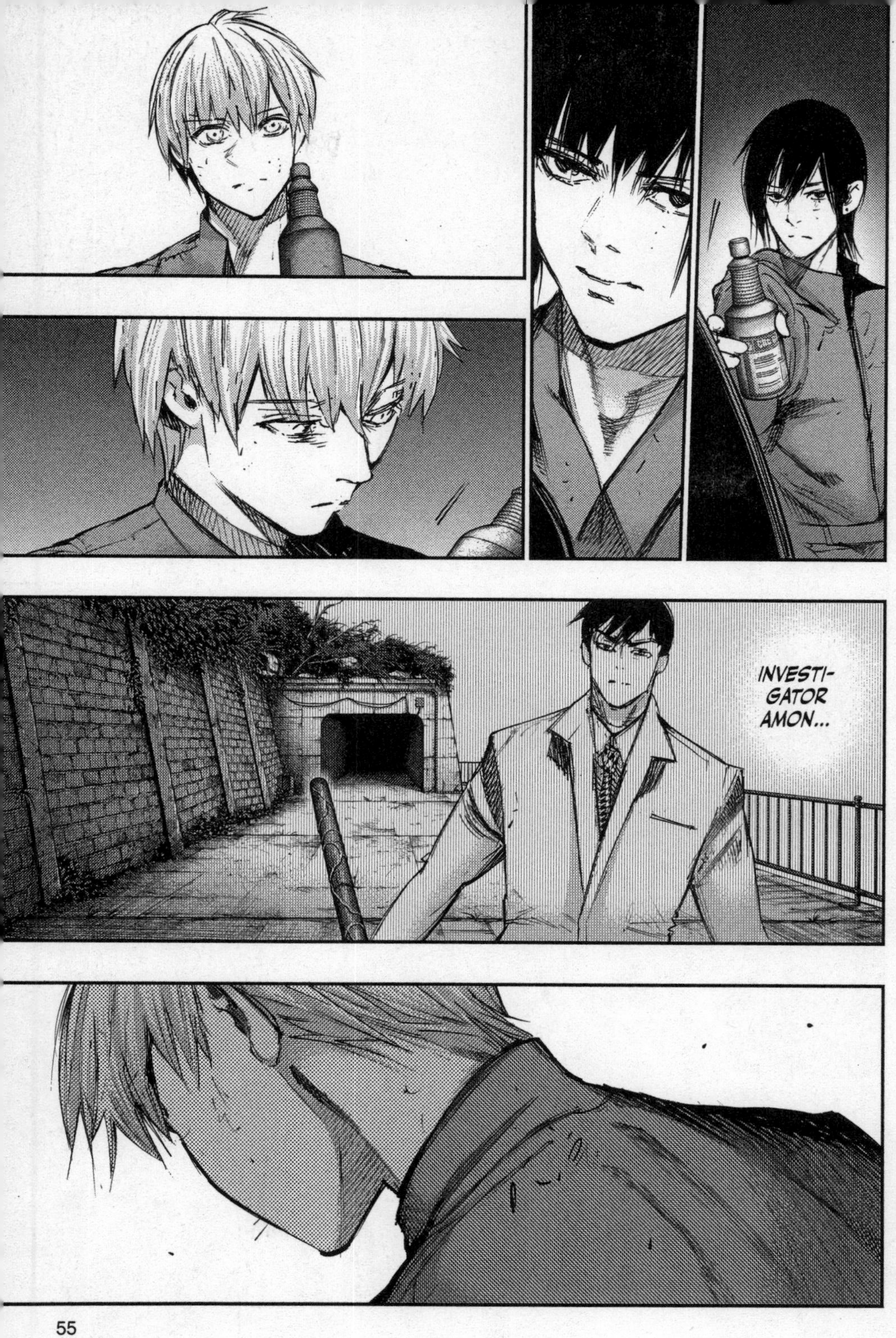
INVESTI-
GATOR
AMON...

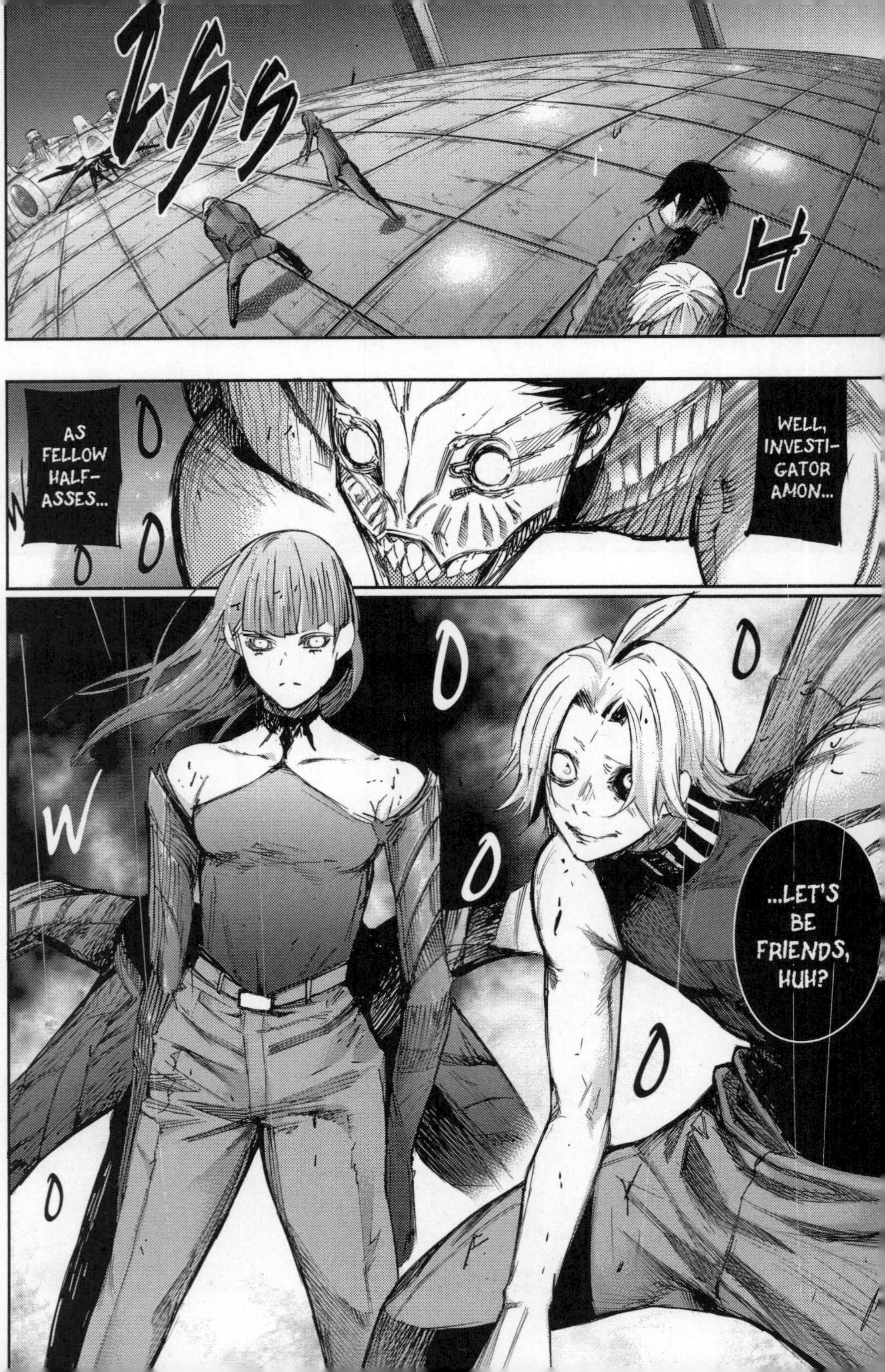
ZSSS
H
WELL, INVESTIGATOR AMON...
AS FELLOW HALF-ASSES...
WOOO
...LET'S BE FRIENDS, HUH?
WOOOOO

ZSH ZSH ZSH ZSH ZSH ZSH ZSH ZSH

ZS

HA

ZSS

SSH

UGH
...

AAH! AH! SHK AH! SHK HA! SHK AH! SHK HA! SHK
SHK AAH! AH! SHK HA! SHK HA! HA! SHK SHK

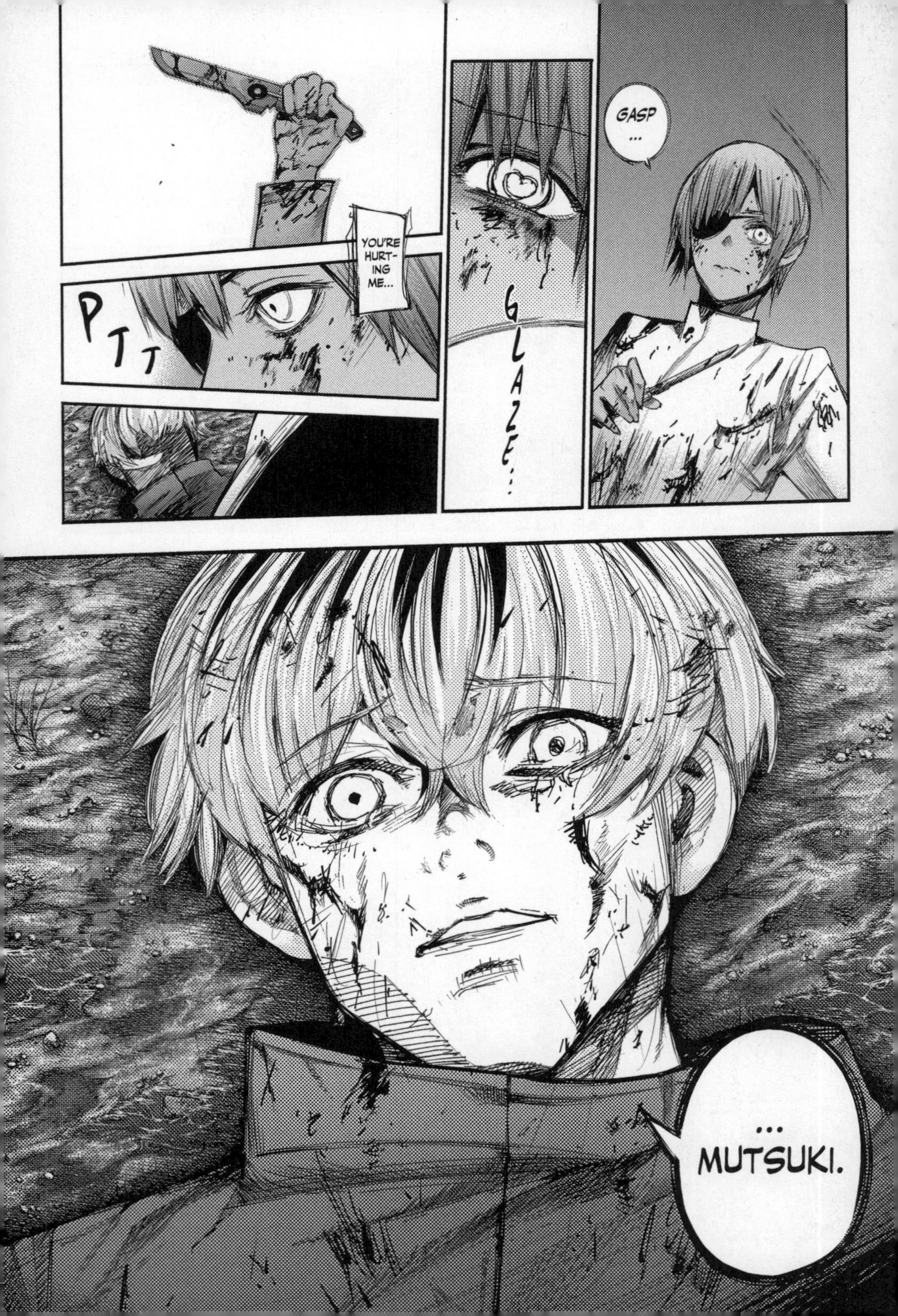
GASP ...
GLAZE...
YOU'RE HURTING ME...
PTTT
... MUTSUKI.

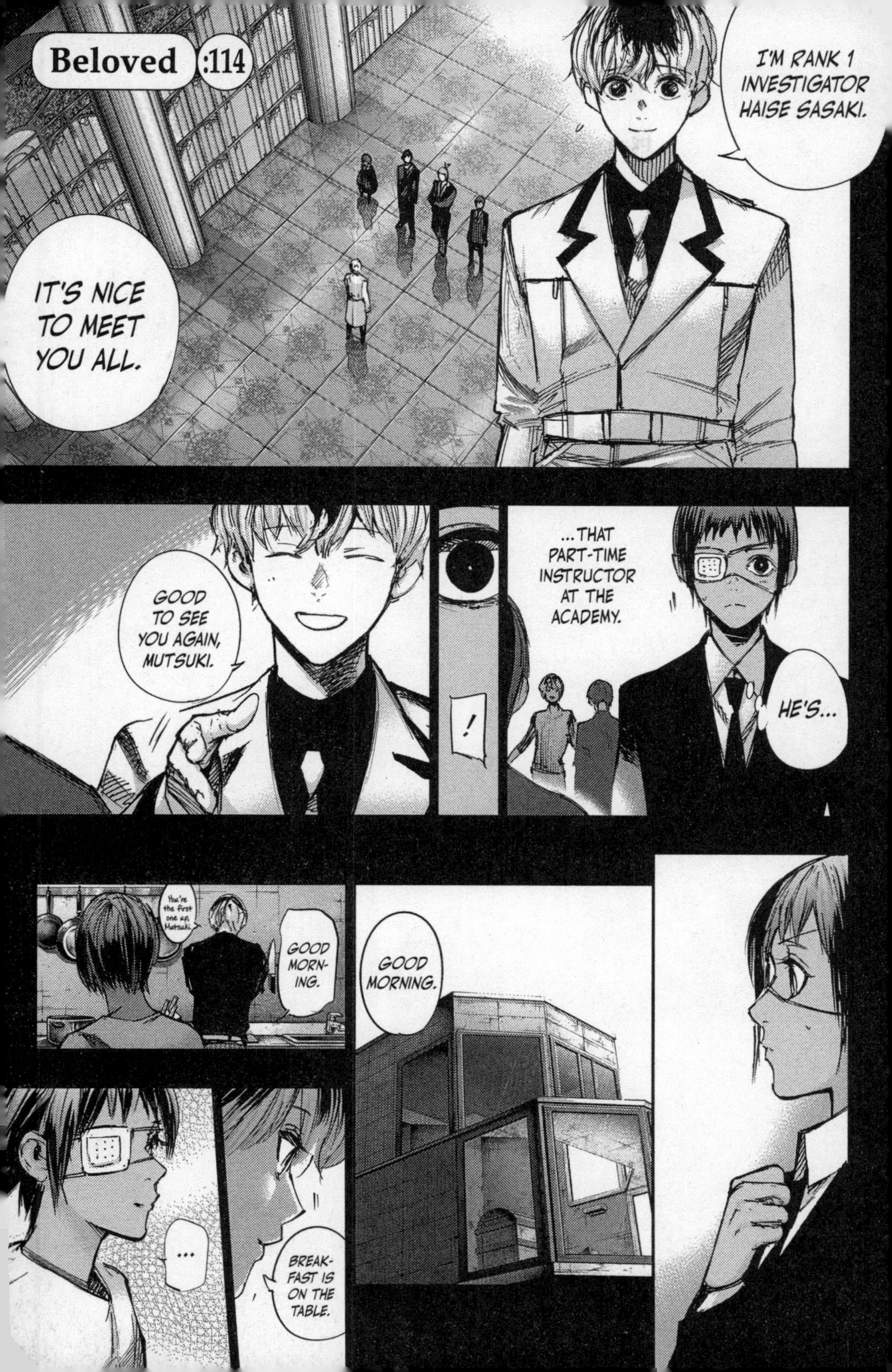
Beloved :114
I'M RANK 1 INVESTIGATOR HAISE SASAKI.
IT'S NICE TO MEET YOU ALL.
HE'S...
...THAT PART-TIME INSTRUCTOR AT THE ACADEMY.
!
GOOD TO SEE YOU AGAIN, MUTSUKI.
GOOD MORNING.
You're the first one up, Mutsuki.
GOOD MORN-ING.
BREAK-FAST IS ON THE TABLE.
...

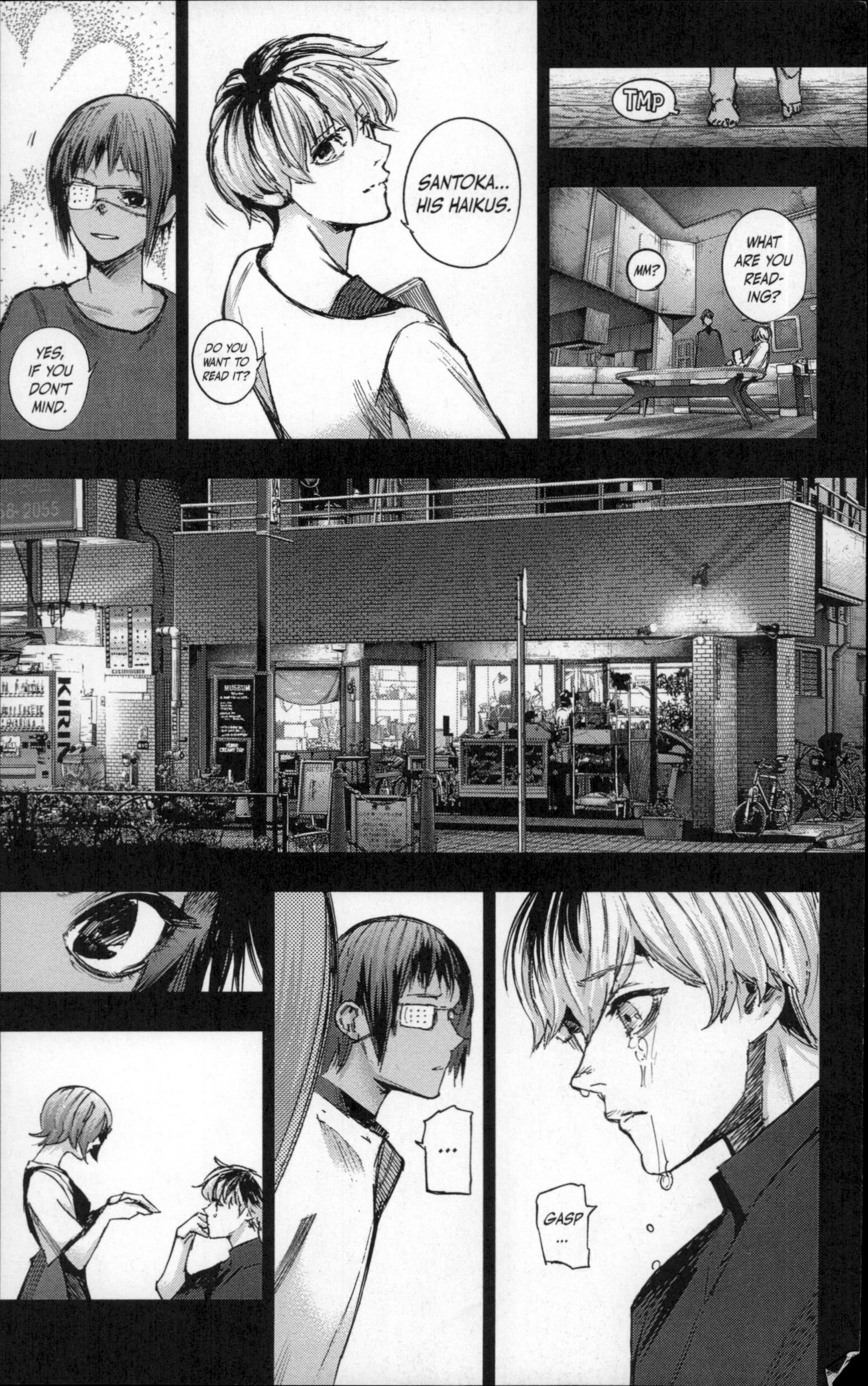
TMP
WHAT ARE YOU READING?
MM?
SANTOKA... HIS HAIKUS.
DO YOU WANT TO READ IT?
YES, IF YOU DON'T MIND.
MUSEUM
KIRIN
GASP...
...

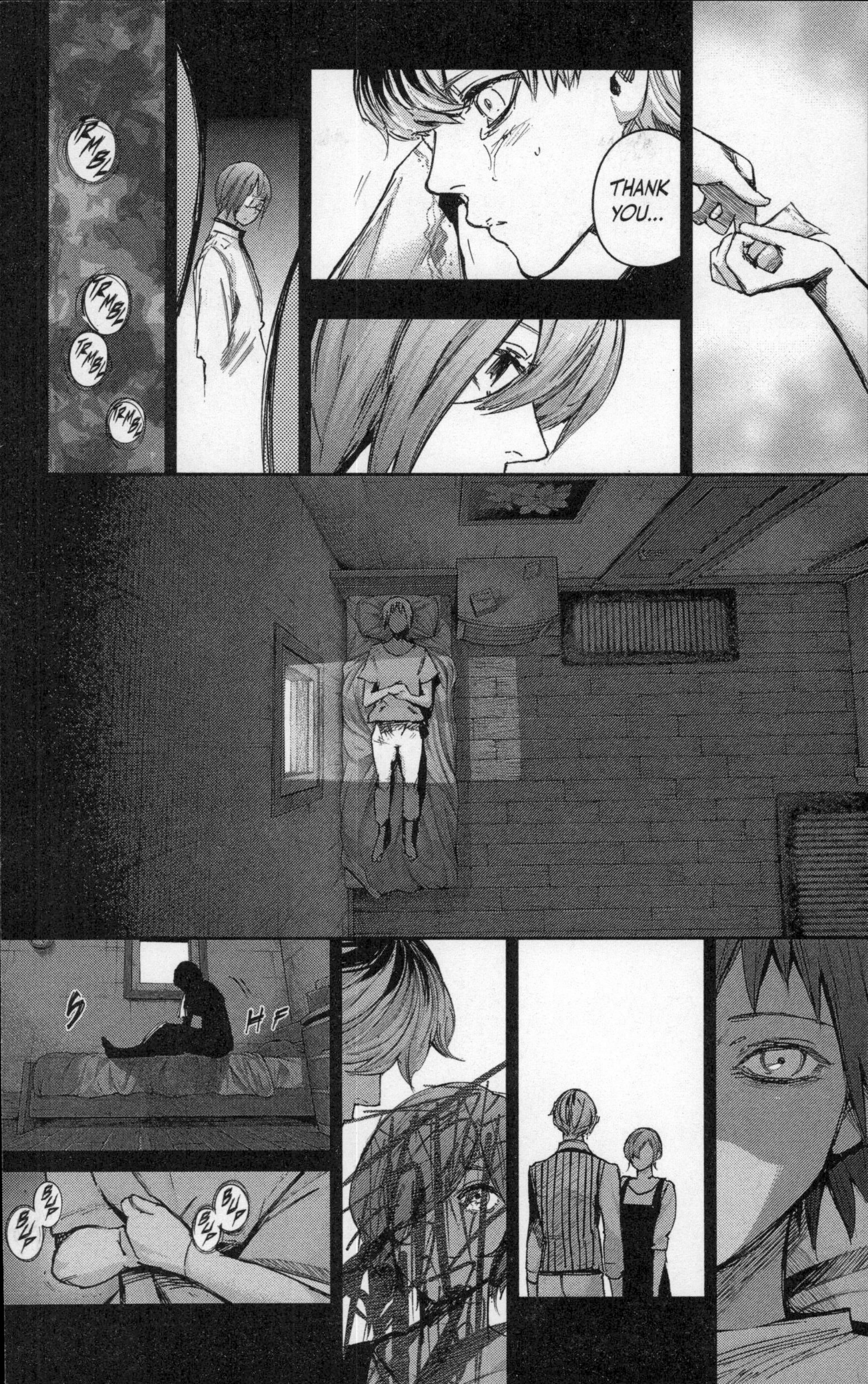
THANK YOU...
TRMBL
TRMBL
TRMBL
TRMBL
S HF
BUP BUP
BUP BUP

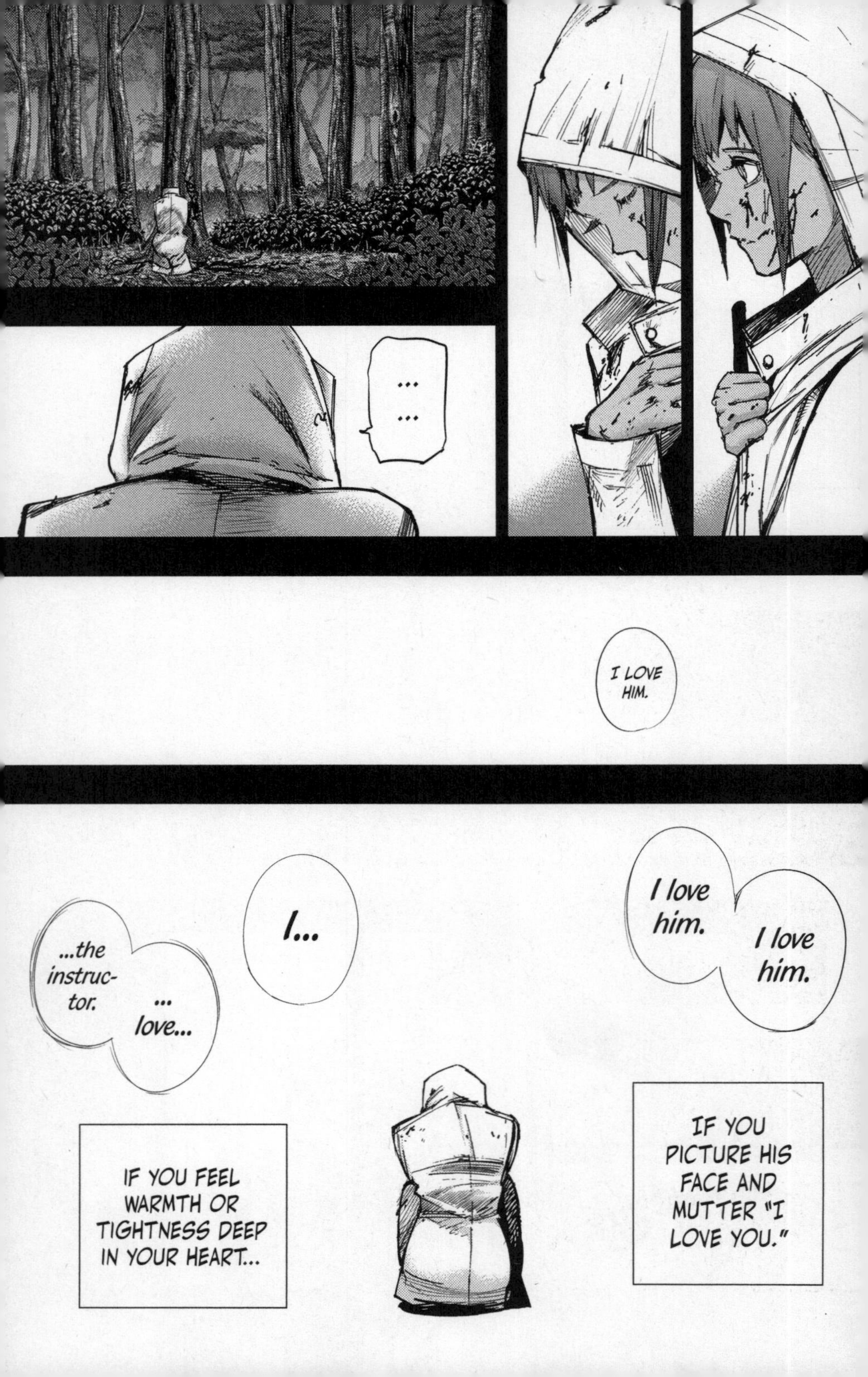
……
……
I LOVE HIM.
I love him.
I love him.
I...
...love...
...the instructor.
IF YOU PICTURE HIS FACE AND MUTTER "I LOVE YOU."
IF YOU FEEL WARMTH OR TIGHTNESS DEEP IN YOUR HEART...

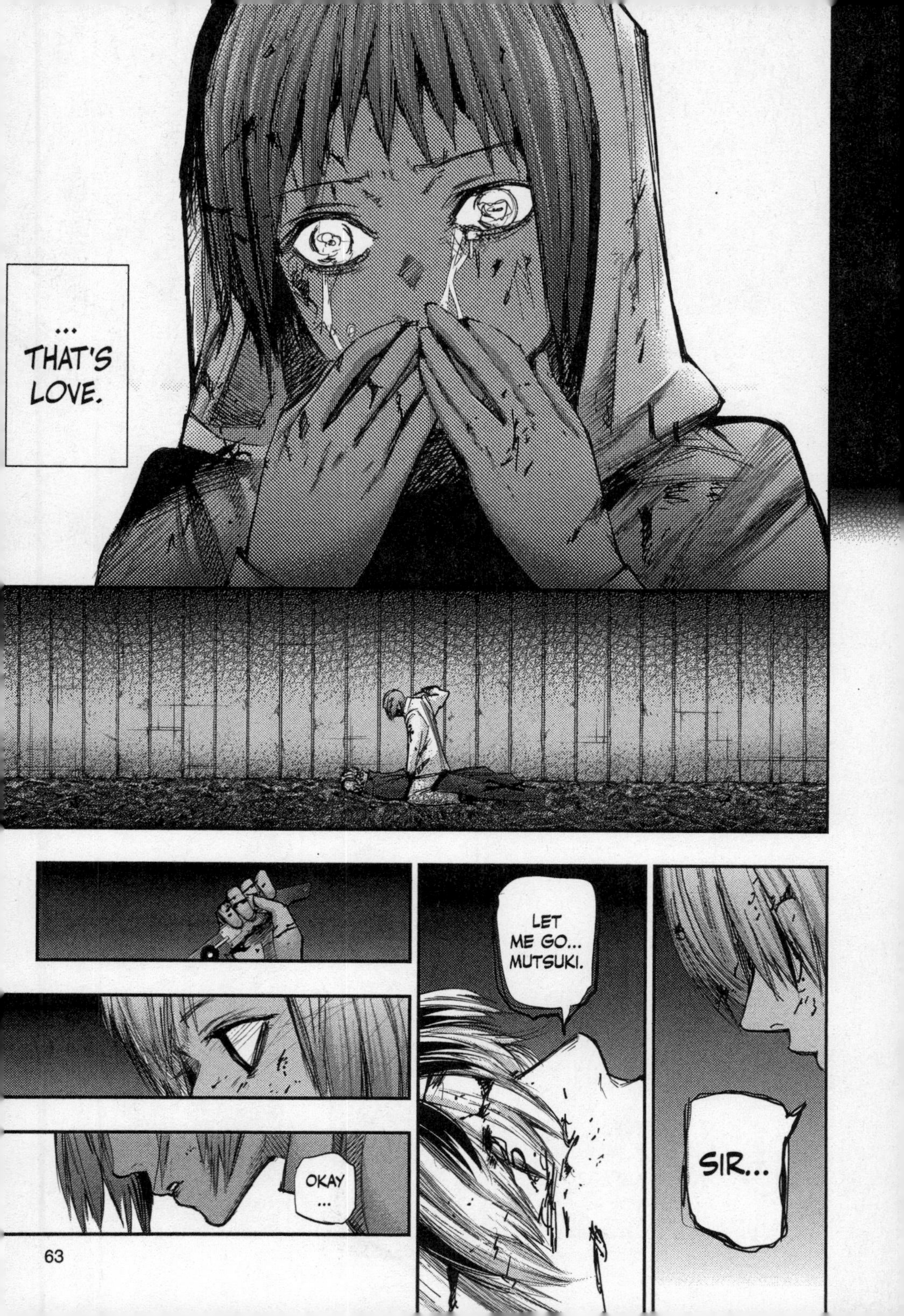
...THAT'S LOVE.
SIR...
LET ME GO... MUTSUKI.
OKAY ...

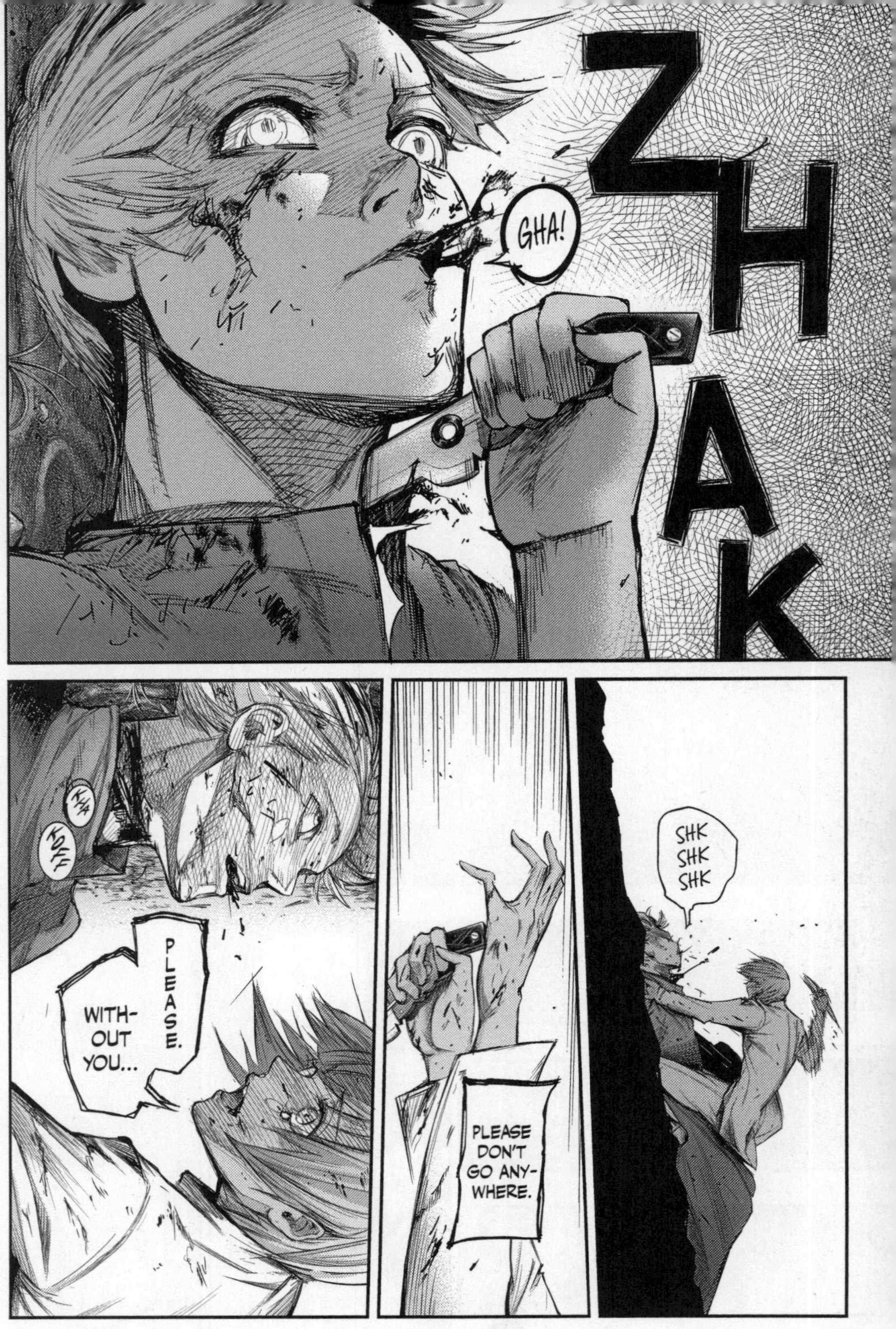

ZHAK
GHA!
SHK SHK SHK
PLEASE DON'T GO ANY-WHERE.
KHA
KOFF
PLEASE.
WITH-OUT YOU...

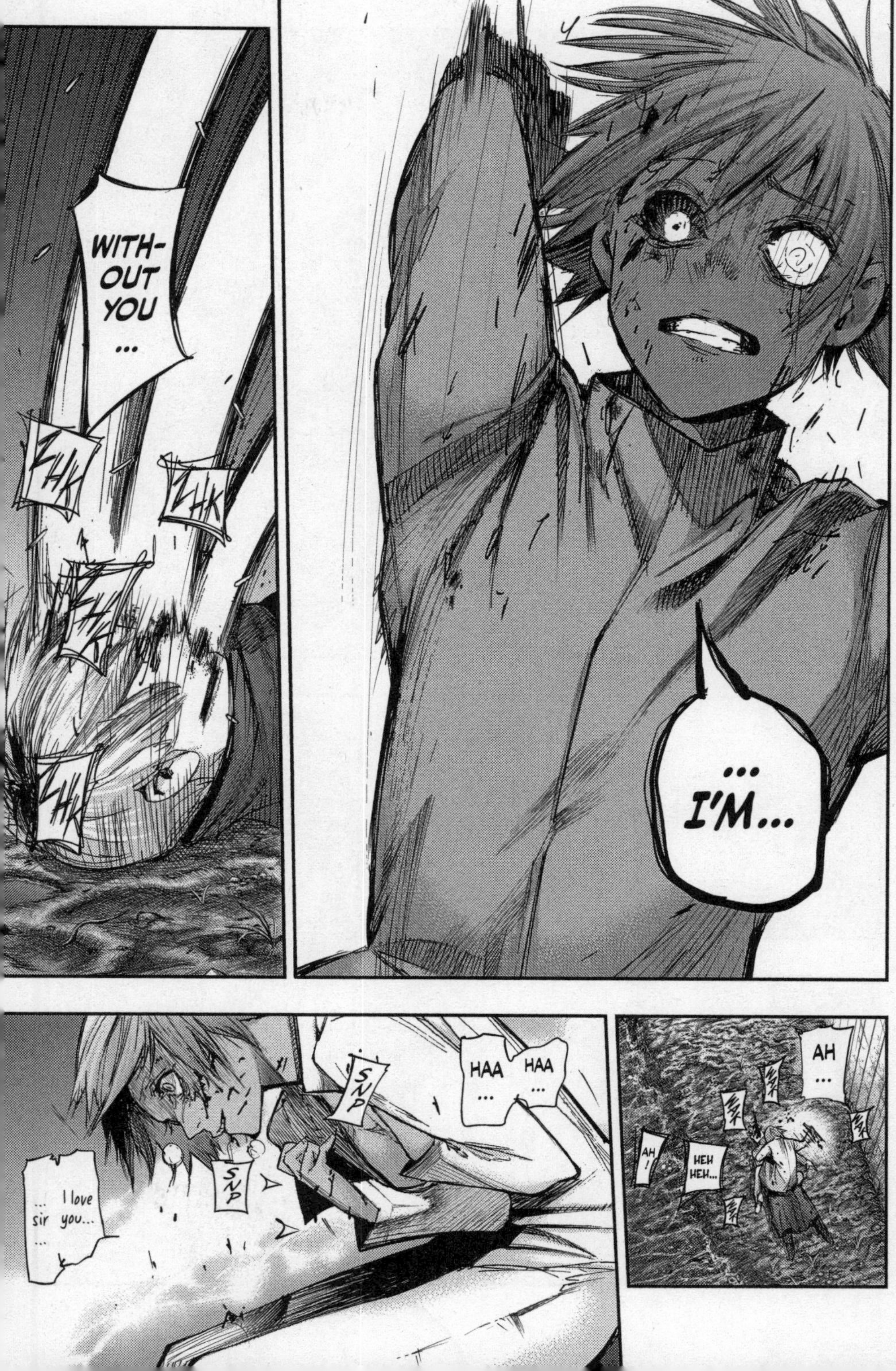
... I'M...
WITH-OUT YOU ...
ZHK
ZHK
ZHK
AH ...
HEH HEH...
AH !
HAA ...
HAA ...
SNP
SNP
... I love you... sir ...

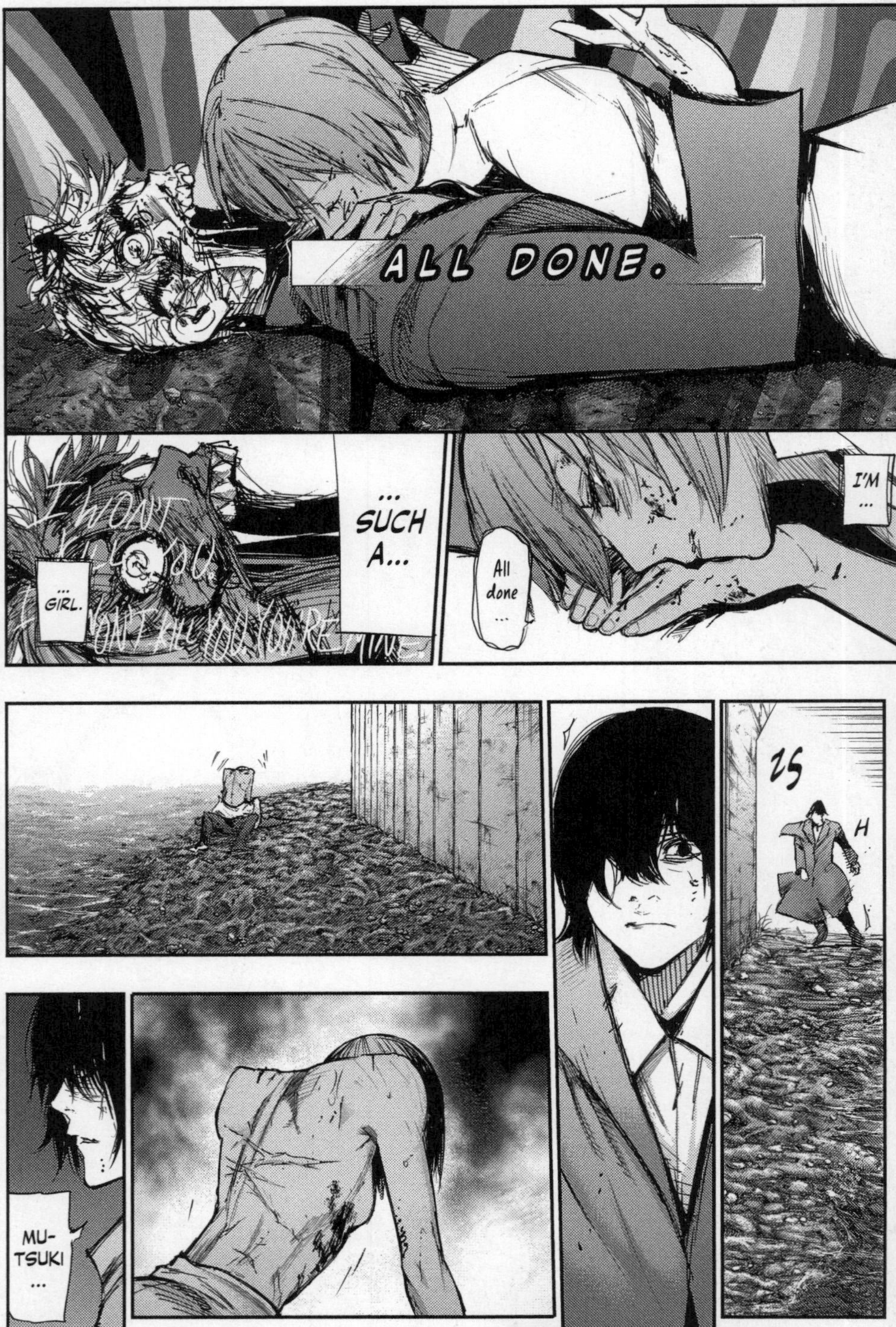
ALL DONE.
I'M ...
All done ...
... SUCH A...
I WON'T KILL YOU.
... GIRL.
ZS
H
MU-TSUKI ...

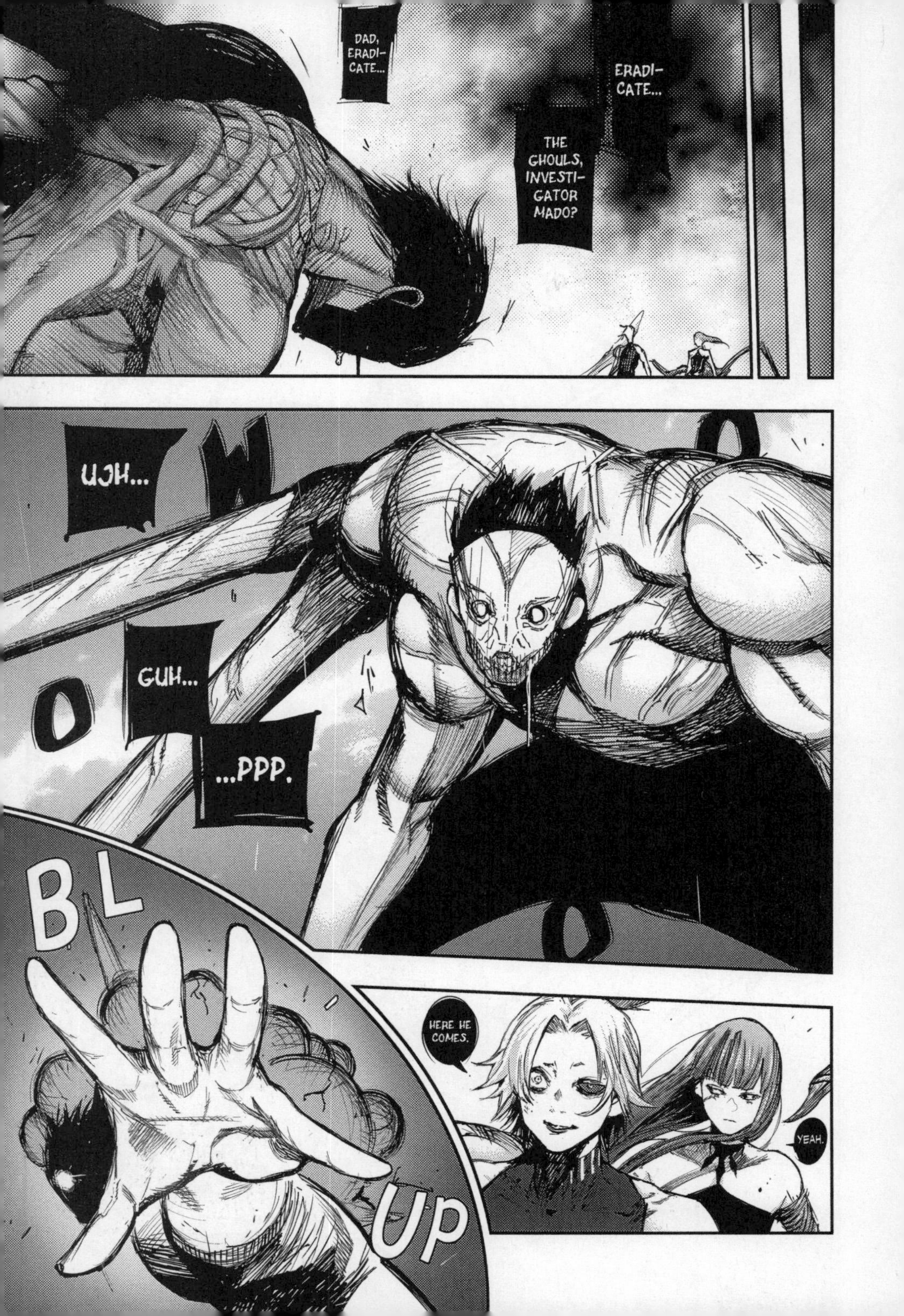
ERADICATE...
THE GHOULS, INVESTIGATOR MADO?
DAD, ERADICATE...
UJH...
GUH...
...PPP.
WOOO
HERE HE COMES.
YEAH.
BLUP

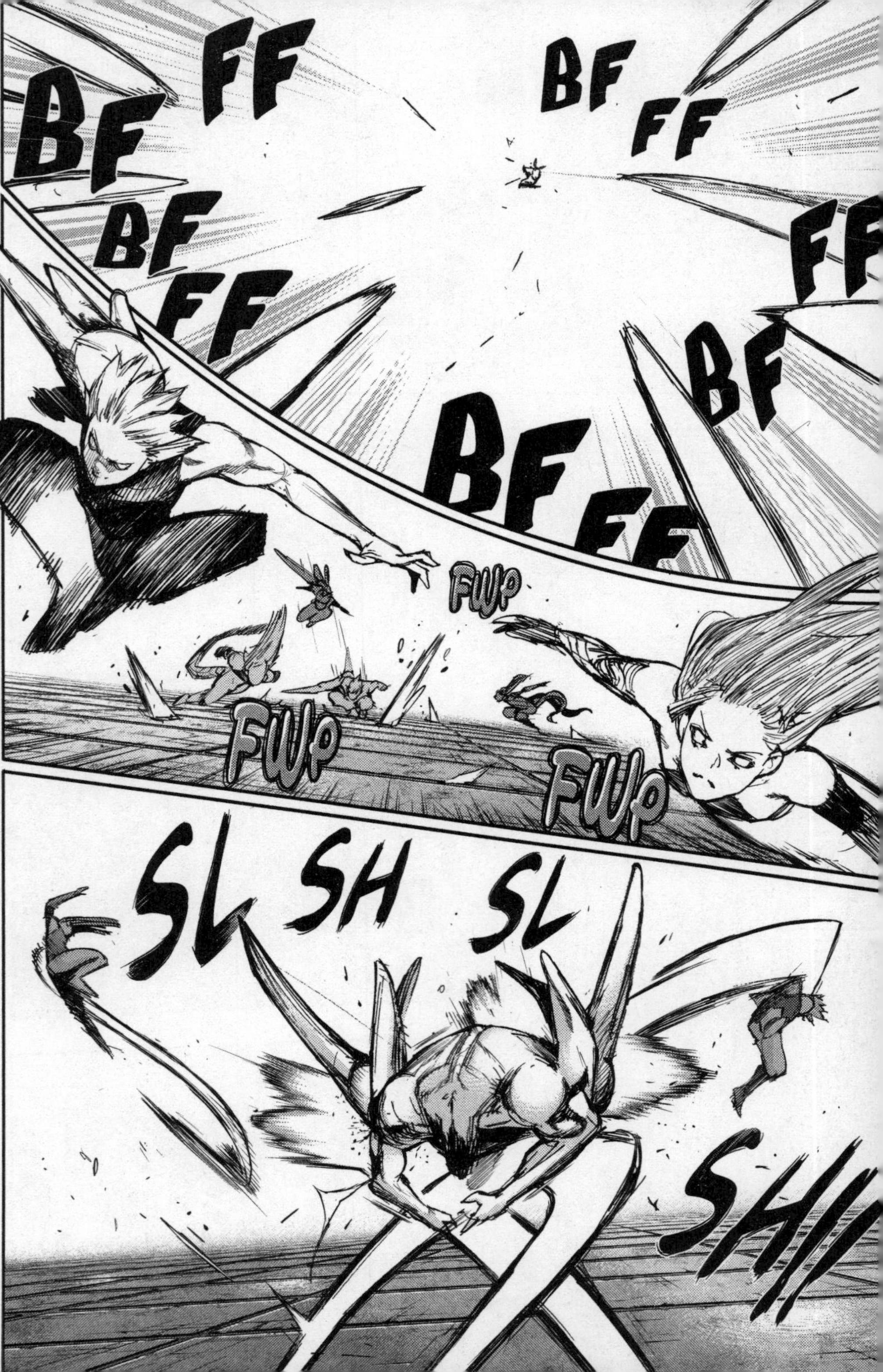
BF
FF
FF
BF
BF
FF
BF
FF
BF
FF
BF
FF
FWP
FWP
FWP
SHH
SL
SH
SL

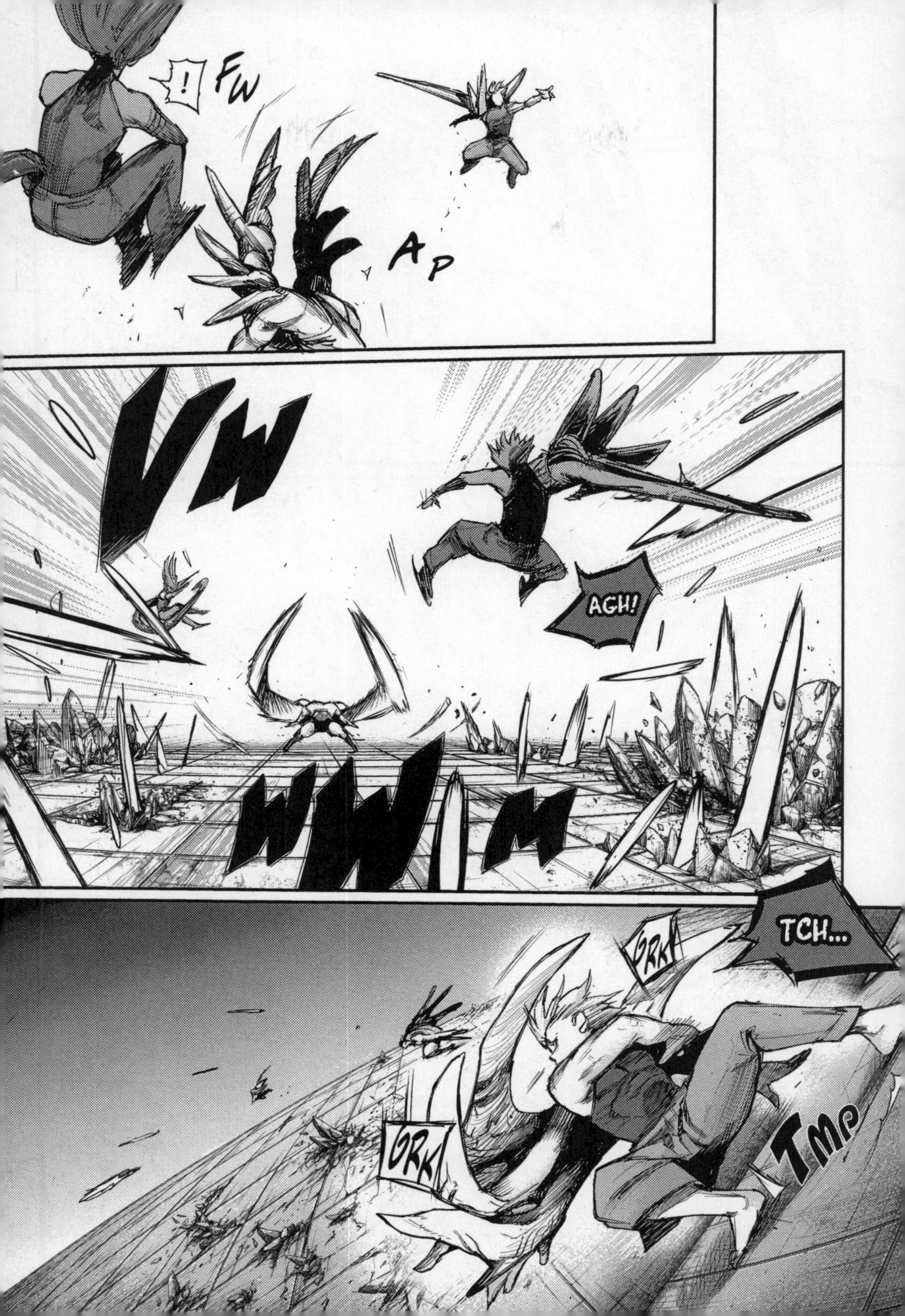
!
FW
AP
AGH!
VW
WWWM
TCH...
GRK
GRK
TMP

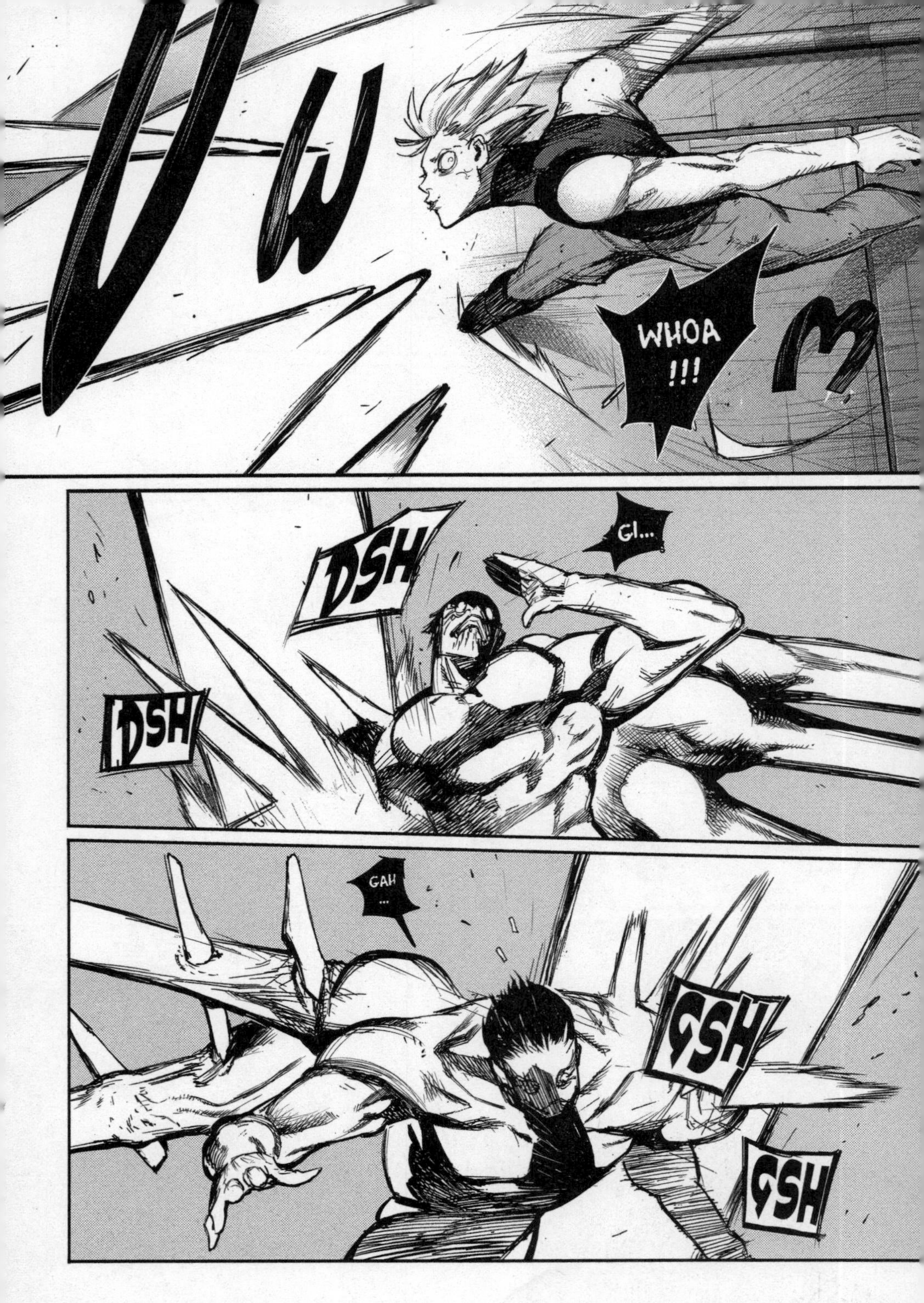
WHOA !!!
GI...
DSH
DSH
GAH ...
GSH
GSH

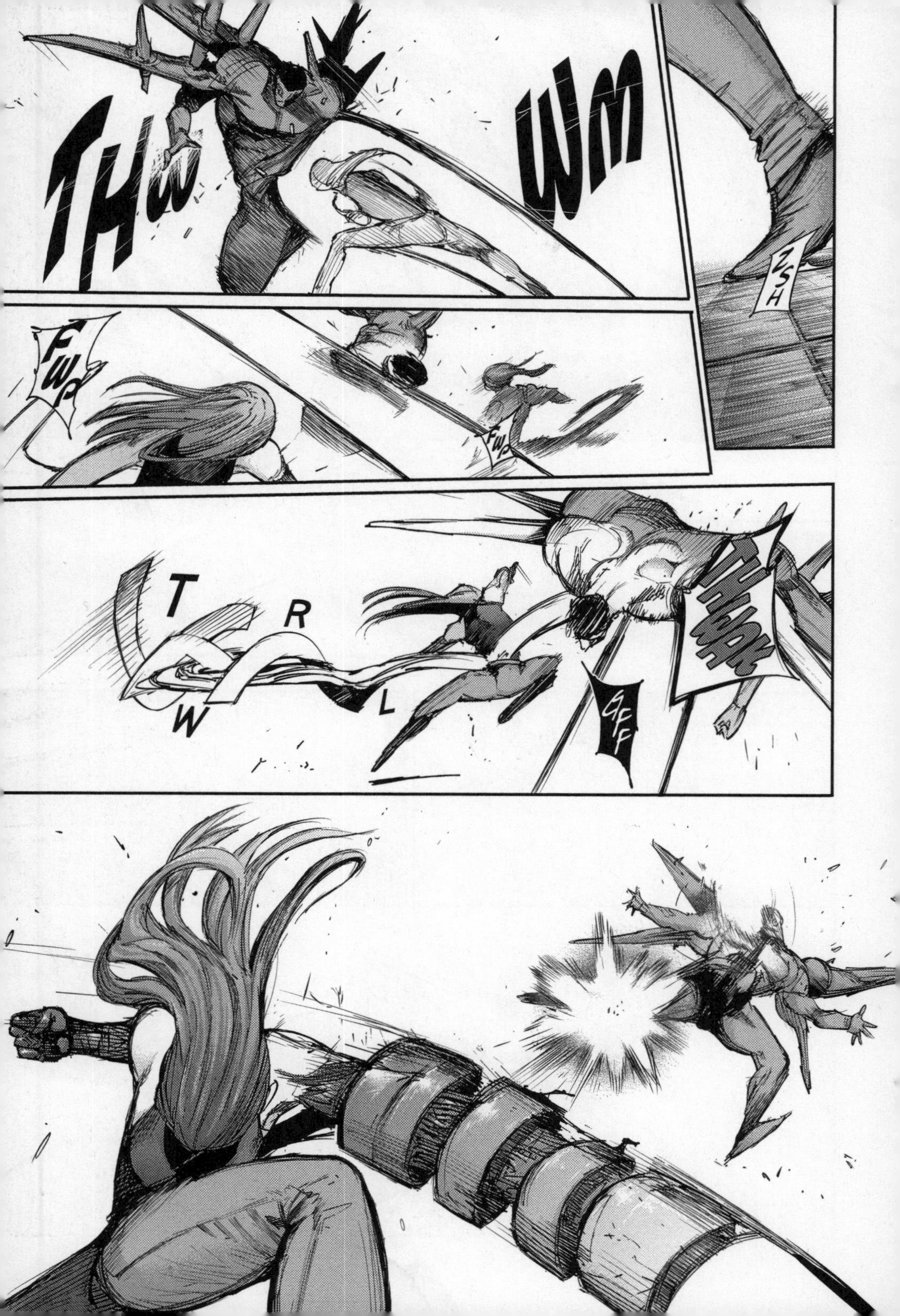
ZSH
THWUM
FWP
FWP
THWAK
GFF
TRWL

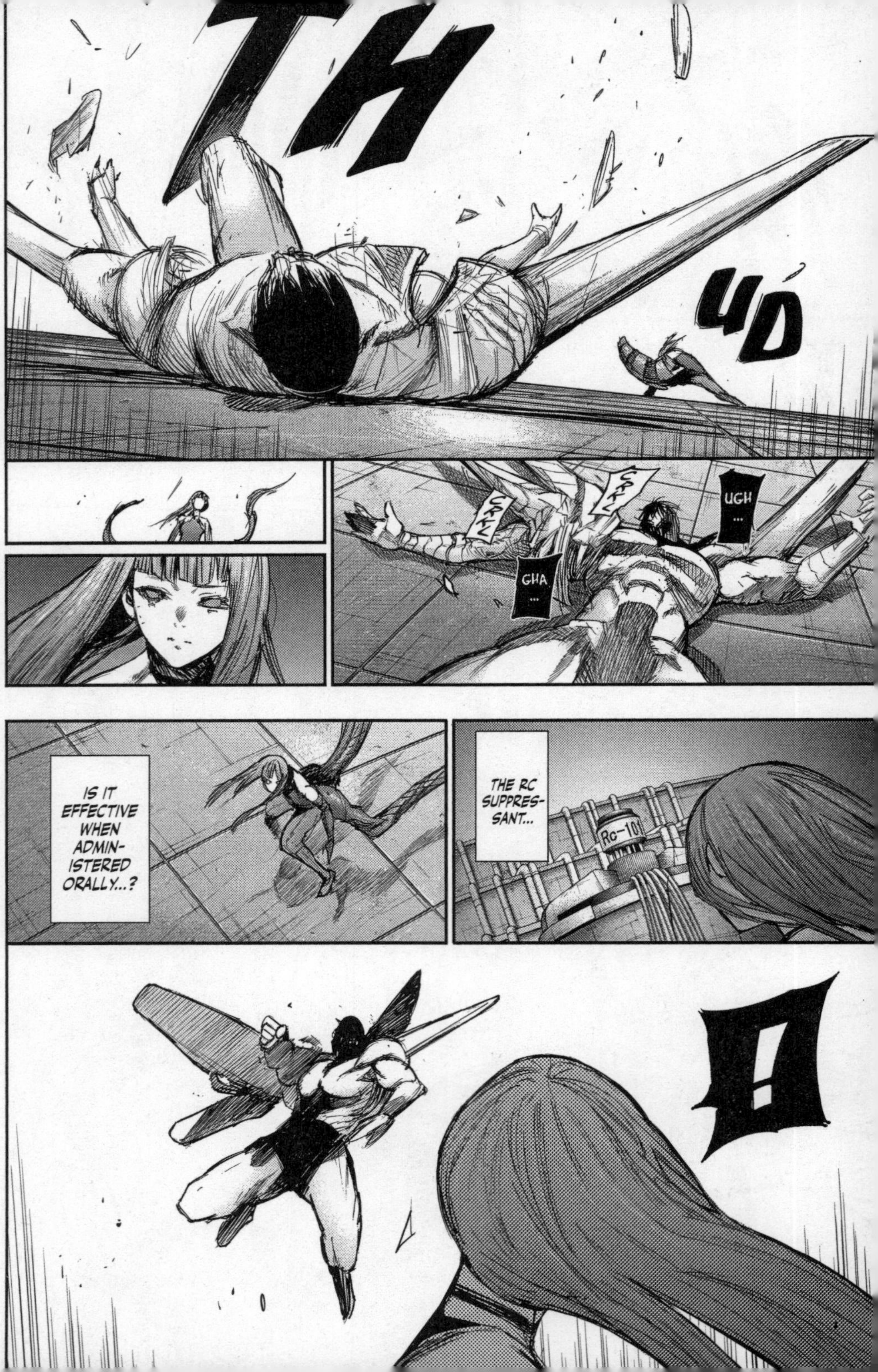
TH
UD
UGH ...
URKL
URKL
GHA ...
THE RC SUPPRES-SANT...
Rc-101
IS IT EFFECTIVE WHEN ADMIN-ISTERED ORALLY...?
!

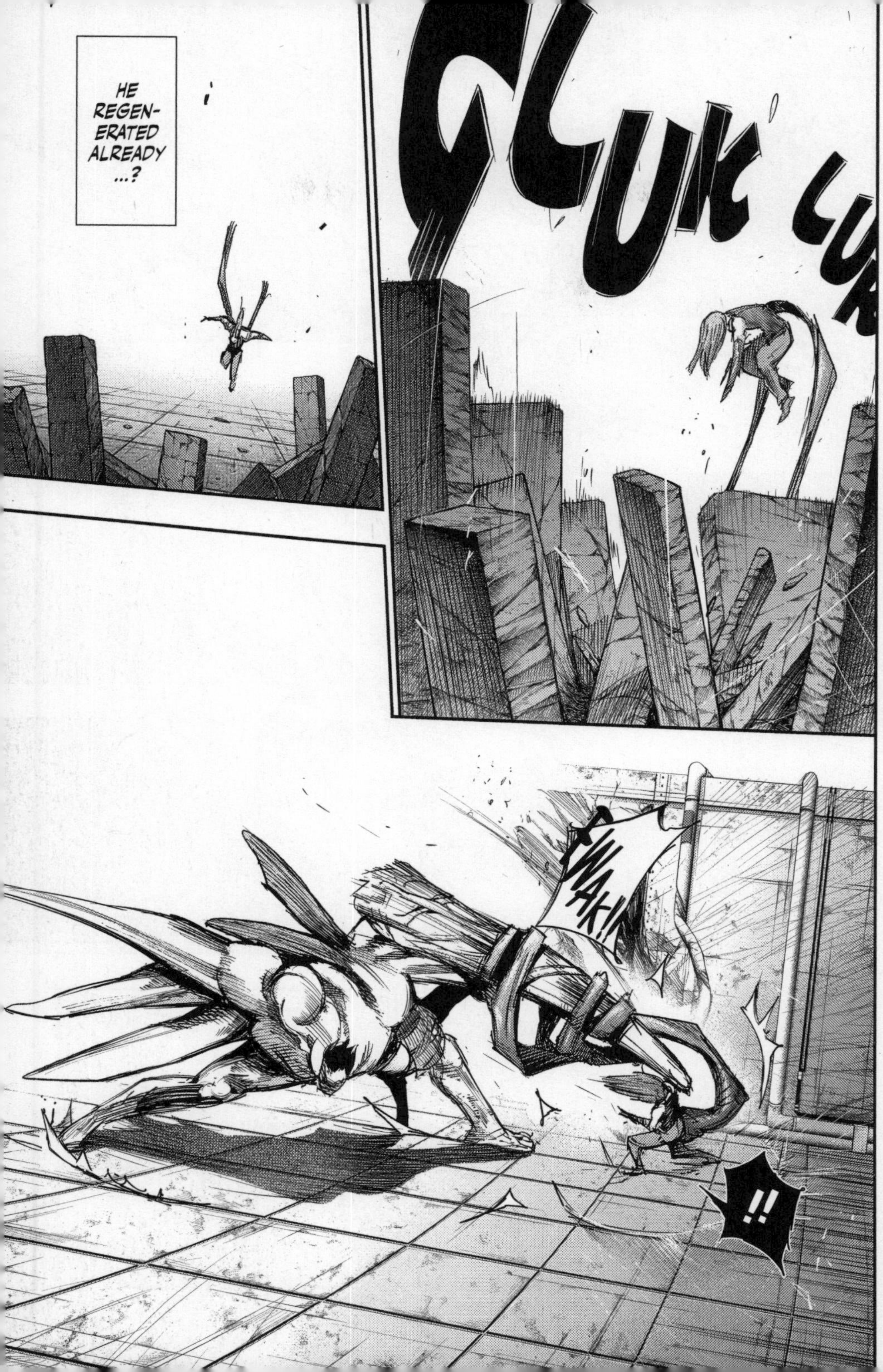
GLUK LUK LUK
HE REGEN-ERATED ALREADY ...?
FWAK!!
!!

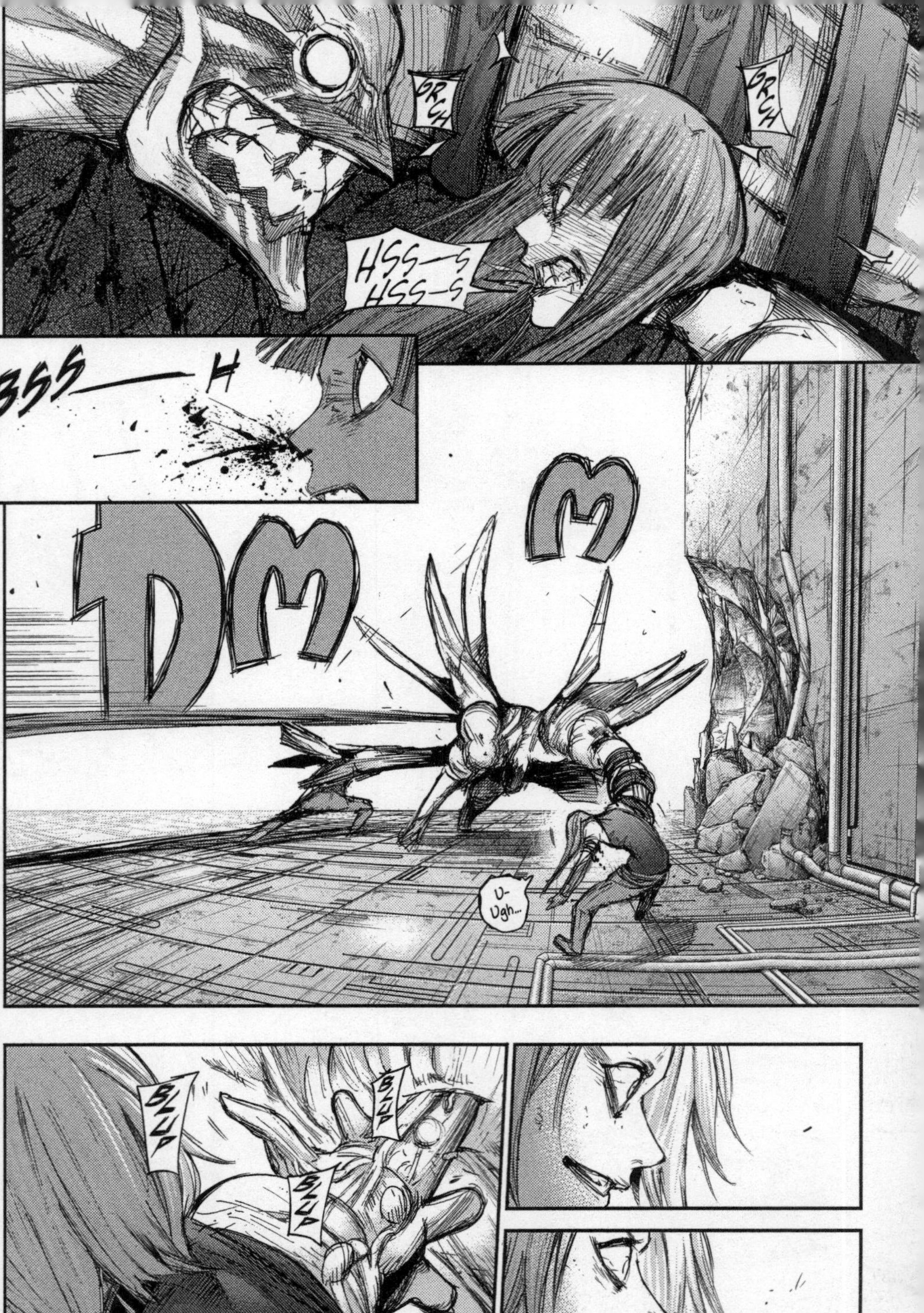
GRCH
GRCH
HSS—S HSS—S
BSS—H
DM M M
U-Ugh...
BLUP
BLUP
BLUP

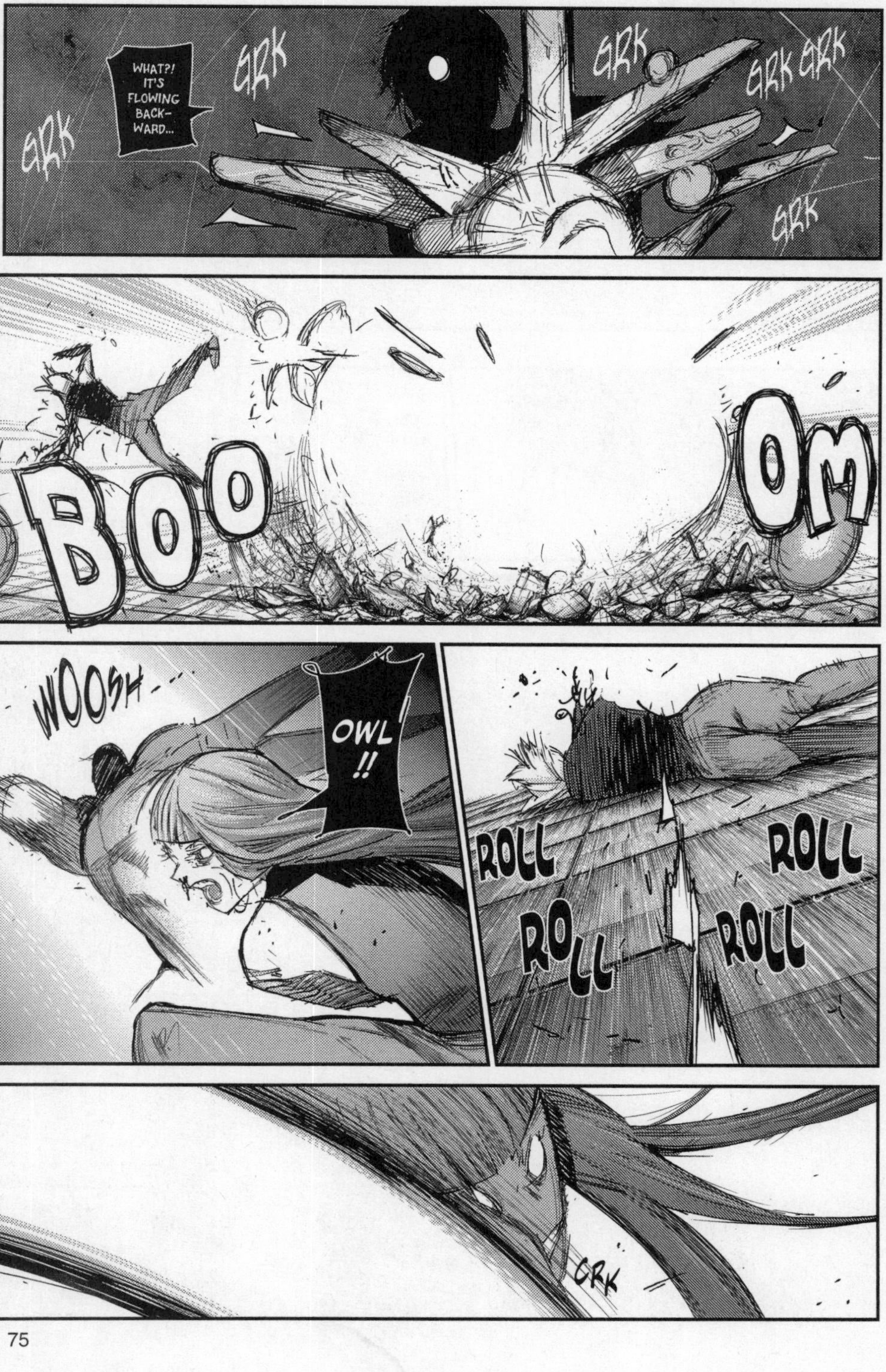
GRK GRK
GRK
GRK
GRK
WHAT?! IT'S FLOWING BACKWARD...
GRK
BOOOM
ROLL
ROLL
ROLL
ROLL
WOOSH
OWL!!
GRK

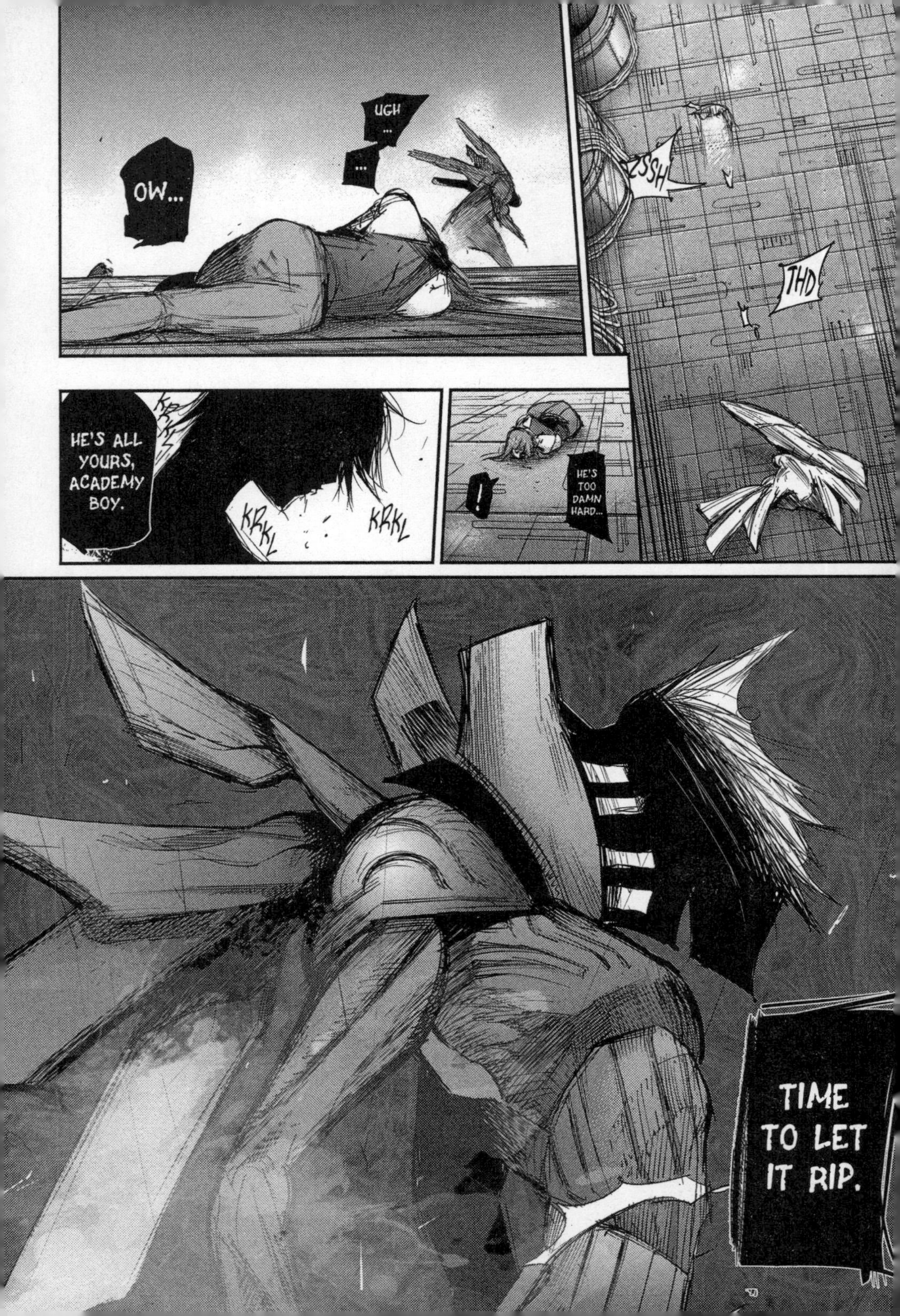
ZSSH
THD
UGH ...
...
OW...
!
HE'S TOO DAMN HARD...
KRKL
HE'S ALL YOURS, ACADEMY BOY.
KRKL
KRKL
TIME TO LET IT RIP.

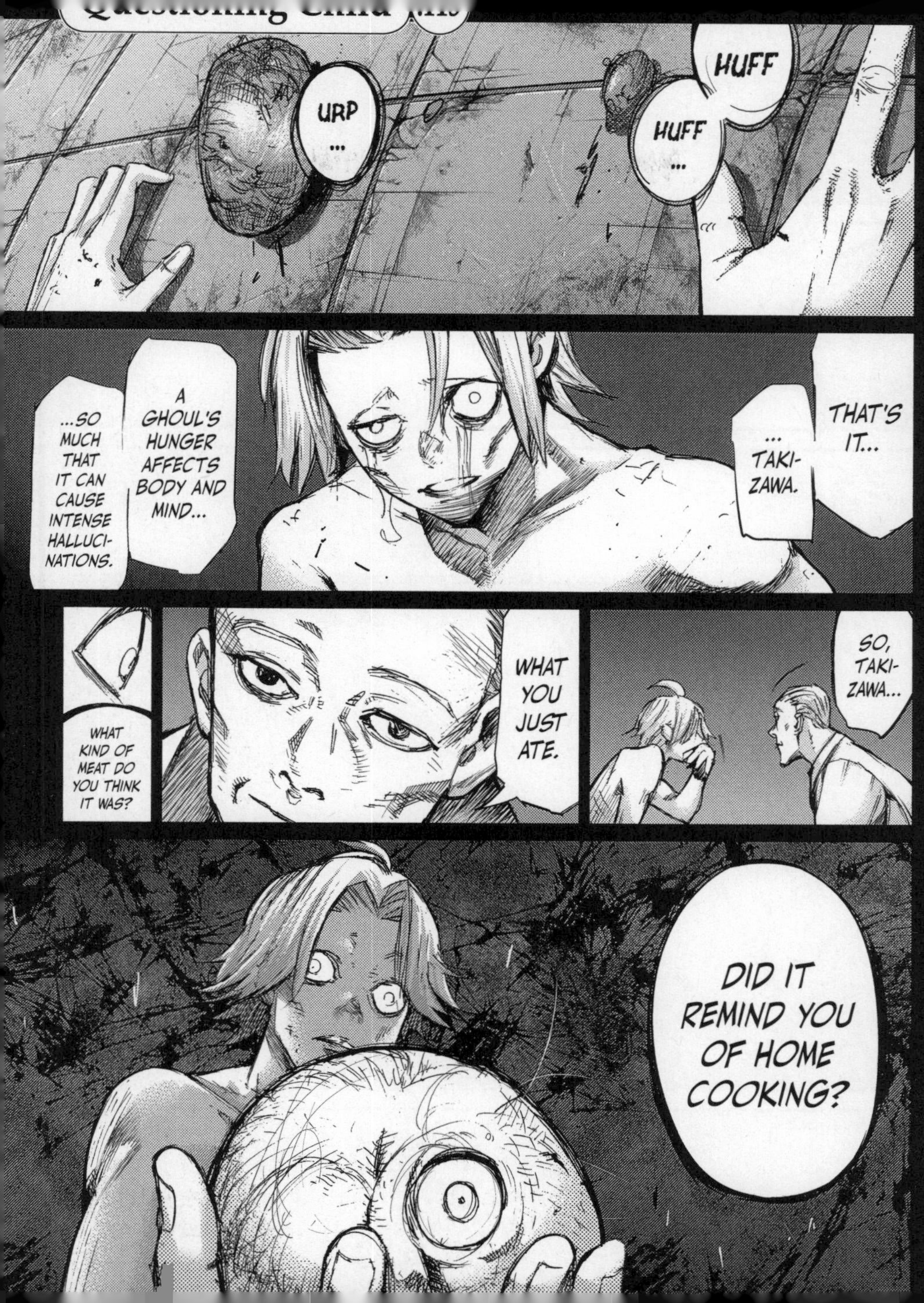
HUFF
HUFF ...
URP ...
THAT'S IT...
... TAKI-ZAWA.
A GHOUL'S HUNGER AFFECTS BODY AND MIND...
...SO MUCH THAT IT CAN CAUSE INTENSE HALLUCI-NATIONS.
SO, TAKI-ZAWA...
WHAT YOU JUST ATE.
WHAT KIND OF MEAT DO YOU THINK IT WAS?
DID IT REMIND YOU OF HOME COOKING?

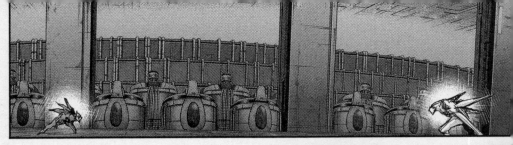

I KNOW WHAT YOU'VE BEEN THROUGH ...

ZS   SH

GRK!

GZK GZK GZK
GZK
GZK
GZK GZK

FWM

... AMON.

I'LL TAKE YOU HOME...

FWP

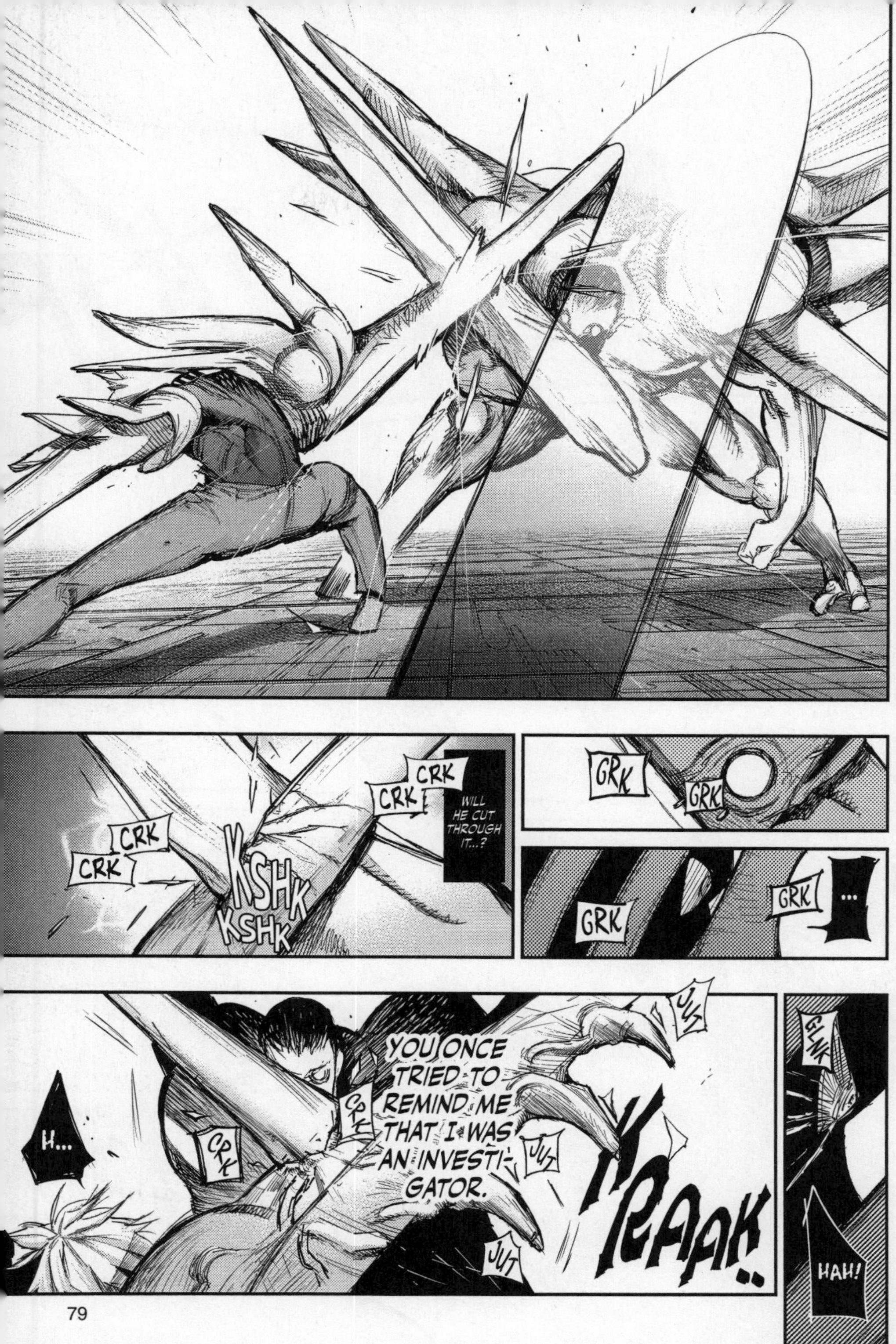
GRK
GRK
...
GRK
GRK
WILL HE CUT THROUGH IT...?
CRK
CRK
KSHK
KSHK
CRK
CRK
GLNK
HAH!
JUT
YOU ONCE TRIED TO REMIND ME THAT I WAS AN INVESTI-GATOR.
JUT
CRK
CRK
KRAAK
JUT
H...

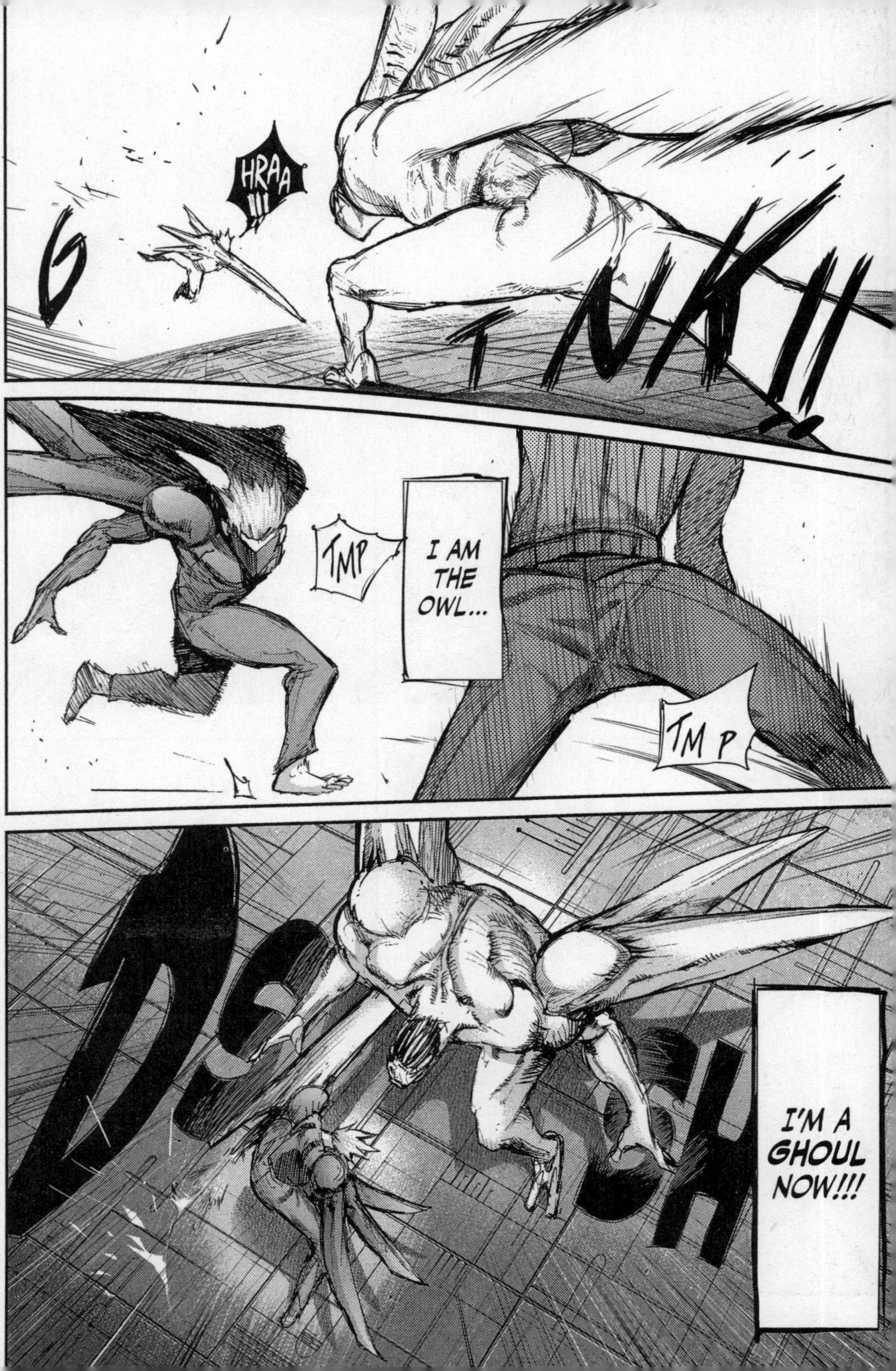
HRAA!!!
G TINK!!
I AM THE OWL...
TMP
TMP
I'M A GHOUL NOW!!!
DSCH

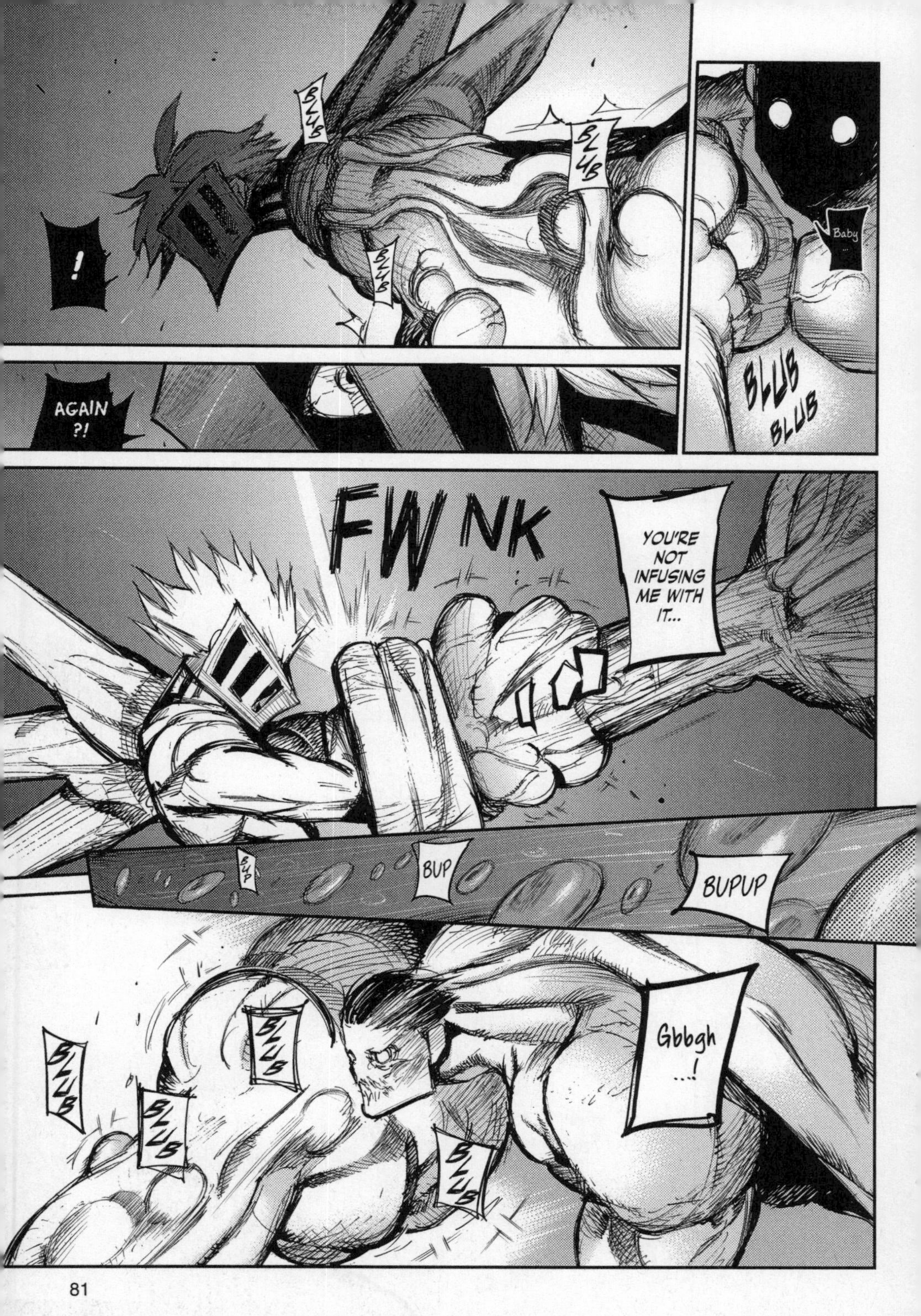
Baby ...
BLUB BLUB
BLUB
BLUB
BLUB
!
AGAIN ?!
FWNK
YOU'RE NOT INFUSING ME WITH IT...
BUPUP
BUP
BUP
Gbbgh ...!
BLUB
BLUB
BLUB
BLUB

I DECIDED...

Dz

SH

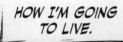

HOW I'M GOING TO LIVE.

URRP ...

DAMN IT, DAMN IT...

SOB ...

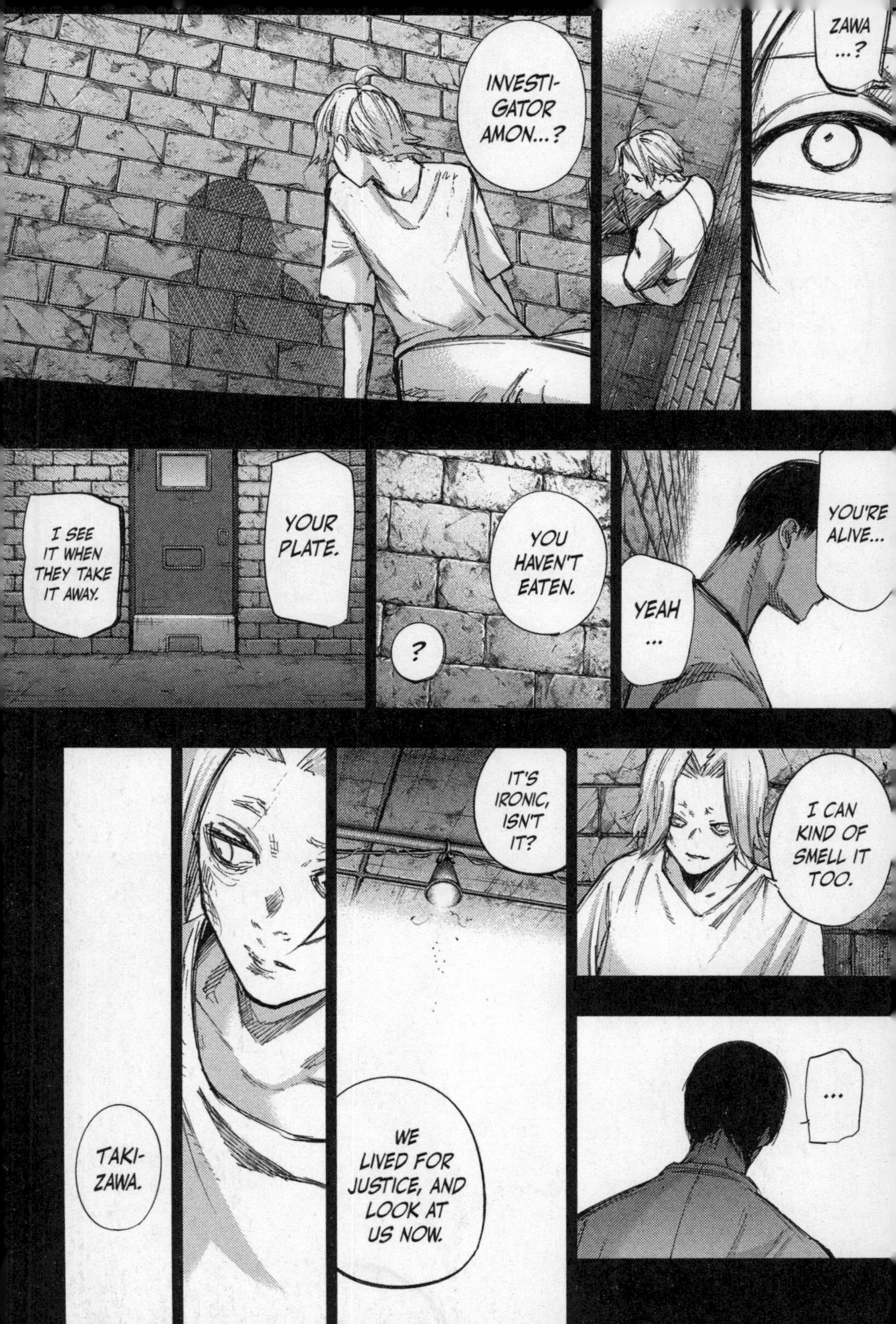
ZAWA ...?
INVESTI-GATOR AMON...?
YOU'RE ALIVE...
YEAH ...
YOU HAVEN'T EATEN.
?
YOUR PLATE.
I SEE IT WHEN THEY TAKE IT AWAY.
I CAN KIND OF SMELL IT TOO.
...
IT'S IRONIC, ISN'T IT?
WE LIVED FOR JUSTICE, AND LOOK AT US NOW.
TAKI-ZAWA.

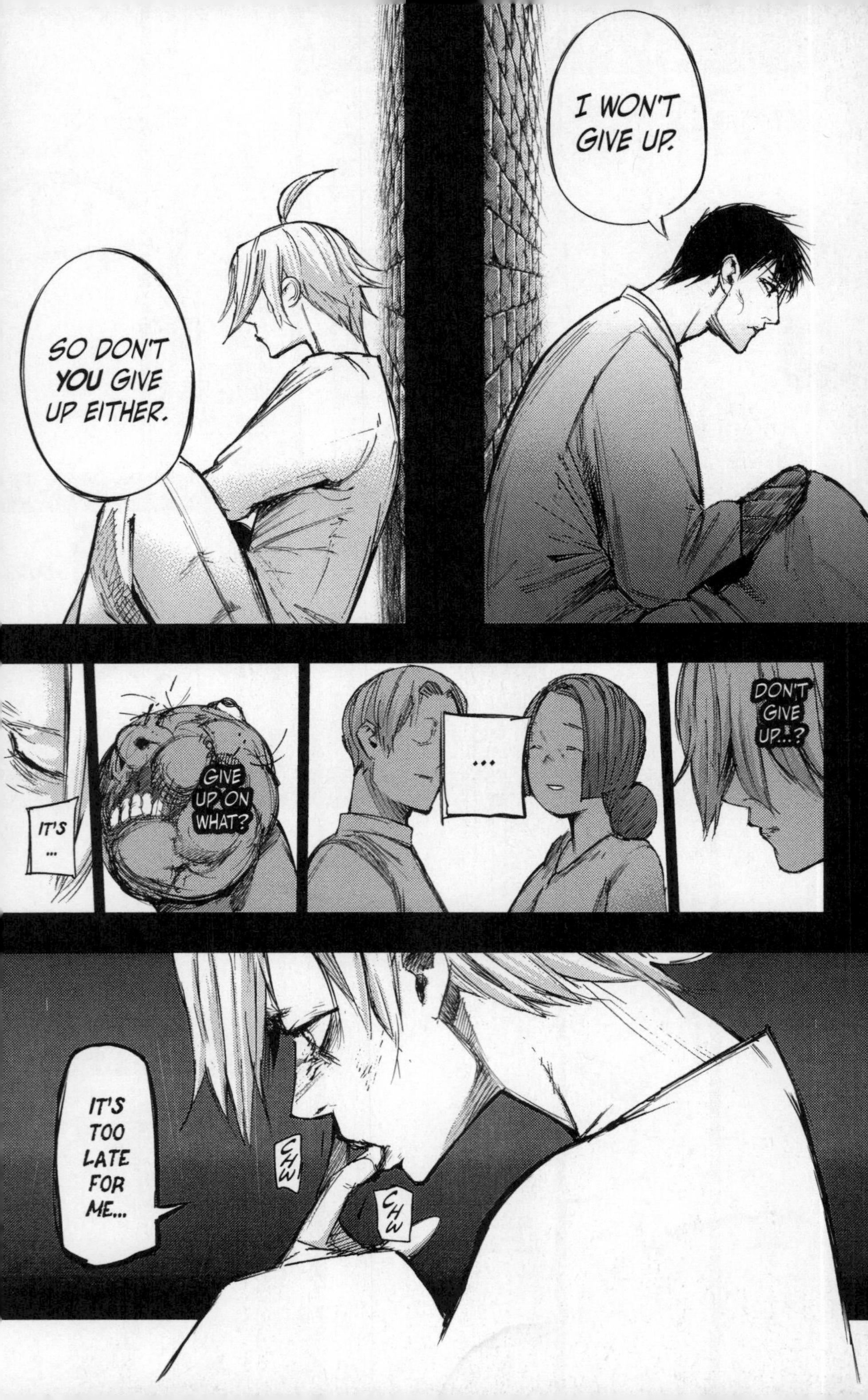
I WON'T GIVE UP.
SO DON'T YOU GIVE UP EITHER.
DON'T GIVE UP...?
...
GIVE UP ON WHAT?
IT'S ...
IT'S TOO LATE FOR ME...
CHW
CHW

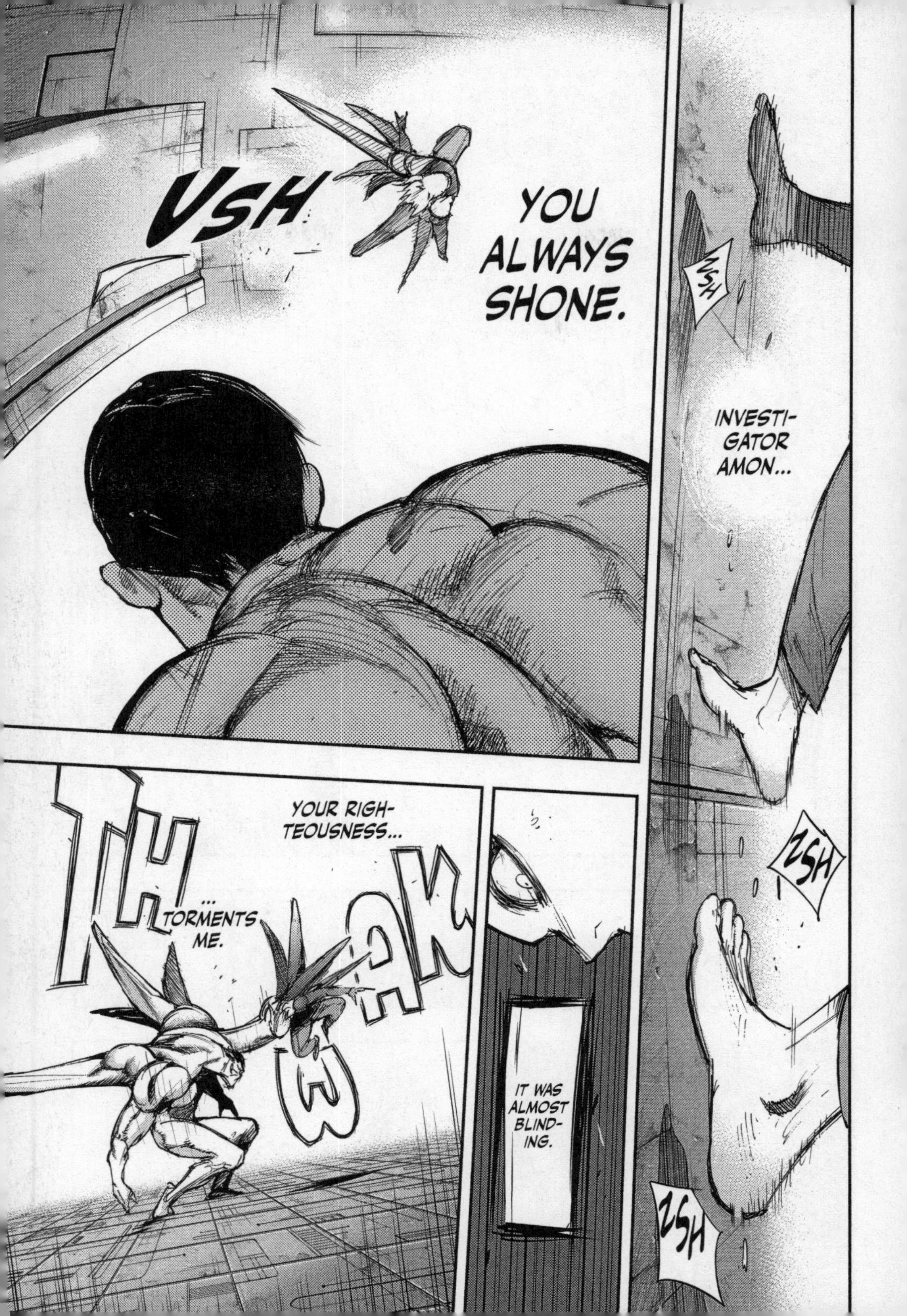
ZSH
INVESTI-GATOR AMON...
ZSH
ZSH
VSH
YOU ALWAYS SHONE.
IT WAS ALMOST BLIND-ING.
YOUR RIGH-TEOUSNESS...
...TORMENTS ME.
THWACK

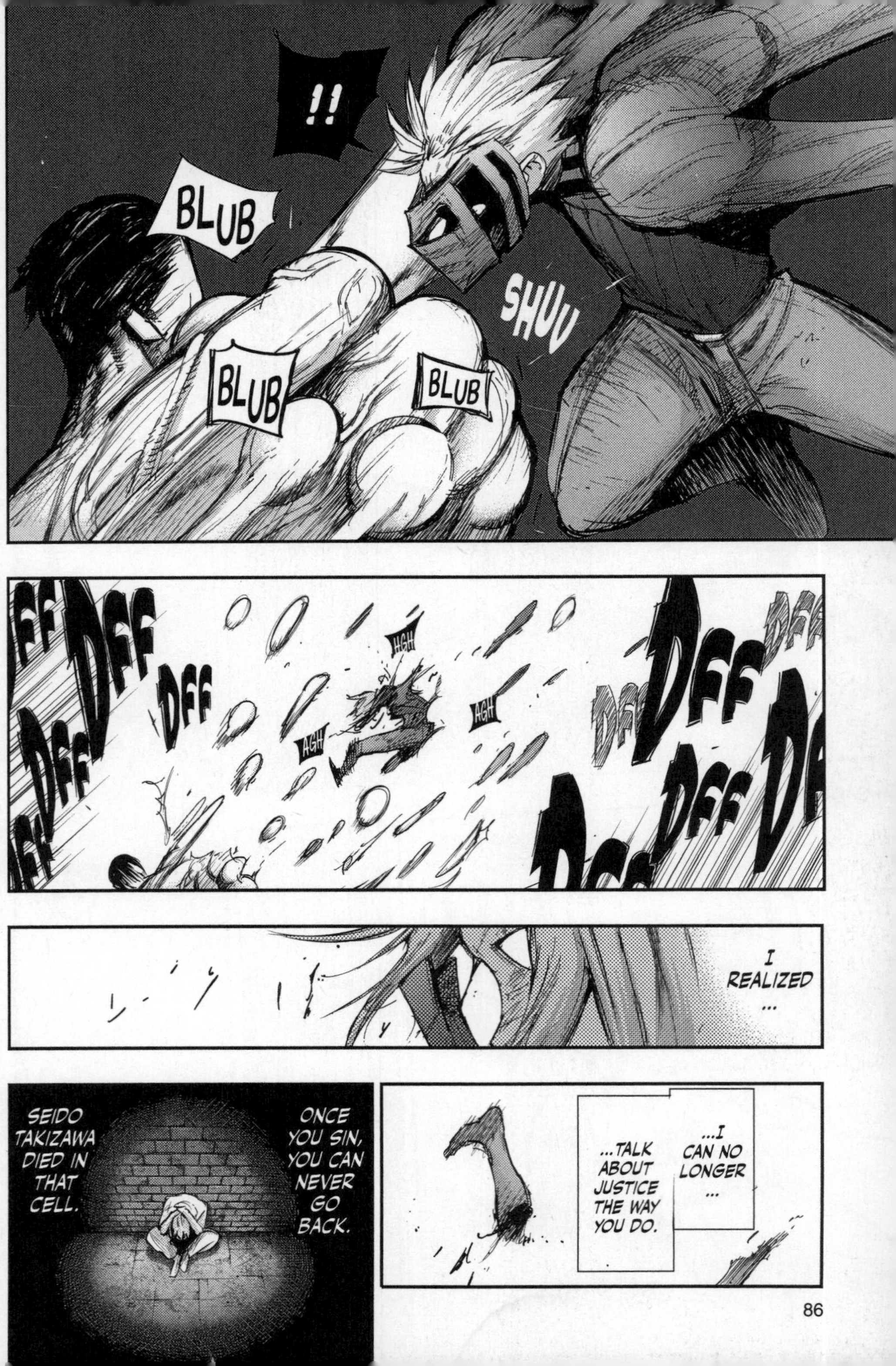
!!
SHUU
BLUB
BLUB
BLUB
DFF DFF DFF DFF
AGH
AGH
AGH
DFF DFF DFF
I REALIZED ...
...I CAN NO LONGER ...
...TALK ABOUT JUSTICE THE WAY YOU DO.
ONCE YOU SIN, YOU CAN NEVER GO BACK.
SEIDO TAKIZAWA DIED IN THAT CELL.

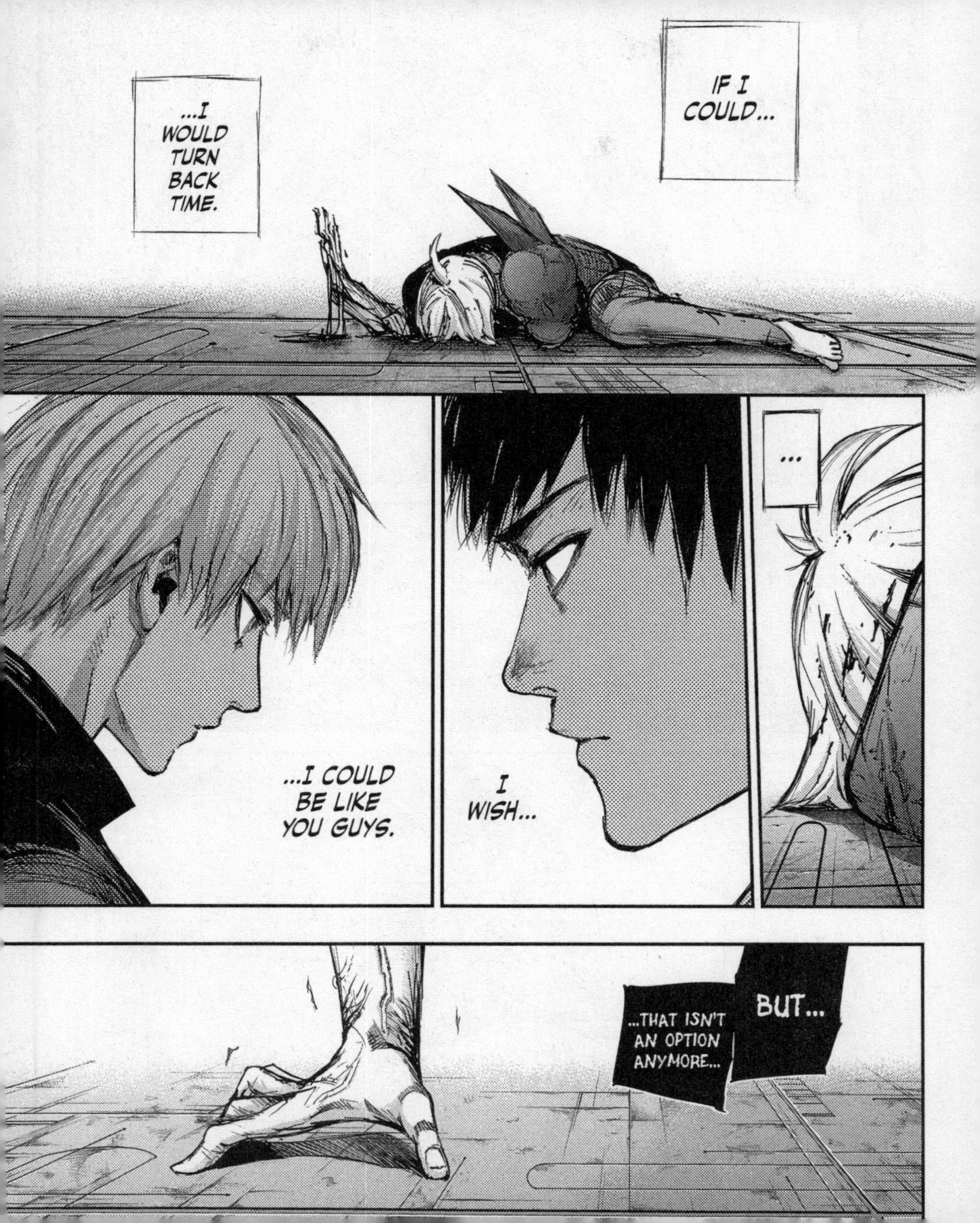
IF I COULD...
...I WOULD TURN BACK TIME.
...
I WISH...
...I COULD BE LIKE YOU GUYS.
BUT...
...THAT ISN'T AN OPTION ANYMORE...

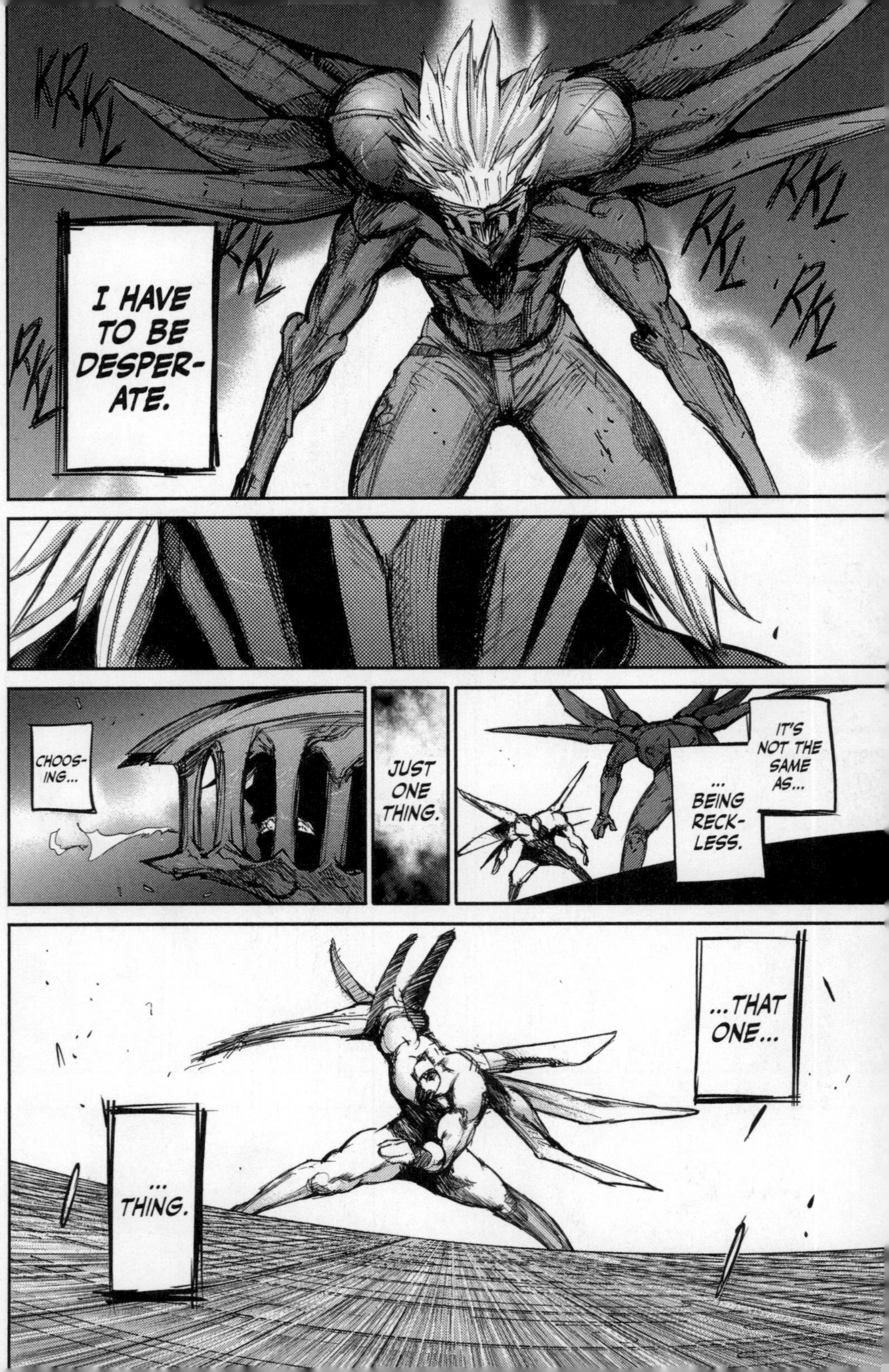

KRKL
I HAVE TO BE DESPER-ATE.
IT'S NOT THE SAME AS...
...BEING RECK-LESS.
JUST ONE THING.
CHOOS-ING...
...THAT ONE...
...THING.

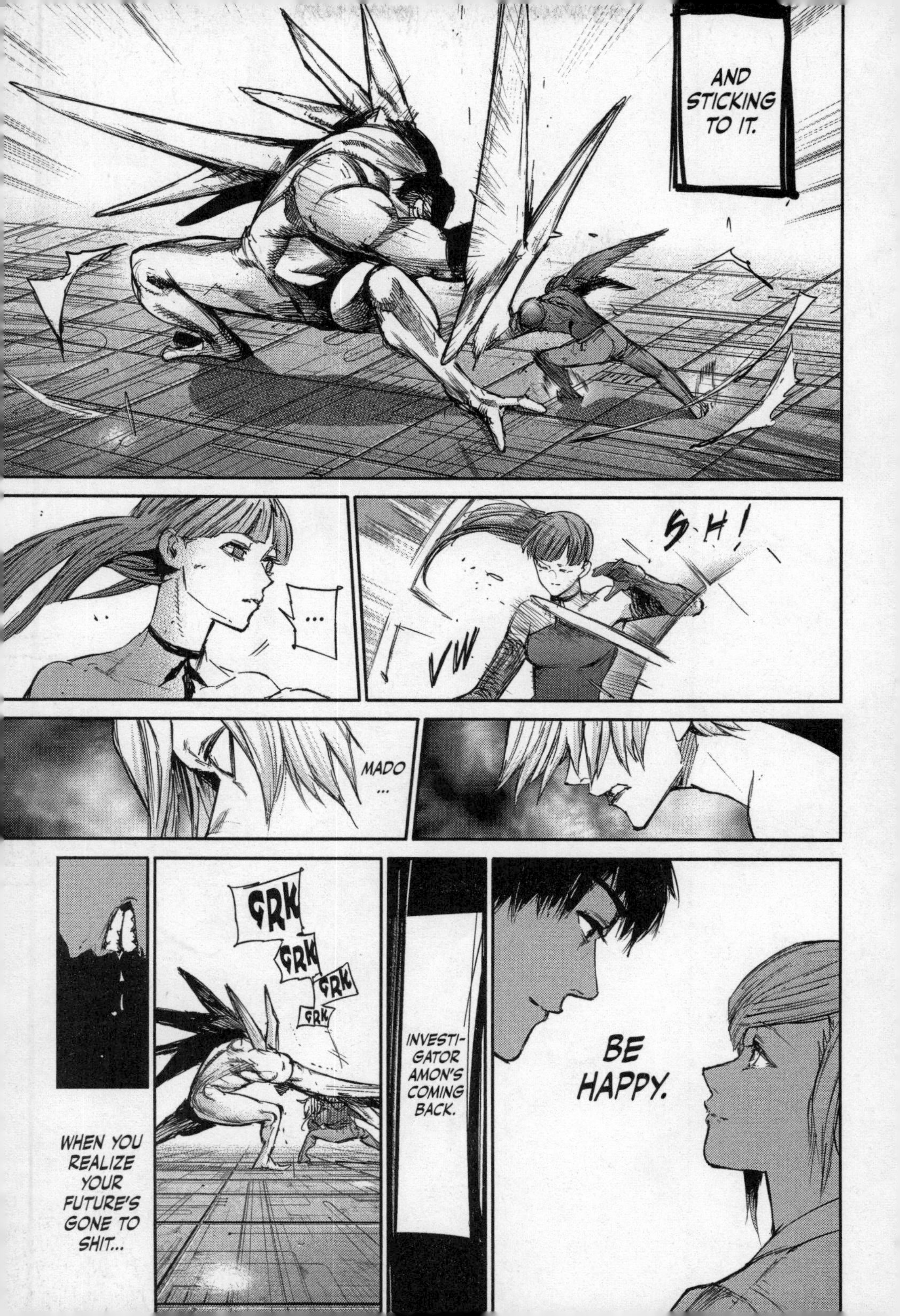
AND STICKING TO IT.
SH!
VW
...
MADO ...
BE HAPPY.
INVESTI-GATOR AMON'S COMING BACK.
GRK
GRK
GRK
GRK
WHEN YOU REALIZE YOUR FUTURE'S GONE TO SHIT...

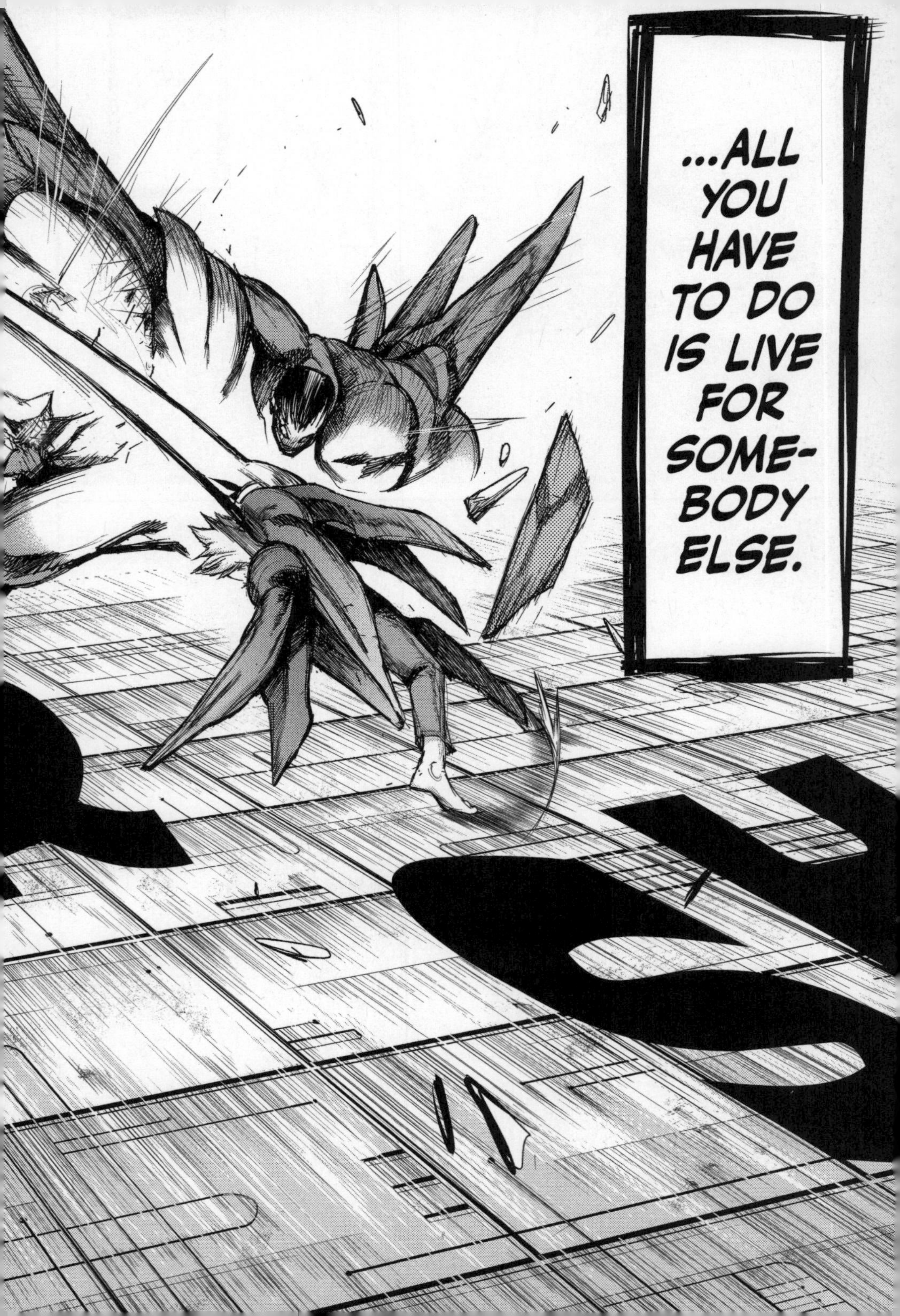
...ALL YOU HAVE TO DO IS LIVE FOR SOME-BODY ELSE.

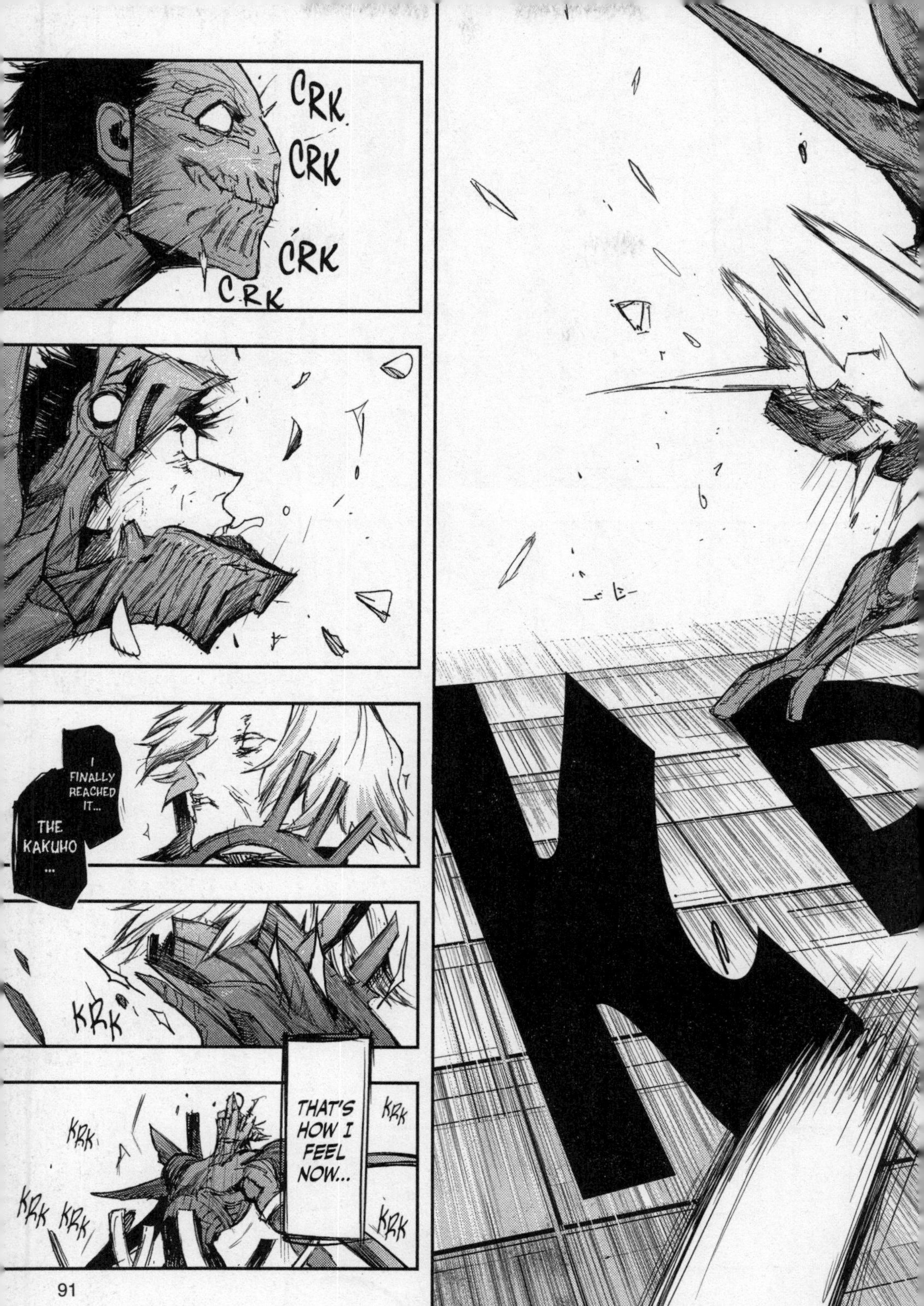
CRK
CRK
CRK
CRK
I FINALLY REACHED IT...
THE KAKUHO...
KRK
KRK
THAT'S HOW I FEEL NOW...
KRK
KRK
KRK KRK

LOOKING AT YOU, INVESTIGATOR AMON...
U-UGH...
DS
G... GUH...
SSH
KPA
KRAK
PA
KRAK
PKA
KRRK
FWP...

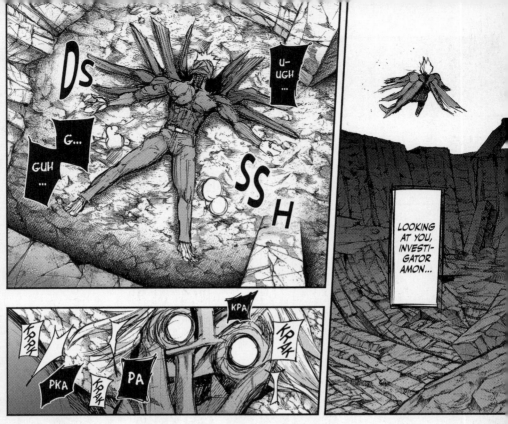

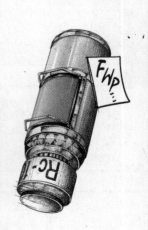

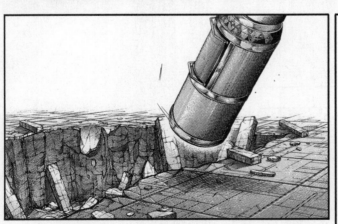

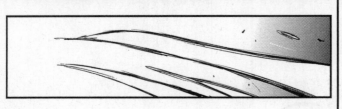

PSSSH...

SPLSH

SPLSH

SPLSH

SPLSH   PLSH   PLSH PLSH PLSH   PLSH

LET'S GO,
INVESTI-
GATOR
AMON.

WELL
DONE.

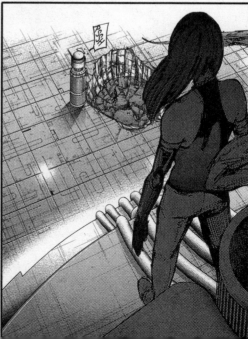

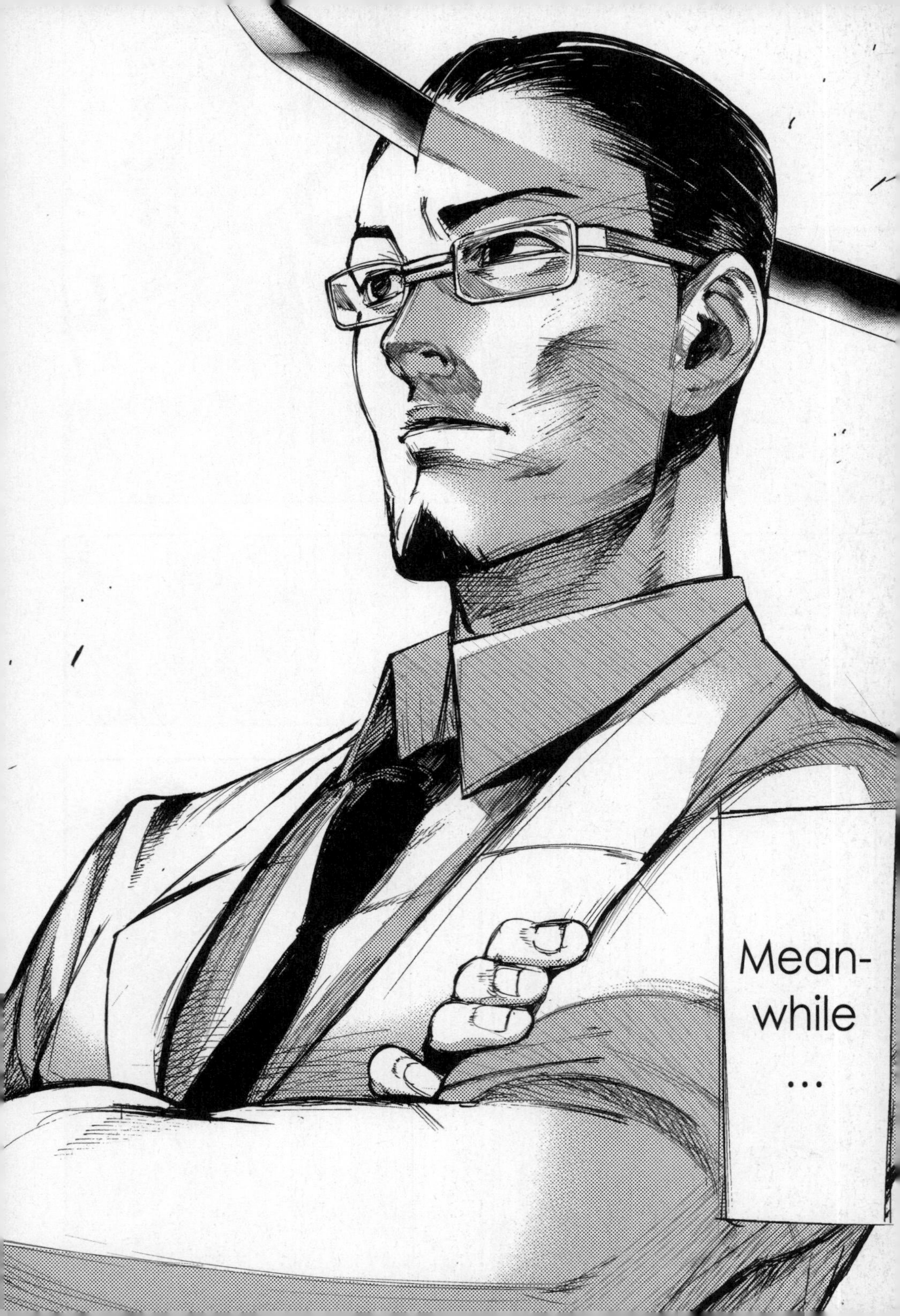
Mean-while...

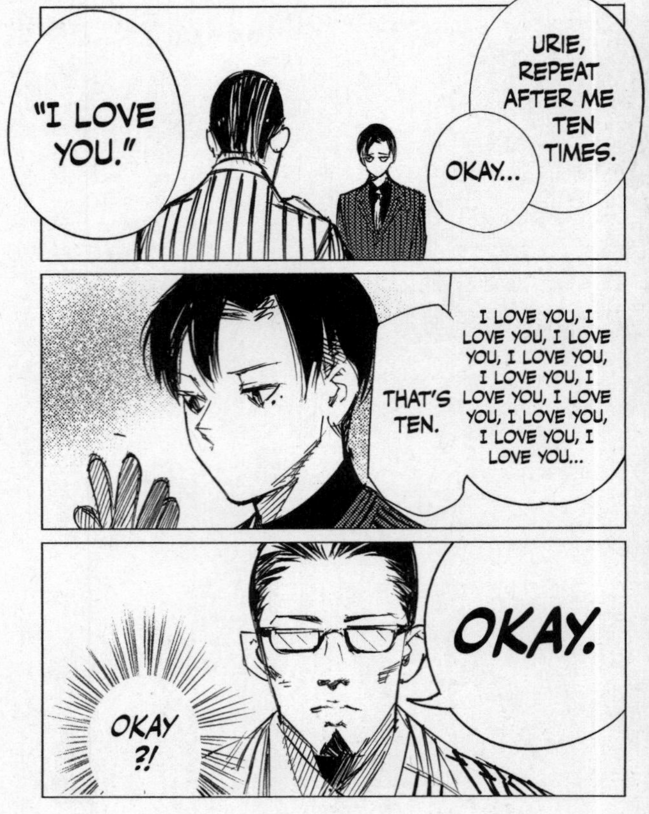
URIE, REPEAT AFTER ME TEN TIMES.
OKAY...
"I LOVE YOU."
I LOVE YOU, I LOVE YOU, I LOVE YOU, I LOVE YOU, I LOVE YOU, I LOVE YOU, I LOVE YOU, I LOVE YOU, I LOVE YOU, I LOVE YOU...
THAT'S TEN.
OKAY.
OKAY ?!

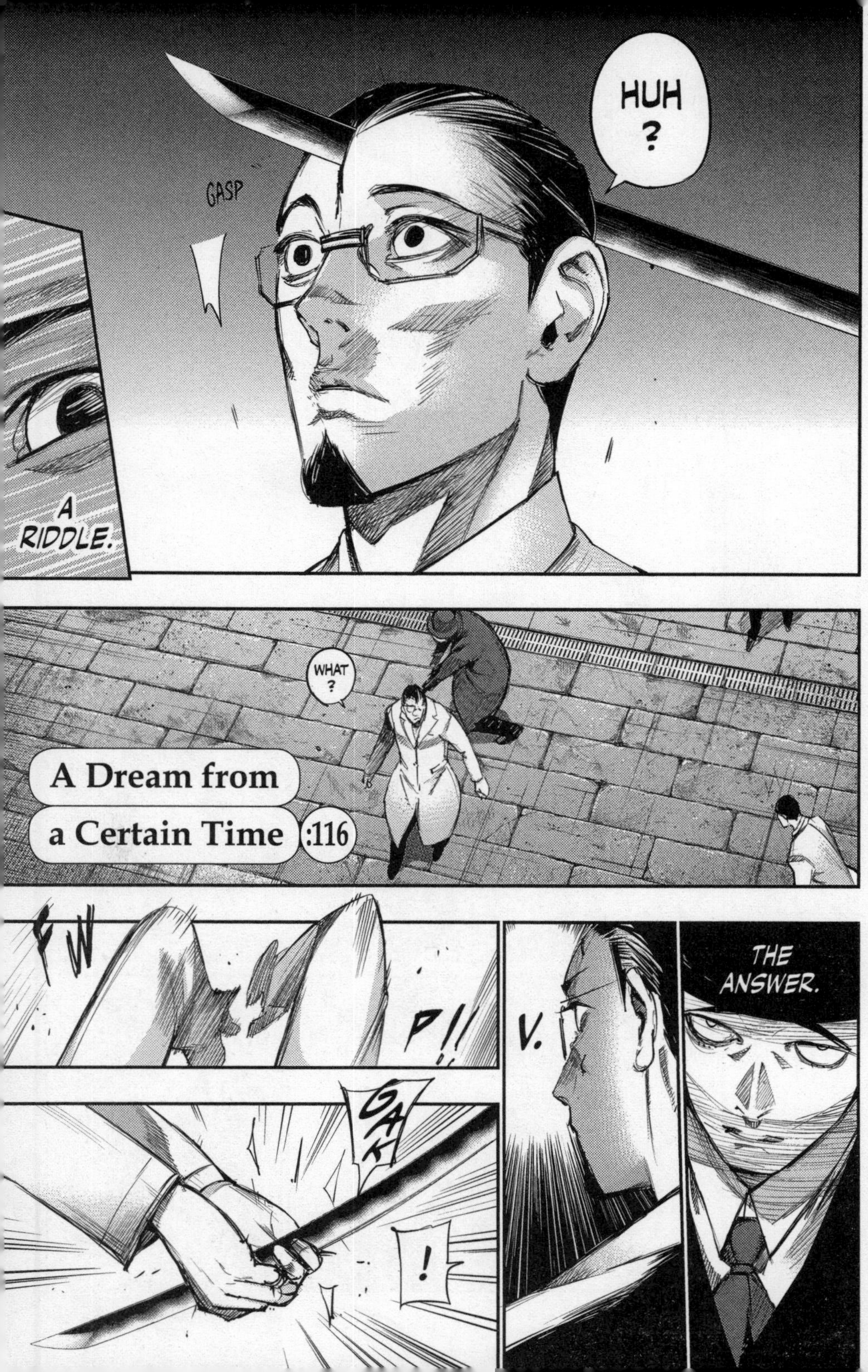
HUH ?
GASP
A RIDDLE.
WHAT ?
A Dream from a Certain Time :116
THE ANSWER.
V.
FW
P!!
GAK
!

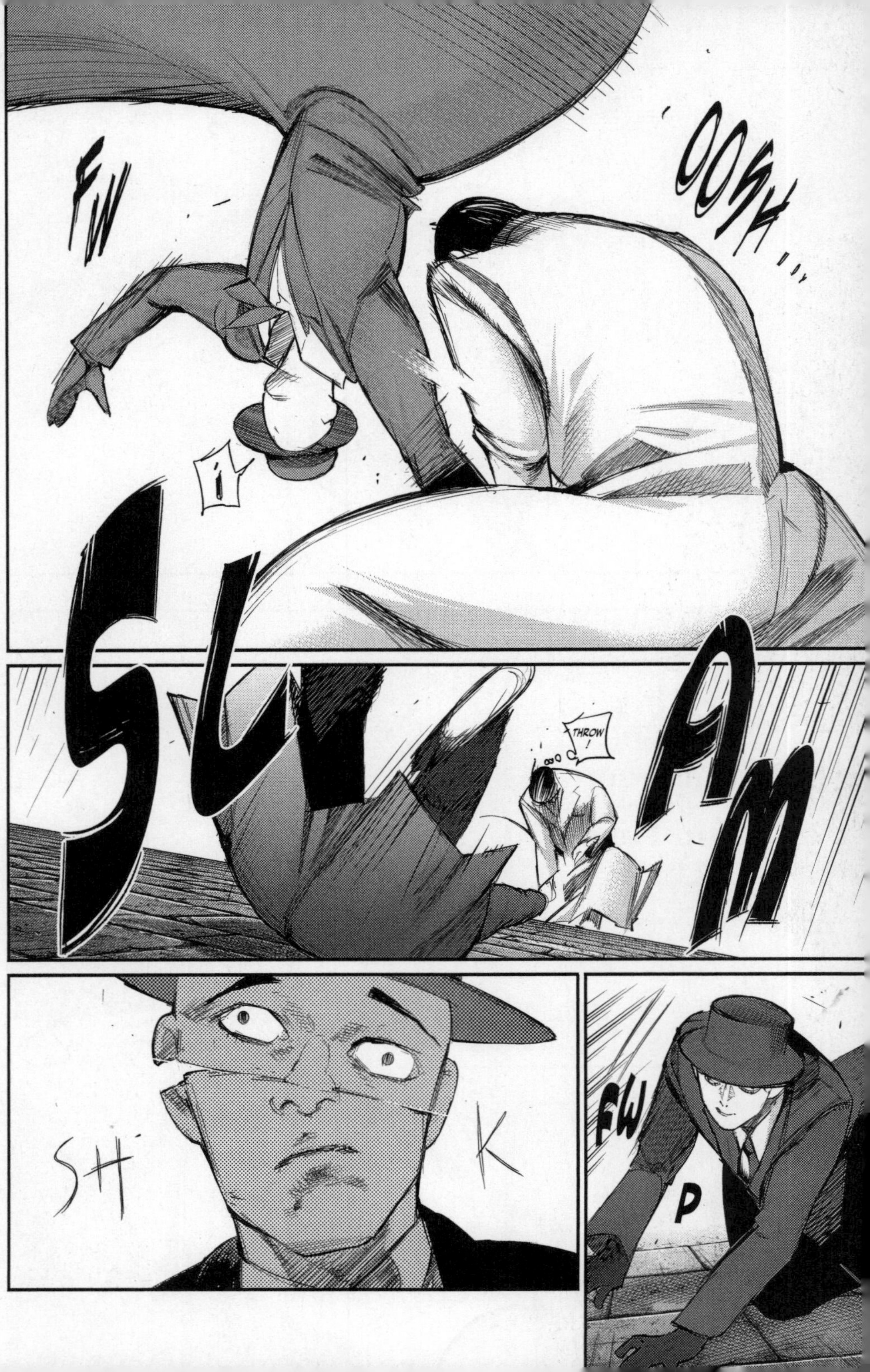
FW
OOSH...
!
SLAM
THROW!
FW
P
SH
K

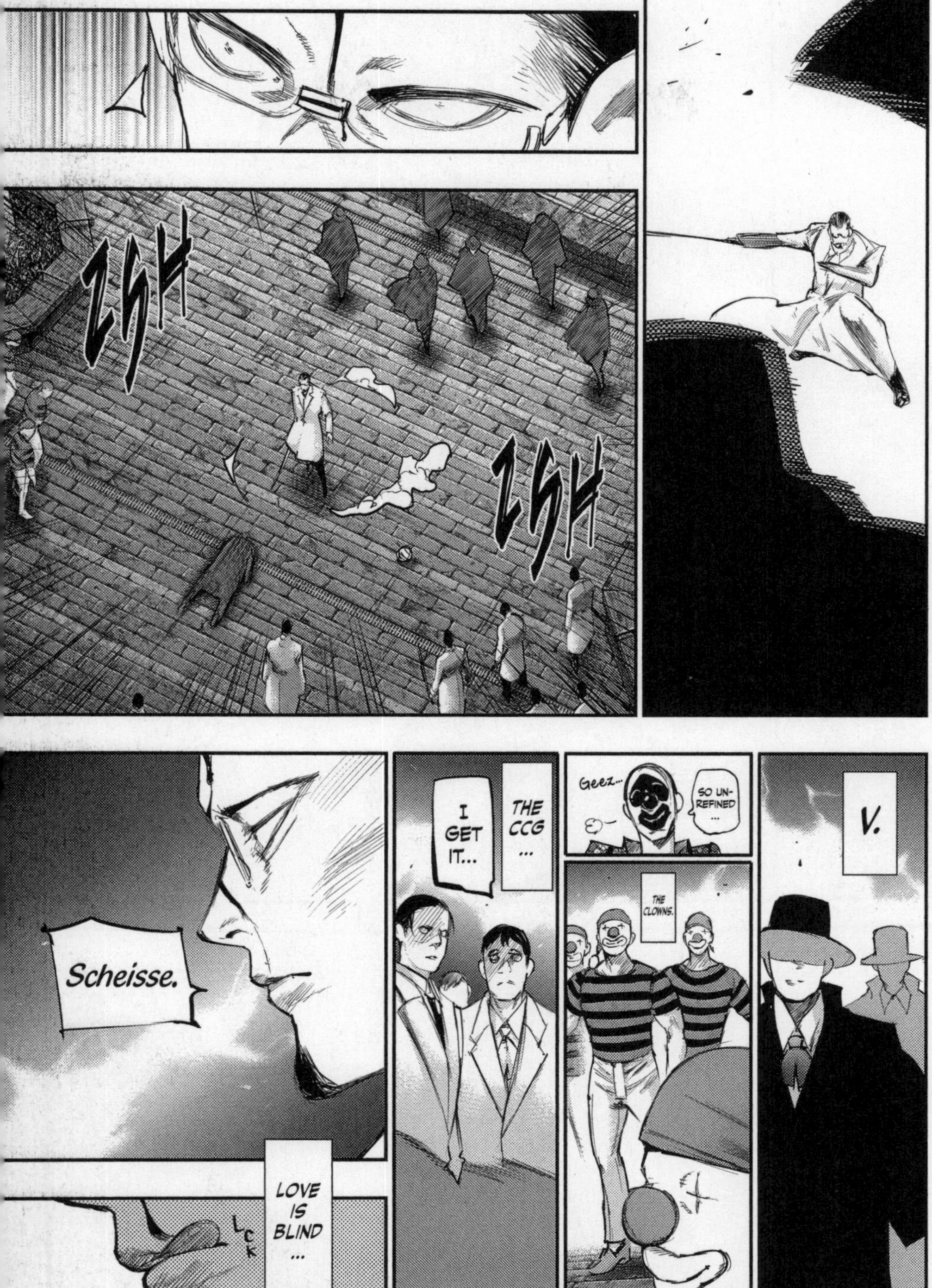
ZSH
ZSH
V.
Geez...
SO UN-REFINED...
THE CLOWNS.
THE CCG...
I GET IT...
Scheisse.
LOVE IS BLIND...
LCK

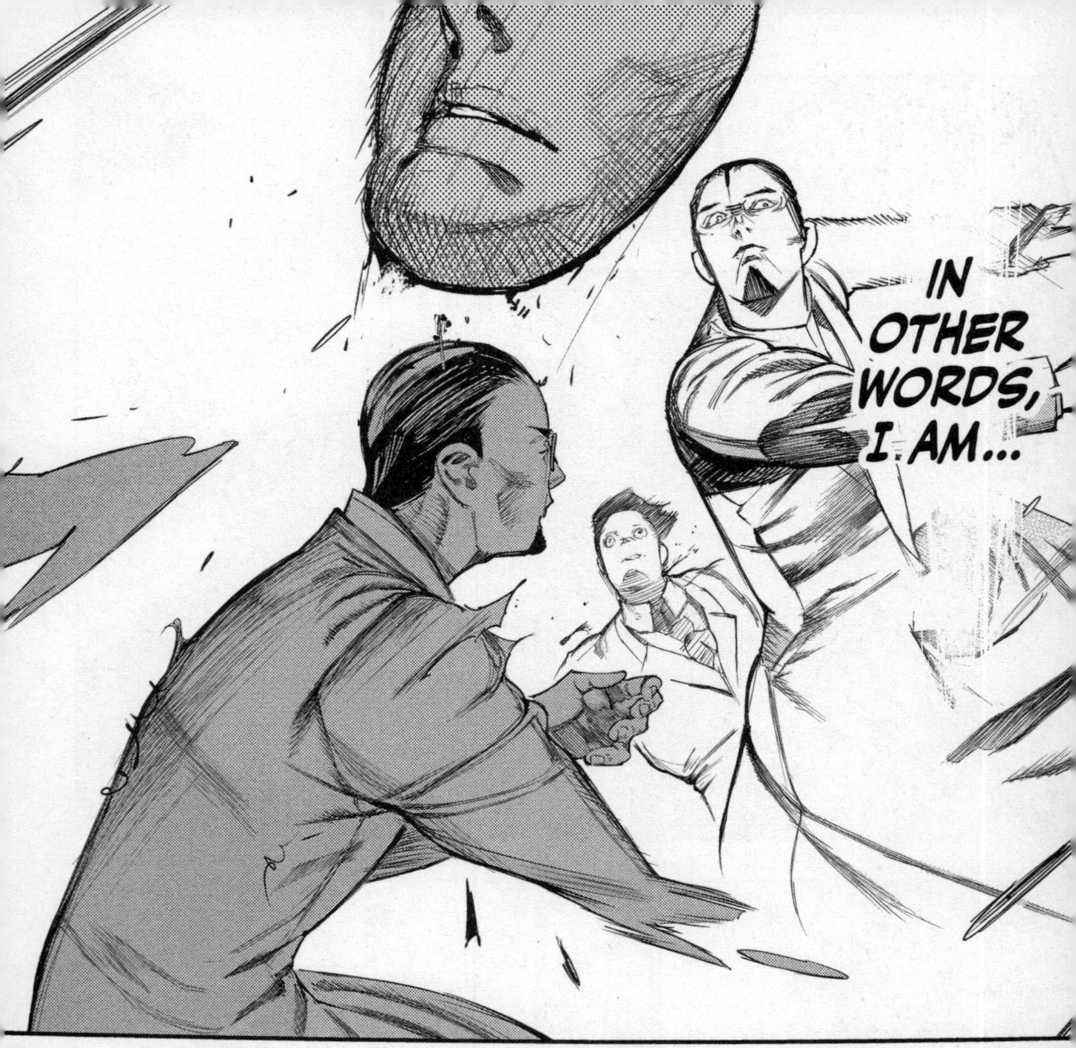
IN OTHER WORDS, I AM...
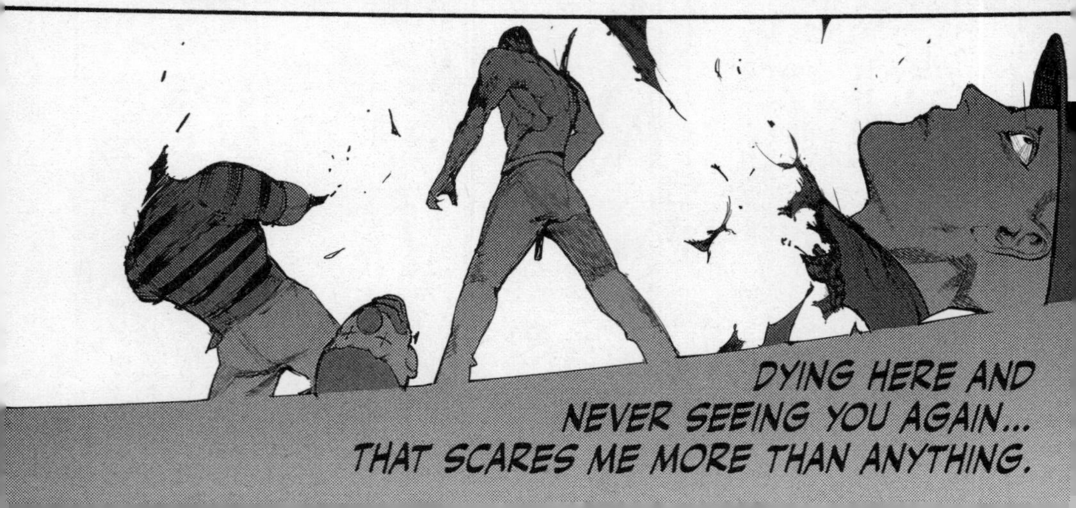
DYING HERE AND NEVER SEEING YOU AGAIN... THAT SCARES ME MORE THAN ANYTHING.

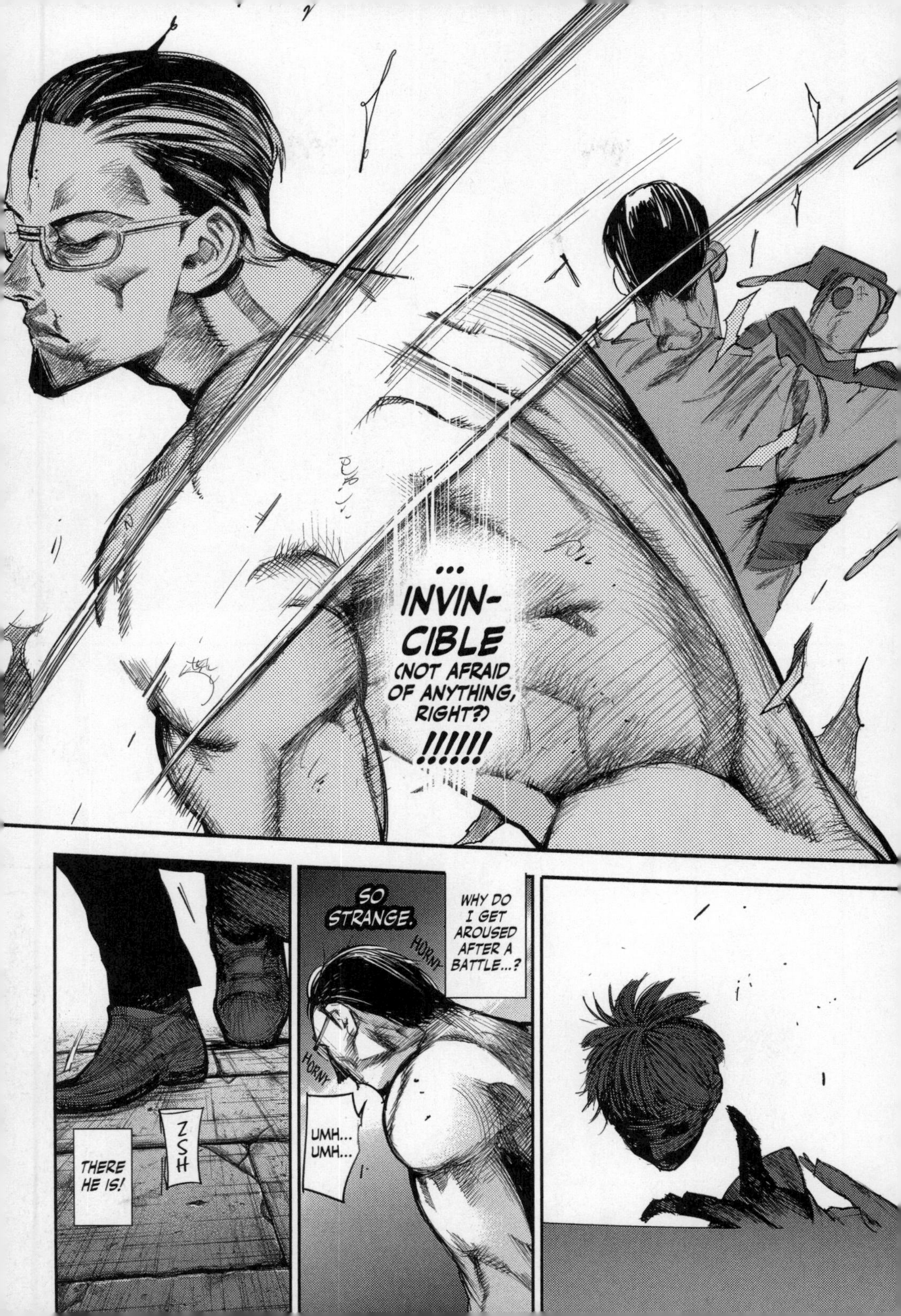
... INVIN-CIBLE (NOT AFRAID OF ANYTHING, RIGHT?) !!!!!!
WHY DO I GET AROUSED AFTER A BATTLE...?
SO STRANGE.
HORNY
HORNY
UMH... UMH...
ZSH
THERE HE IS!

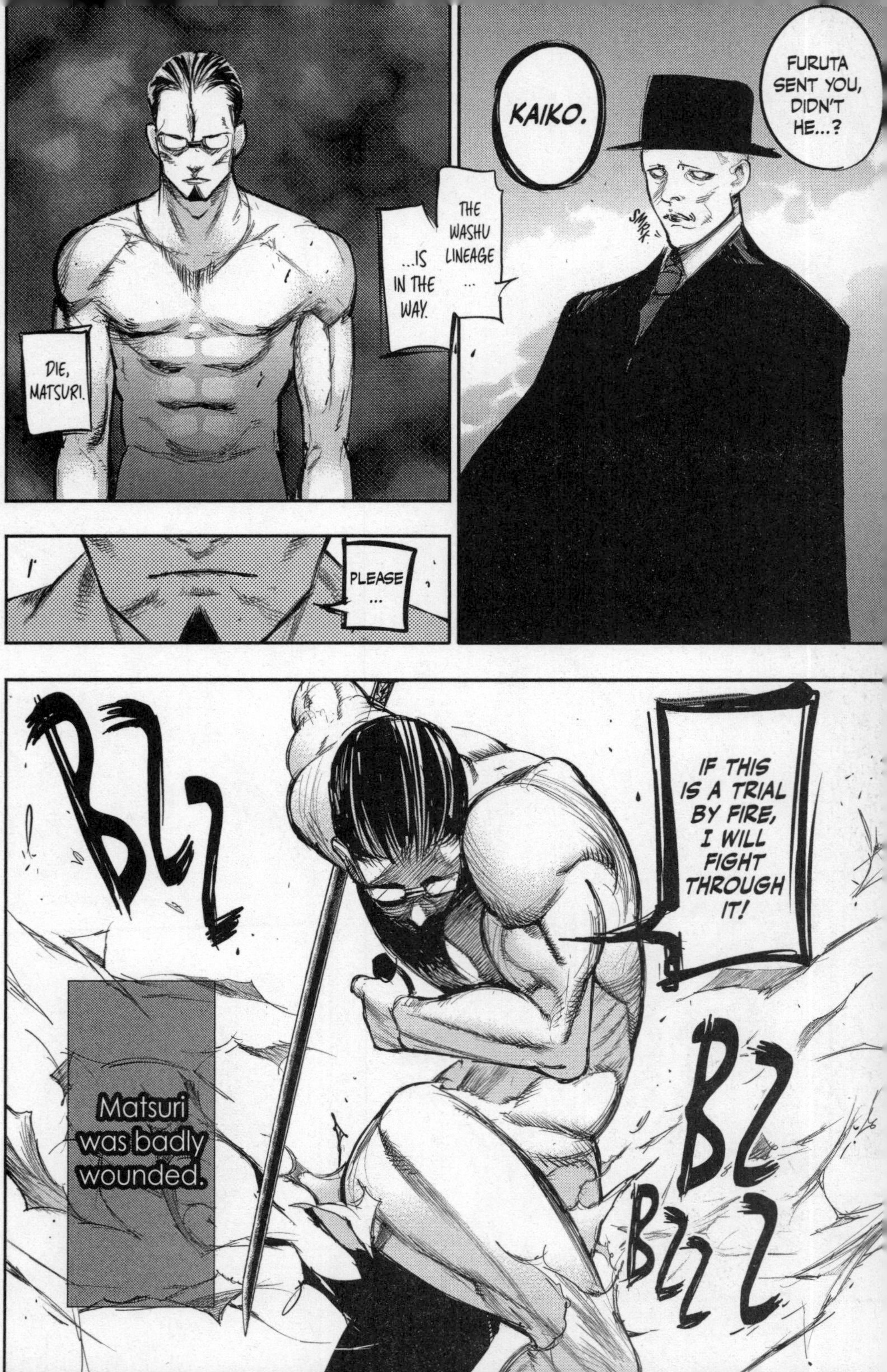
FURUTA SENT YOU, DIDN'T HE...?
KAIKO.
SMRK
THE WASHU LINEAGE ...
...IS IN THE WAY.
DIE, MATSURI.
PLEASE ...
IF THIS IS A TRIAL BY FIRE, I WILL FIGHT THROUGH IT!
BZZ
BZ
BZZ
Matsuri was badly wounded.

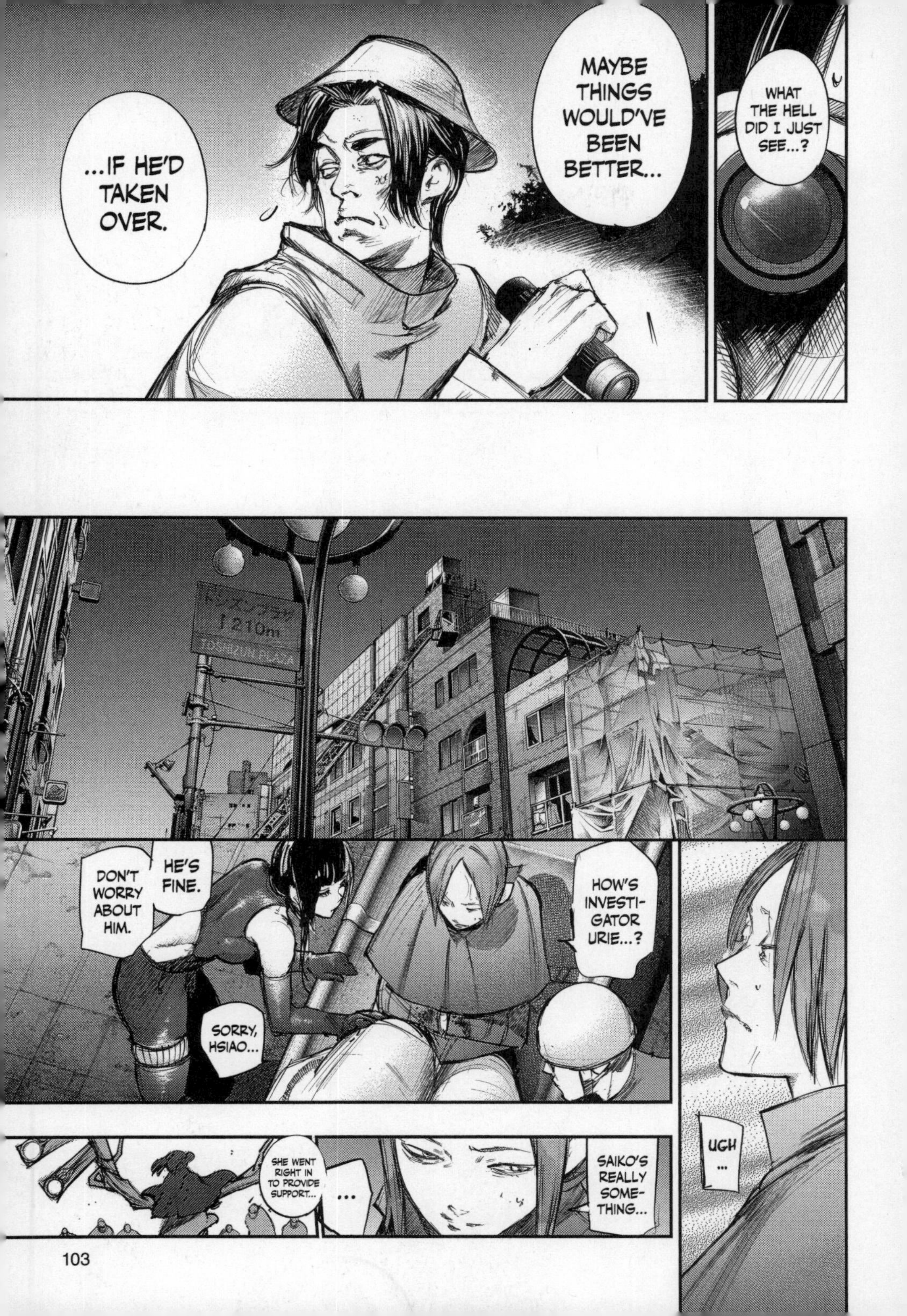
WHAT THE HELL DID I JUST SEE...?
MAYBE THINGS WOULD'VE BEEN BETTER...
...IF HE'D TAKEN OVER.
トシズンプラザ
210m
TOSHIZUN PLAZA
UGH ...
HOW'S INVESTIGATOR URIE...?
HE'S FINE.
DON'T WORRY ABOUT HIM.
SORRY, HSIAO...
SAIKO'S REALLY SOMETHING...
...
SHE WENT RIGHT IN TO PROVIDE SUPPORT...

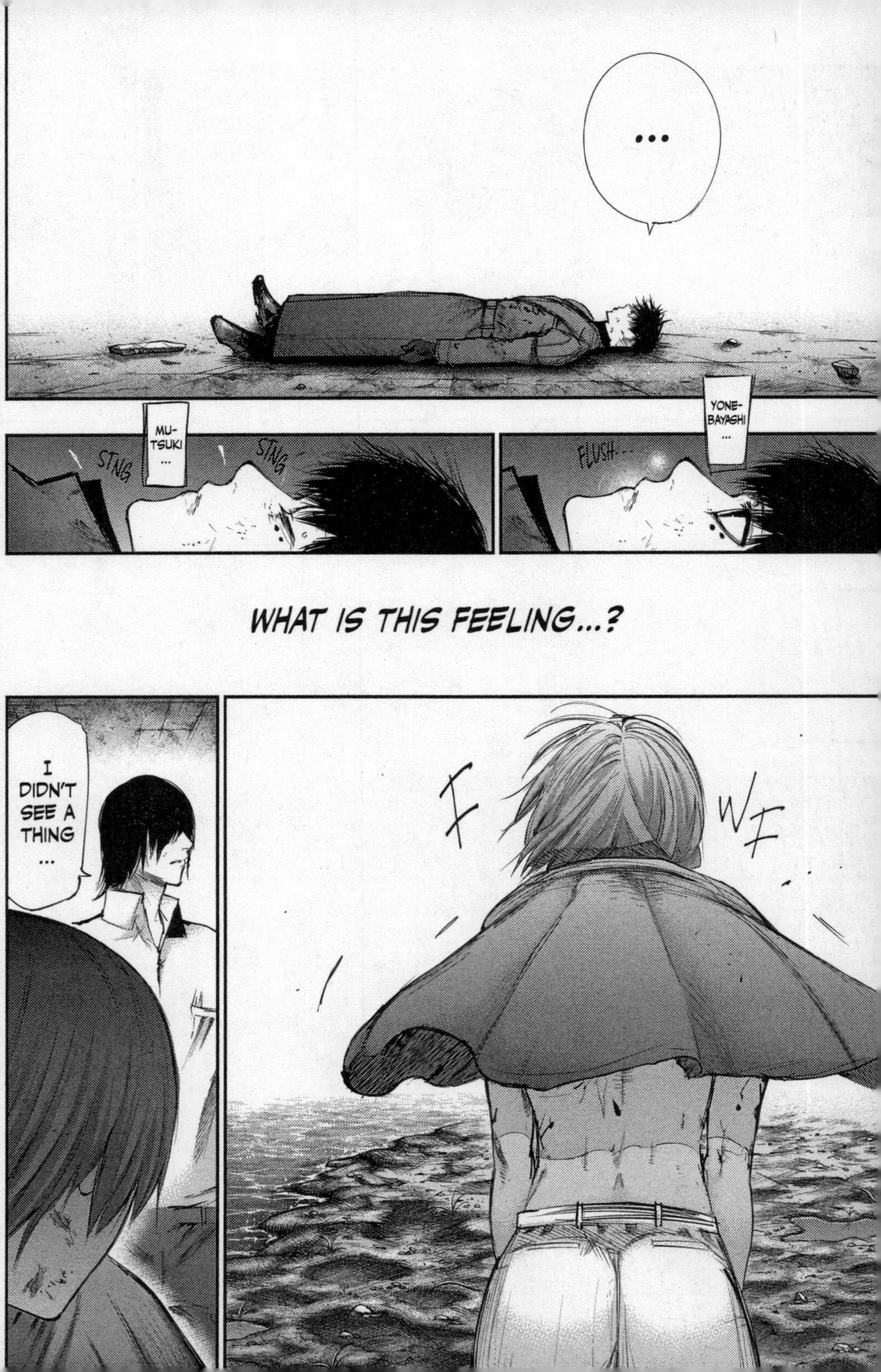
...
YONE-BAYASHI ...
FLUSH...
MU-TSUKI ...
STNG
STNG
WHAT IS THIS FEELING...?
F
WF
I DIDN'T SEE A THING ...

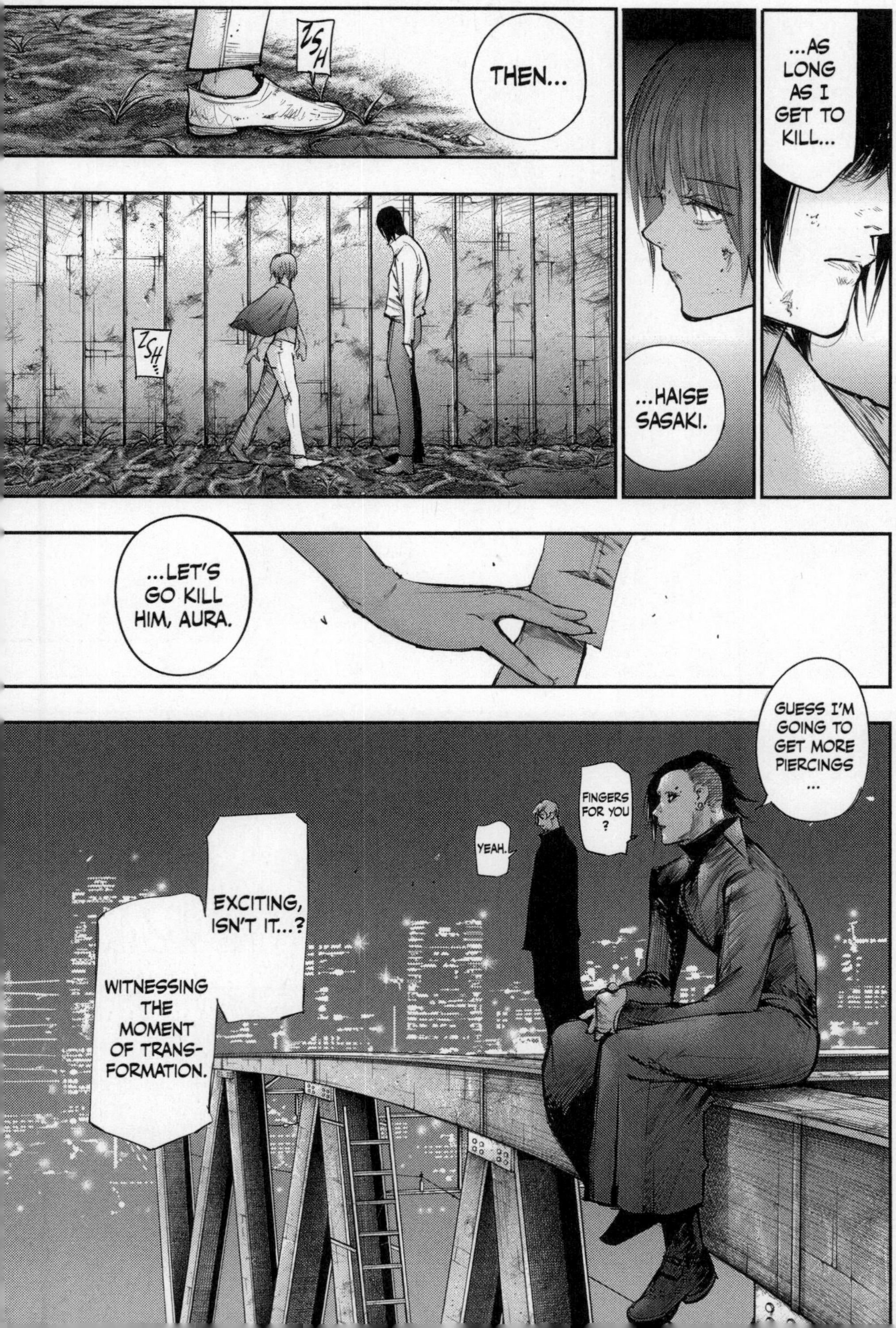
...AS LONG AS I GET TO KILL...
...HAISE SASAKI.
ZSH
THEN...
ZSH...
...LET'S GO KILL HIM, AURA.
GUESS I'M GOING TO GET MORE PIERCINGS ...
FINGERS FOR YOU?
YEAH...
EXCITING, ISN'T IT...?
WITNESSING THE MOMENT OF TRANS-FORMATION.

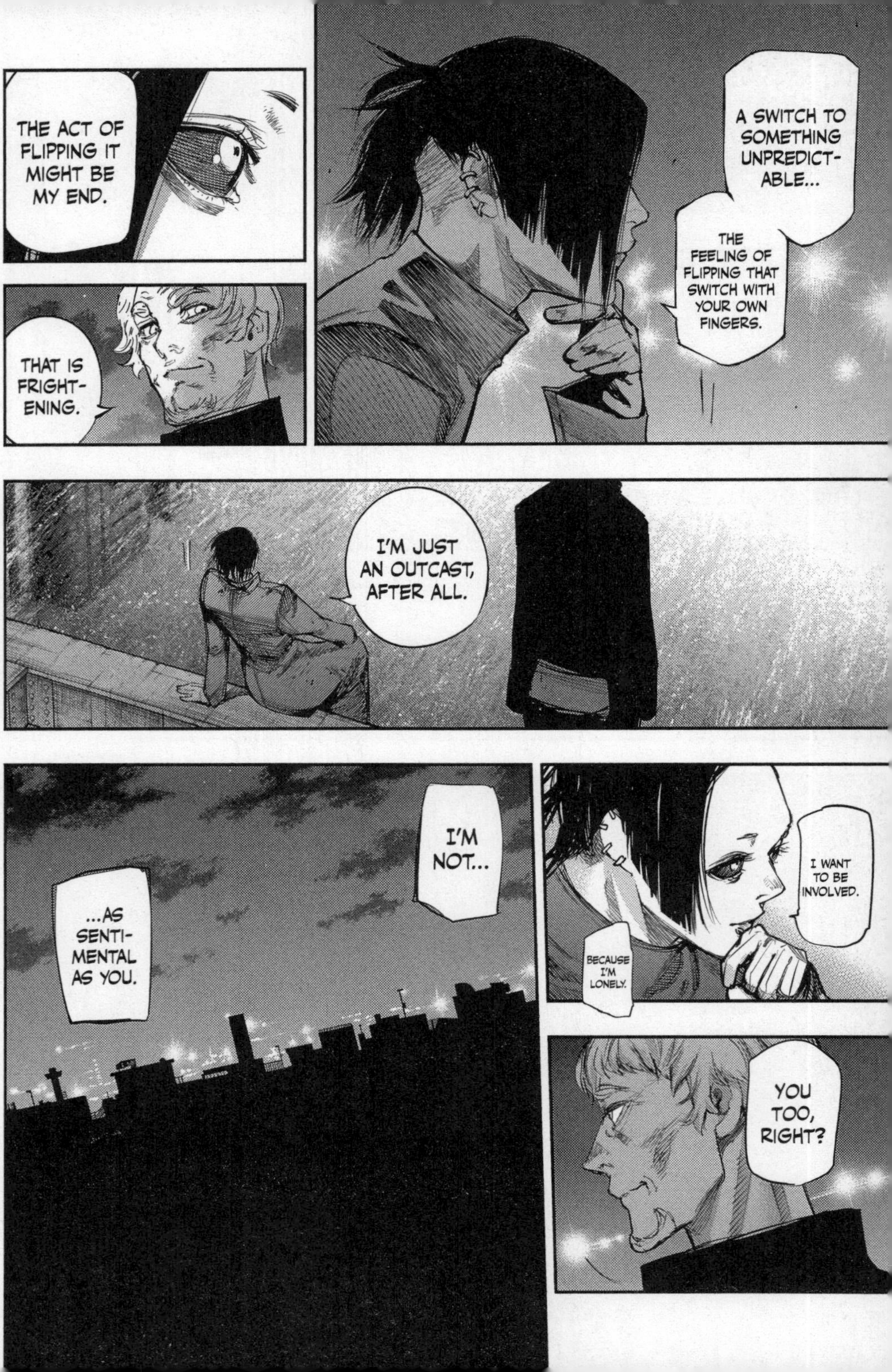
A SWITCH TO SOMETHING UNPREDICT-ABLE...
THE FEELING OF FLIPPING THAT SWITCH WITH YOUR OWN FINGERS.
THE ACT OF FLIPPING IT MIGHT BE MY END.
THAT IS FRIGHT-ENING.
I'M JUST AN OUTCAST, AFTER ALL.
I WANT TO BE INVOLVED.
BECAUSE I'M LONELY.
YOU TOO, RIGHT?
I'M NOT...
...AS SENTI-MENTAL AS YOU.

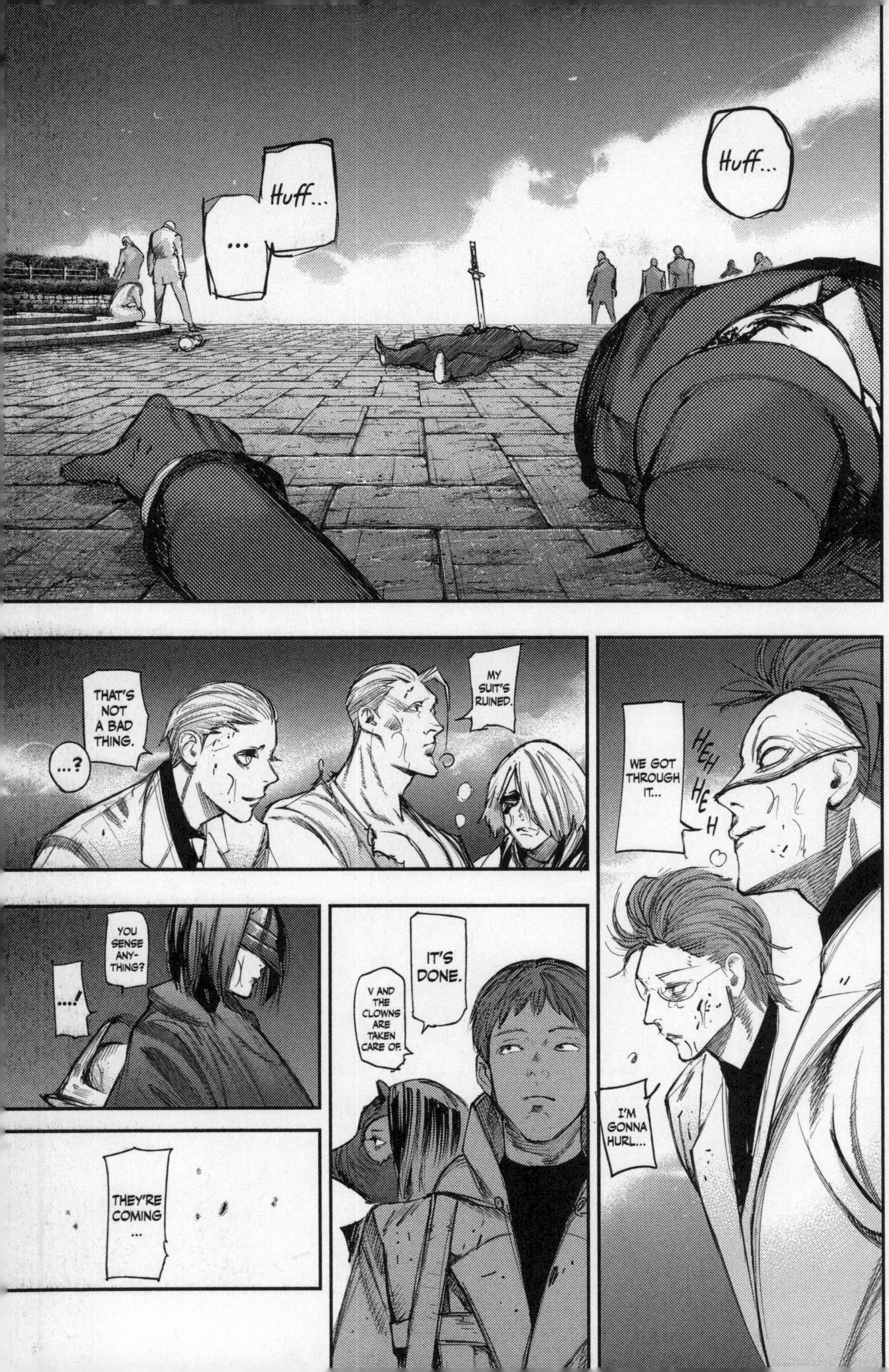

Huff...
Huff...
...
WE GOT THROUGH IT...
HEH HEH HEH
I'M GONNA HURL...
MY SUIT'S RUINED.
THAT'S NOT A BAD THING.
...?
IT'S DONE.
V AND THE CLOWNS ARE TAKEN CARE OF.
YOU SENSE ANYTHING?
...!
THEY'RE COMING ...

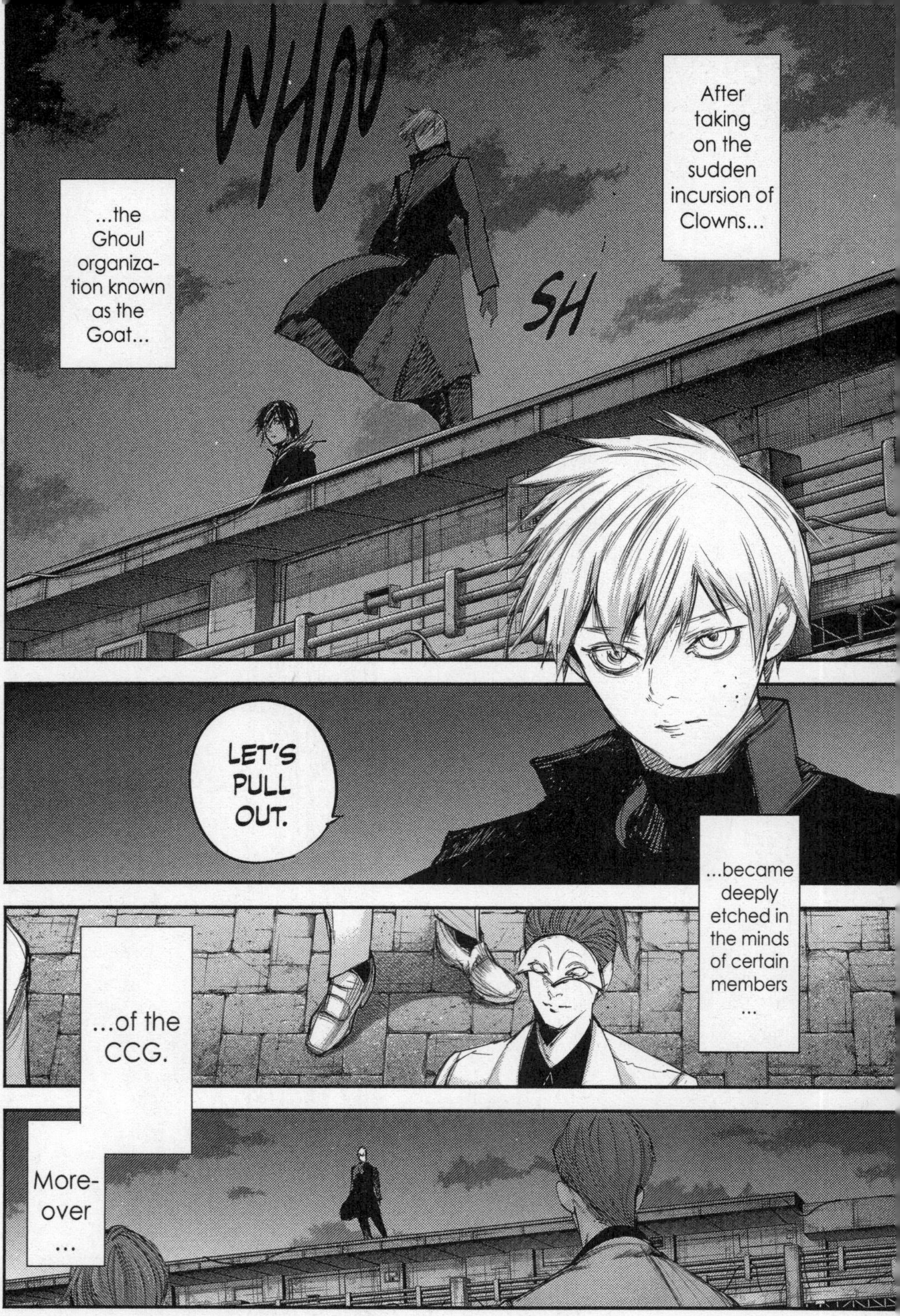
After taking on the sudden incursion of Clowns...
WHOO
...the Ghoul organization known as the Goat...
SH
...became deeply etched in the minds of certain members ...
LET'S PULL OUT.
...of the CCG.
More-over ...

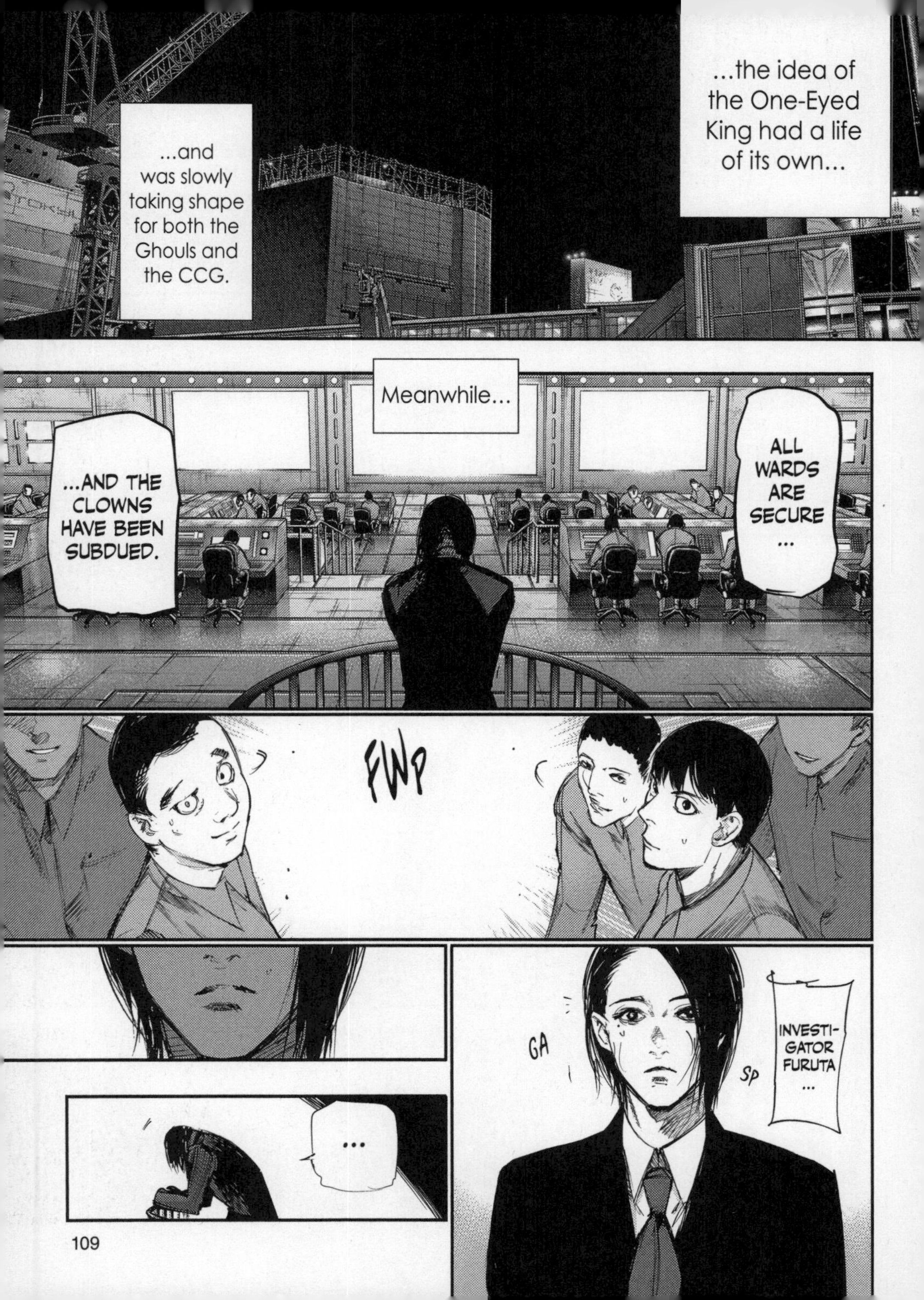
...the idea of the One-Eyed King had a life of its own...
...and was slowly taking shape for both the Ghouls and the CCG.
Meanwhile...
ALL WARDS ARE SECURE...
...AND THE CLOWNS HAVE BEEN SUBDUED.
FWP
INVESTI-GATOR FURUTA...
SP
GA
...

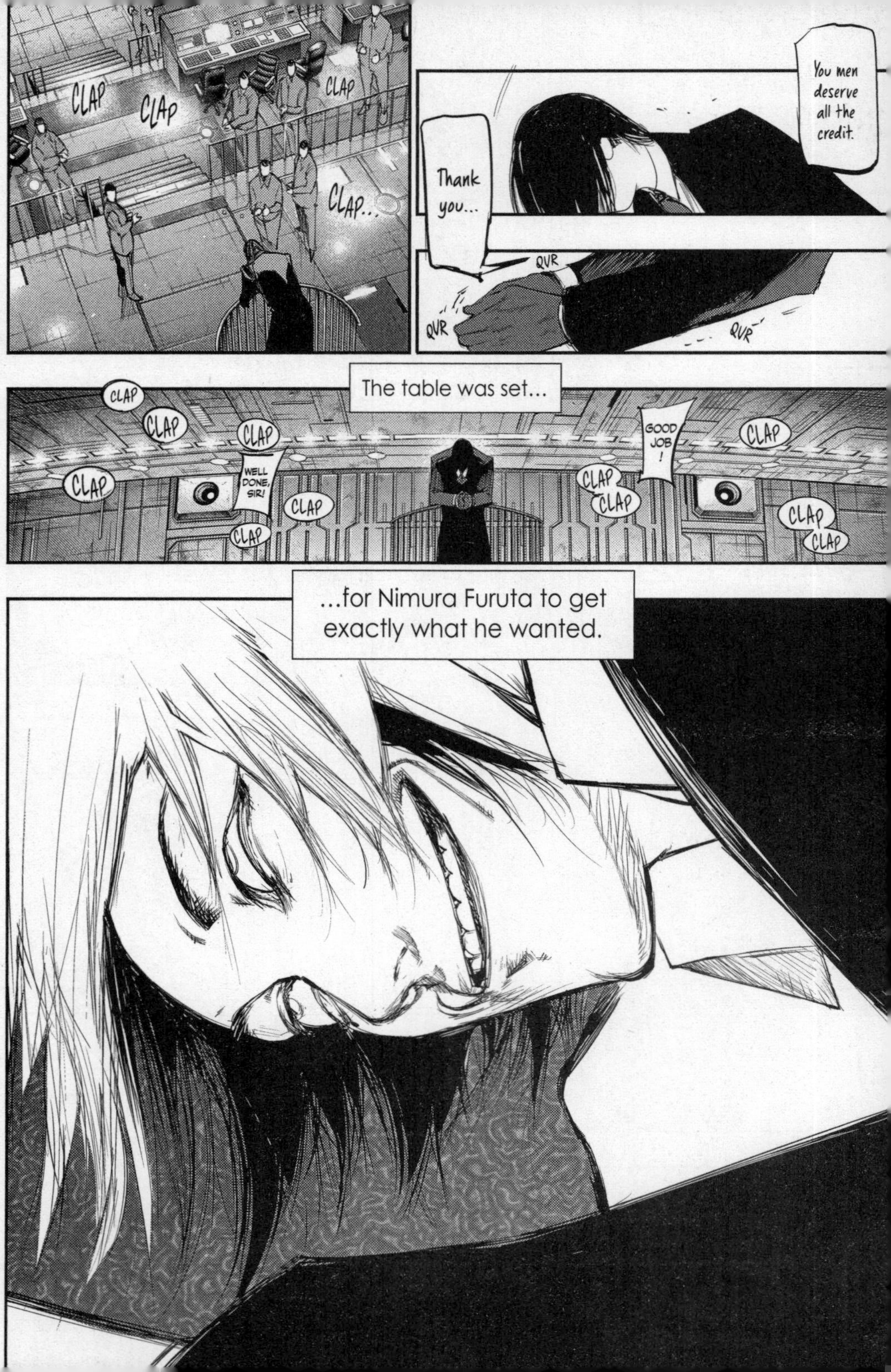
You men deserve all the credit.
Thank you...
QVR
QVR
QVR
CLAP
CLAP
CLAP
CLAP...
The table was set...
CLAP
GOOD JOB!
CLAP
CLAP
CLAP
CLAP
CLAP
CLAP
CLAP
WELL DONE, SIR!
CLAP
CLAP
CLAP
...for Nimura Furuta to get exactly what he wanted.

BEEP...
BEEP...
BEEP...
BEEP...
BEEP...
BEEP...

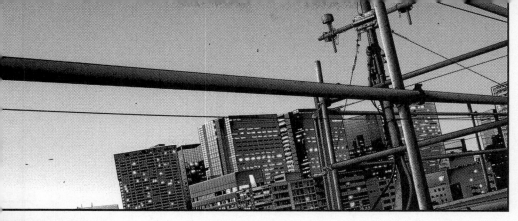

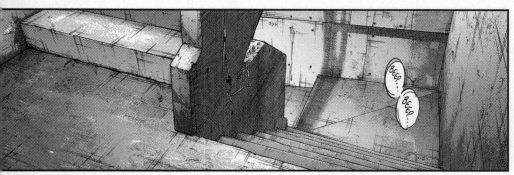

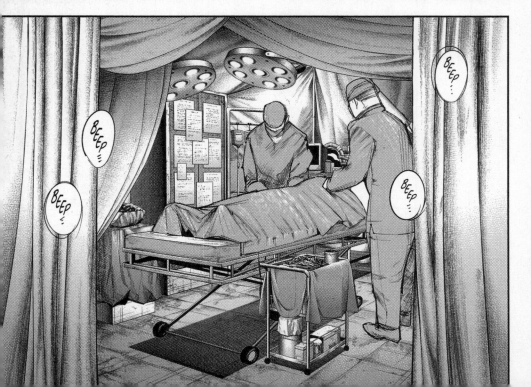

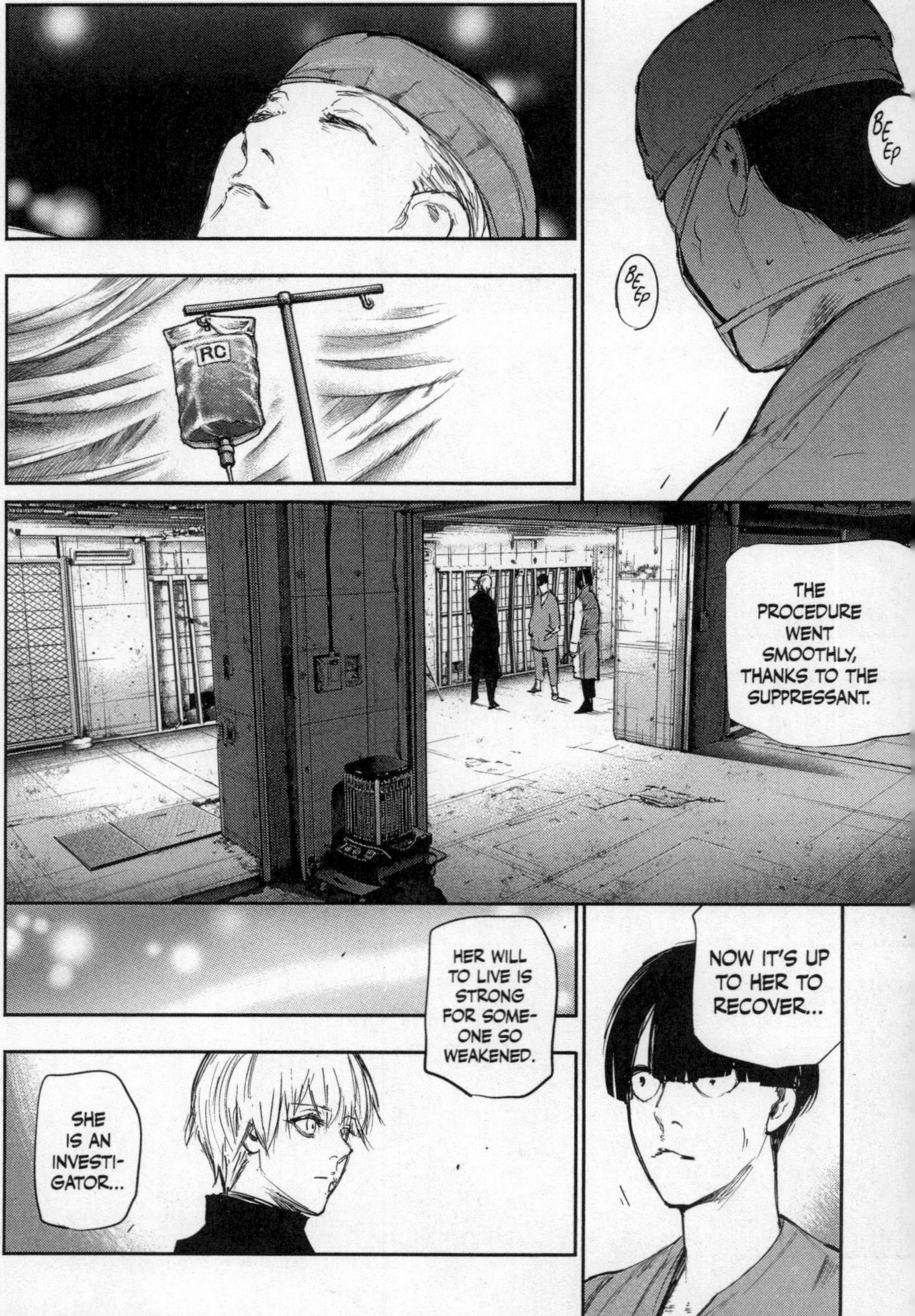
BEEP
BEEP
RC
THE PROCEDURE WENT SMOOTHLY, THANKS TO THE SUPPRESSANT.
NOW IT'S UP TO HER TO RECOVER...
HER WILL TO LIVE IS STRONG FOR SOME-ONE SO WEAKENED.
SHE IS AN INVESTI-GATOR...

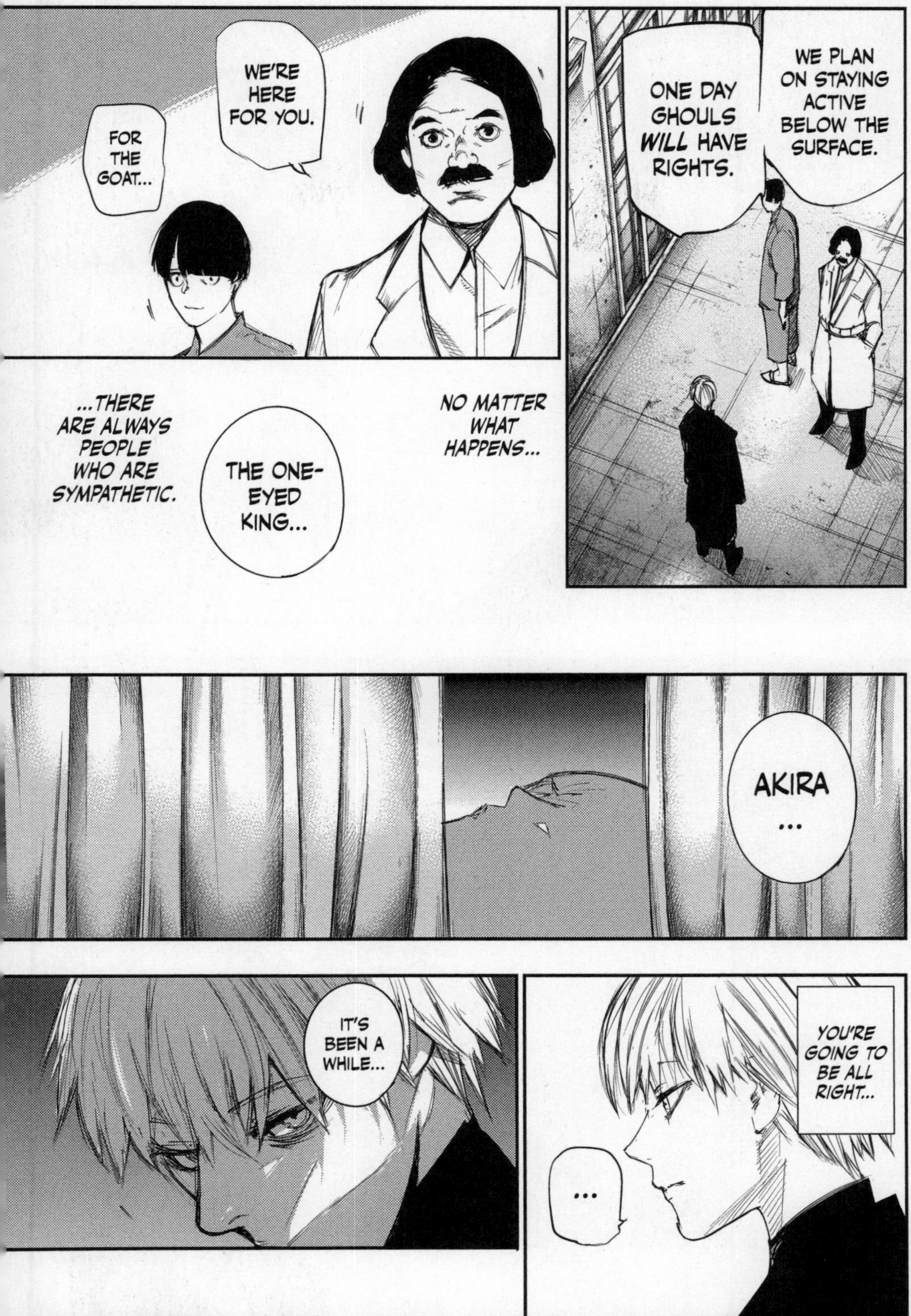
WE PLAN ON STAYING ACTIVE BELOW THE SURFACE.
ONE DAY GHOULS *WILL* HAVE RIGHTS.
WE'RE HERE FOR YOU.
FOR THE GOAT...
NO MATTER WHAT HAPPENS...
THE ONE-EYED KING...
...THERE ARE ALWAYS PEOPLE WHO ARE SYMPATHETIC.
AKIRA ...
YOU'RE GOING TO BE ALL RIGHT...
...
IT'S BEEN A WHILE...

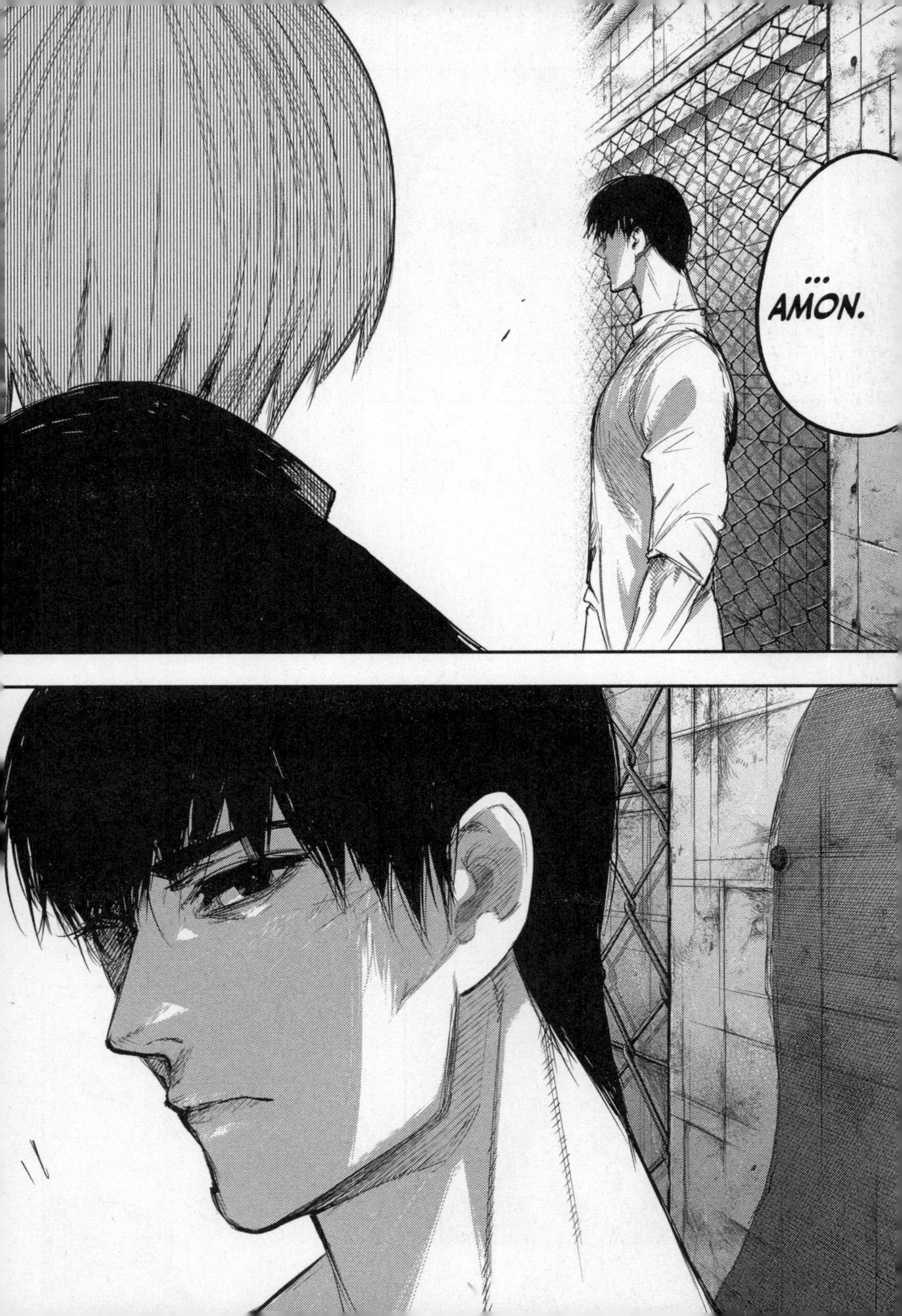
... AMON.

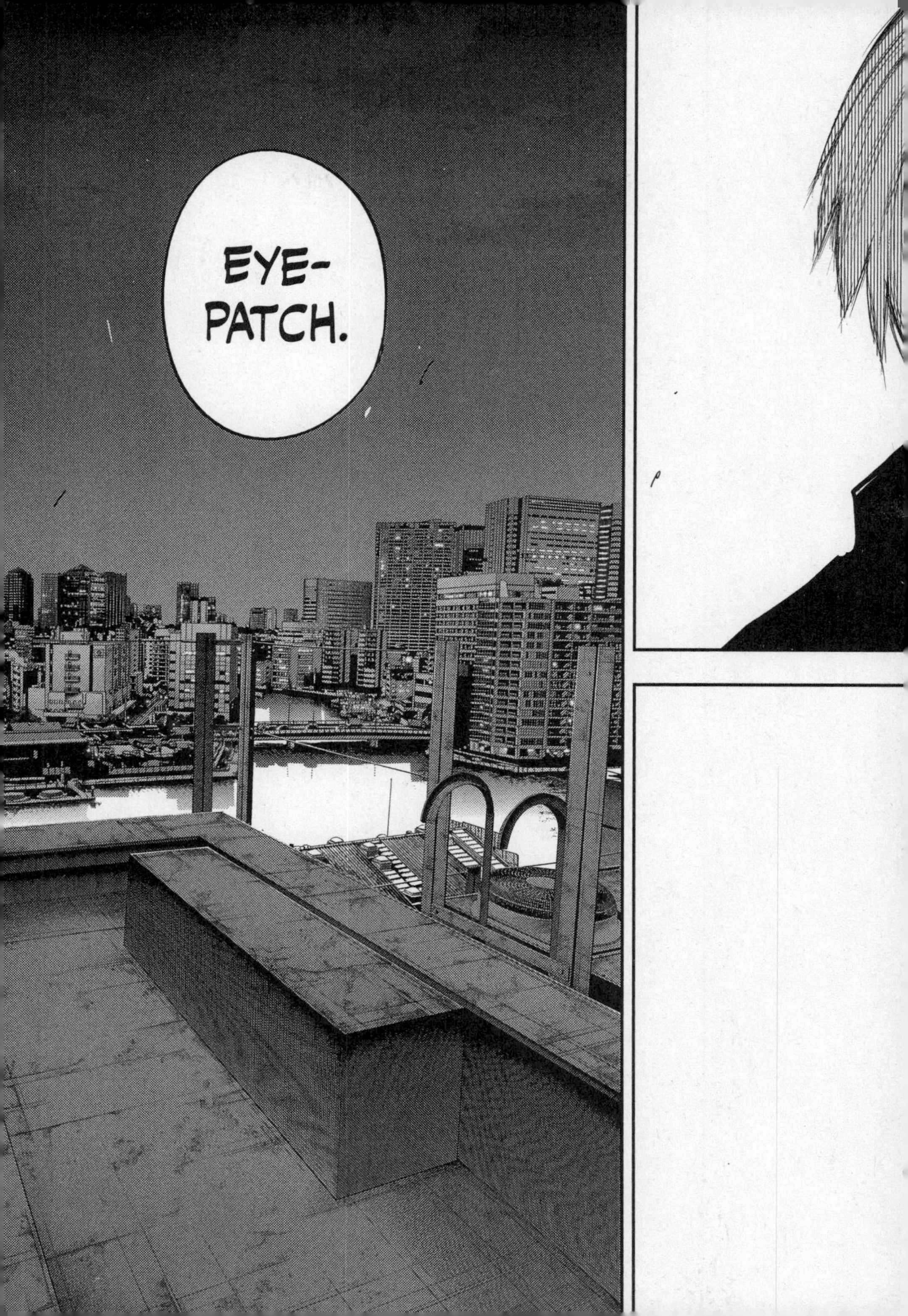
EYE-PATCH.

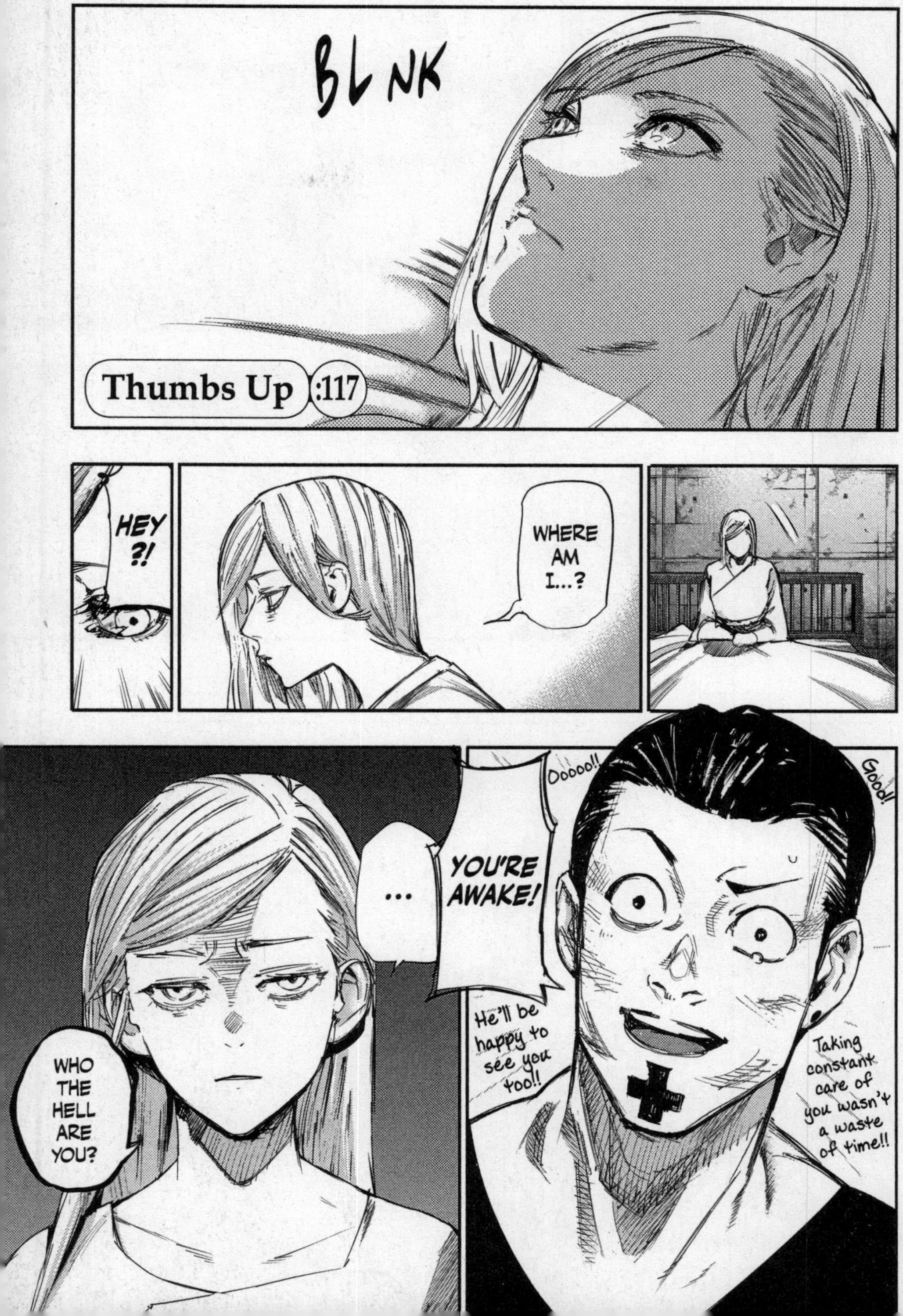
BLNK
Thumbs Up :117
WHERE AM I...?
HEY ?!
Good!
Ooooo!!
YOU'RE AWAKE!
Taking constant care of you wasn't a waste of time!!
He'll be happy to see you too!!
...
WHO THE HELL ARE YOU?

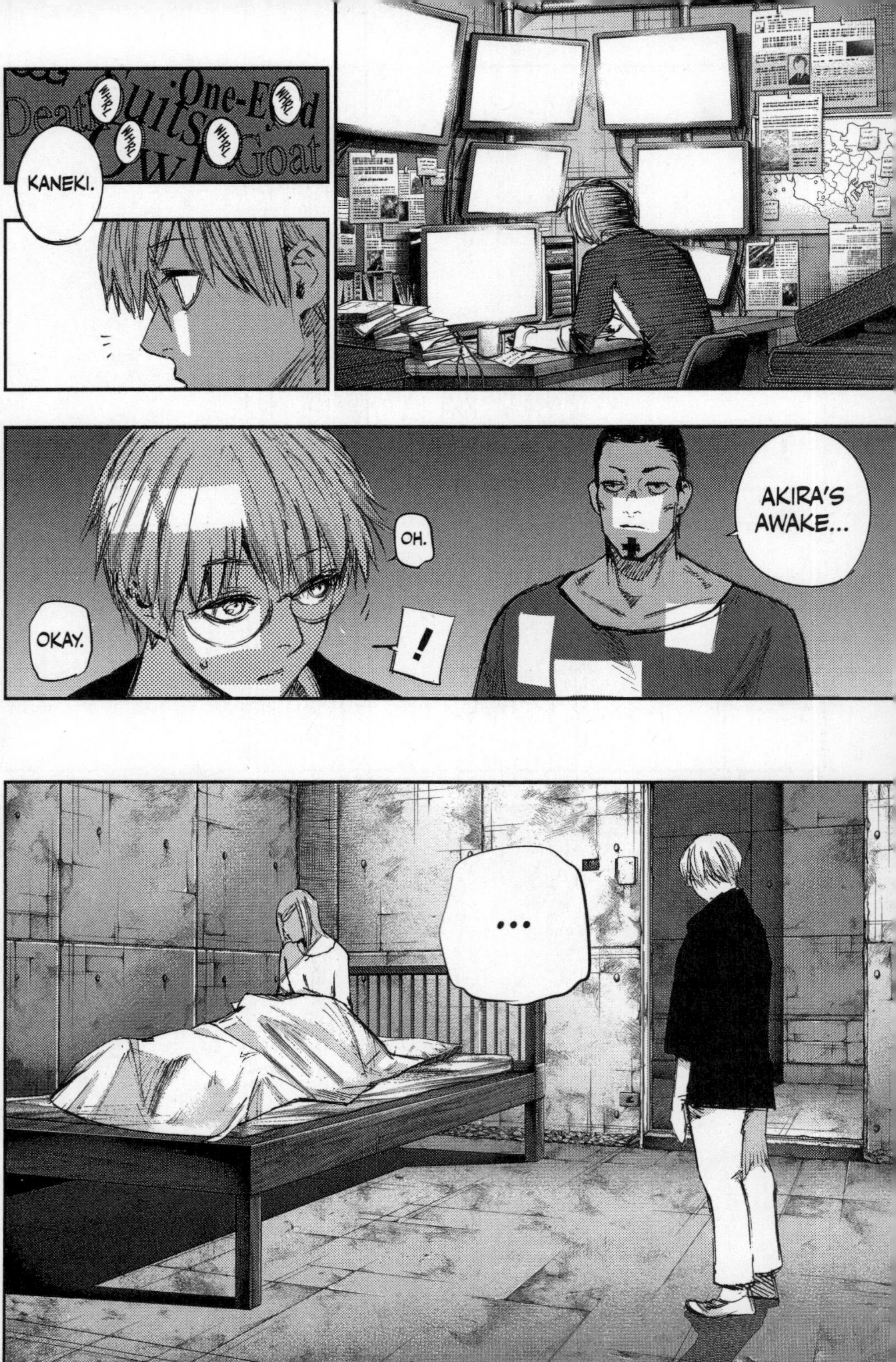
Owl
Goat
KANEKI.
AKIRA'S AWAKE...
!
OH.
OKAY.
...

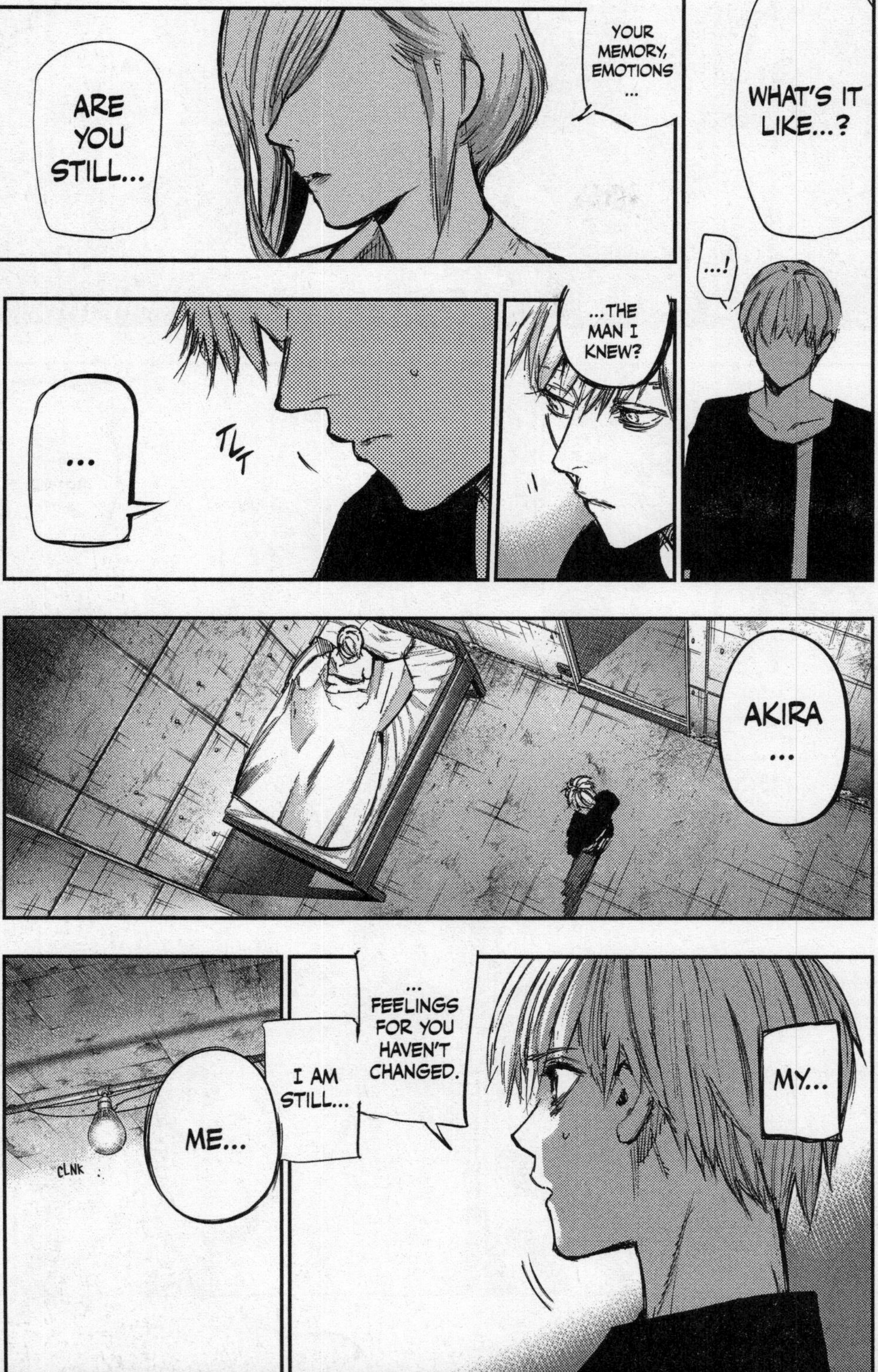
WHAT'S IT LIKE...?
YOUR MEMORY, EMOTIONS ...
ARE YOU STILL...
...!
...THE MAN I KNEW?
TLK
...
AKIRA ...
MY...
... FEELINGS FOR YOU HAVEN'T CHANGED.
I AM STILL...
ME...
CLNK

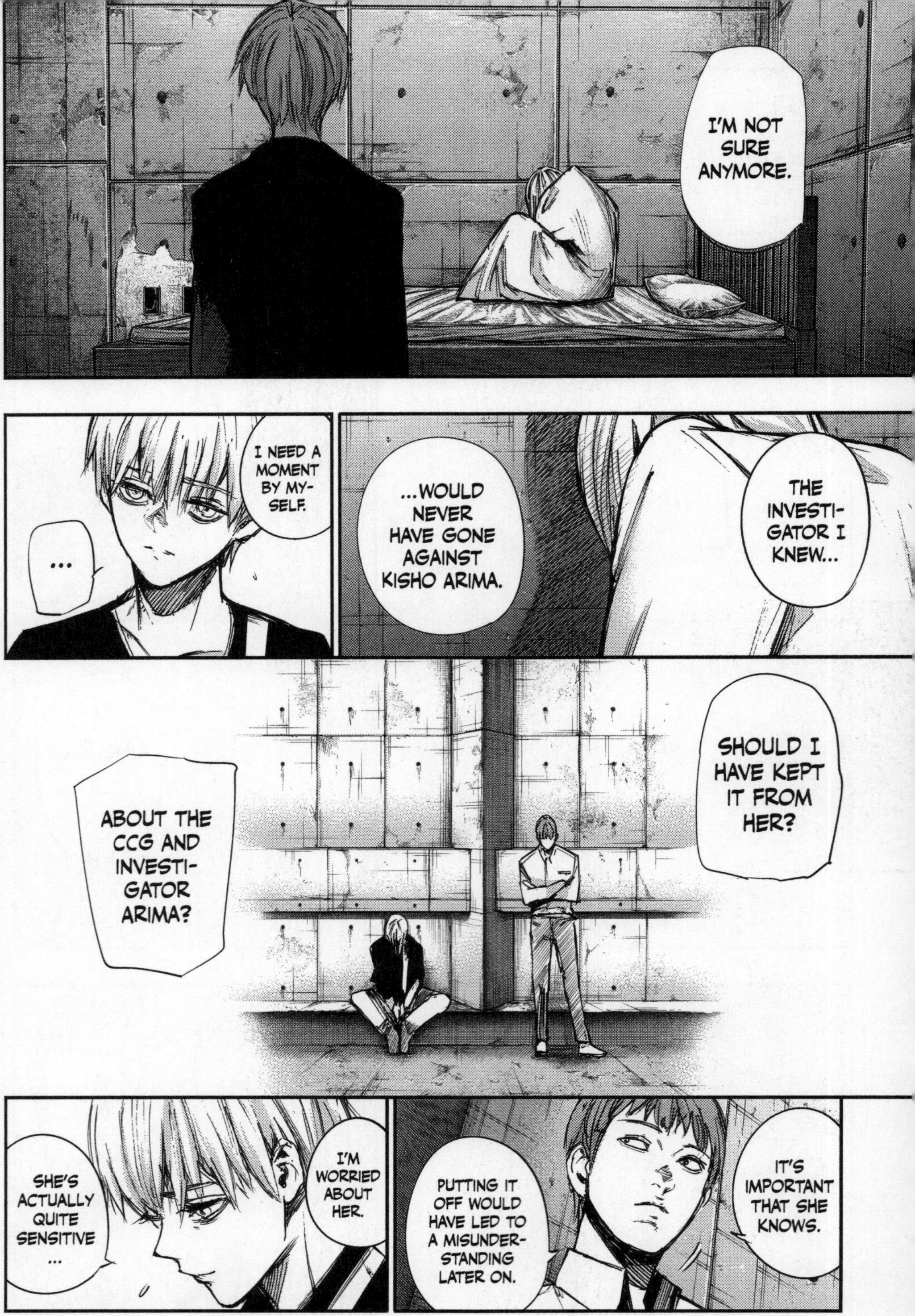
I'M NOT SURE ANYMORE.
THE INVESTI-GATOR I KNEW...
...WOULD NEVER HAVE GONE AGAINST KISHO ARIMA.
I NEED A MOMENT BY MY-SELF.
...
SHOULD I HAVE KEPT IT FROM HER?
ABOUT THE CCG AND INVESTI-GATOR ARIMA?
IT'S IMPORTANT THAT SHE KNOWS.
PUTTING IT OFF WOULD HAVE LED TO A MISUNDER-STANDING LATER ON.
I'M WORRIED ABOUT HER.
SHE'S ACTUALLY QUITE SENSITIVE ...

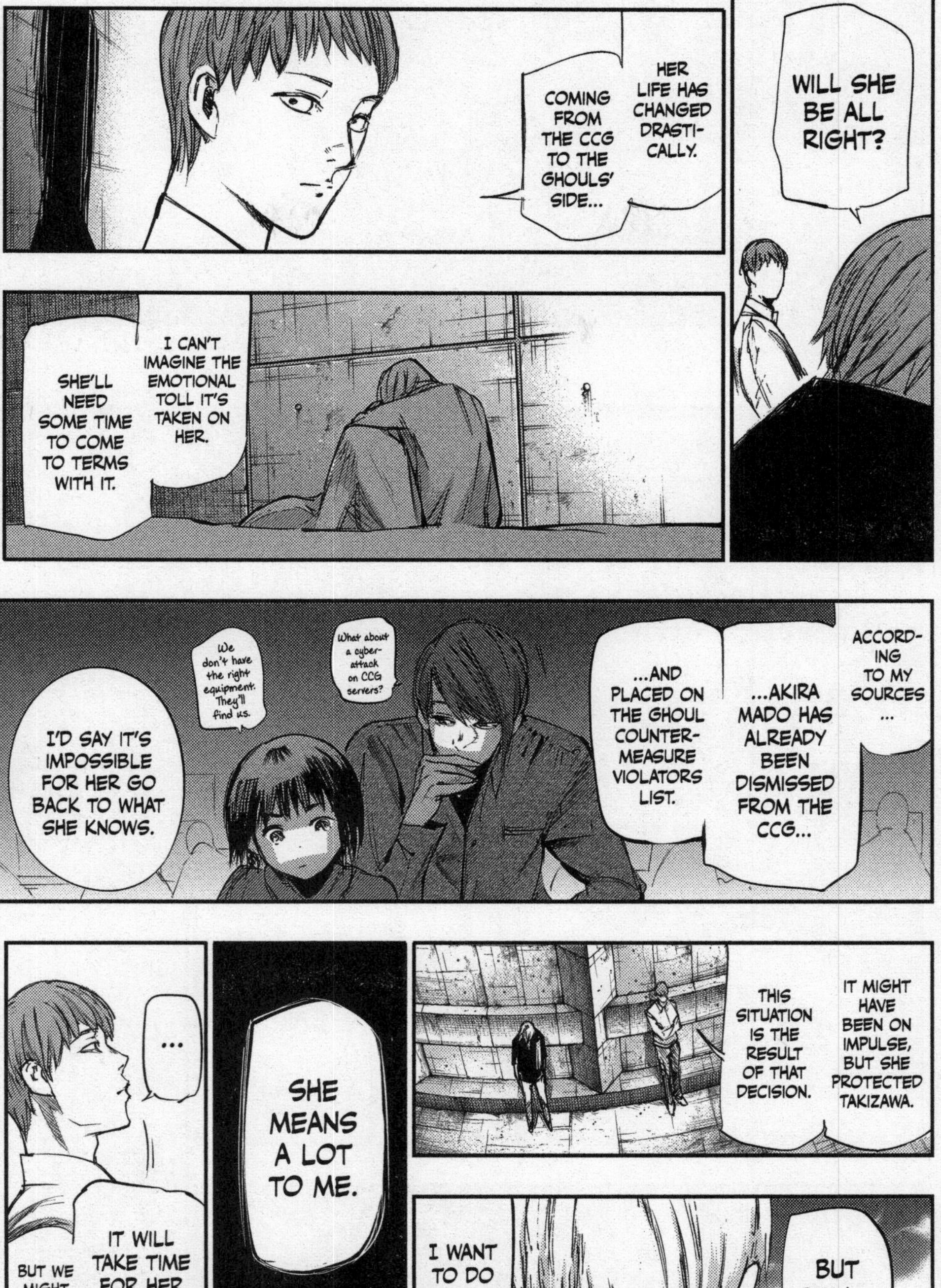

WILL SHE BE ALL RIGHT?
HER LIFE HAS CHANGED DRASTICALLY.
COMING FROM THE CCG TO THE GHOULS' SIDE...
I CAN'T IMAGINE THE EMOTIONAL TOLL IT'S TAKEN ON HER.
SHE'LL NEED SOME TIME TO COME TO TERMS WITH IT.
ACCORDING TO MY SOURCES...
...AKIRA MADO HAS ALREADY BEEN DISMISSED FROM THE CCG...
...AND PLACED ON THE GHOUL COUNTERMEASURE VIOLATORS LIST.
What about a cyber-attack on CCG servers?
We don't have the right equipment. They'll find us.
I'D SAY IT'S IMPOSSIBLE FOR HER GO BACK TO WHAT SHE KNOWS.
IT MIGHT HAVE BEEN ON IMPULSE, BUT SHE PROTECTED TAKIZAWA.
THIS SITUATION IS THE RESULT OF THAT DECISION.
BUT STILL...
I WANT TO DO EVERYTHING I CAN.
SHE MEANS A LOT TO ME.
...
IT WILL TAKE TIME FOR HER TO ACCEPT THINGS.
BUT WE MIGHT BE ABLE TO SPEED IT UP.

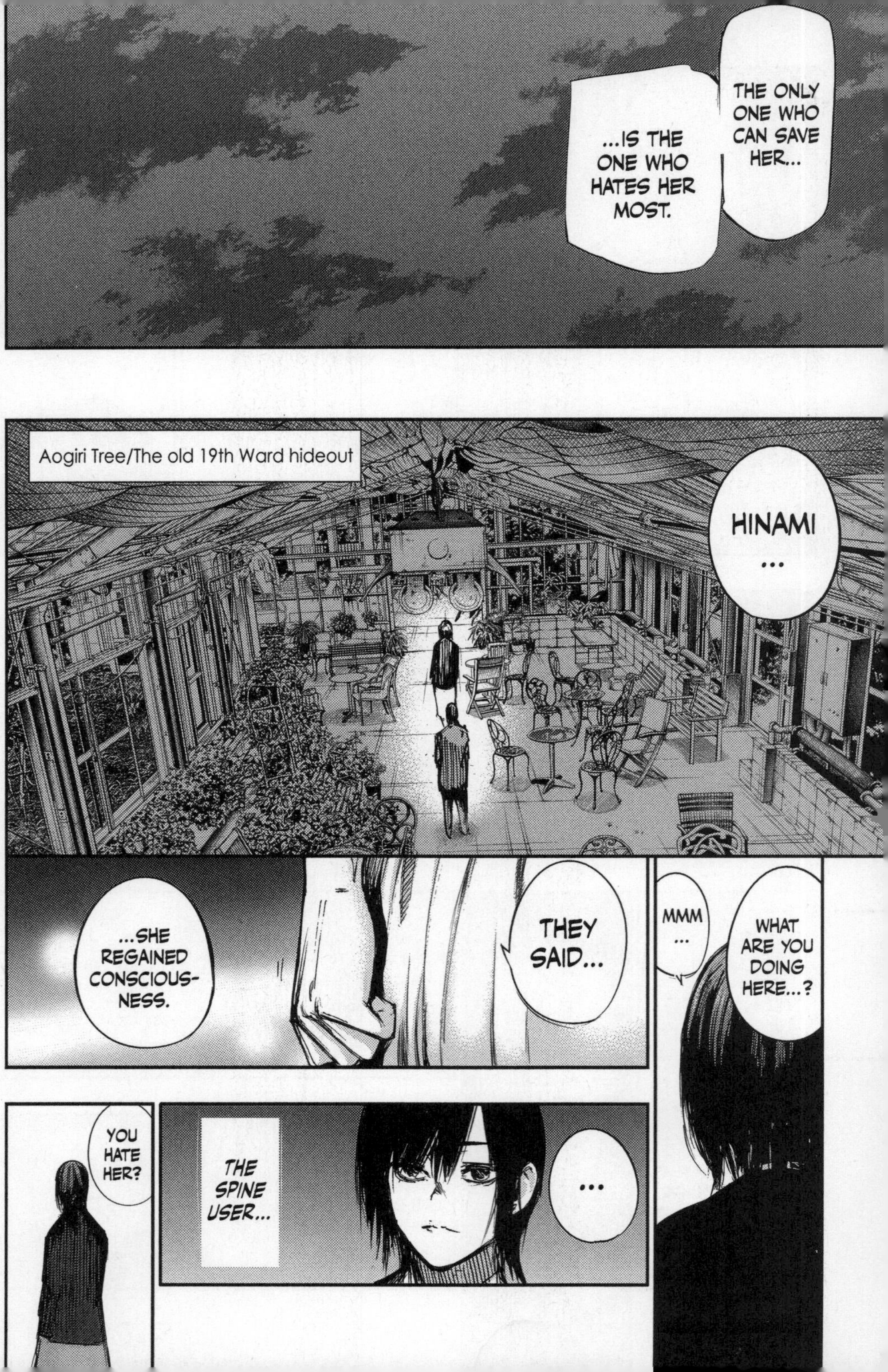
THE ONLY ONE WHO CAN SAVE HER...
...IS THE ONE WHO HATES HER MOST.
HINAMI ...
Aogiri Tree/The old 19th Ward hideout
WHAT ARE YOU DOING HERE...?
MMM ...
THEY SAID...
...SHE REGAINED CONSCIOUS-NESS.
...
THE SPINE USER...
YOU HATE HER?

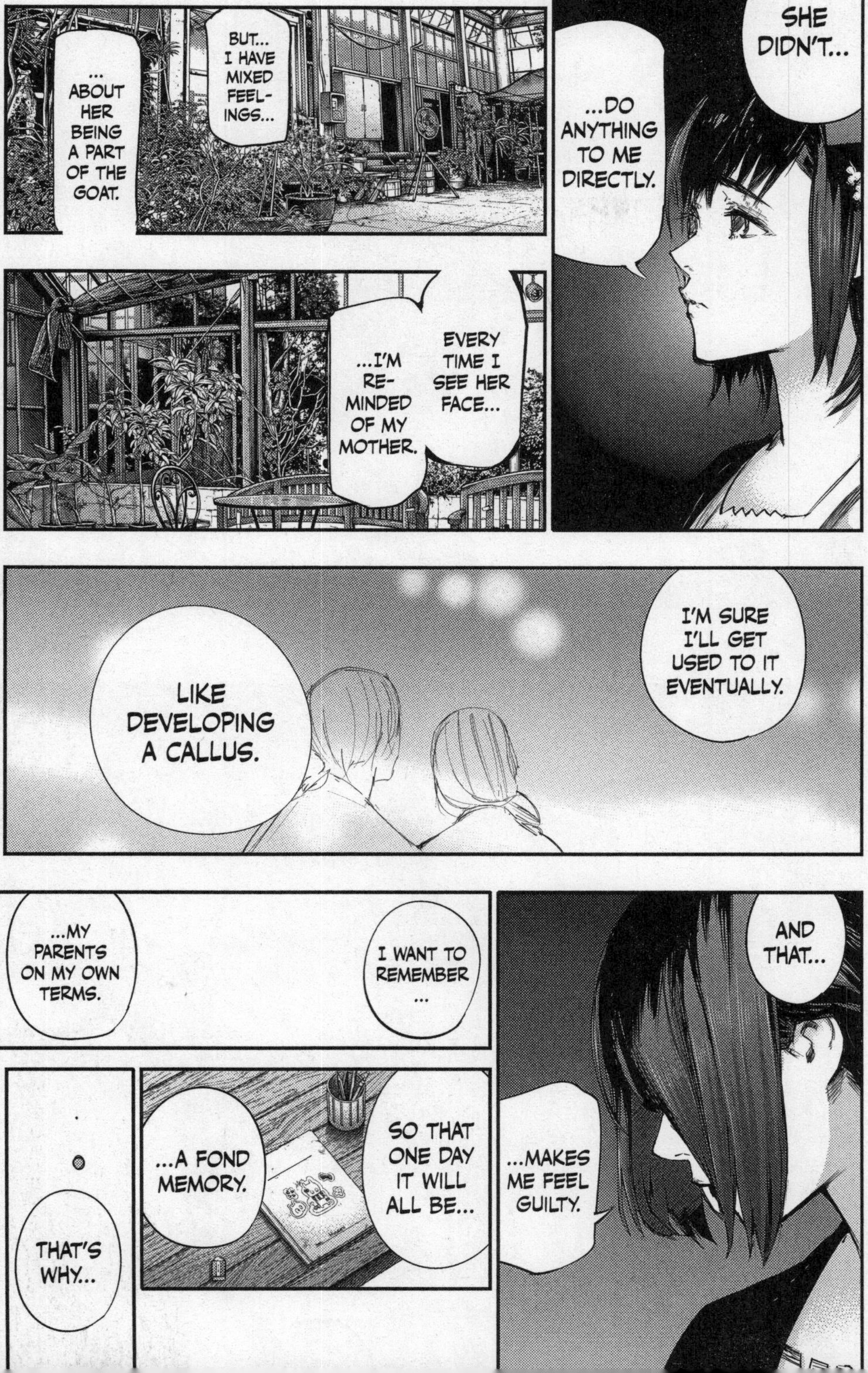
SHE DIDN'T...
...DO ANYTHING TO ME DIRECTLY.
BUT... I HAVE MIXED FEEL-INGS...
...ABOUT HER BEING A PART OF THE GOAT.
EVERY TIME I SEE HER FACE...
...I'M RE-MINDED OF MY MOTHER.
I'M SURE I'LL GET USED TO IT EVENTUALLY.
LIKE DEVELOPING A CALLUS.
AND THAT...
...MAKES ME FEEL GUILTY.
I WANT TO REMEMBER...
...MY PARENTS ON MY OWN TERMS.
SO THAT ONE DAY IT WILL ALL BE...
...A FOND MEMORY.
THAT'S WHY...

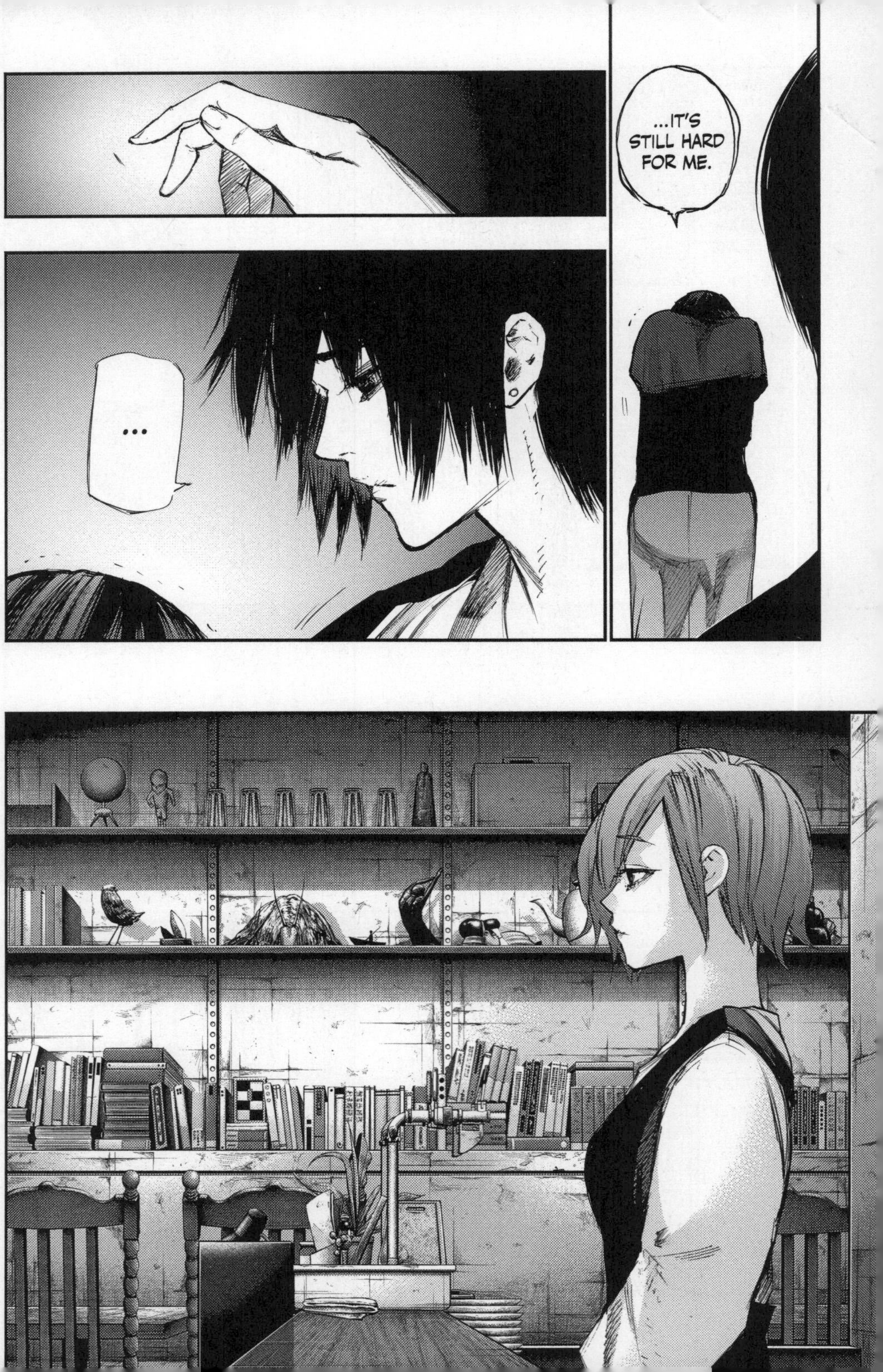
...IT'S STILL HARD FOR ME.
...

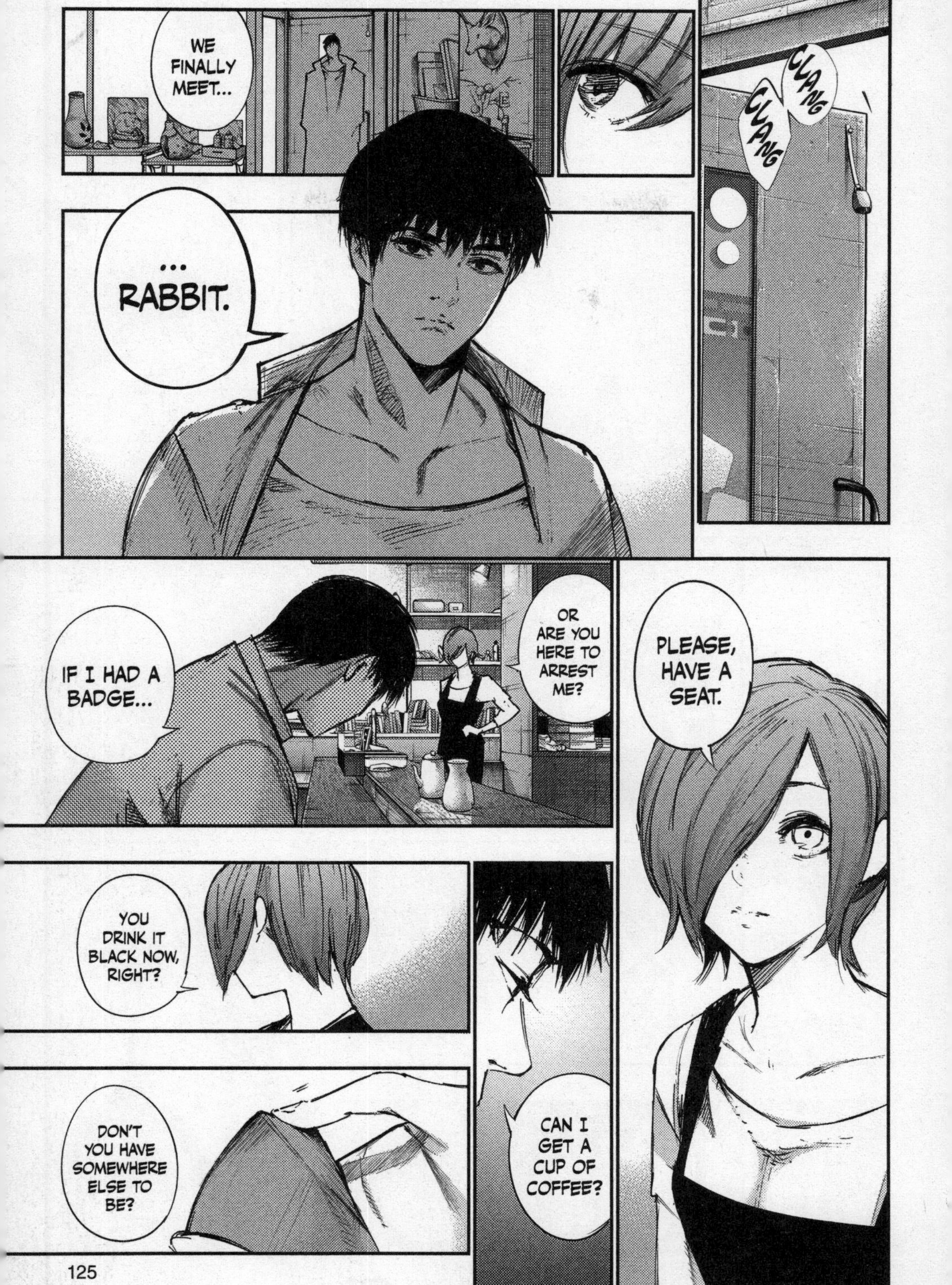
CLANG
CLANG
WE FINALLY MEET...
...RABBIT.
PLEASE, HAVE A SEAT.
OR ARE YOU HERE TO ARREST ME?
IF I HAD A BADGE...
CAN I GET A CUP OF COFFEE?
YOU DRINK IT BLACK NOW, RIGHT?
DON'T YOU HAVE SOMEWHERE ELSE TO BE?

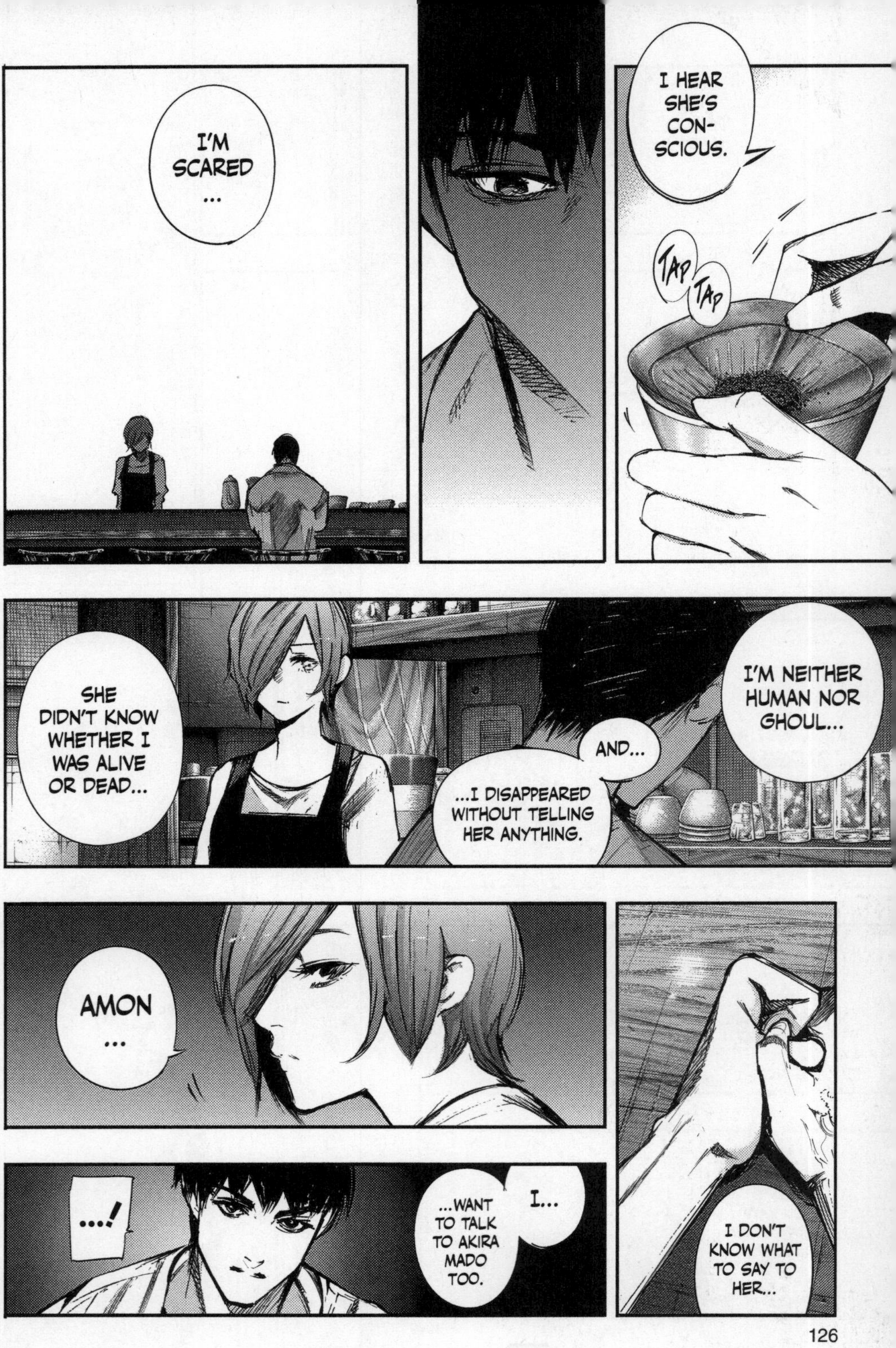
I HEAR SHE'S CON- SCIOUS.
TAP TAP
I'M SCARED ...
I'M NEITHER HUMAN NOR GHOUL...
AND...
...I DISAPPEARED WITHOUT TELLING HER ANYTHING.
SHE DIDN'T KNOW WHETHER I WAS ALIVE OR DEAD...
I DON'T KNOW WHAT TO SAY TO HER...
AMON ...
I...
...WANT TO TALK TO AKIRA MADO TOO.
...!

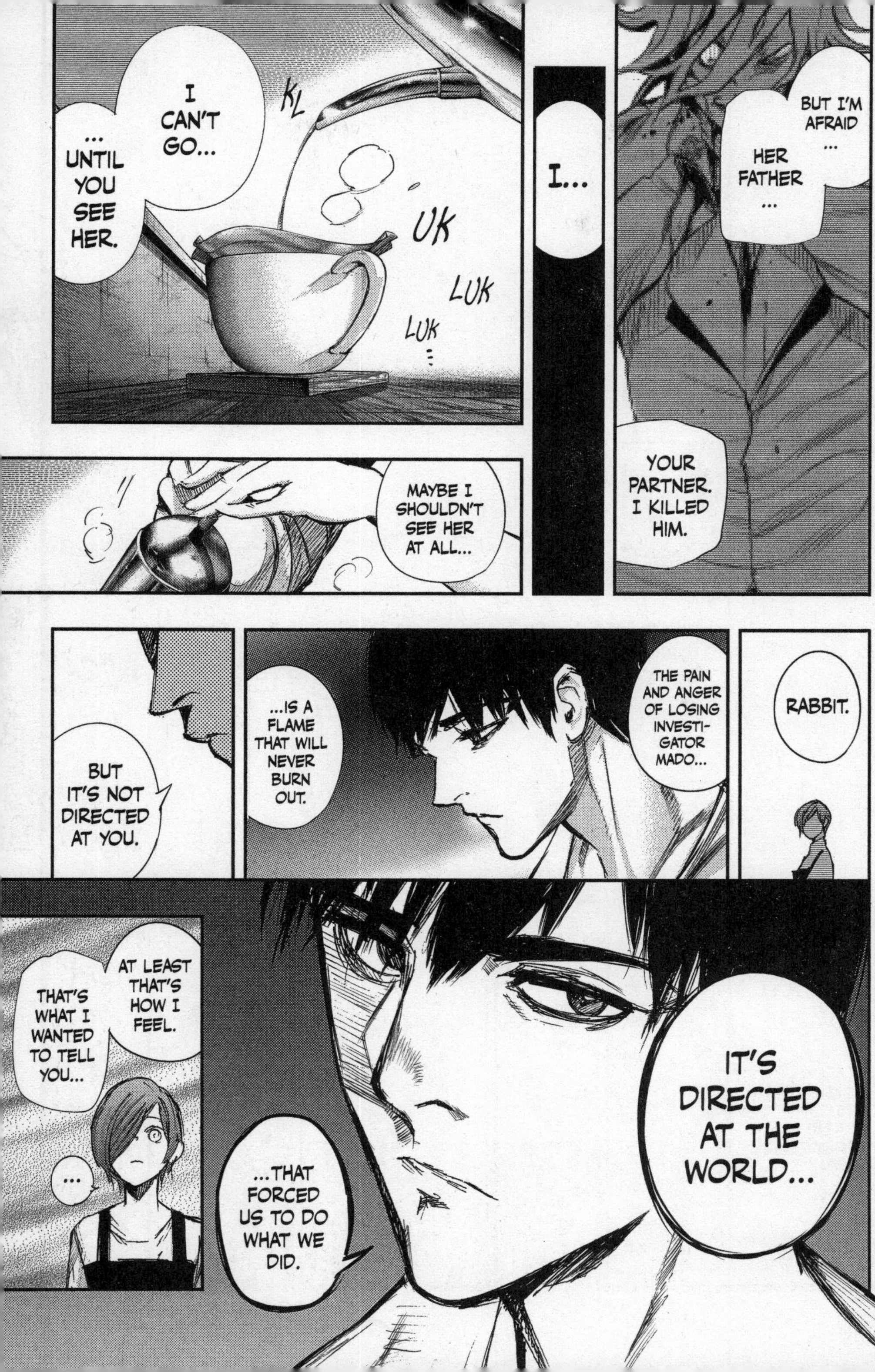
BUT I'M AFRAID ... HER FATHER ...
YOUR PARTNER. I KILLED HIM.
I...
I CAN'T GO...
... UNTIL YOU SEE HER.
KL
UK
LUK
LUK
MAYBE I SHOULDN'T SEE HER AT ALL...
RABBIT.
THE PAIN AND ANGER OF LOSING INVESTI-GATOR MADO...
...IS A FLAME THAT WILL NEVER BURN OUT.
BUT IT'S NOT DIRECTED AT YOU.
IT'S DIRECTED AT THE WORLD...
...THAT FORCED US TO DO WHAT WE DID.
AT LEAST THAT'S HOW I FEEL.
THAT'S WHAT I WANTED TO TELL YOU...
...

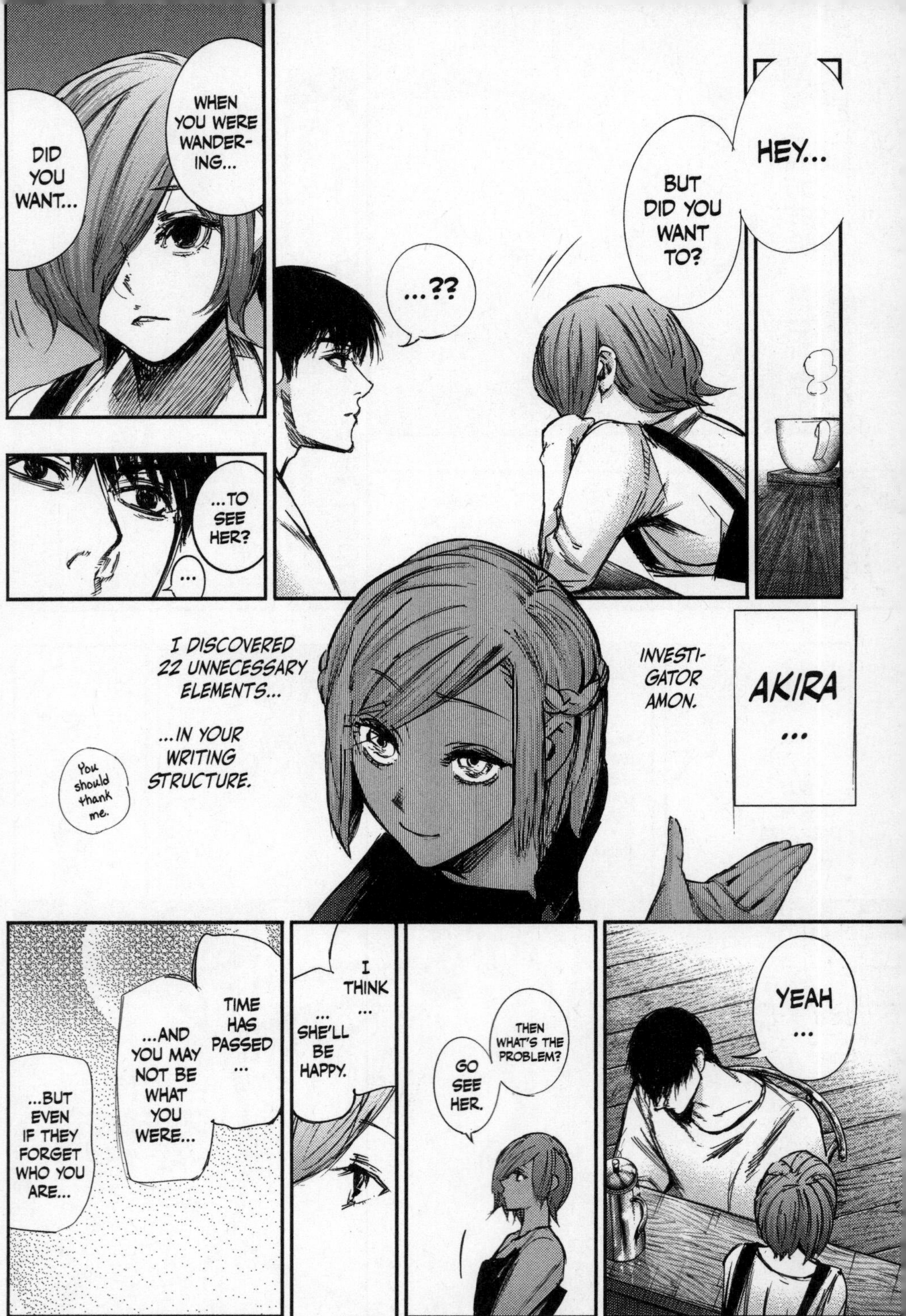
HEY...
BUT DID YOU WANT TO?
...??
WHEN YOU WERE WANDER-ING...
DID YOU WANT...
...TO SEE HER?
...
AKIRA ...
INVESTI-GATOR AMON.
I DISCOVERED 22 UNNECESSARY ELEMENTS...
...IN YOUR WRITING STRUCTURE.
You should thank me.
YEAH ...
THEN WHAT'S THE PROBLEM?
GO SEE HER.
I THINK ...
... SHE'LL BE HAPPY.
TIME HAS PASSED ...
...AND YOU MAY NOT BE WHAT YOU WERE...
...BUT EVEN IF THEY FORGET WHO YOU ARE...

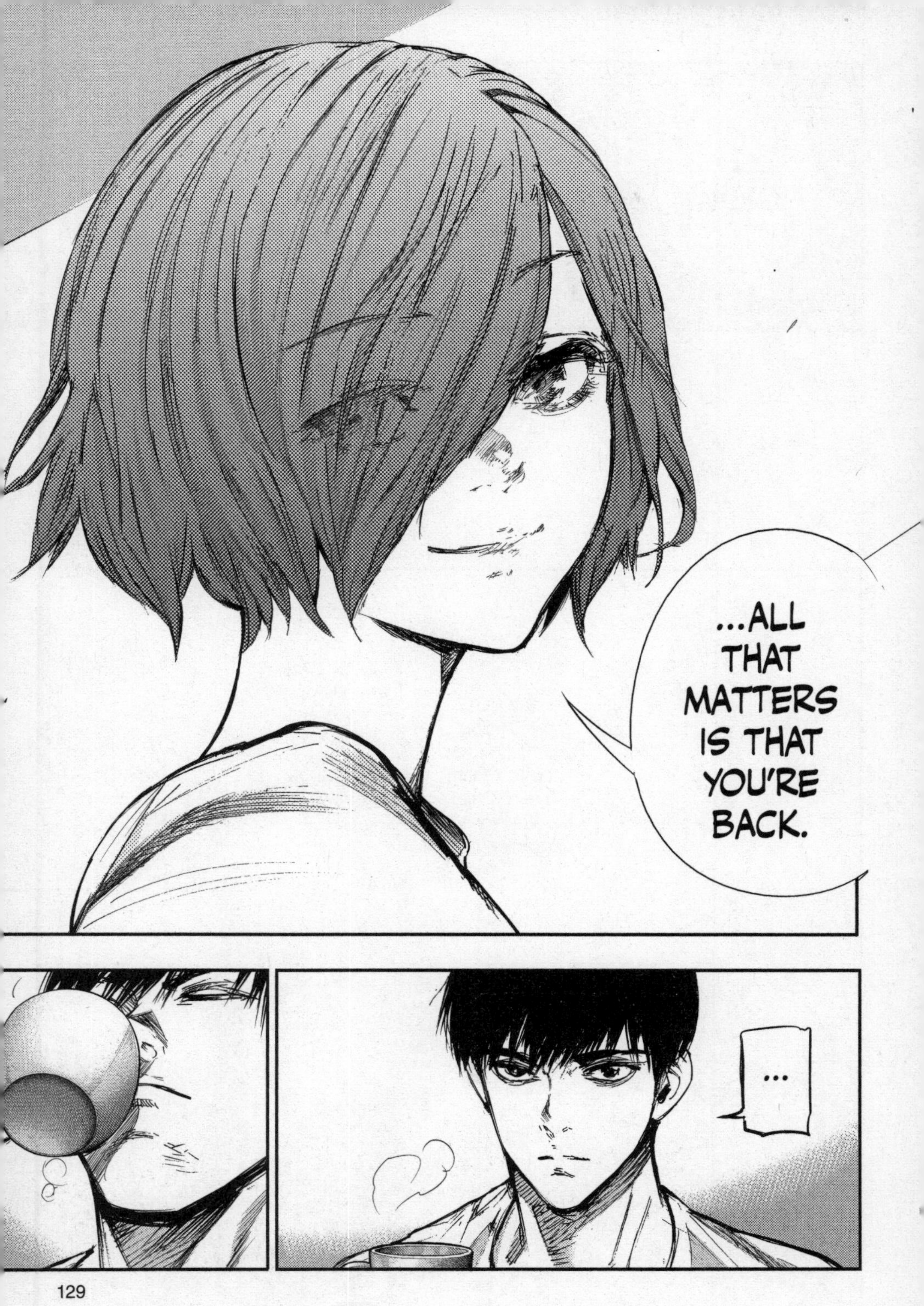
...ALL THAT MATTERS IS THAT YOU'RE BACK.
...

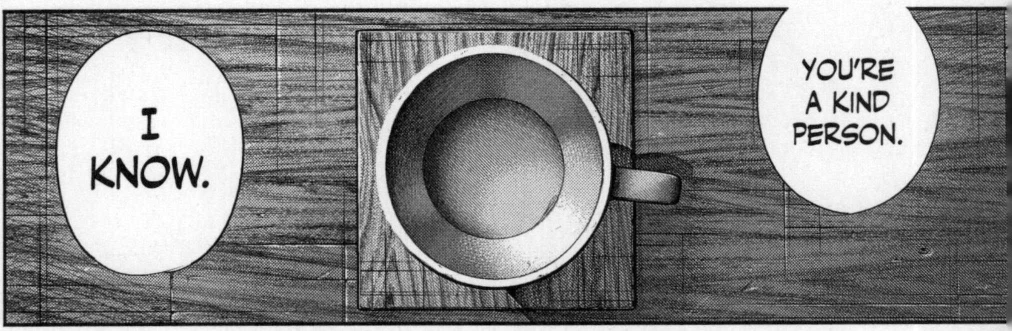
YOU'RE A KIND PERSON.
I KNOW.

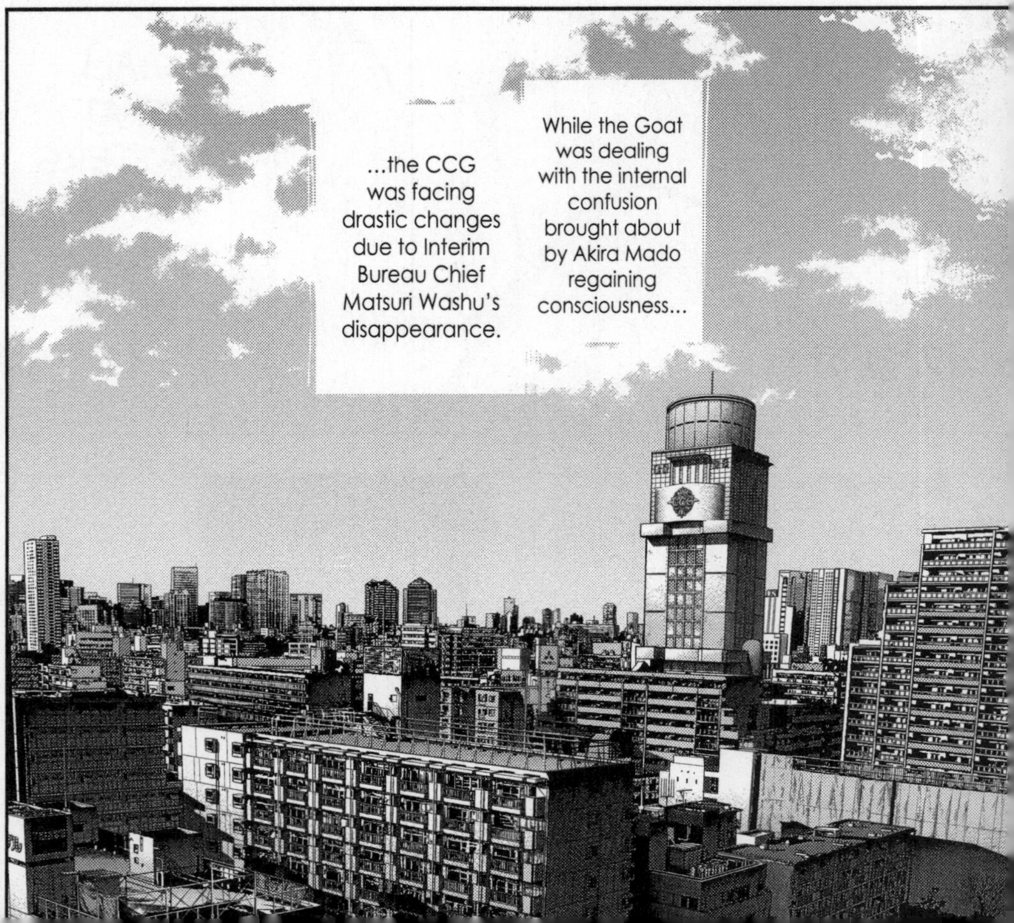
While the Goat was dealing with the internal confusion brought about by Akira Mado regaining consciousness...
...the CCG was facing drastic changes due to Interim Bureau Chief Matsuri Washu's disappearance.

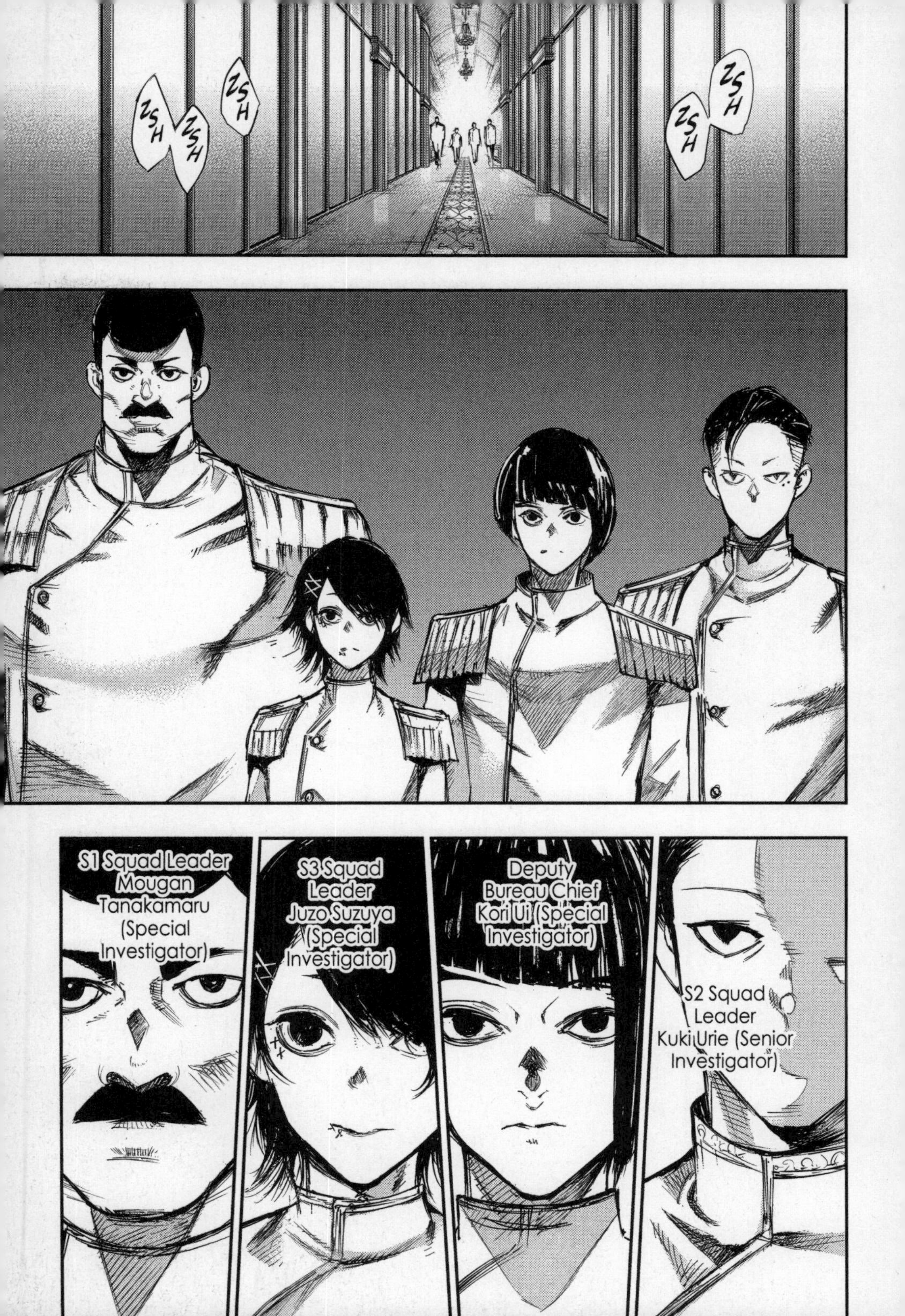
ZSH
ZSH
ZSH
ZSH
ZSH
S2 Squad Leader Kuki Urie (Senior Investigator)
Deputy Bureau Chief Kori Ui (Special Investigator)
S3 Squad Leader Juzo Suzuya (Special Investigator)
S1 Squad Leader Mougan Tanakamaru (Special Investigator)

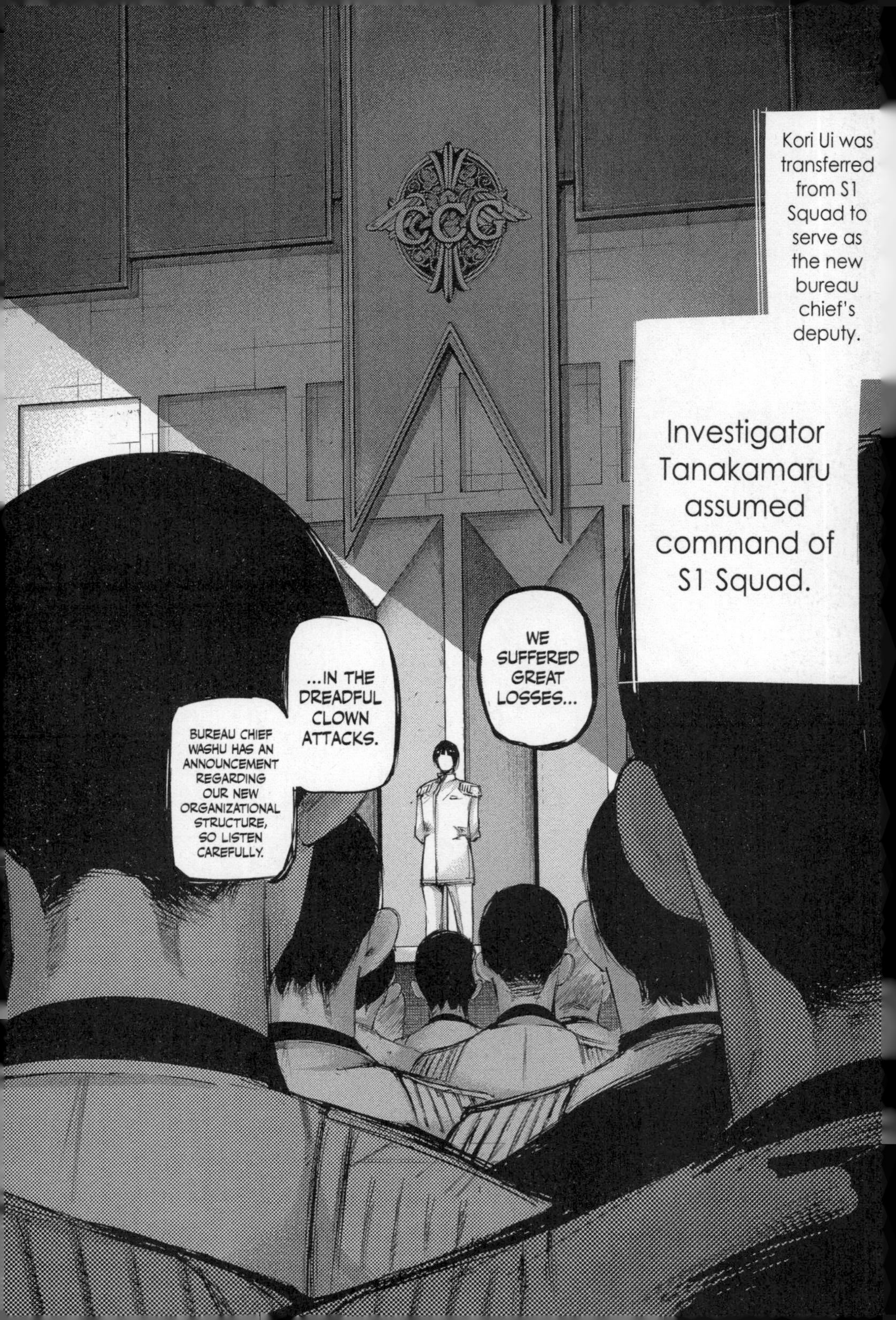
CCG
Kori Ui was transferred from S1 Squad to serve as the new bureau chief's deputy.
Investigator Tanakamaru assumed command of S1 Squad.
WE SUFFERED GREAT LOSSES...
...IN THE DREADFUL CLOWN ATTACKS.
BUREAU CHIEF WASHU HAS AN ANNOUNCEMENT REGARDING OUR NEW ORGANIZATIONAL STRUCTURE, SO LISTEN CAREFULLY.

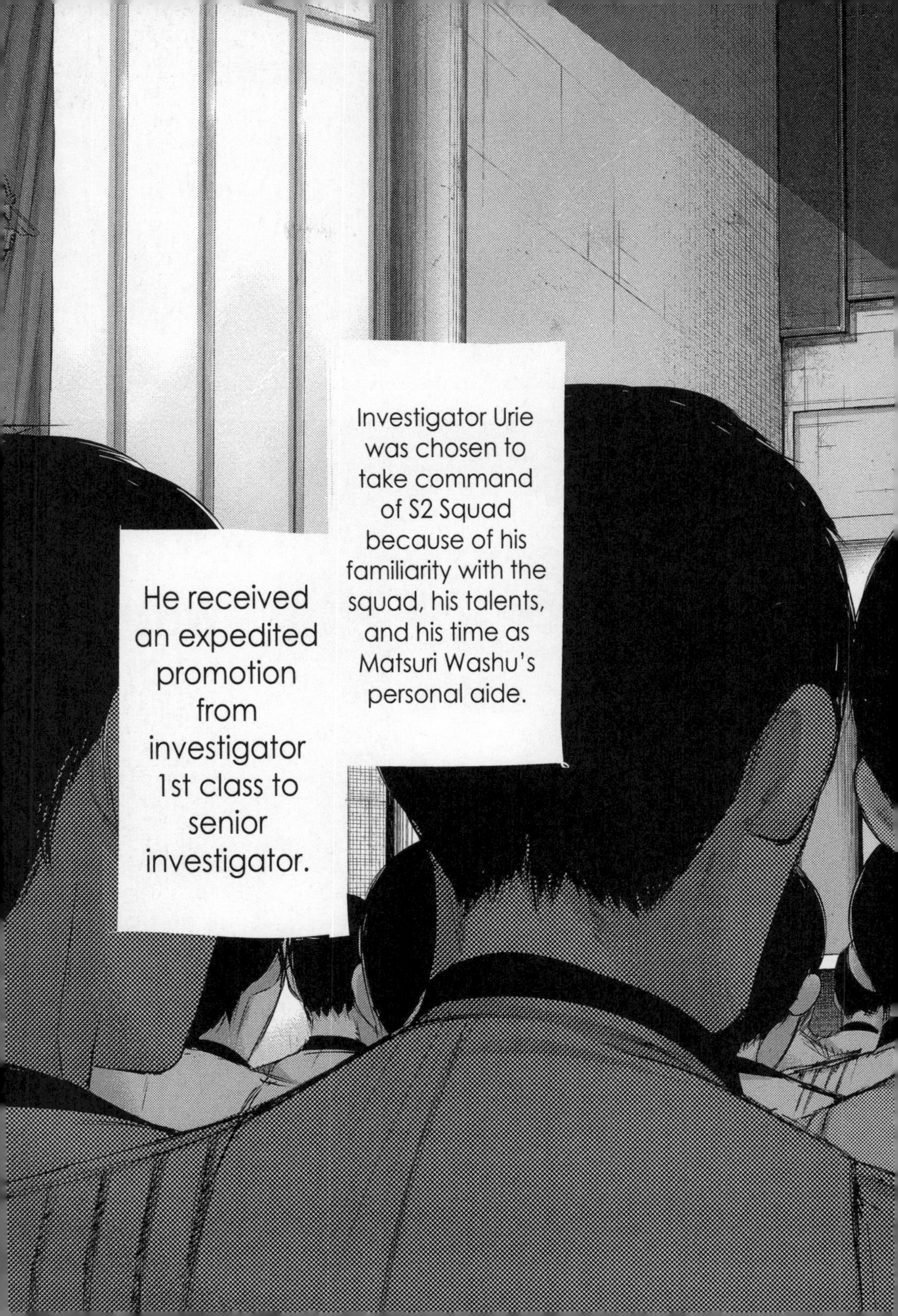
Investigator Urie was chosen to take command of S2 Squad because of his familiarity with the squad, his talents, and his time as Matsuri Washu's personal aide.
He received an expedited promotion from investigator 1st class to senior investigator.

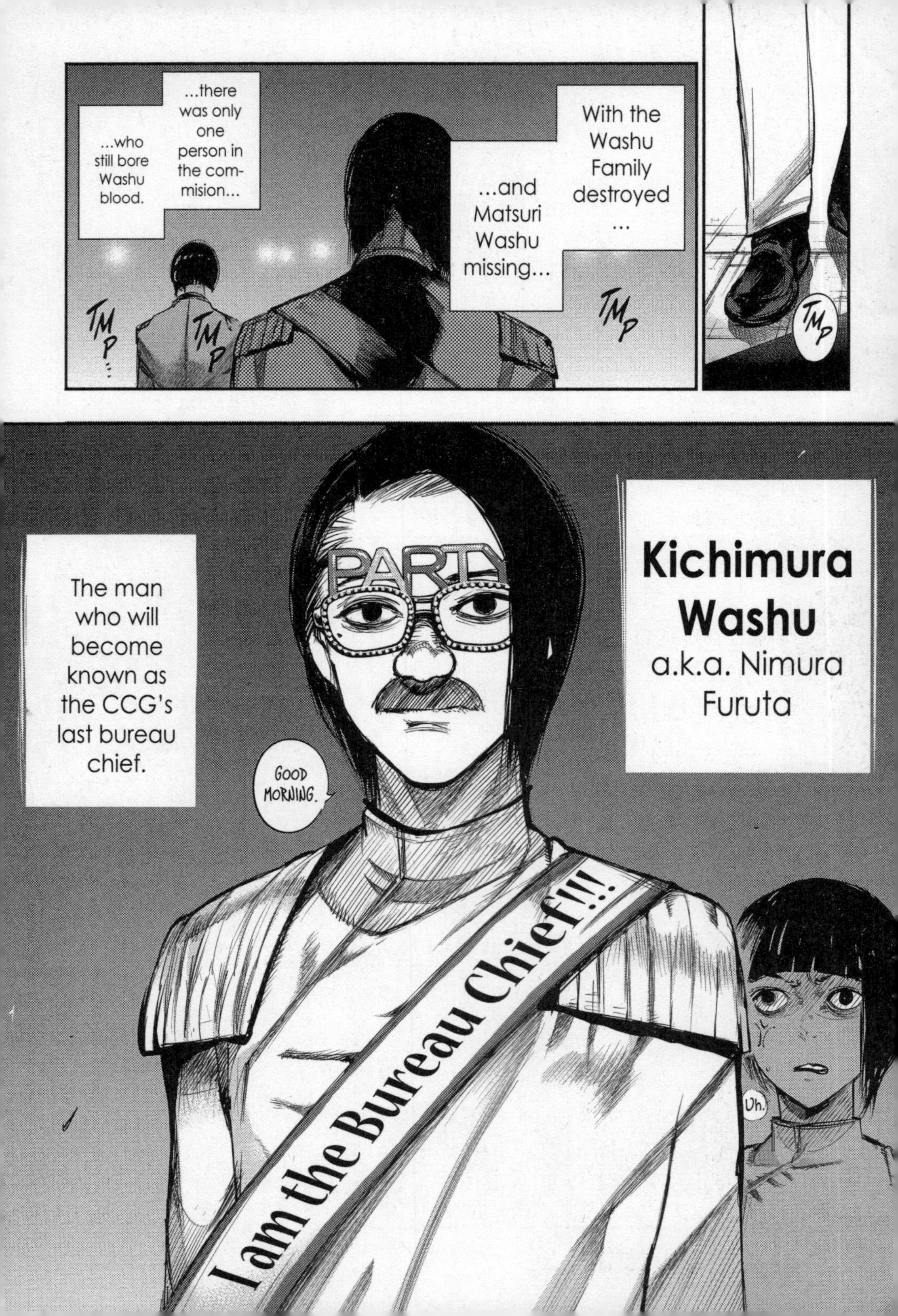
TMP
With the Washu Family destroyed ...
...and Matsuri Washu missing...
...there was only one person in the com-mision...
...who still bore Washu blood.
TMP
TMP
TMP...
Kichimura Washu
a.k.a. Nimura Furuta
The man who will become known as the CCG's last bureau chief.
PARTY
GOOD MORNING.
I am the Bureau Chief!!!
Uh.

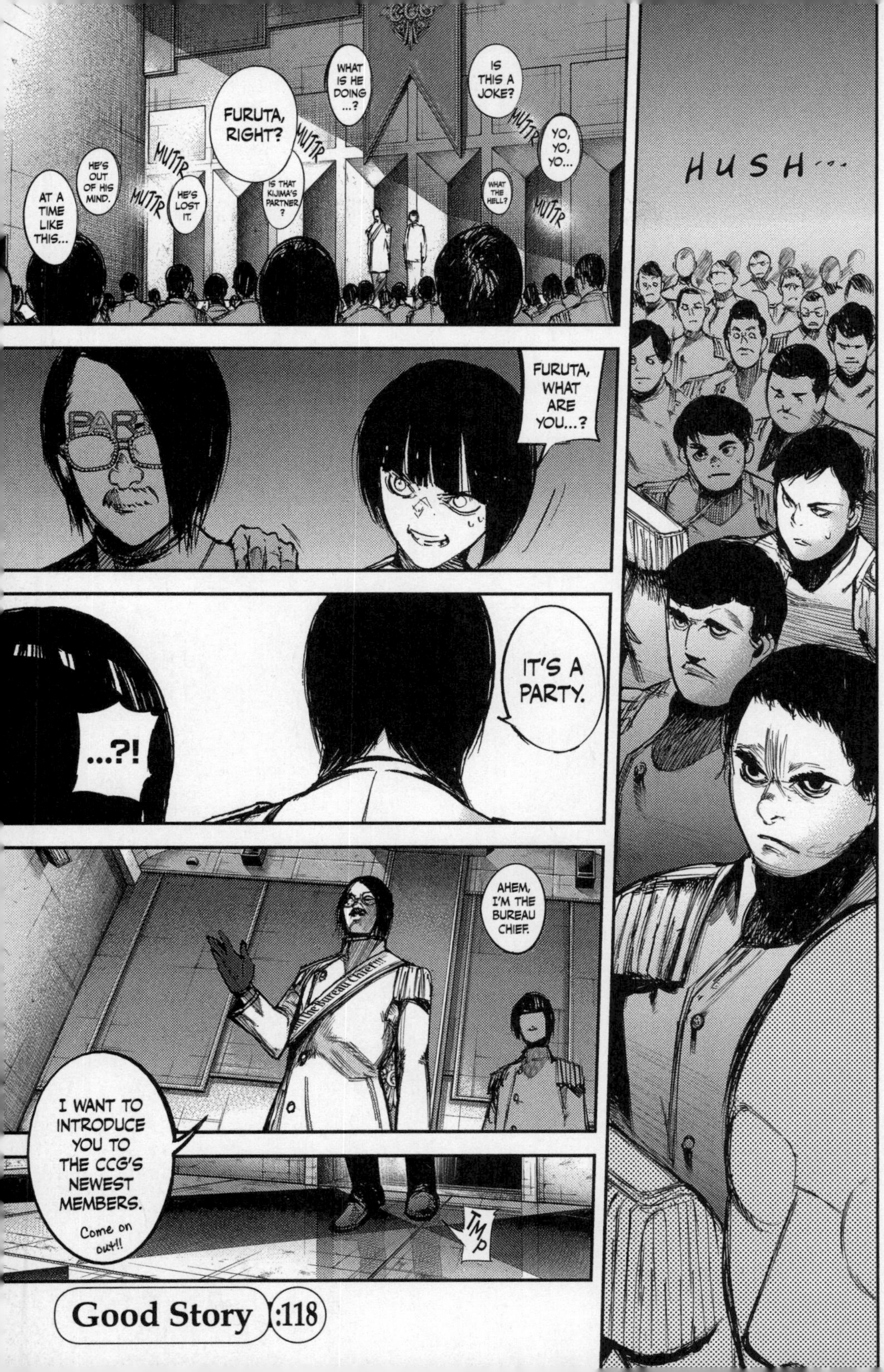
HUSH...
IS THIS A JOKE?
MUTTR
YO, YO, YO...
WHAT IS HE DOING ...?
WHAT THE HELL?
MUTTR
FURUTA, RIGHT?
MUTTR
IS THAT KIJIMA'S PARTNER ?
HE'S OUT OF HIS MIND.
MUTTR
HE'S LOST IT.
MUTTR
AT A TIME LIKE THIS...
FURUTA, WHAT ARE YOU...?
IT'S A PARTY.
...?!
AHEM, I'M THE BUREAU CHIEF.
I WANT TO INTRODUCE YOU TO THE CCG'S NEWEST MEMBERS.
Come on out!!
TMP

Good Story :118

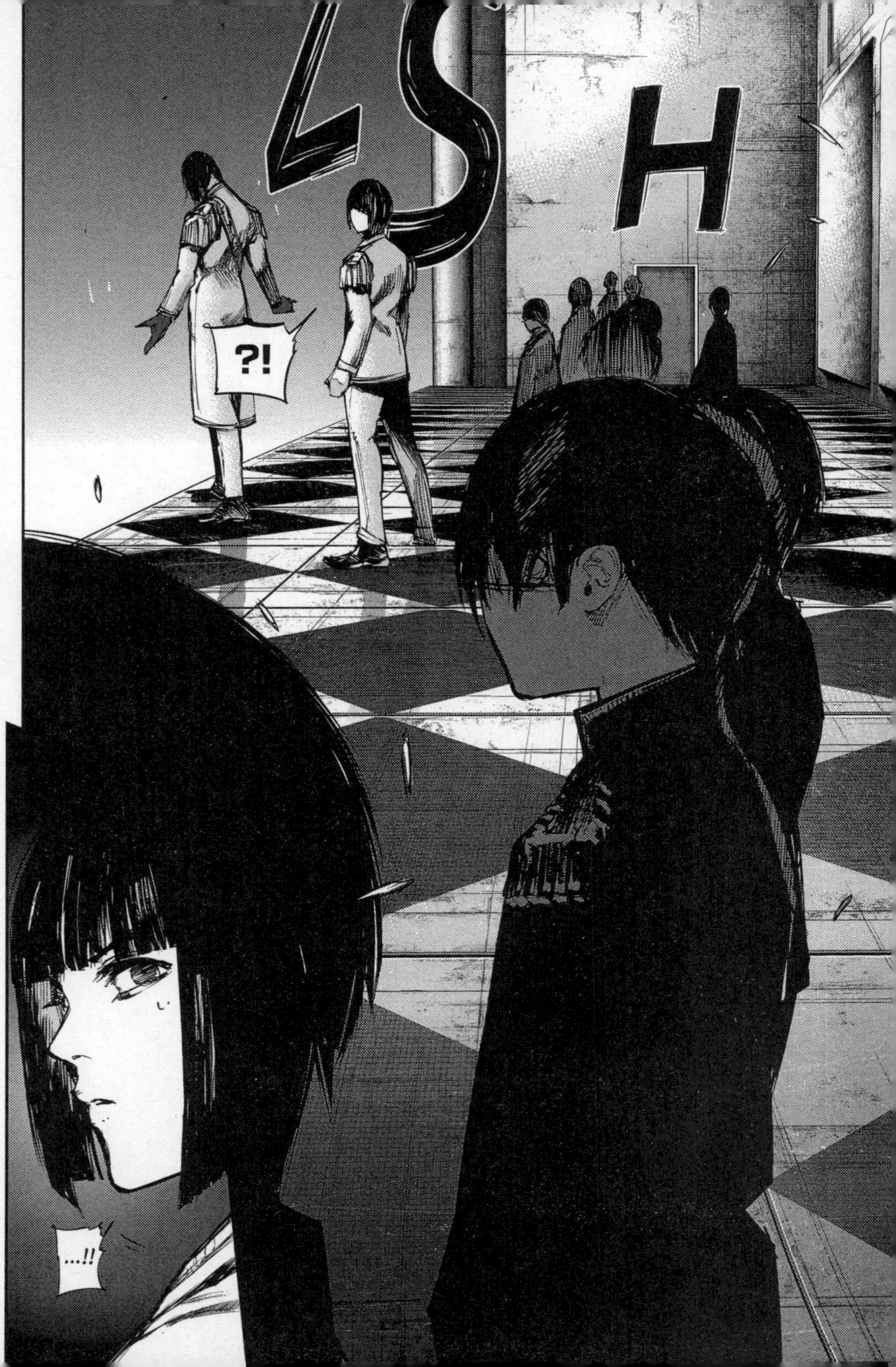

ZSH
?!
...!!

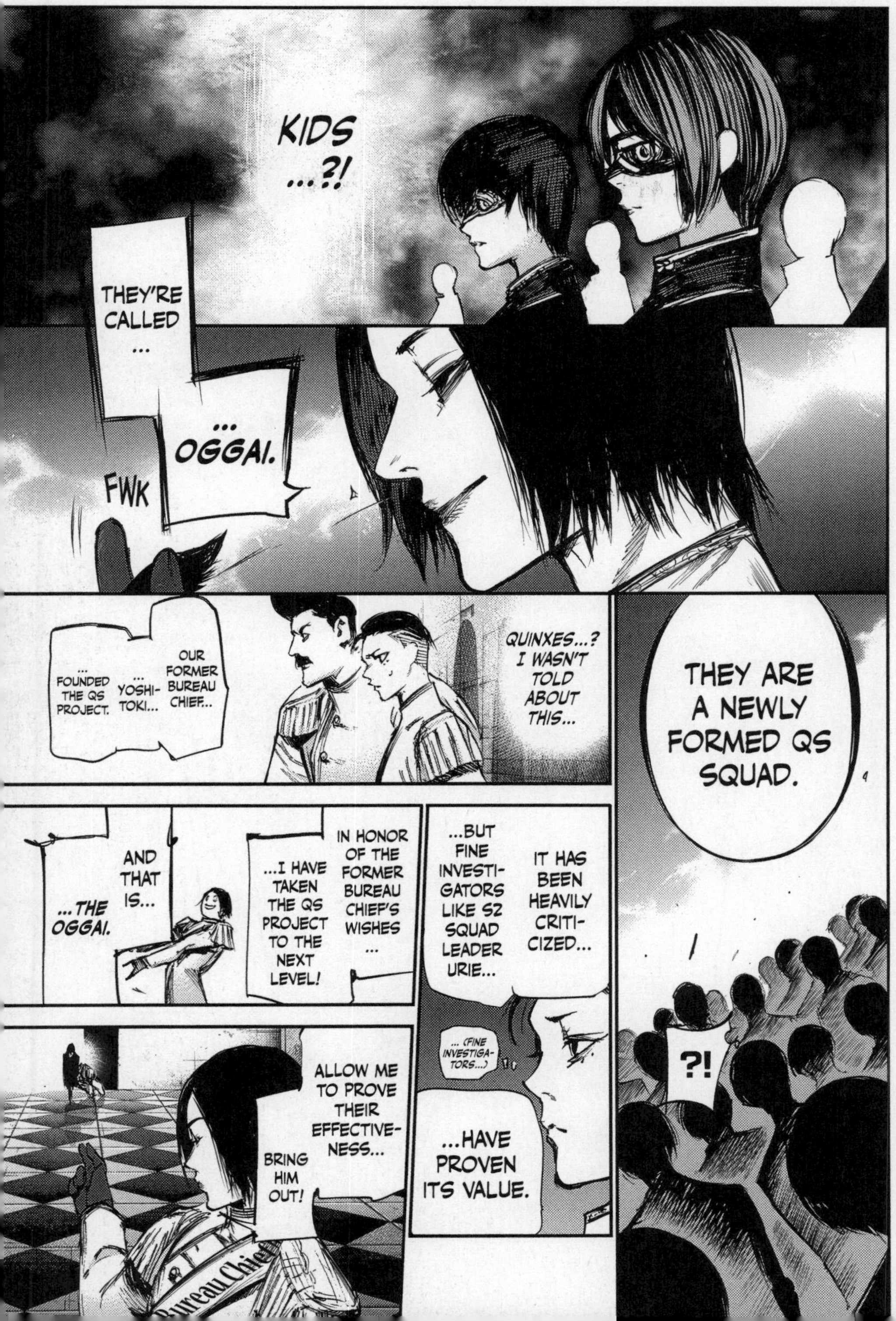
KIDS ...?!
THEY'RE CALLED ...
... OGGAI.
FWK
THEY ARE A NEWLY FORMED QS SQUAD.
?!
QUINXES...? I WASN'T TOLD ABOUT THIS...
OUR FORMER BUREAU CHIEF...
... YOSHITOKI...
... FOUNDED THE QS PROJECT.
IT HAS BEEN HEAVILY CRITICIZED...
...BUT FINE INVESTIGATORS LIKE S2 SQUAD LEADER URIE...
... (FINE INVESTIGATORS...)
...HAVE PROVEN ITS VALUE.
IN HONOR OF THE FORMER BUREAU CHIEF'S WISHES ...
...I HAVE TAKEN THE QS PROJECT TO THE NEXT LEVEL!
AND THAT IS...
...THE OGGAI.
ALLOW ME TO PROVE THEIR EFFECTIVENESS...
BRING HIM OUT!
Bureau Chief

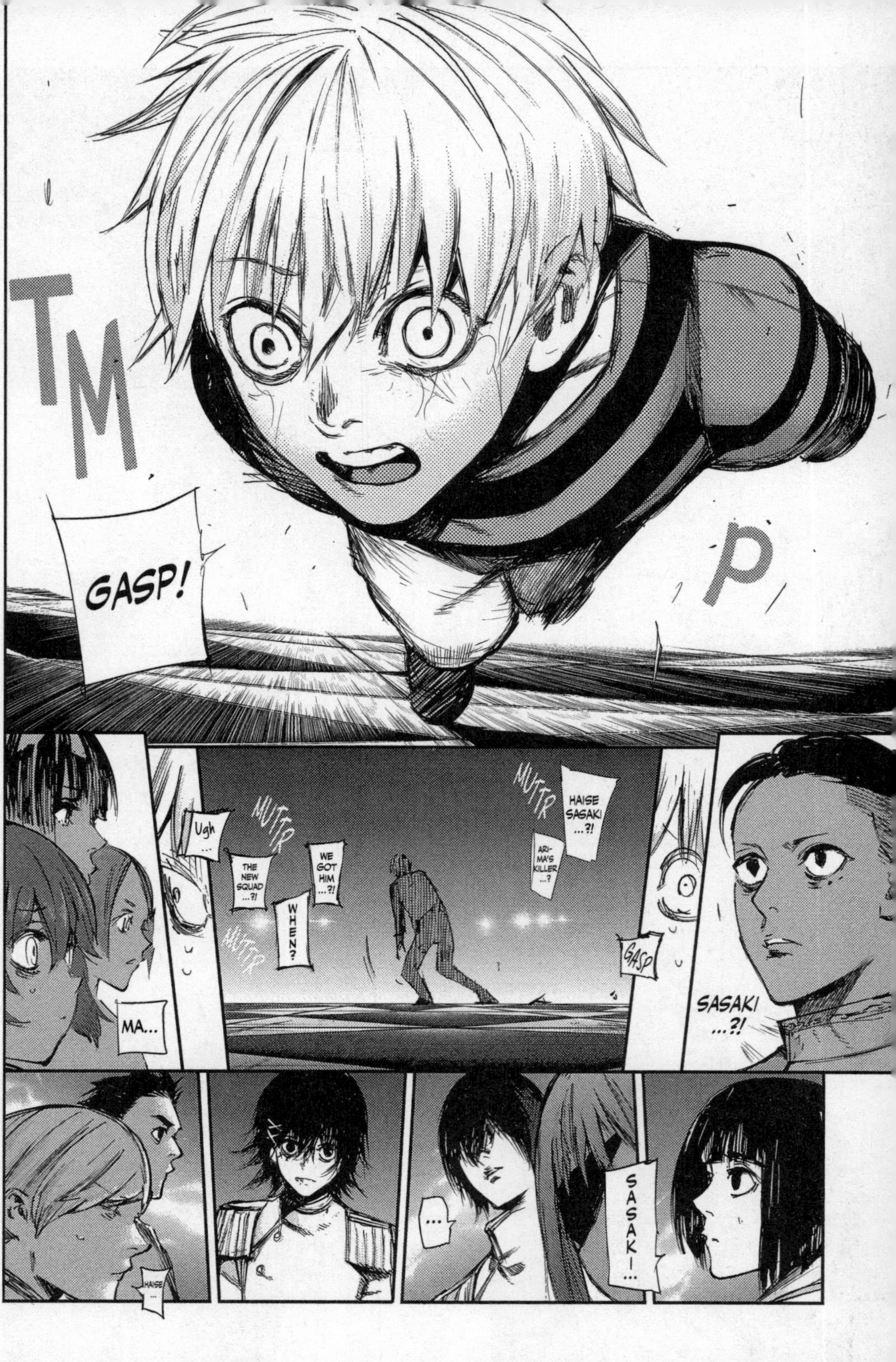
TMP
GASP!
SASAKI ...?!
GASP
MUTTR
HAISE SASAKI ...?!
ARI-MA'S KILLER ...?
WE GOT HIM ...?!
WHEN?
THE NEW SQUAD ...?!
MUTTR
MUTTR
Ugh ...
MA...
SASAKI ...
...
HAISE ...

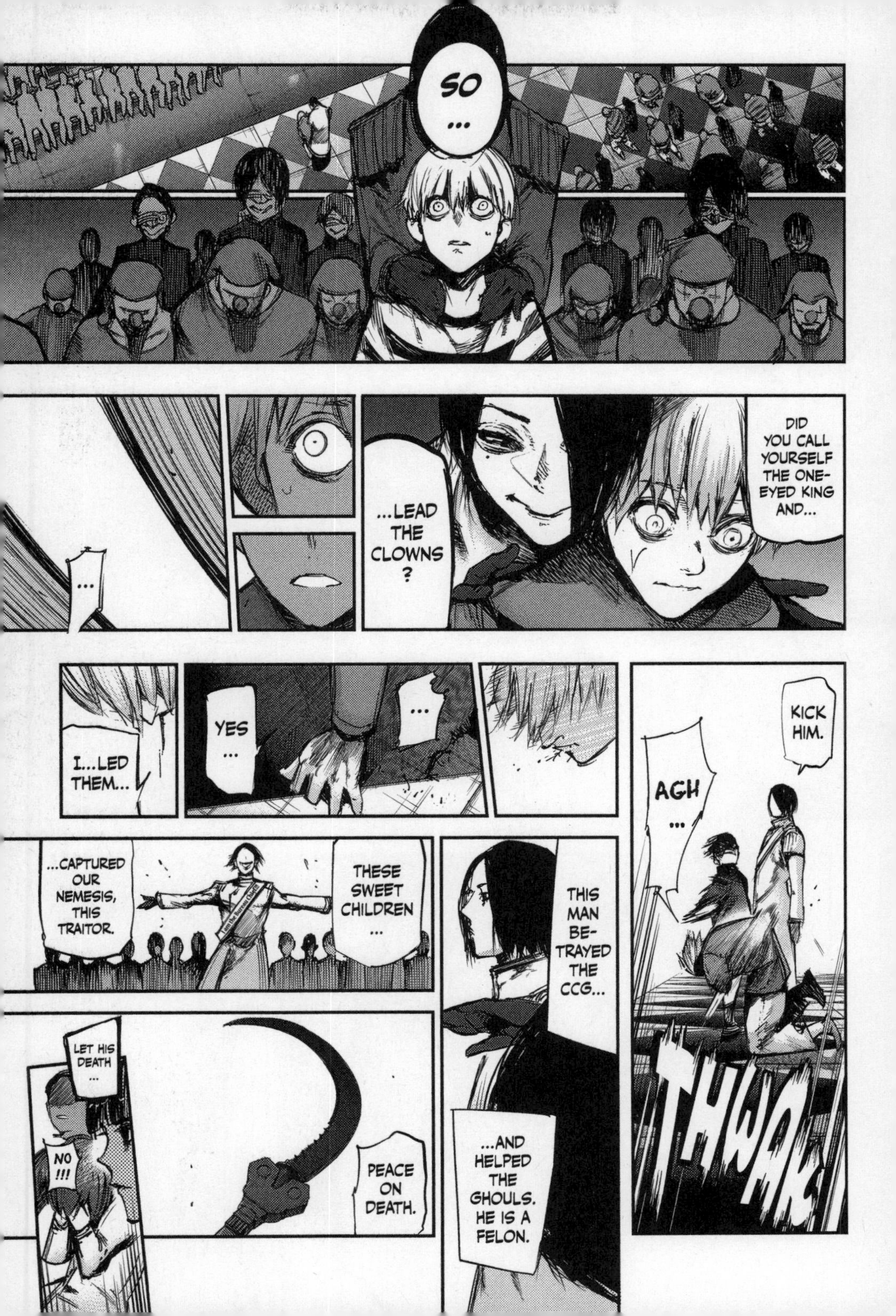
SO ...
DID YOU CALL YOURSELF THE ONE-EYED KING AND...
...LEAD THE CLOWNS ?
...
KICK HIM.
AGH ...
THWAK!
...
YES ...
I...LED THEM...
THIS MAN BE-TRAYED THE CCG...
...AND HELPED THE GHOULS. HE IS A FELON.
THESE SWEET CHILDREN ...
...CAPTURED OUR NEMESIS, THIS TRAITOR.
PEACE ON DEATH.
LET HIS DEATH ...
NO !!!

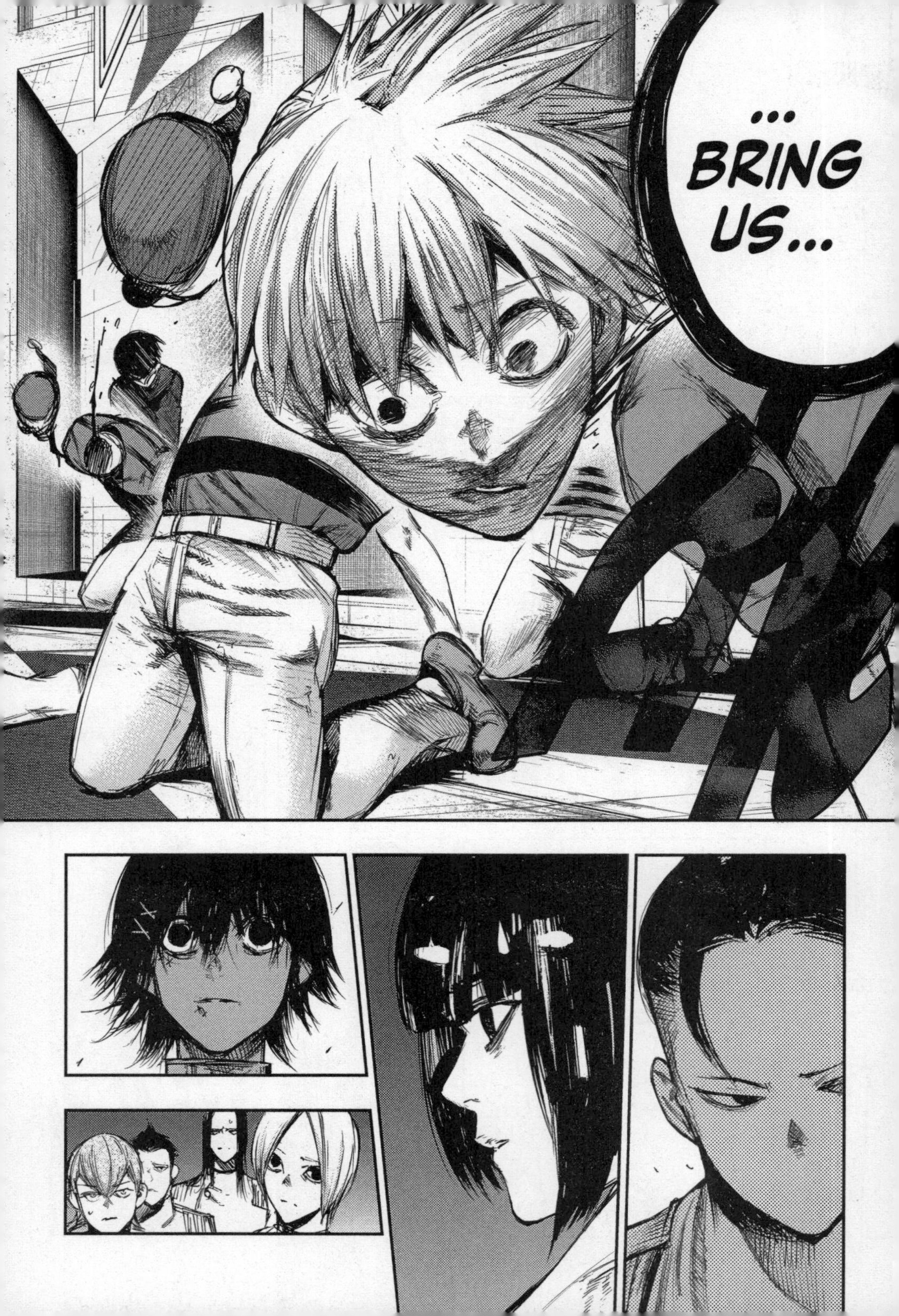
...BRING US...

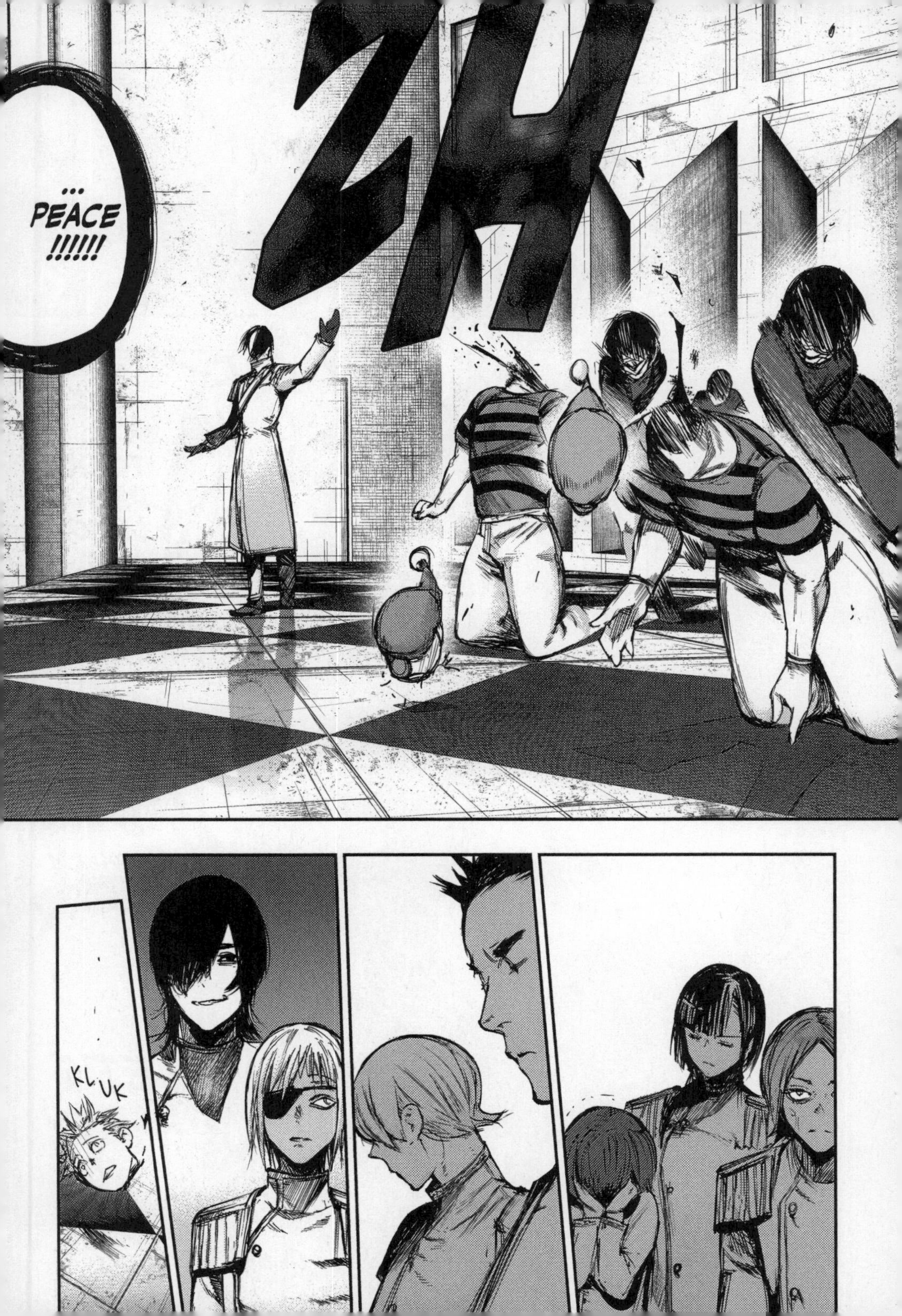
ZH
...PEACE!!!!!!
KLUK

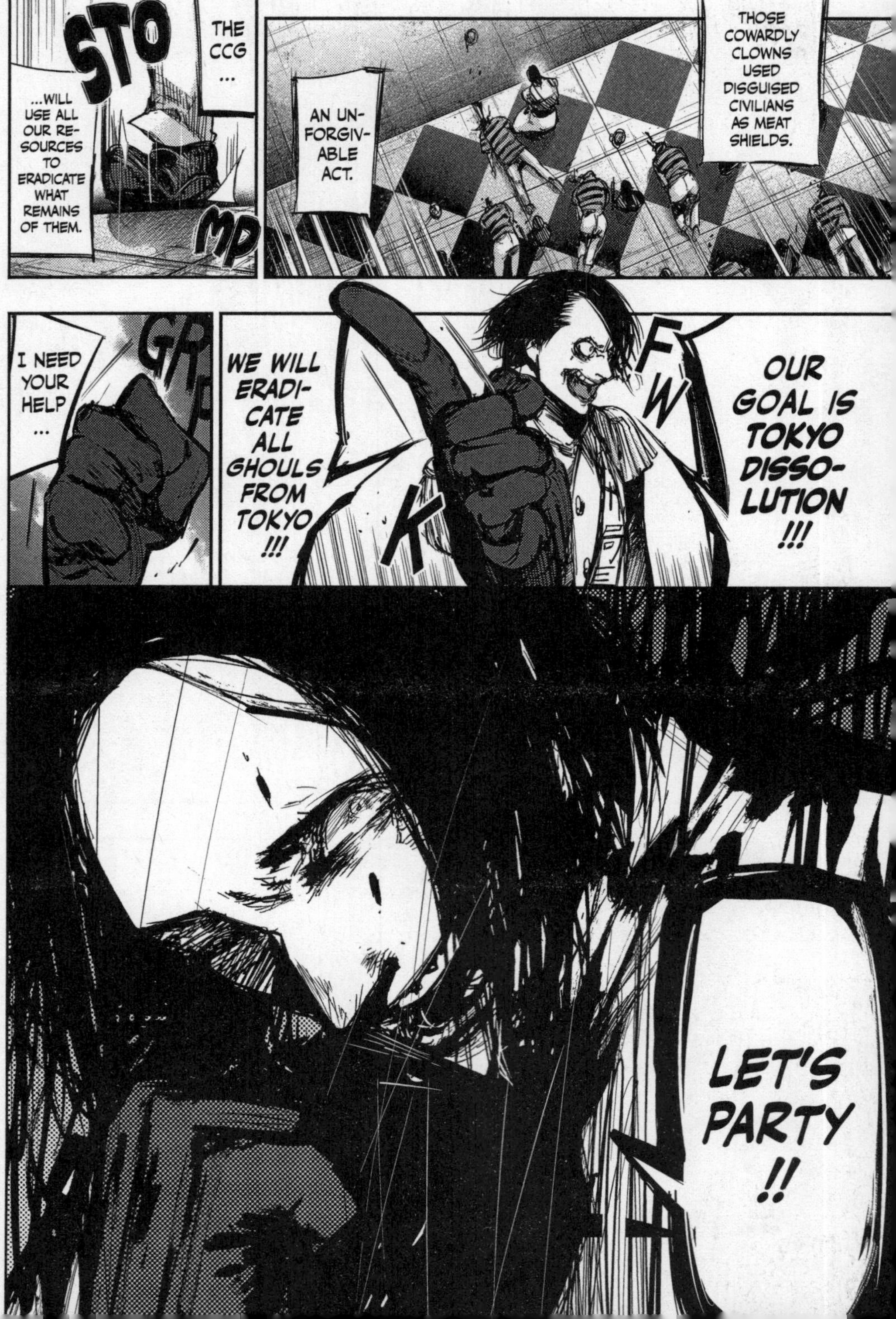
THOSE COWARDLY CLOWNS USED DISGUISED CIVILIANS AS MEAT SHIELDS.
AN UNFORGIVABLE ACT.
THE CCG...
...WILL USE ALL OUR RESOURCES TO ERADICATE WHAT REMAINS OF THEM.
STO
MP
OUR GOAL IS TOKYO DISSOLUTION!!!
FW
K
WE WILL ERADICATE ALL GHOULS FROM TOKYO!!!
GR
I NEED YOUR HELP...
LET'S PARTY!!

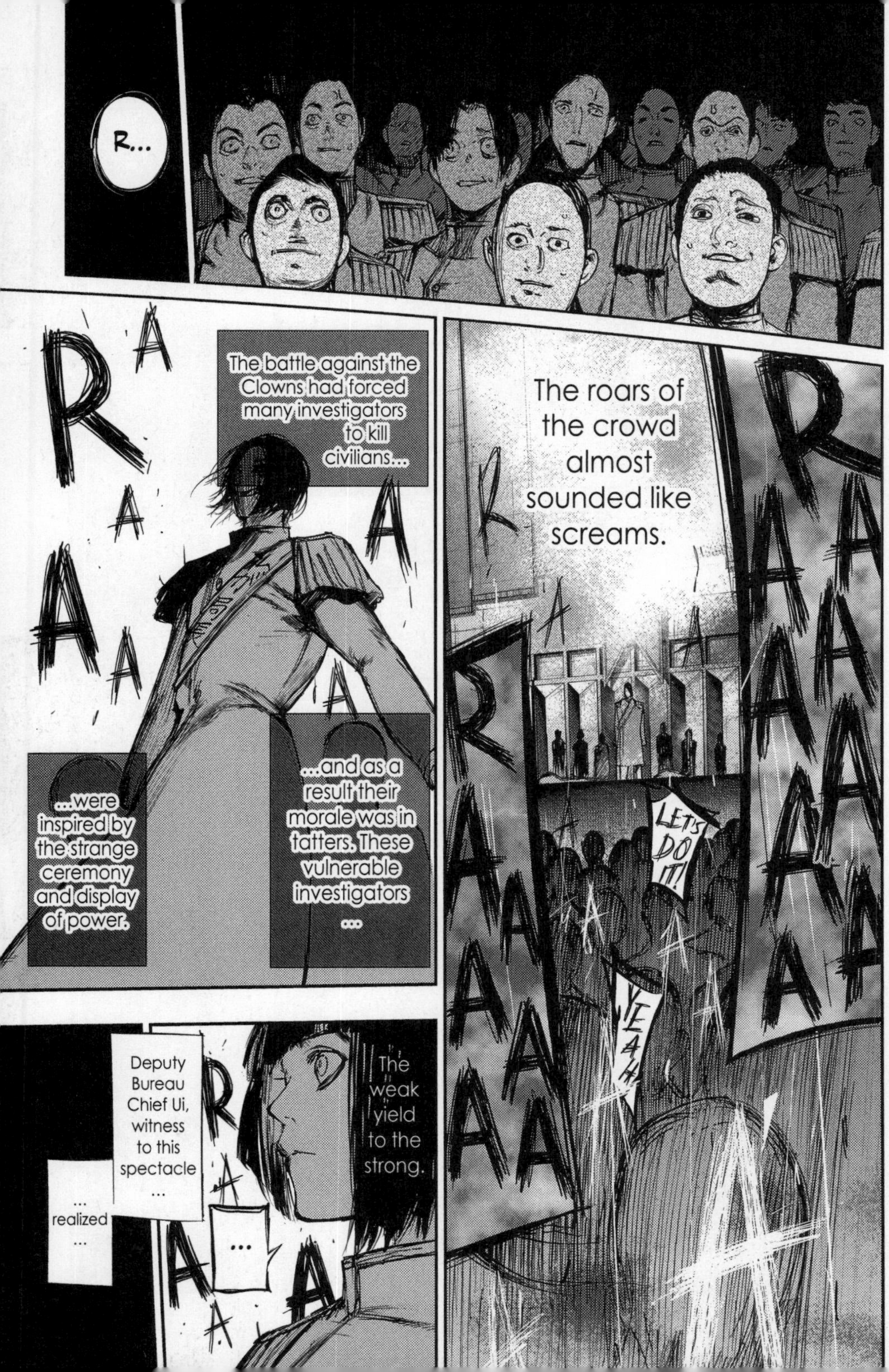
R...
RAAAAAAAAA
The roars of the crowd almost sounded like screams.
LET'S DO IT!
YEAH
RAAAAAA
The battle against the Clowns had forced many investigators to kill civilians...
...and as a result their morale was in tatters. These vulnerable investigators ...
...were inspired by the strange ceremony and display of power.
RAAA
The weak yield to the strong.
Deputy Bureau Chief Ui, witness to this spectacle ...
... realized ...
...

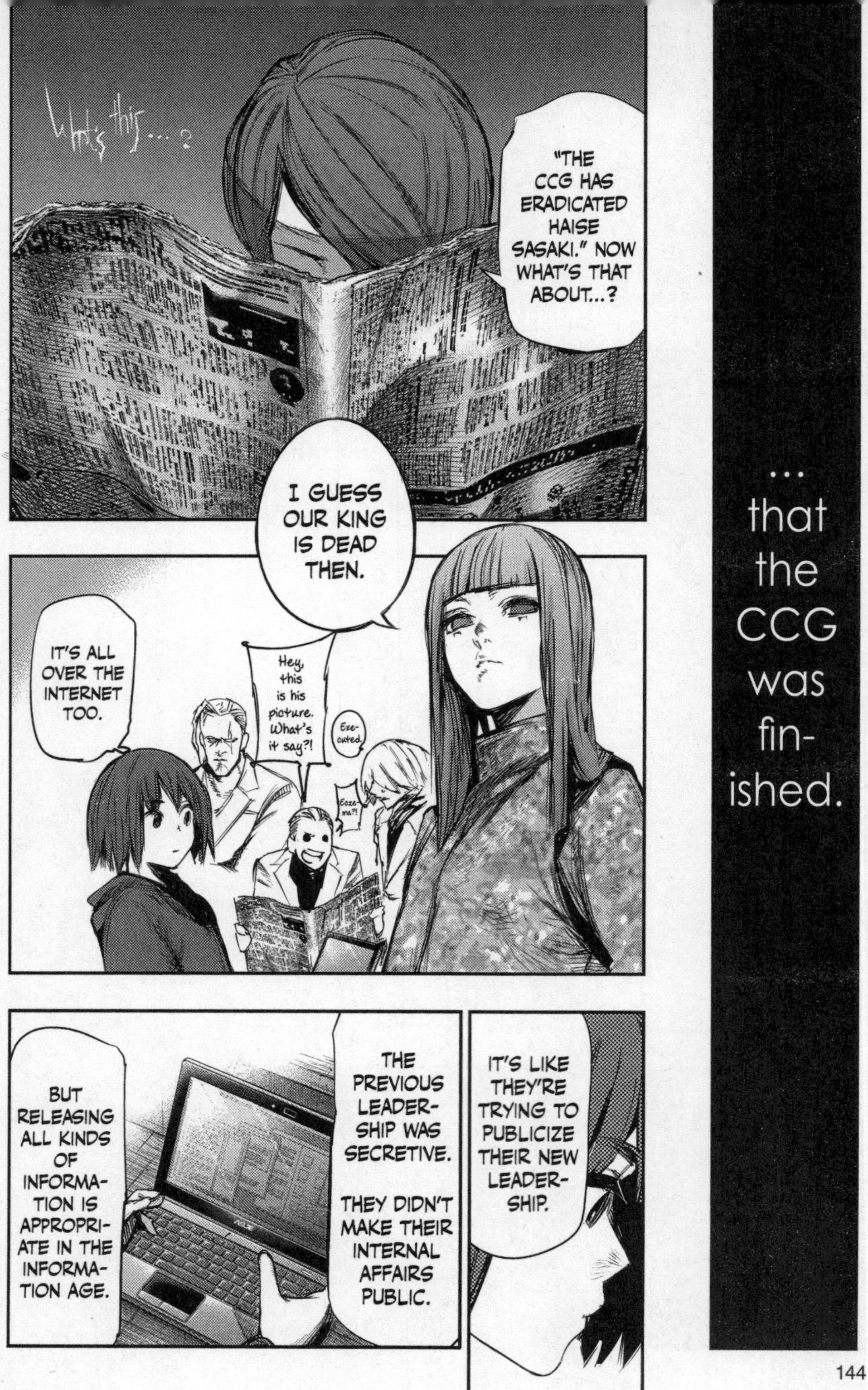
... that the CCG was fin-ished.
What's this...?
"THE CCG HAS ERADICATED HAISE SASAKI." NOW WHAT'S THAT ABOUT...?
I GUESS OUR KING IS DEAD THEN.
IT'S ALL OVER THE INTERNET TOO.
Hey, this is his picture. What's it say?!
Exe-cuted.
IT'S LIKE THEY'RE TRYING TO PUBLICIZE THEIR NEW LEADER-SHIP.
THE PREVIOUS LEADER-SHIP WAS SECRETIVE.
THEY DIDN'T MAKE THEIR INTERNAL AFFAIRS PUBLIC.
BUT RELEASING ALL KINDS OF INFORMA-TION IS APPROPRI-ATE IN THE INFORMA-TION AGE.

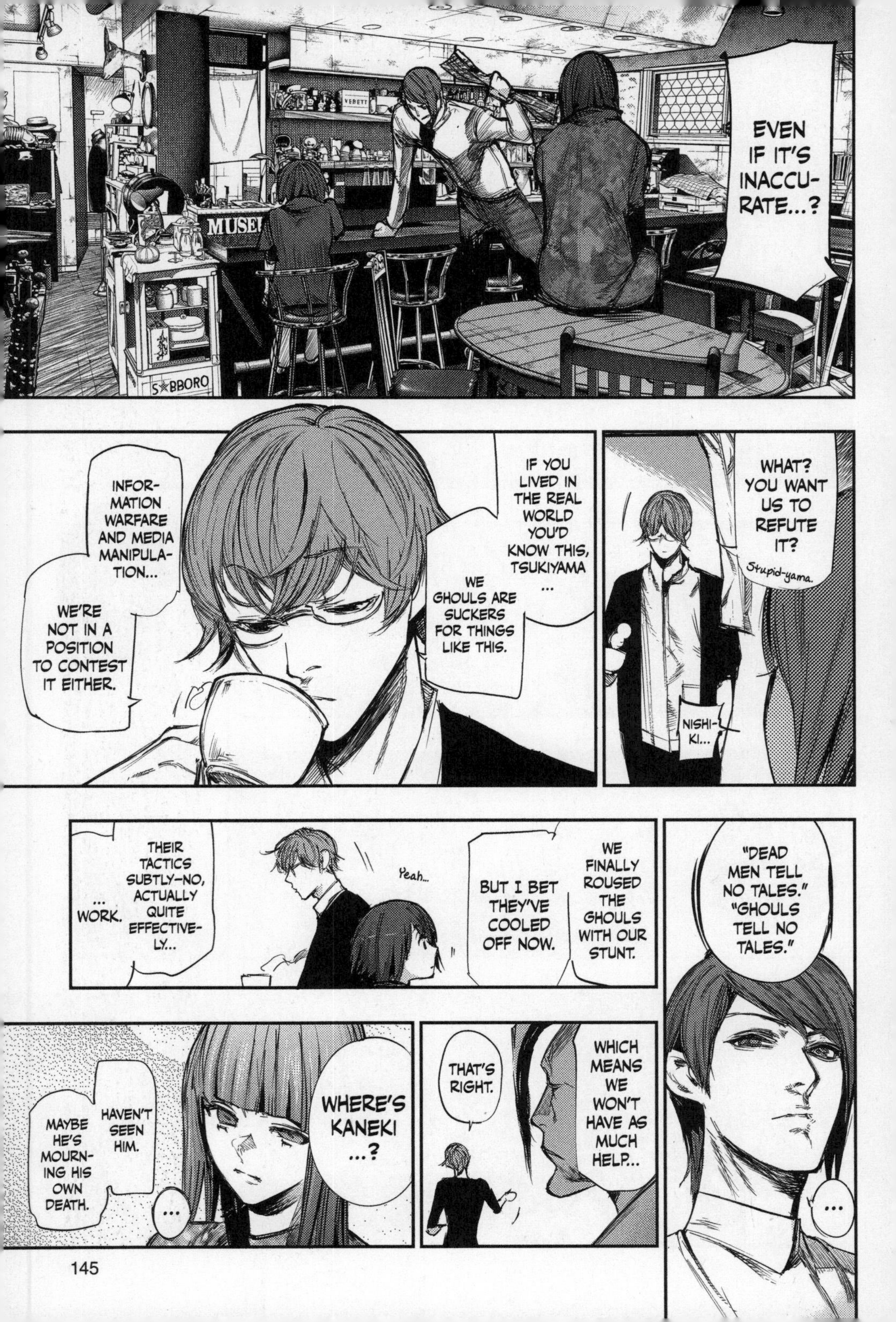
EVEN IF IT'S INACCURATE...?
WHAT? YOU WANT US TO REFUTE IT?
Stupid-yama.
NISHIKI...
IF YOU LIVED IN THE REAL WORLD YOU'D KNOW THIS, TSUKIYAMA...
WE GHOULS ARE SUCKERS FOR THINGS LIKE THIS.
INFORMATION WARFARE AND MEDIA MANIPULATION...
WE'RE NOT IN A POSITION TO CONTEST IT EITHER.
"DEAD MEN TELL NO TALES." "GHOULS TELL NO TALES."
WE FINALLY ROUSED THE GHOULS WITH OUR STUNT.
BUT I BET THEY'VE COOLED OFF NOW.
Yeah...
THEIR TACTICS SUBTLY—NO, ACTUALLY QUITE EFFECTIVELY...
...WORK.
...
WHICH MEANS WE WON'T HAVE AS MUCH HELP...
THAT'S RIGHT.
WHERE'S KANEKI...?
HAVEN'T SEEN HIM.
MAYBE HE'S MOURNING HIS OWN DEATH.
...

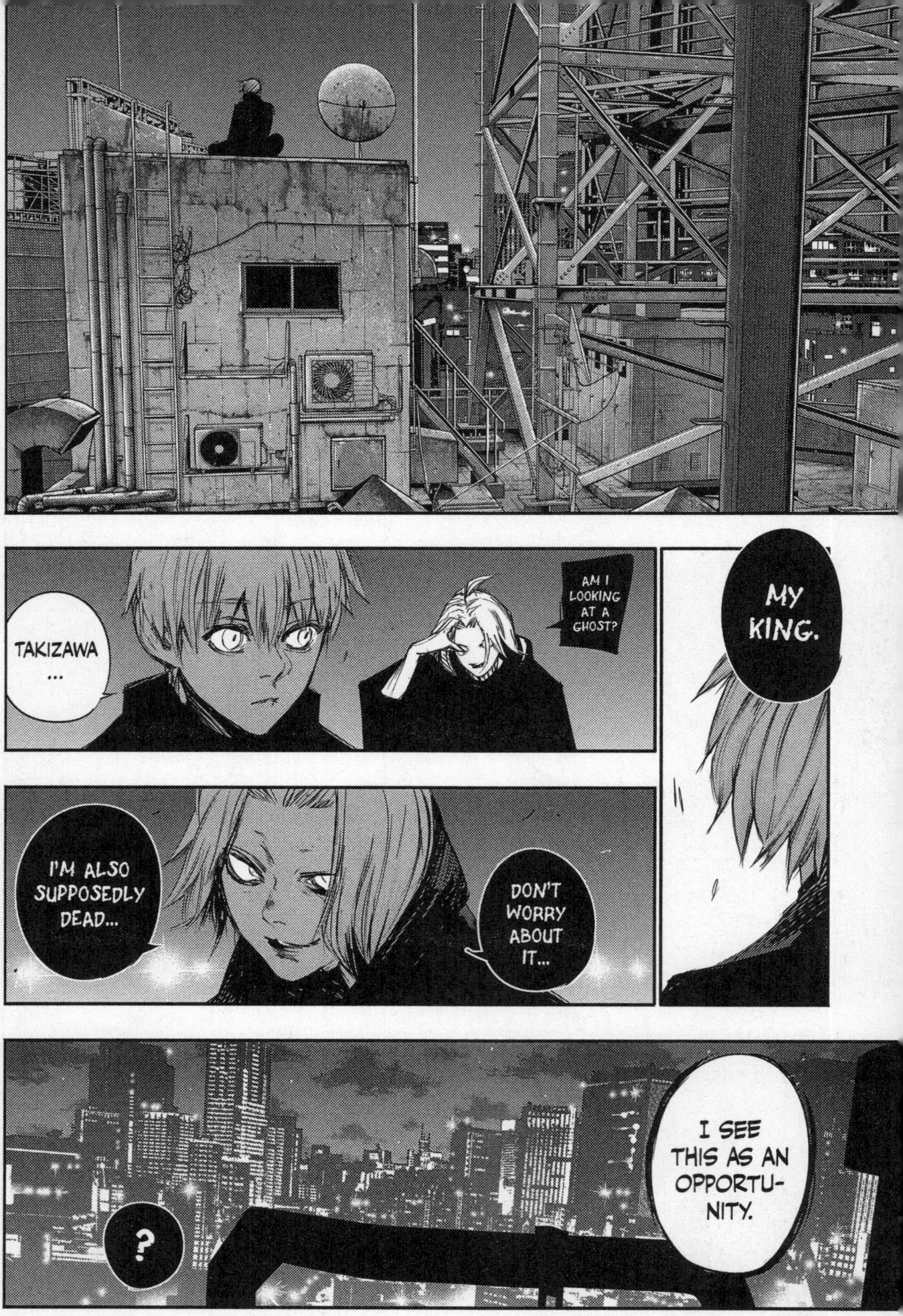
MY KING.
AM I LOOKING AT A GHOST?
TAKIZAWA ...
DON'T WORRY ABOUT IT...
I'M ALSO SUPPOSEDLY DEAD...
I SEE THIS AS AN OPPORTU-NITY.
?

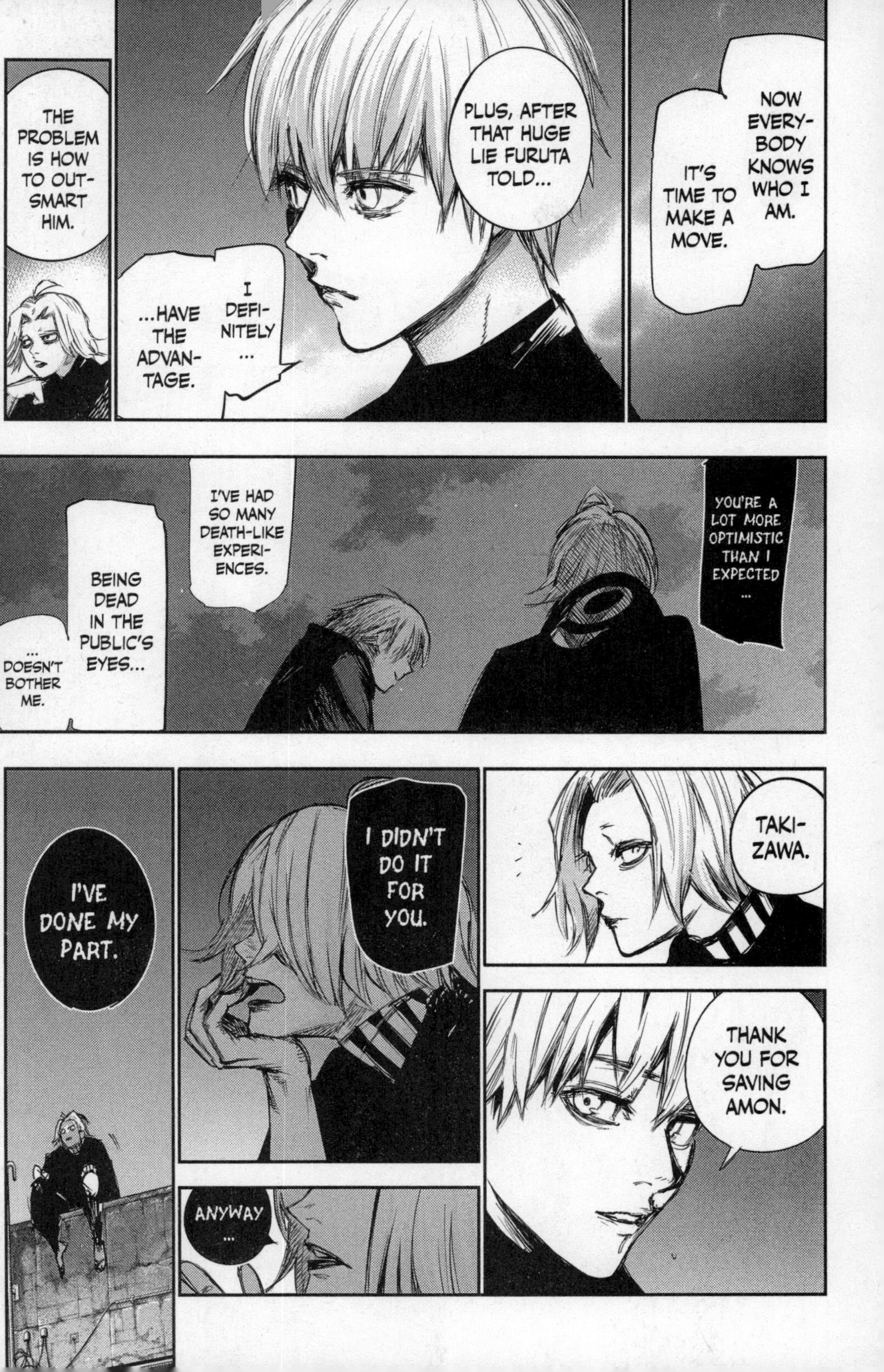
NOW EVERYBODY KNOWS WHO I AM.
IT'S TIME TO MAKE A MOVE.
PLUS, AFTER THAT HUGE LIE FURUTA TOLD...
I DEFINITELY...
...HAVE THE ADVANTAGE.
THE PROBLEM IS HOW TO OUTSMART HIM.
YOU'RE A LOT MORE OPTIMISTIC THAN I EXPECTED...
I'VE HAD SO MANY DEATH-LIKE EXPERIENCES.
BEING DEAD IN THE PUBLIC'S EYES...
...DOESN'T BOTHER ME.
TAKIZAWA.
THANK YOU FOR SAVING AMON.
I DIDN'T DO IT FOR YOU.
ANYWAY...
I'VE DONE MY PART.

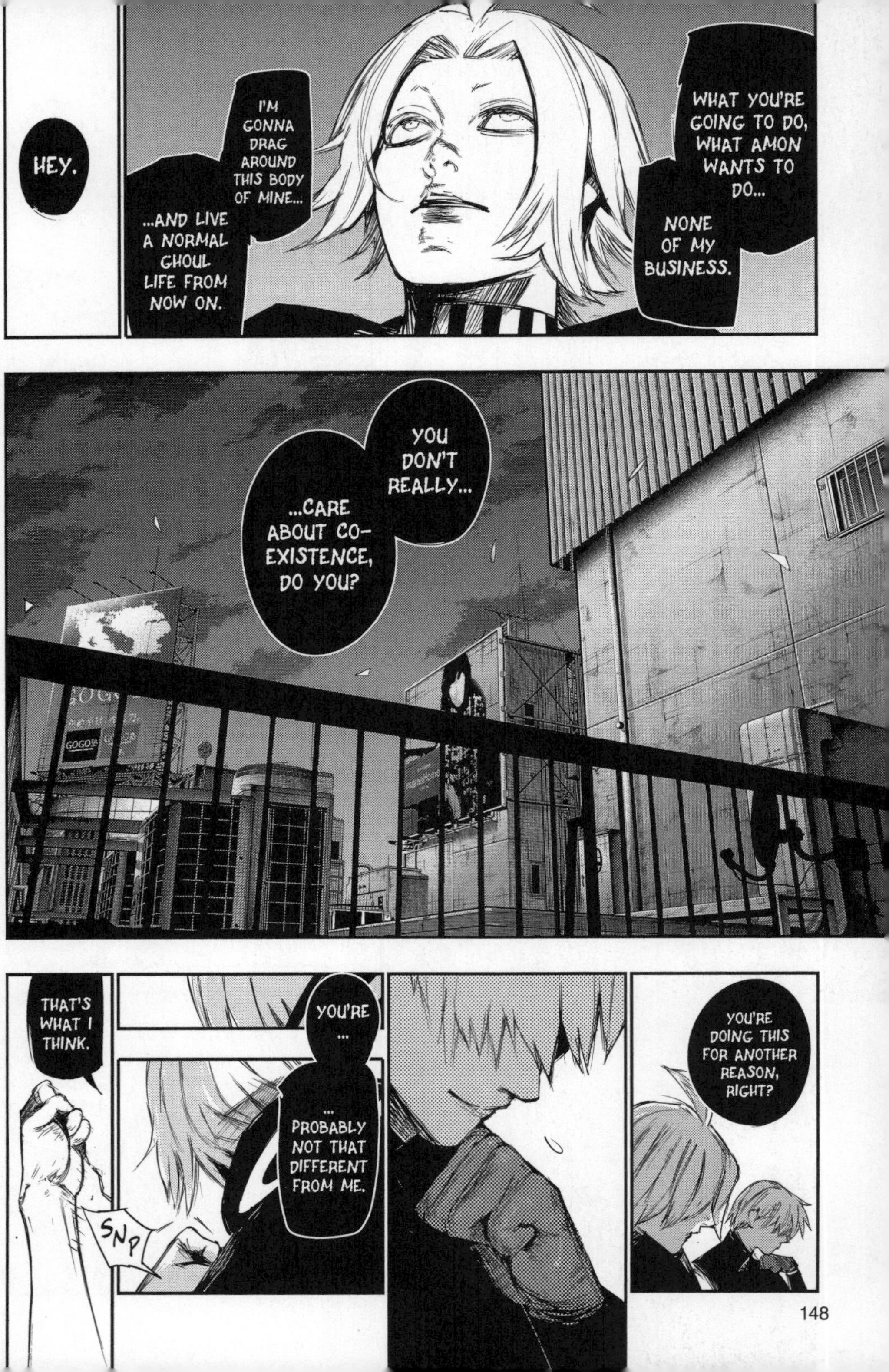
WHAT YOU'RE GOING TO DO, WHAT AMON WANTS TO DO...
NONE OF MY BUSINESS.
I'M GONNA DRAG AROUND THIS BODY OF MINE...
...AND LIVE A NORMAL GHOUL LIFE FROM NOW ON.
HEY.
YOU DON'T REALLY...
...CARE ABOUT CO-EXISTENCE, DO YOU?
YOU'RE DOING THIS FOR ANOTHER REASON, RIGHT?
YOU'RE ...
... PROBABLY NOT THAT DIFFERENT FROM ME.
THAT'S WHAT I THINK.
SNP

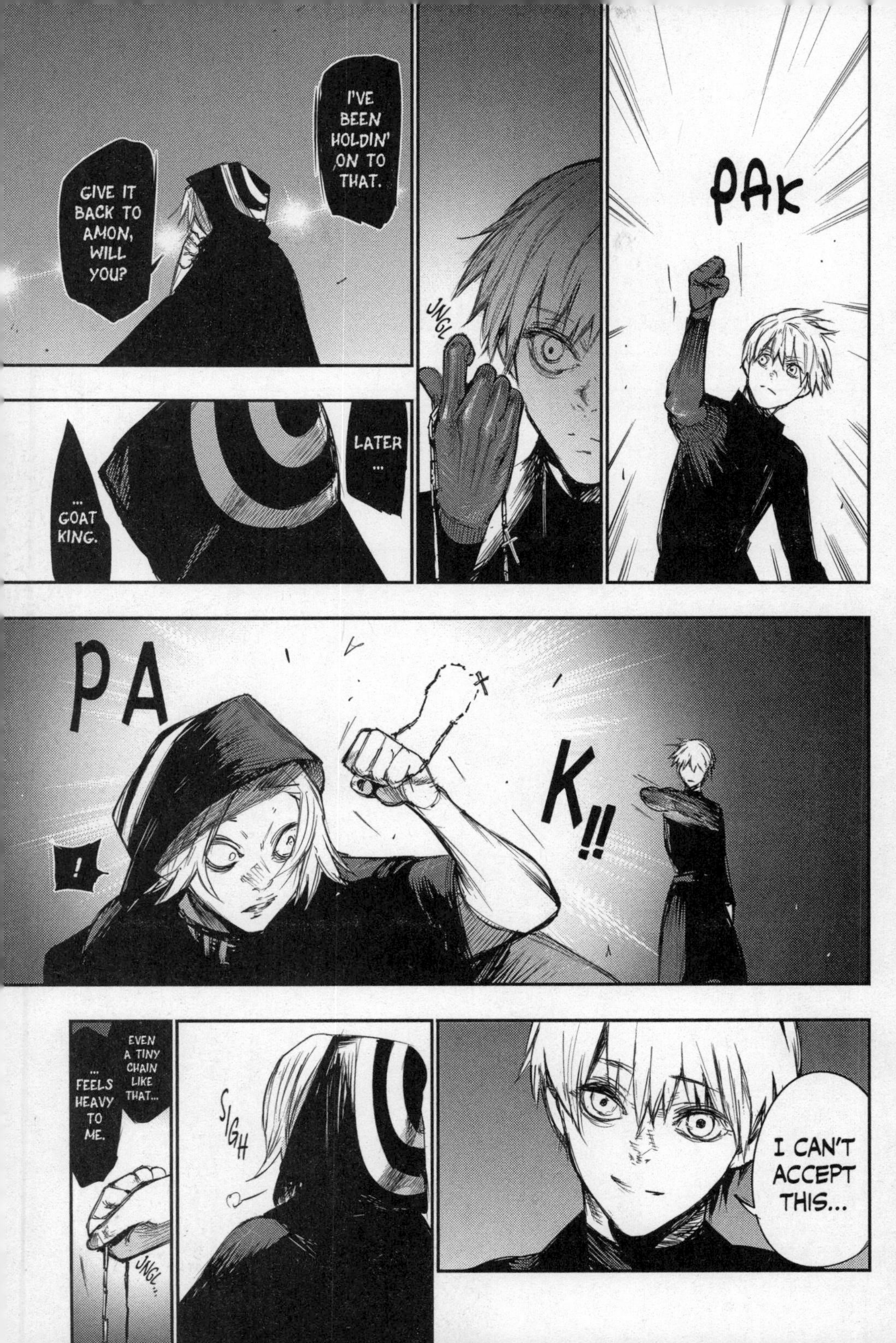
PAK
JNGL
I'VE BEEN HOLDIN' ON TO THAT.
GIVE IT BACK TO AMON, WILL YOU?
LATER...
... GOAT KING.
PA
K!!
!
I CAN'T ACCEPT THIS...
SIGH
EVEN A TINY CHAIN LIKE THAT...
... FEELS HEAVY TO ME.
JNGL...

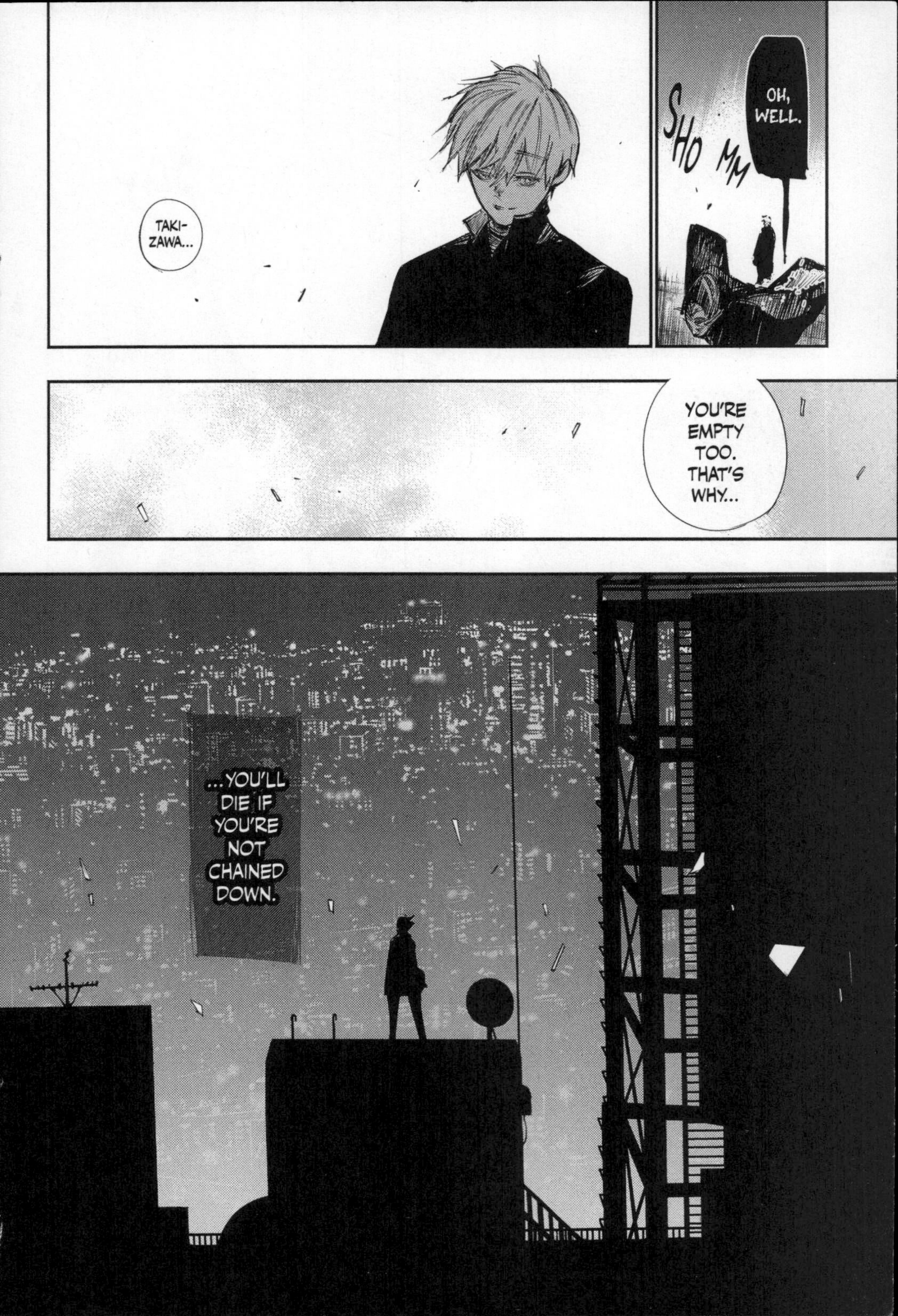
OH, WELL.
SHOMM
TAKI-ZAWA...
YOU'RE EMPTY TOO. THAT'S WHY...
...YOU'LL DIE IF YOU'RE NOT CHAINED DOWN.

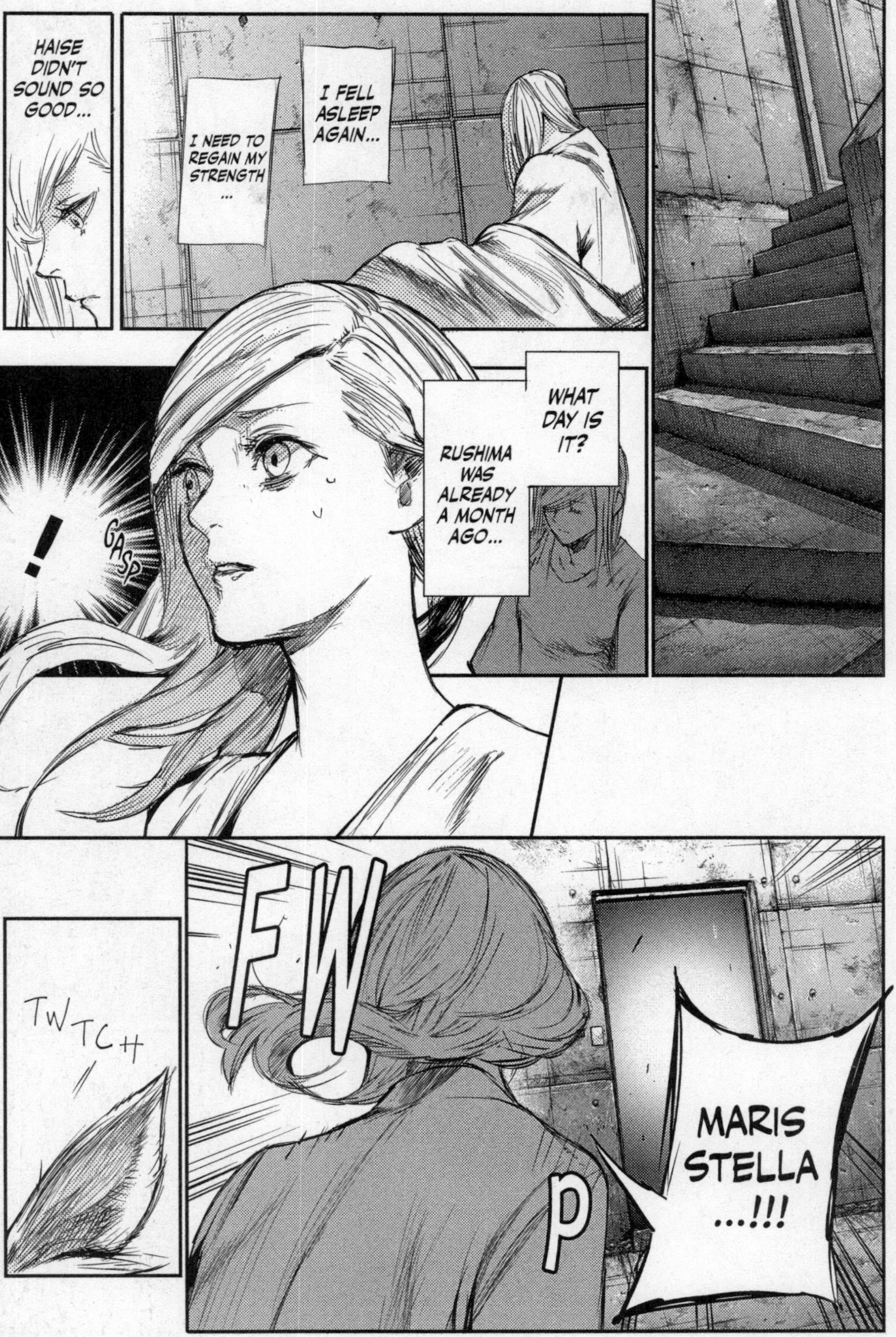
I FELL ASLEEP AGAIN...
I NEED TO REGAIN MY STRENGTH ...
HAISE DIDN'T SOUND SO GOOD...
WHAT DAY IS IT?
RUSHIMA WAS ALREADY A MONTH AGO...
GASP
!
FWP
MARIS STELLA ...!!!
TWTCH

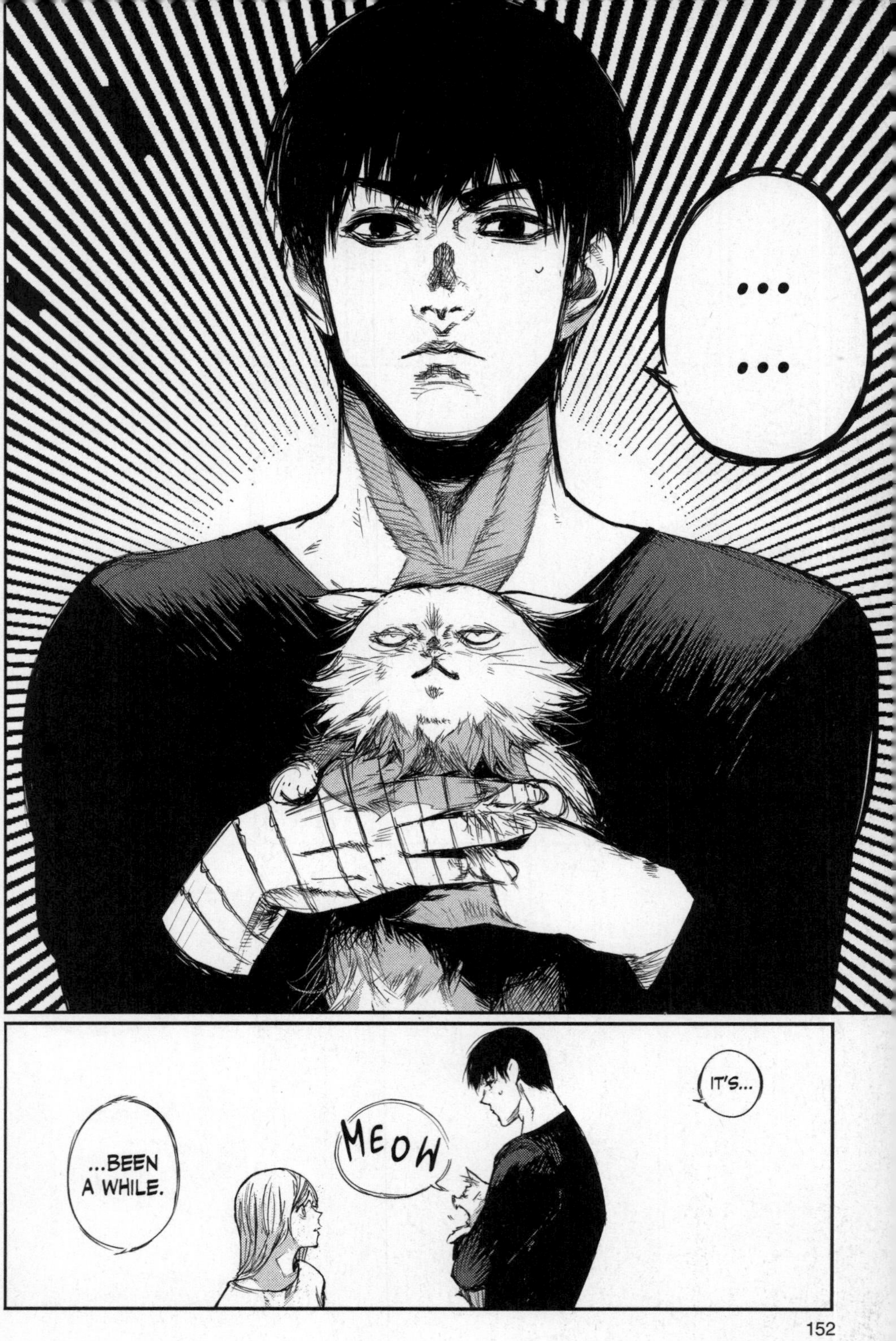
...
...
IT'S...
MEOW
...BEEN A WHILE.

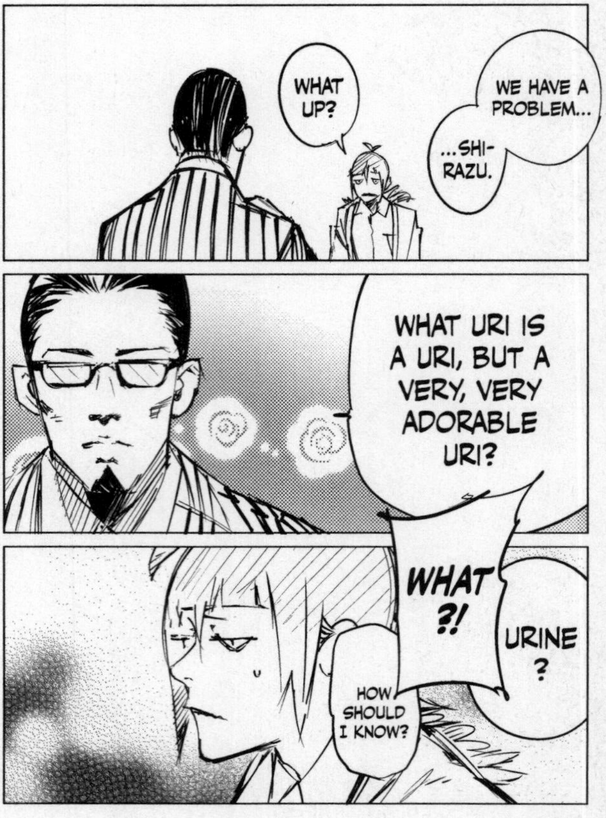
WE HAVE A PROBLEM...
...SHI-RAZU.
WHAT UP?
WHAT URI IS A URI, BUT A VERY, VERY ADORABLE URI?
URINE?
WHAT?!
HOW SHOULD I KNOW?

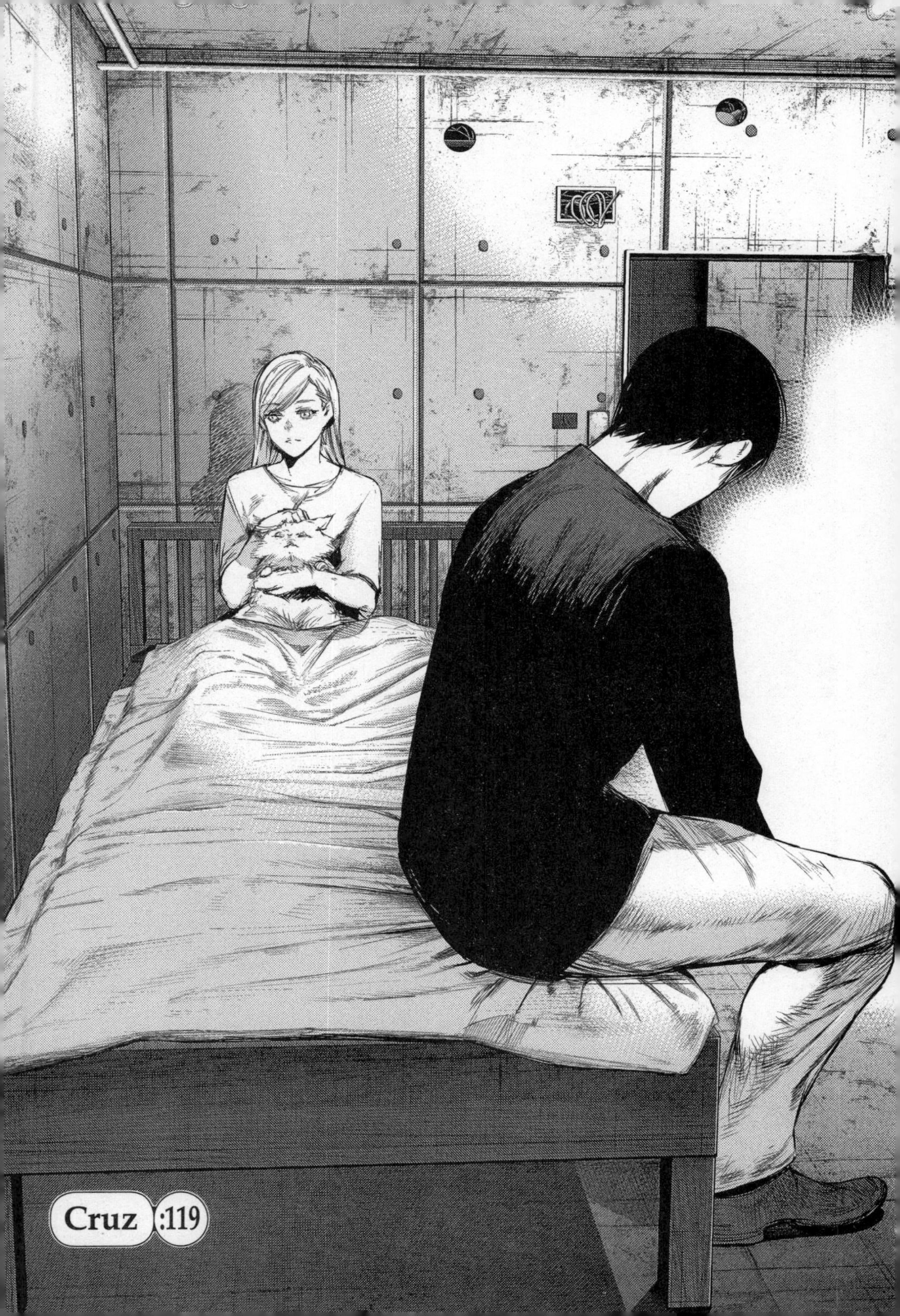
Cruz :119

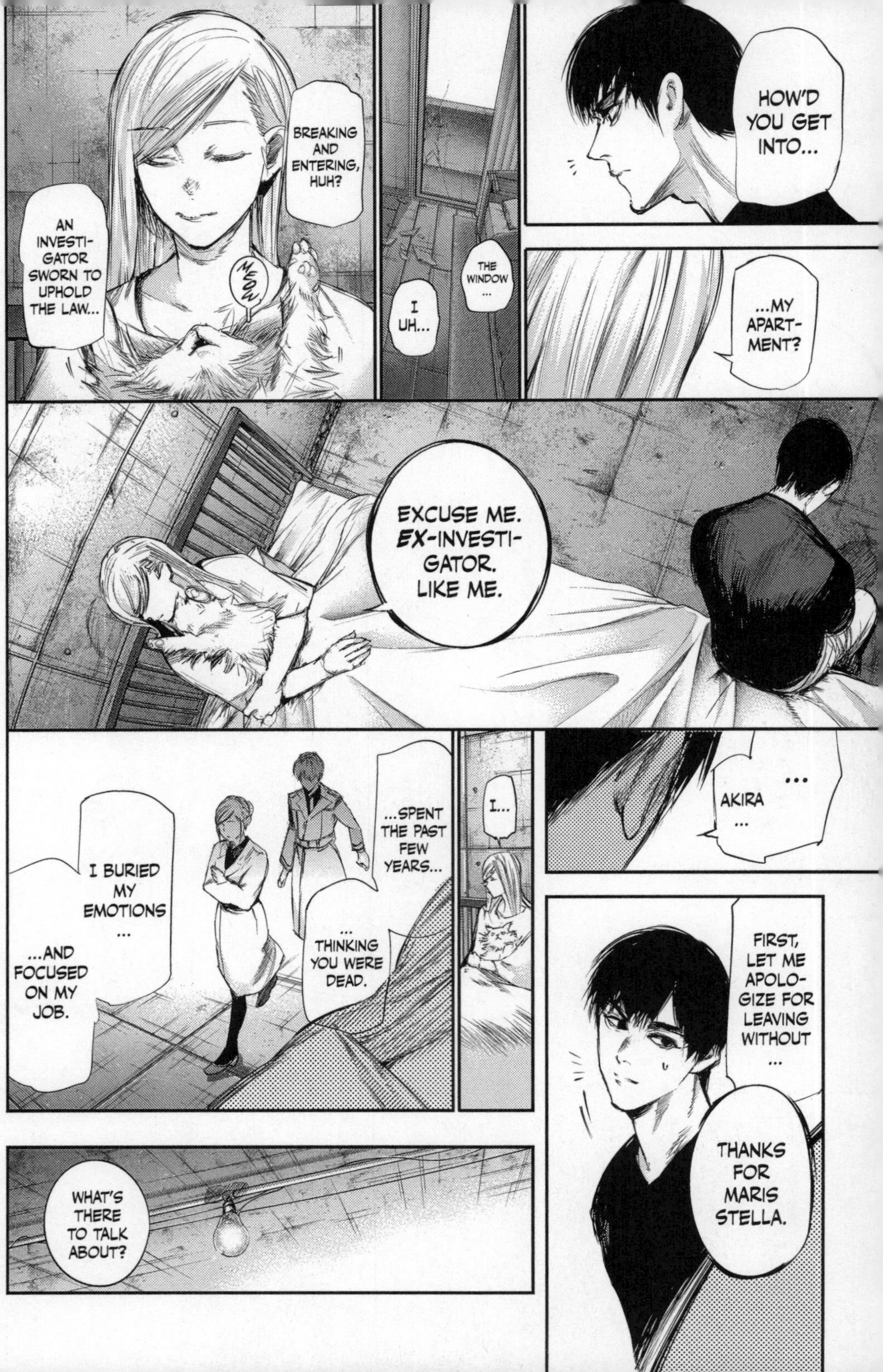
HOW'D YOU GET INTO...
...MY APARTMENT?
THE WINDOW...
I UH...
BREAKING AND ENTERING, HUH?
MEOW
AN INVESTIGATOR SWORN TO UPHOLD THE LAW...
EXCUSE ME. EX-INVESTIGATOR. LIKE ME.
... AKIRA ...
I...
...SPENT THE PAST FEW YEARS...
...THINKING YOU WERE DEAD.
I BURIED MY EMOTIONS...
...AND FOCUSED ON MY JOB.
WHAT'S THERE TO TALK ABOUT?
FIRST, LET ME APOLOGIZE FOR LEAVING WITHOUT...
THANKS FOR MARIS STELLA.

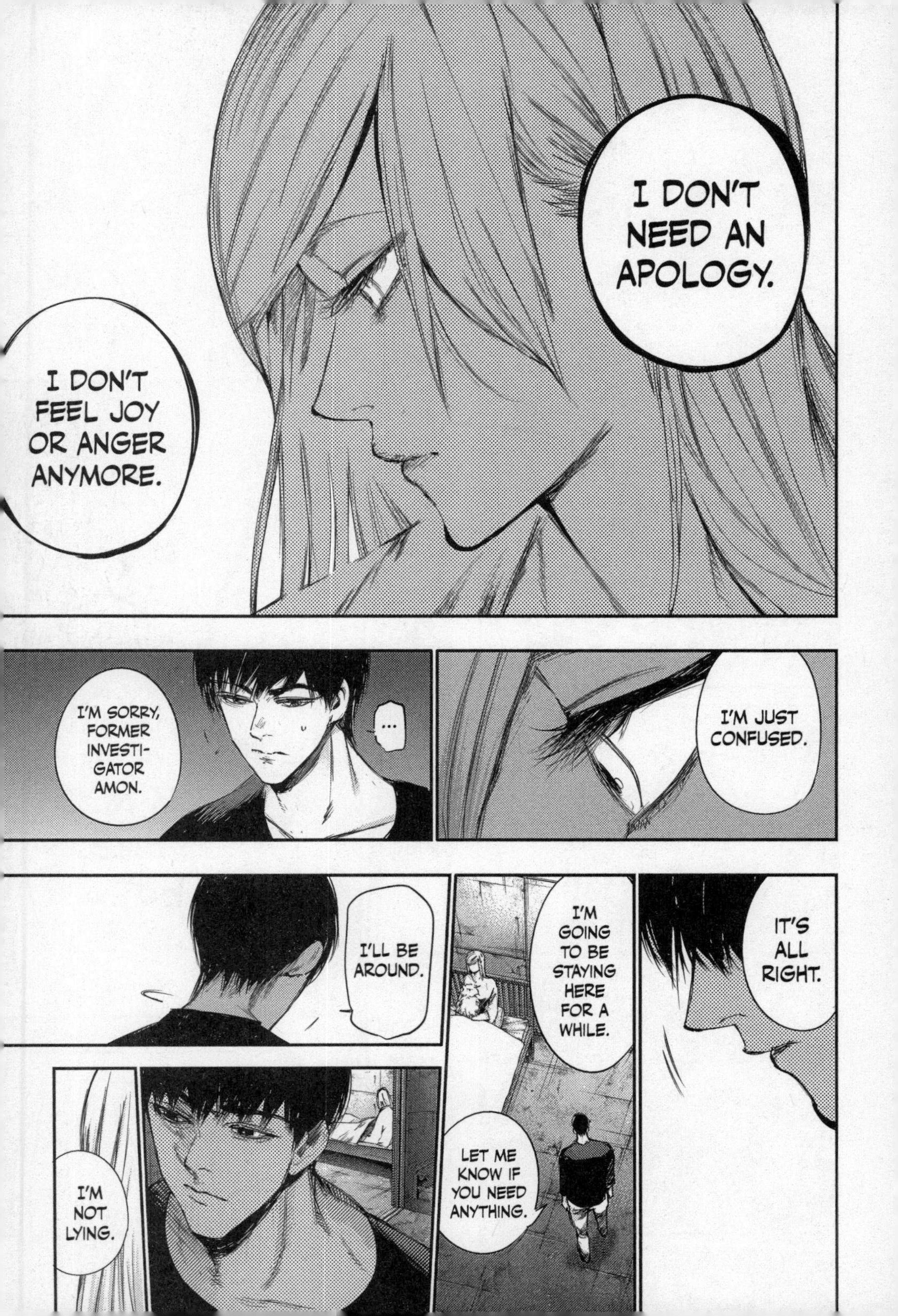
I DON'T NEED AN APOLOGY.
I DON'T FEEL JOY OR ANGER ANYMORE.
I'M JUST CONFUSED.
...
I'M SORRY, FORMER INVESTI-GATOR AMON.
IT'S ALL RIGHT.
I'M GOING TO BE STAYING HERE FOR A WHILE.
LET ME KNOW IF YOU NEED ANYTHING.
I'LL BE AROUND.
I'M NOT LYING.

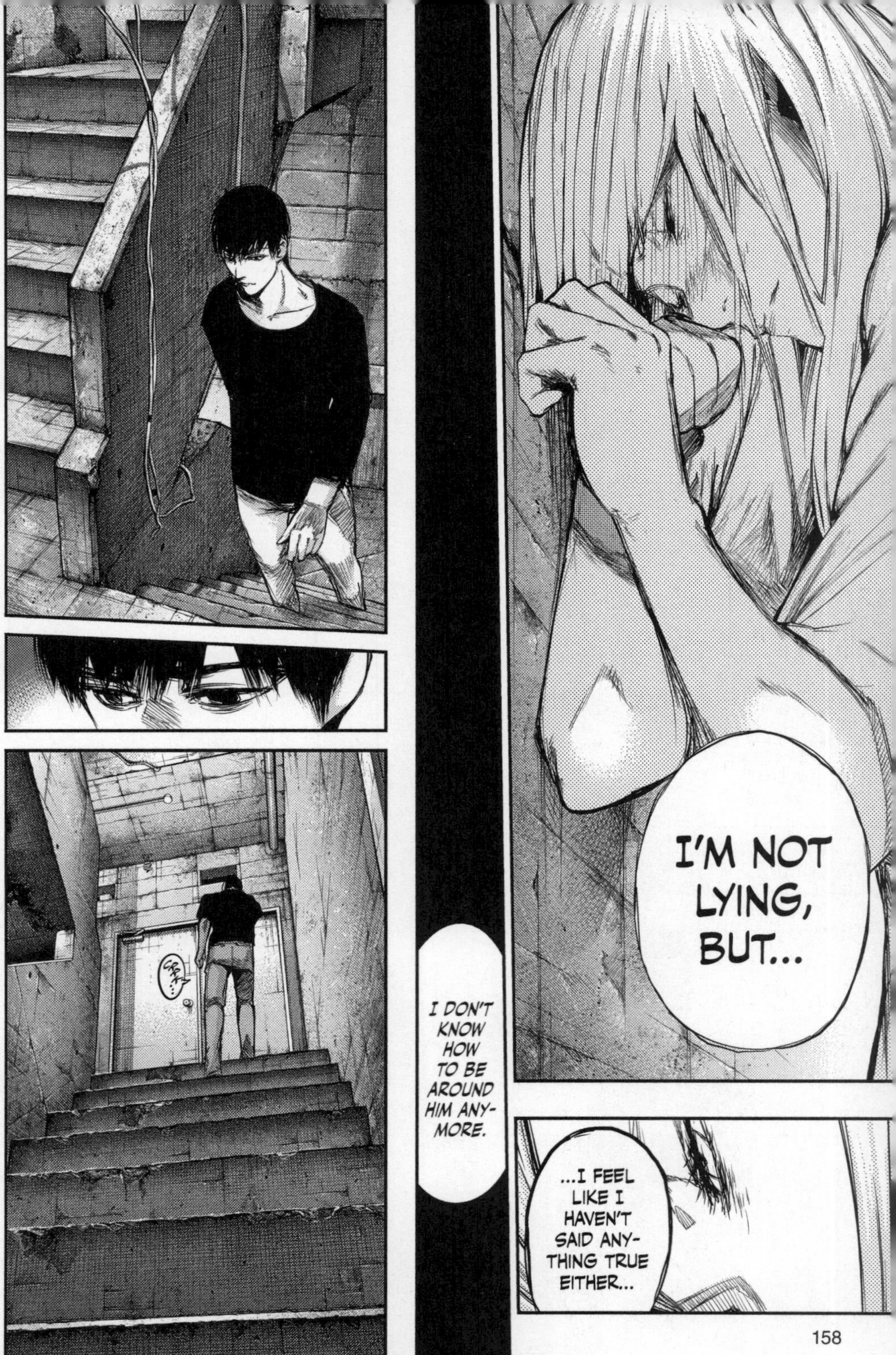
I'M NOT LYING, BUT...
...I FEEL LIKE I HAVEN'T SAID ANYTHING TRUE EITHER...
I DON'T KNOW HOW TO BE AROUND HIM ANYMORE.
CRKK...

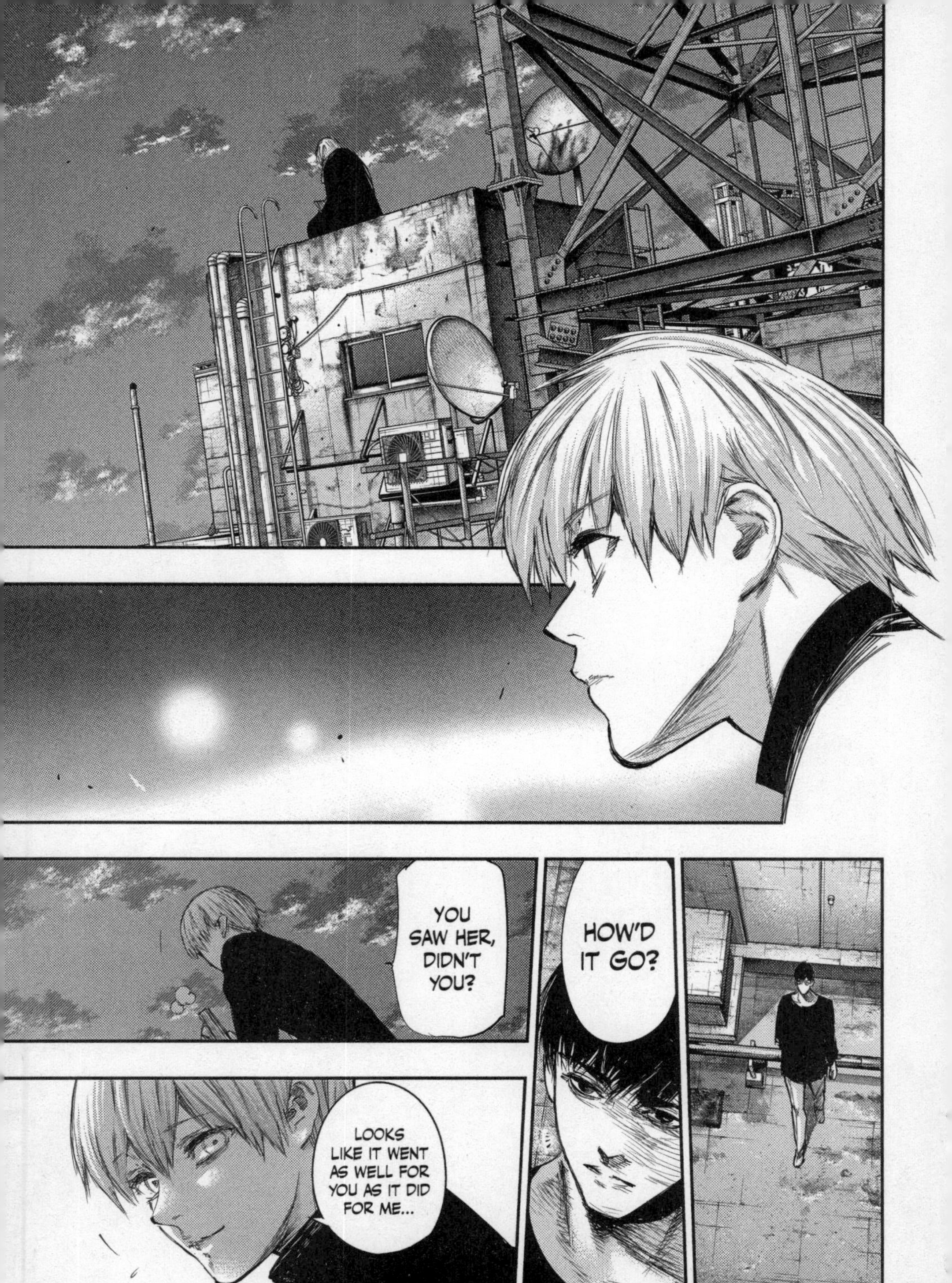
HOW'D IT GO?
YOU SAW HER, DIDN'T YOU?
LOOKS LIKE IT WENT AS WELL FOR YOU AS IT DID FOR ME...

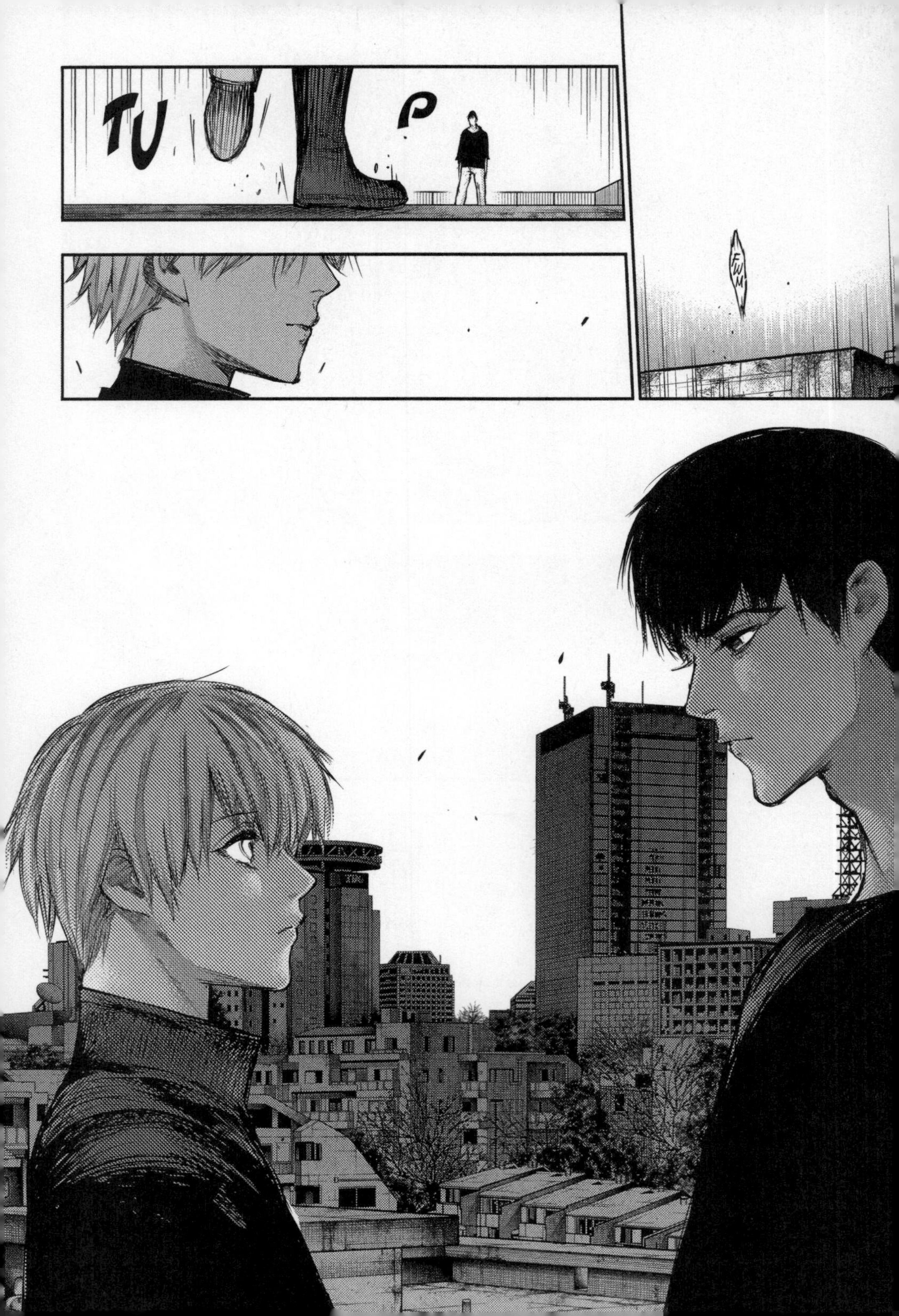
FWM
TU P

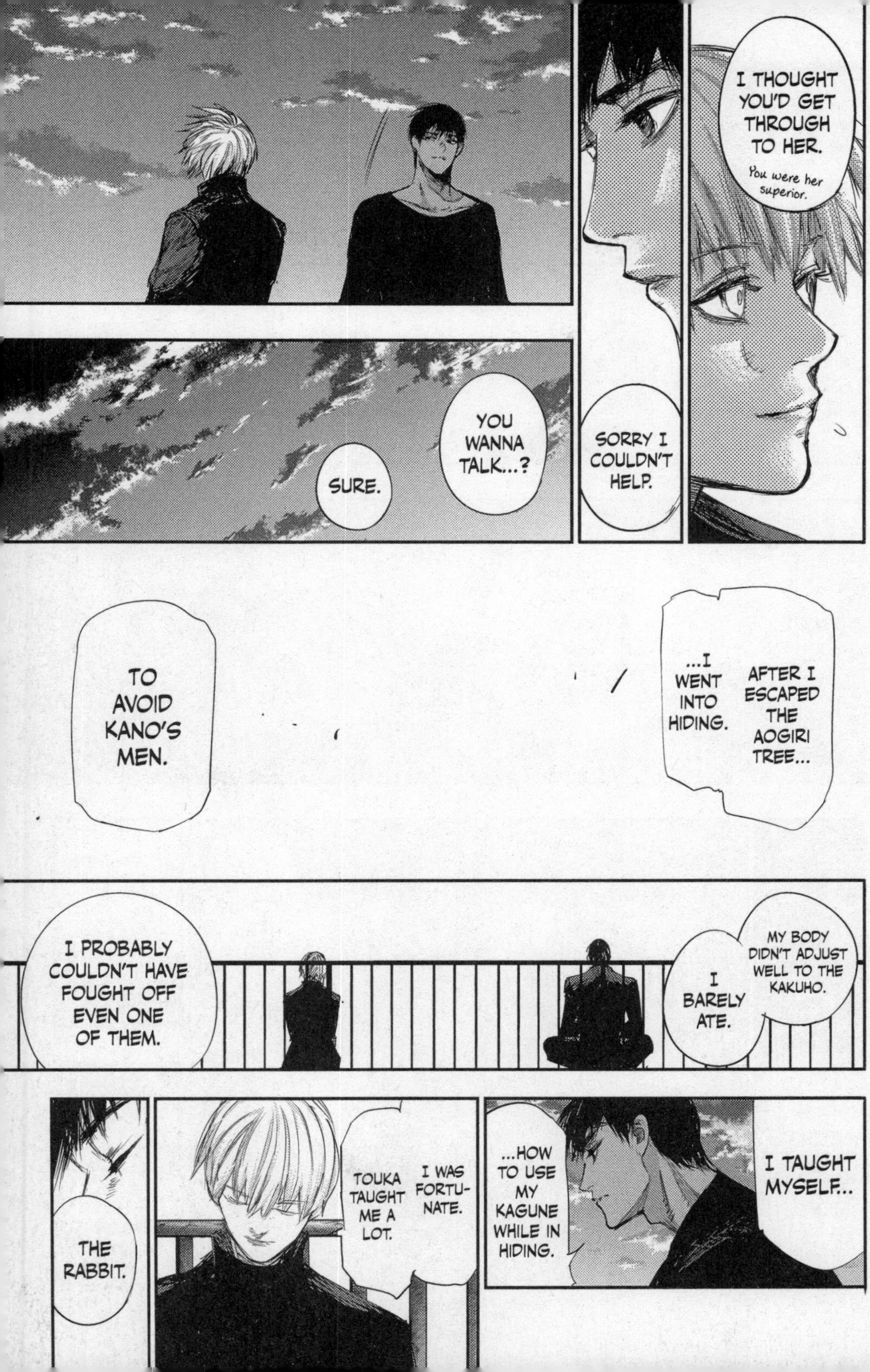
I THOUGHT YOU'D GET THROUGH TO HER.
You were her superior.
SORRY I COULDN'T HELP.
YOU WANNA TALK...?
SURE.
AFTER I ESCAPED THE AOGIRI TREE...
...I WENT INTO HIDING.
TO AVOID KANO'S MEN.
MY BODY DIDN'T ADJUST WELL TO THE KAKUHO.
I BARELY ATE.
I PROBABLY COULDN'T HAVE FOUGHT OFF EVEN ONE OF THEM.
I TAUGHT MYSELF...
...HOW TO USE MY KAGUNE WHILE IN HIDING.
I WAS FORTU-NATE.
TOUKA TAUGHT ME A LOT.
THE RABBIT.

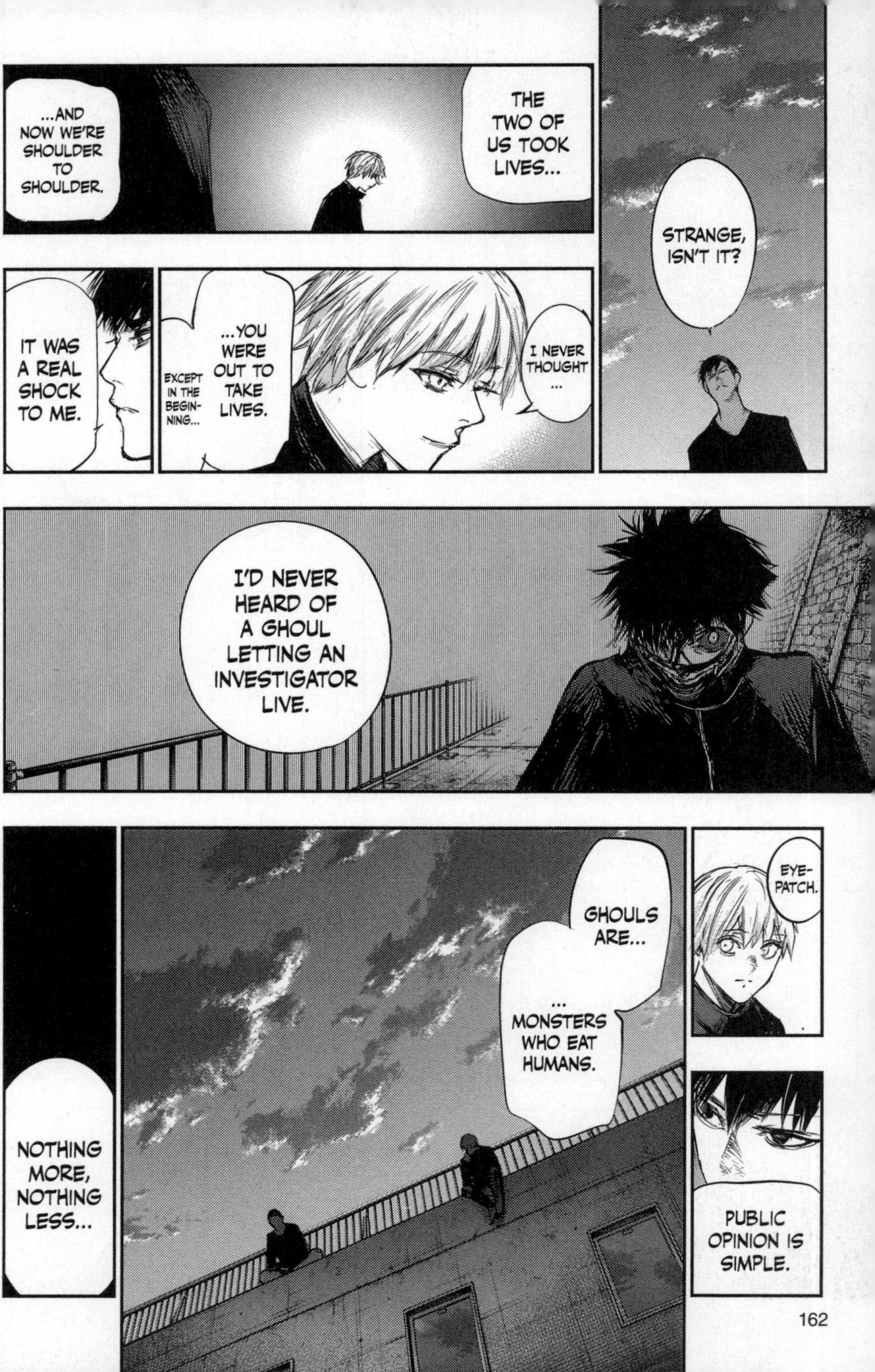

STRANGE, ISN'T IT?
THE TWO OF US TOOK LIVES...
...AND NOW WE'RE SHOULDER TO SHOULDER.
I NEVER THOUGHT...
...YOU WERE OUT TO TAKE LIVES.
EXCEPT IN THE BEGINNING...
IT WAS A REAL SHOCK TO ME.
I'D NEVER HEARD OF A GHOUL LETTING AN INVESTIGATOR LIVE.
EYE-PATCH.
PUBLIC OPINION IS SIMPLE.
GHOULS ARE...
...MONSTERS WHO EAT HUMANS.
NOTHING MORE, NOTHING LESS...

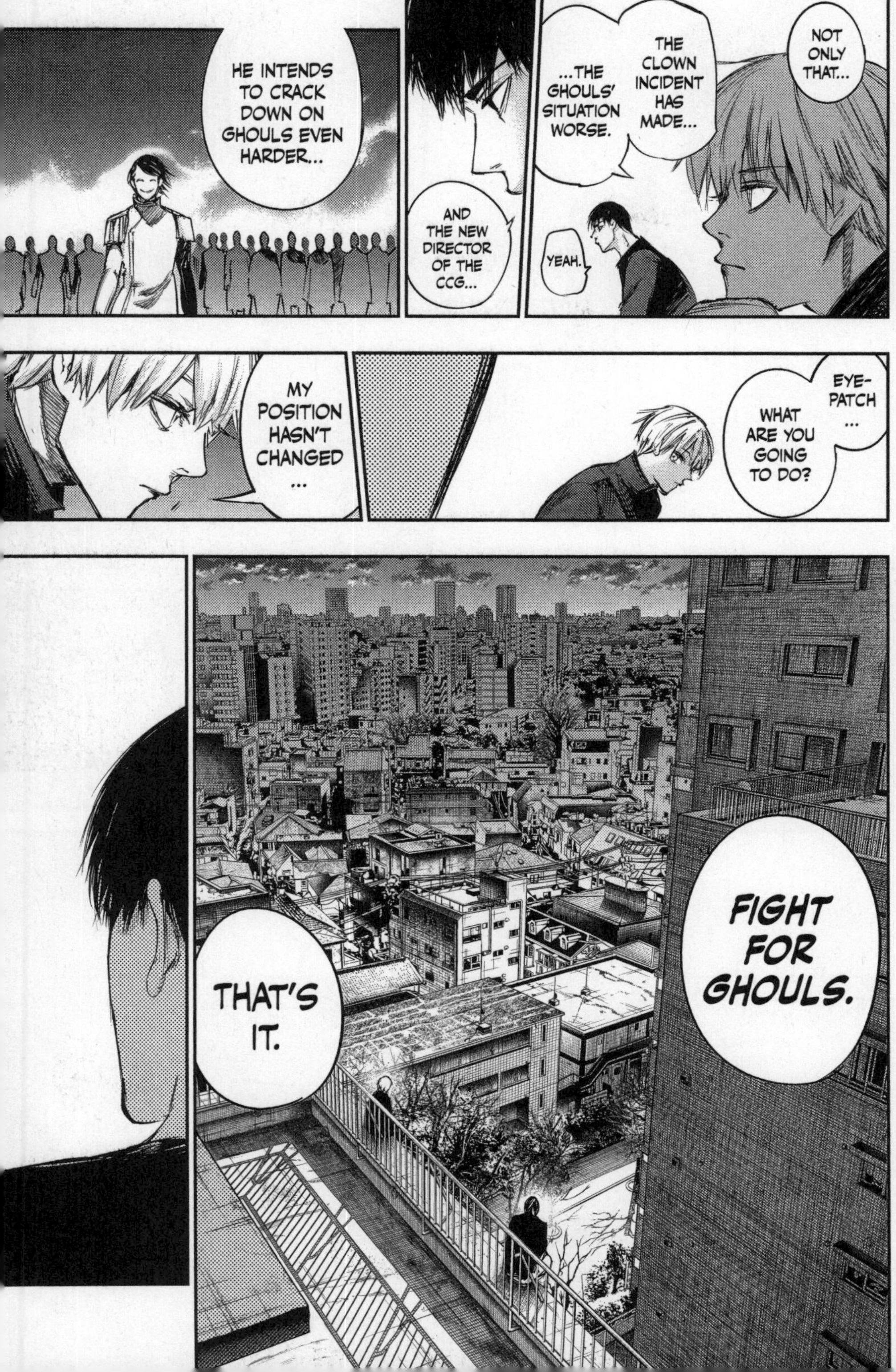
NOT ONLY THAT...
THE CLOWN INCIDENT HAS MADE...
...THE GHOULS' SITUATION WORSE.
YEAH.
AND THE NEW DIRECTOR OF THE CCG...
HE INTENDS TO CRACK DOWN ON GHOULS EVEN HARDER...
EYE-PATCH...
WHAT ARE YOU GOING TO DO?
MY POSITION HASN'T CHANGED...
FIGHT FOR GHOULS.
THAT'S IT.

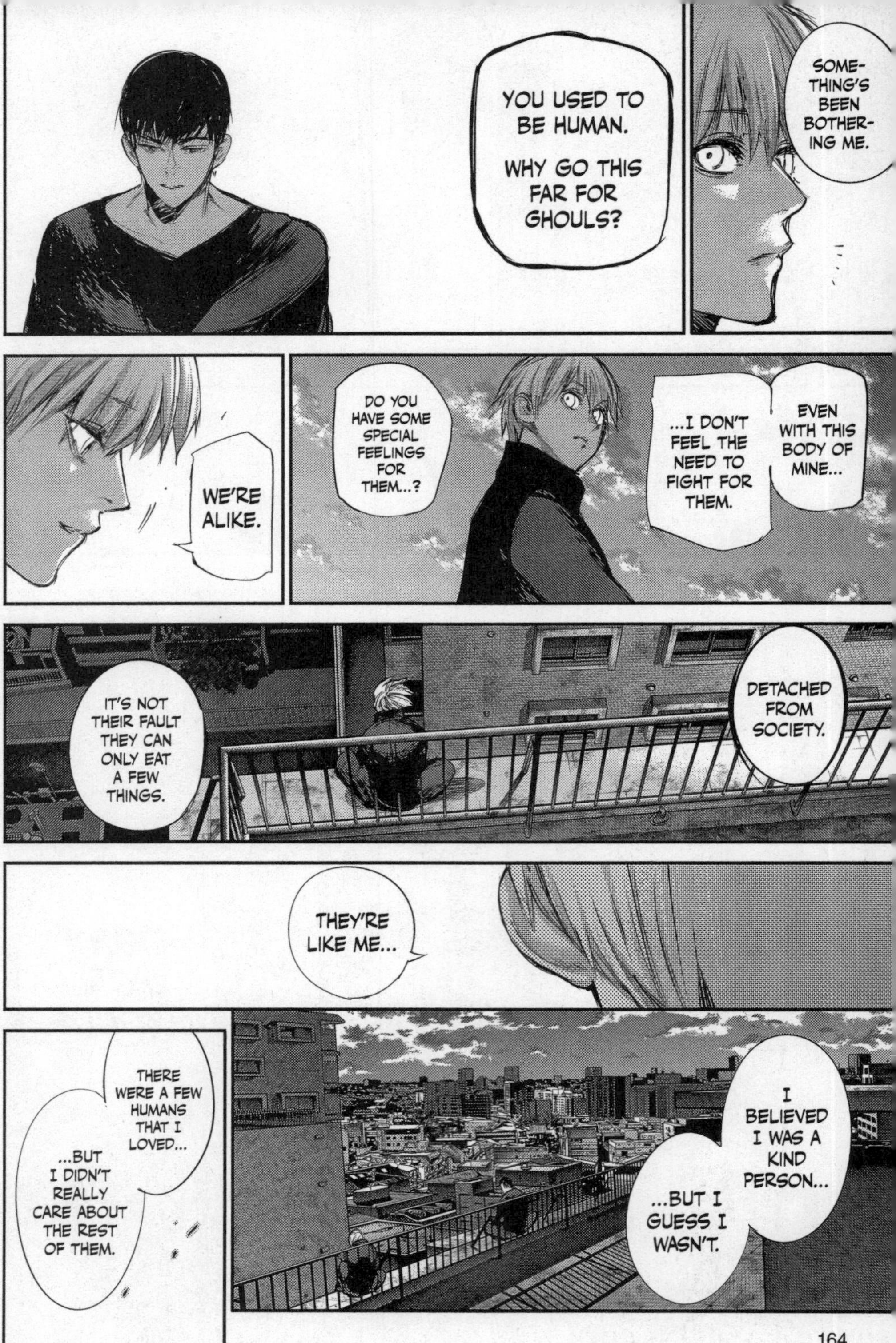
SOMETHING'S BEEN BOTHERING ME.
YOU USED TO BE HUMAN.
WHY GO THIS FAR FOR GHOULS?
EVEN WITH THIS BODY OF MINE...
...I DON'T FEEL THE NEED TO FIGHT FOR THEM.
DO YOU HAVE SOME SPECIAL FEELINGS FOR THEM...?
WE'RE ALIKE.
DETACHED FROM SOCIETY.
IT'S NOT THEIR FAULT THEY CAN ONLY EAT A FEW THINGS.
THEY'RE LIKE ME...
I BELIEVED I WAS A KIND PERSON...
...BUT I GUESS I WASN'T.
THERE WERE A FEW HUMANS THAT I LOVED...
...BUT I DIDN'T REALLY CARE ABOUT THE REST OF THEM.

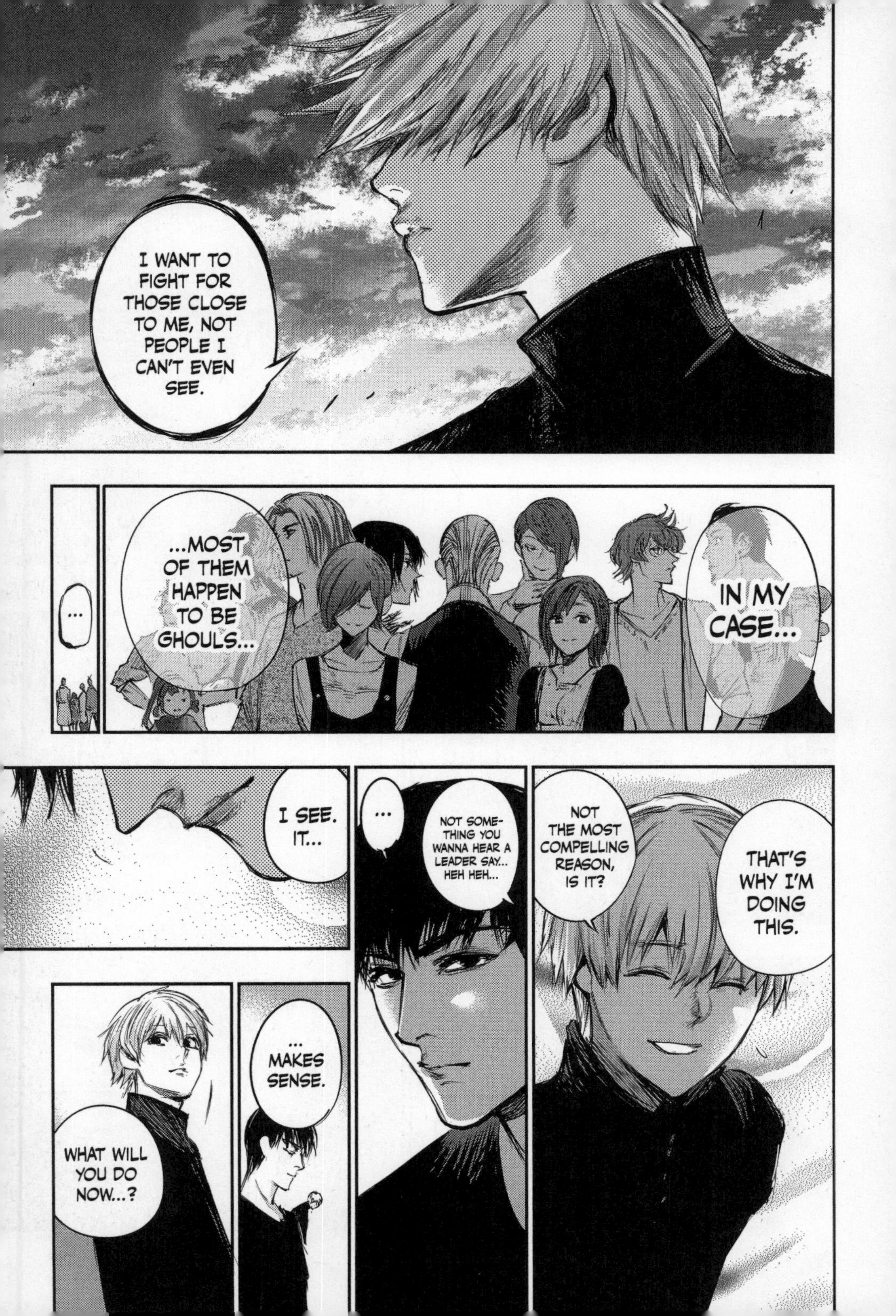

I WANT TO FIGHT FOR THOSE CLOSE TO ME, NOT PEOPLE I CAN'T EVEN SEE.
IN MY CASE...
...MOST OF THEM HAPPEN TO BE GHOULS...
...
THAT'S WHY I'M DOING THIS.
NOT THE MOST COMPELLING REASON, IS IT?
NOT SOME-THING YOU WANNA HEAR A LEADER SAY... HEH HEH...
...
I SEE. IT...
...MAKES SENSE.
WHAT WILL YOU DO NOW...?

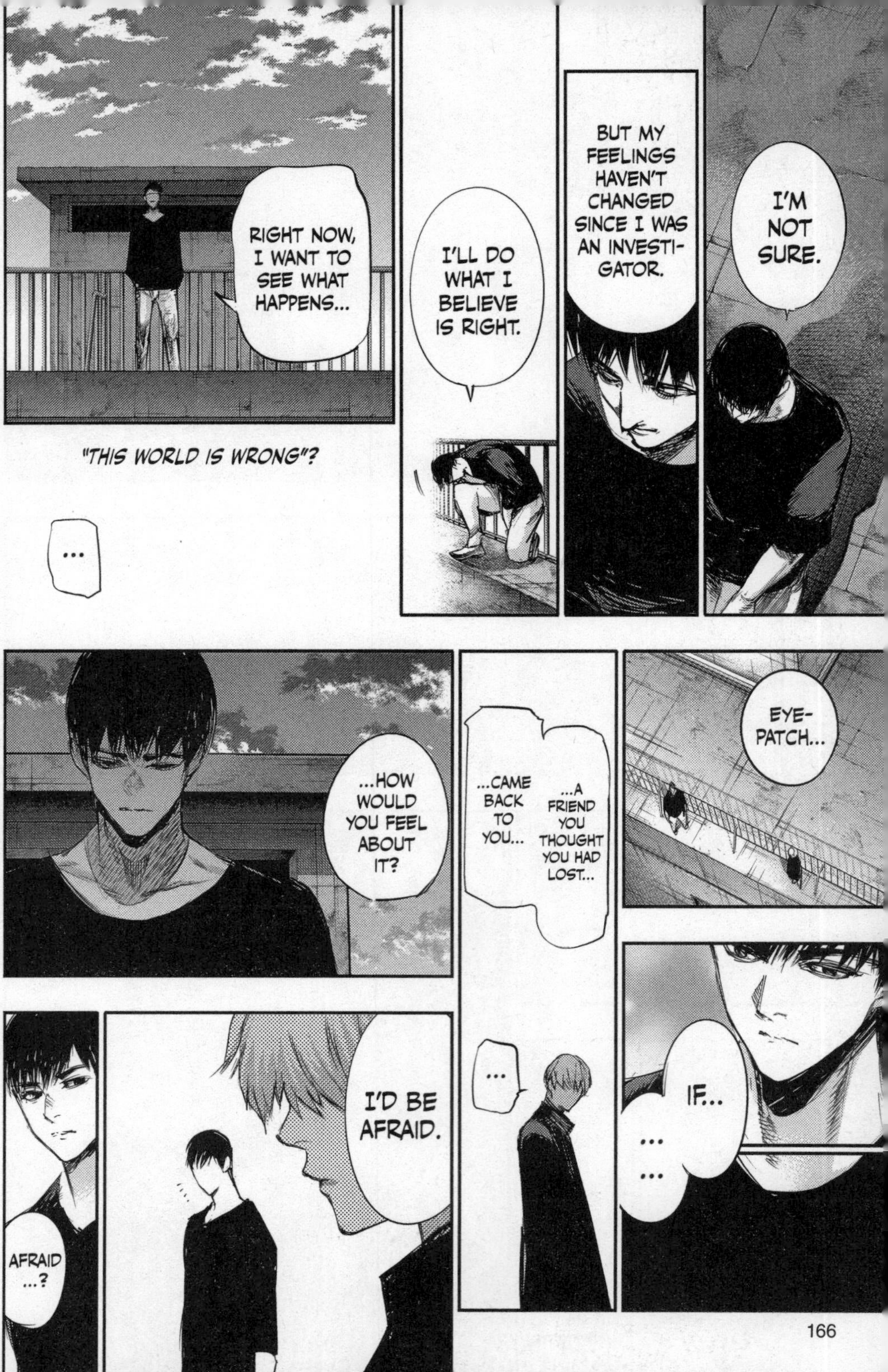

I'M NOT SURE.
BUT MY FEELINGS HAVEN'T CHANGED SINCE I WAS AN INVESTIGATOR.
I'LL DO WHAT I BELIEVE IS RIGHT.
RIGHT NOW, I WANT TO SEE WHAT HAPPENS...
"THIS WORLD IS WRONG"?
...
EYE-PATCH...
IF...
...
...
...A FRIEND YOU THOUGHT YOU HAD LOST...
...CAME BACK TO YOU...
...
...HOW WOULD YOU FEEL ABOUT IT?
I'D BE AFRAID.
AFRAID ...?

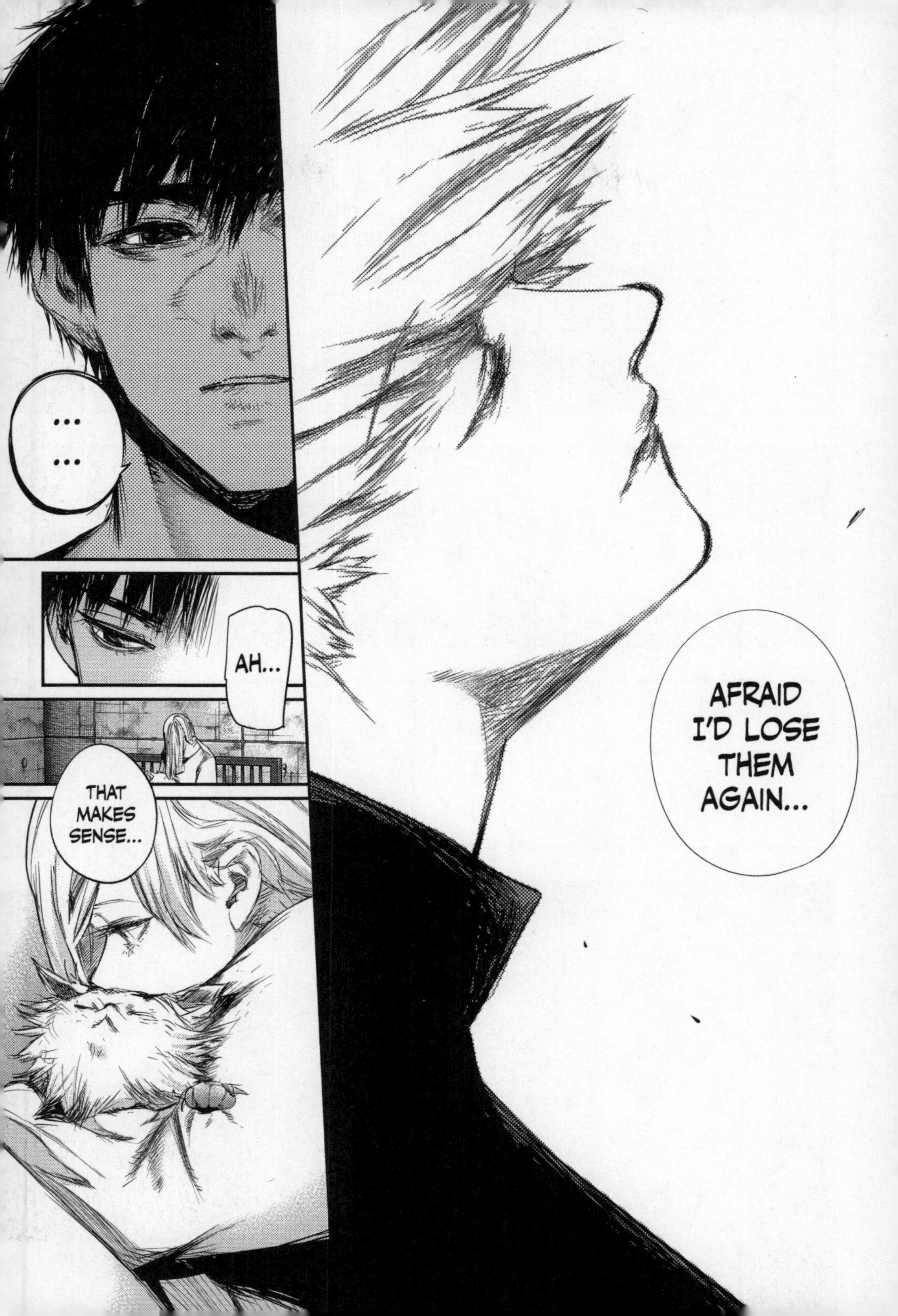
AFRAID I'D LOSE THEM AGAIN...
... ...
AH...
THAT MAKES SENSE...

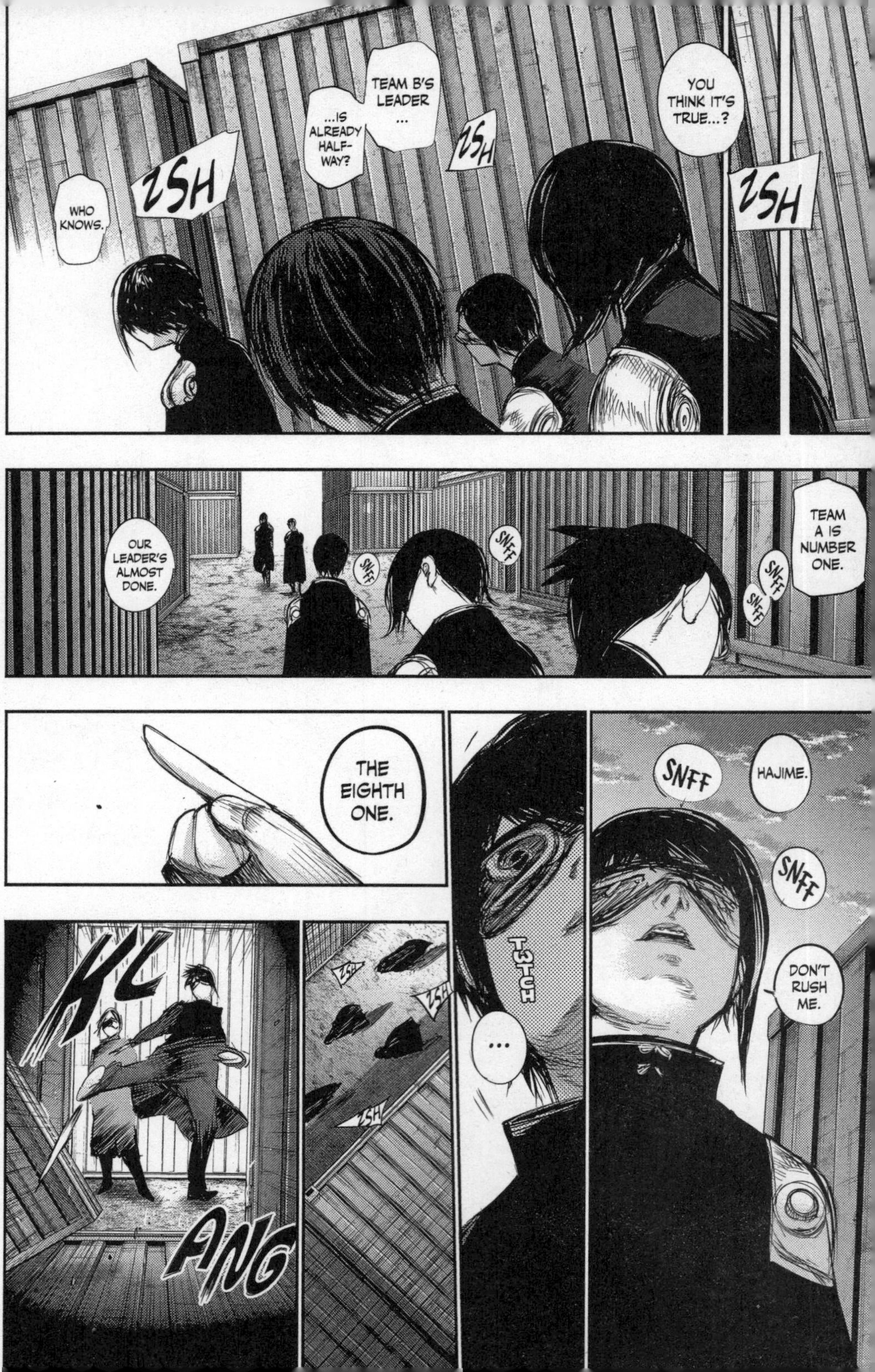
YOU THINK IT'S TRUE...?
ZSH
TEAM B'S LEADER ...
...IS ALREADY HALF-WAY?
ZSH
ZSH
WHO KNOWS.
TEAM A IS NUMBER ONE.
SNFF
SNFF
SNFF
OUR LEADER'S ALMOST DONE.
SNFF
HAJIME.
SNFF
DON'T RUSH ME.
TWTCH
...
THE EIGHTH ONE.
ZSH
ZSH
ZSH
KLANG

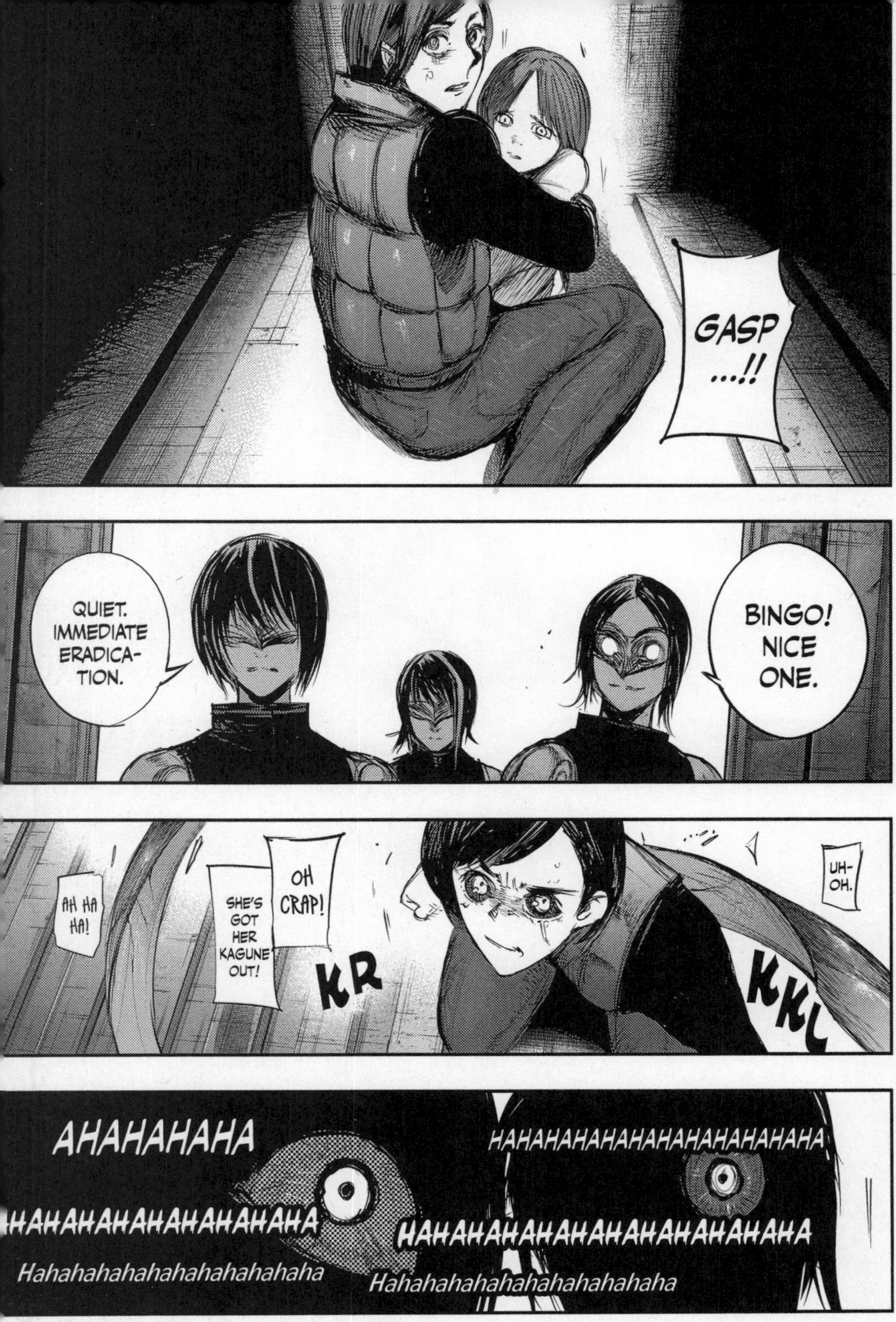
GASP ...!!
BINGO! NICE ONE.
QUIET. IMMEDIATE ERADICA-TION.
UH-OH.
KKL
OH CRAP!
SHE'S GOT HER KAGUNE OUT!
KR
AH HA HA!
HAHAHAHAHAHAHAHAHAHAHAHAHA
AHAHAHAHA
HAHAHAHAHAHAHAHAHAHAHAHAHA
HAHAHAHAHAHAHAHAHAHA
Hahahahahahahahahahahahaha
Hahahahahahahahahahahahaha

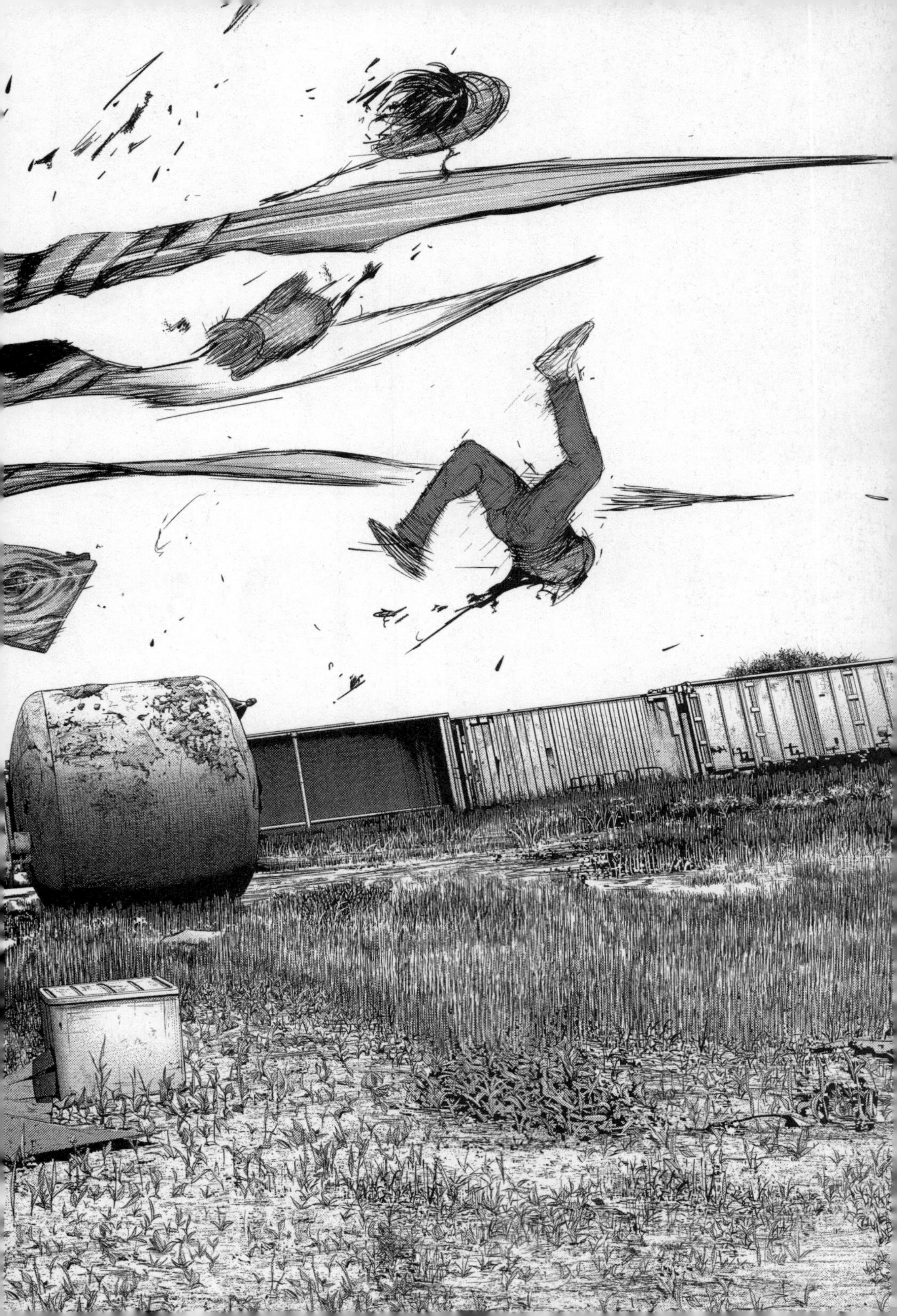

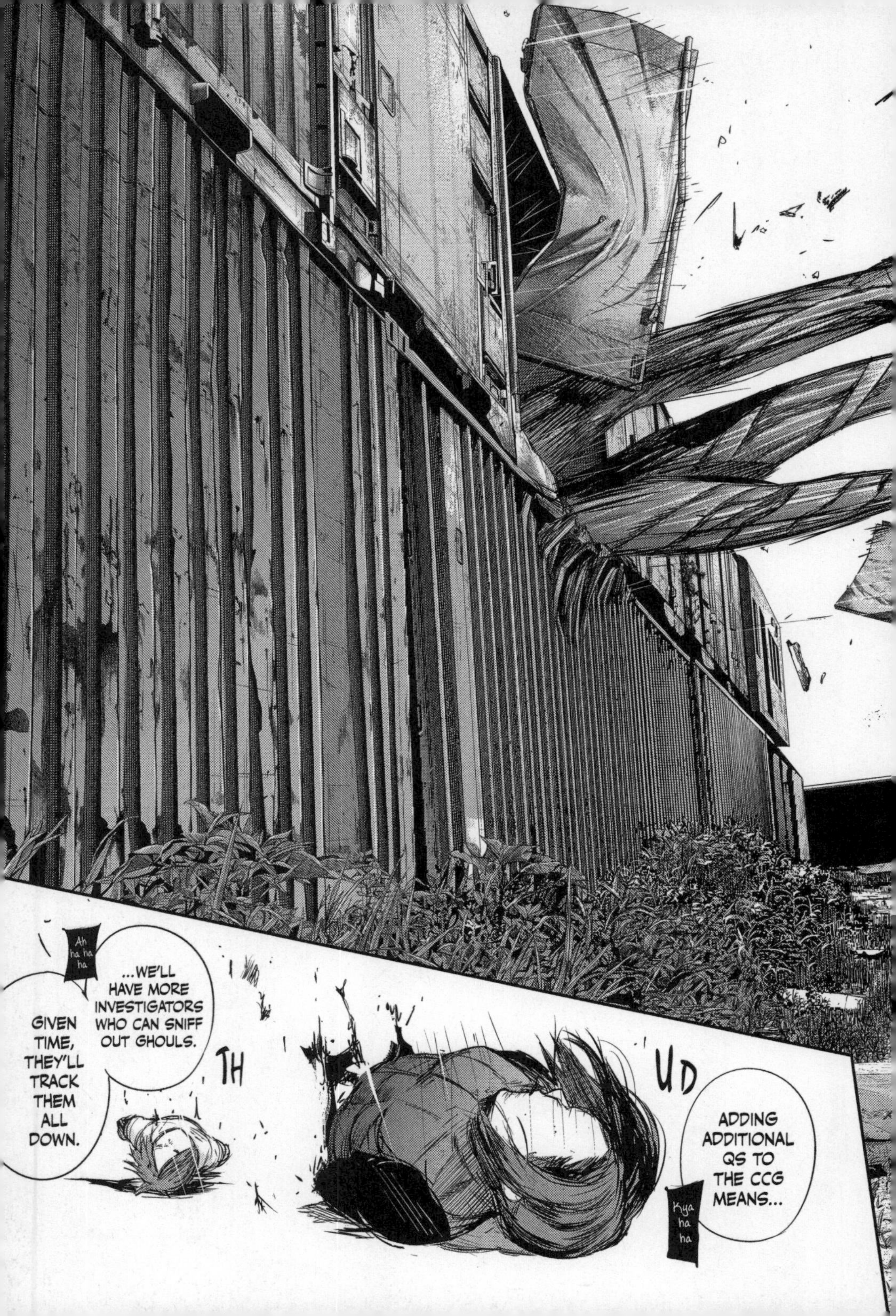
ADDING ADDITIONAL QS TO THE CCG MEANS...
Kya ha ha ha
TH UD
...WE'LL HAVE MORE INVESTIGATORS WHO CAN SNIFF OUT GHOULS.
Ah ha ha ha
GIVEN TIME, THEY'LL TRACK THEM ALL DOWN.

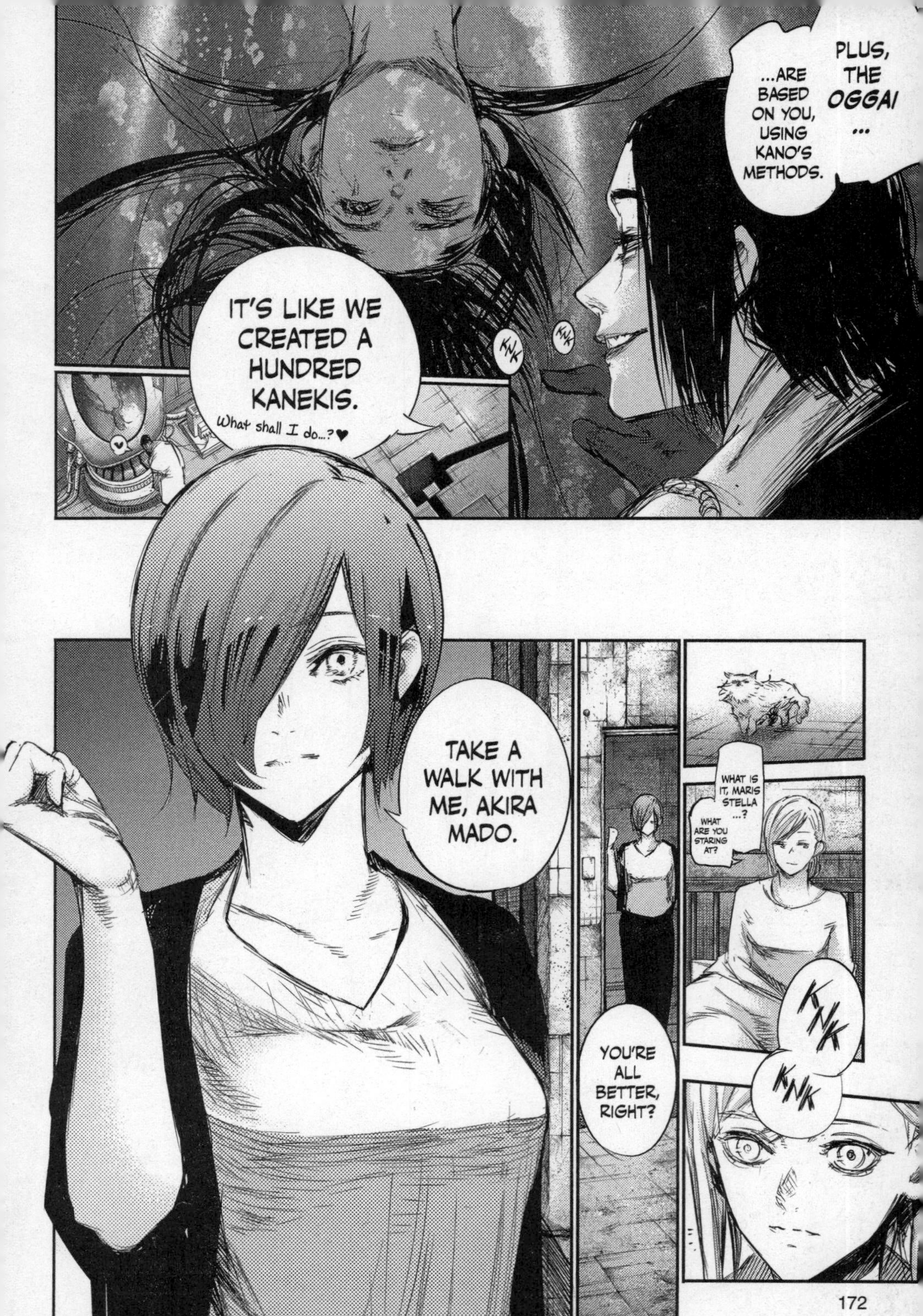
PLUS, THE OGGAI ...
...ARE BASED ON YOU, USING KANO'S METHODS.
KNK
KNK
IT'S LIKE WE CREATED A HUNDRED KANEKIS.
What shall I do...?♥
WHAT IS IT, MARIS STELLA ...?
WHAT ARE YOU STARING AT?
KNK
KNK
YOU'RE ALL BETTER, RIGHT?
TAKE A WALK WITH ME, AKIRA MADO.

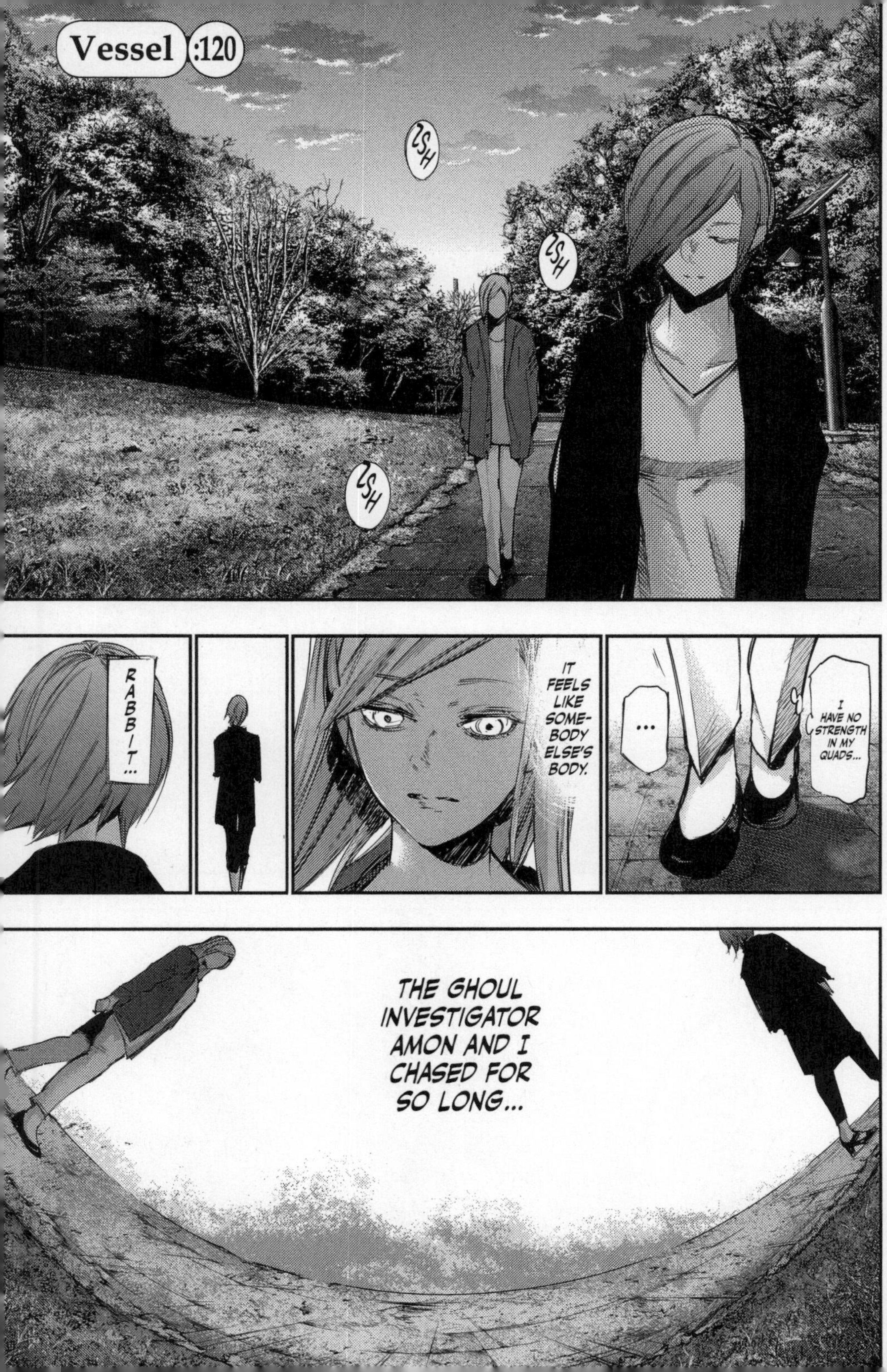
Vessel :120
ZSH
ZSH
ZSH
I HAVE NO STRENGTH IN MY QUADS...
...
IT FEELS LIKE SOMEBODY ELSE'S BODY.
RABBIT...
THE GHOUL INVESTIGATOR AMON AND I CHASED FOR SO LONG...

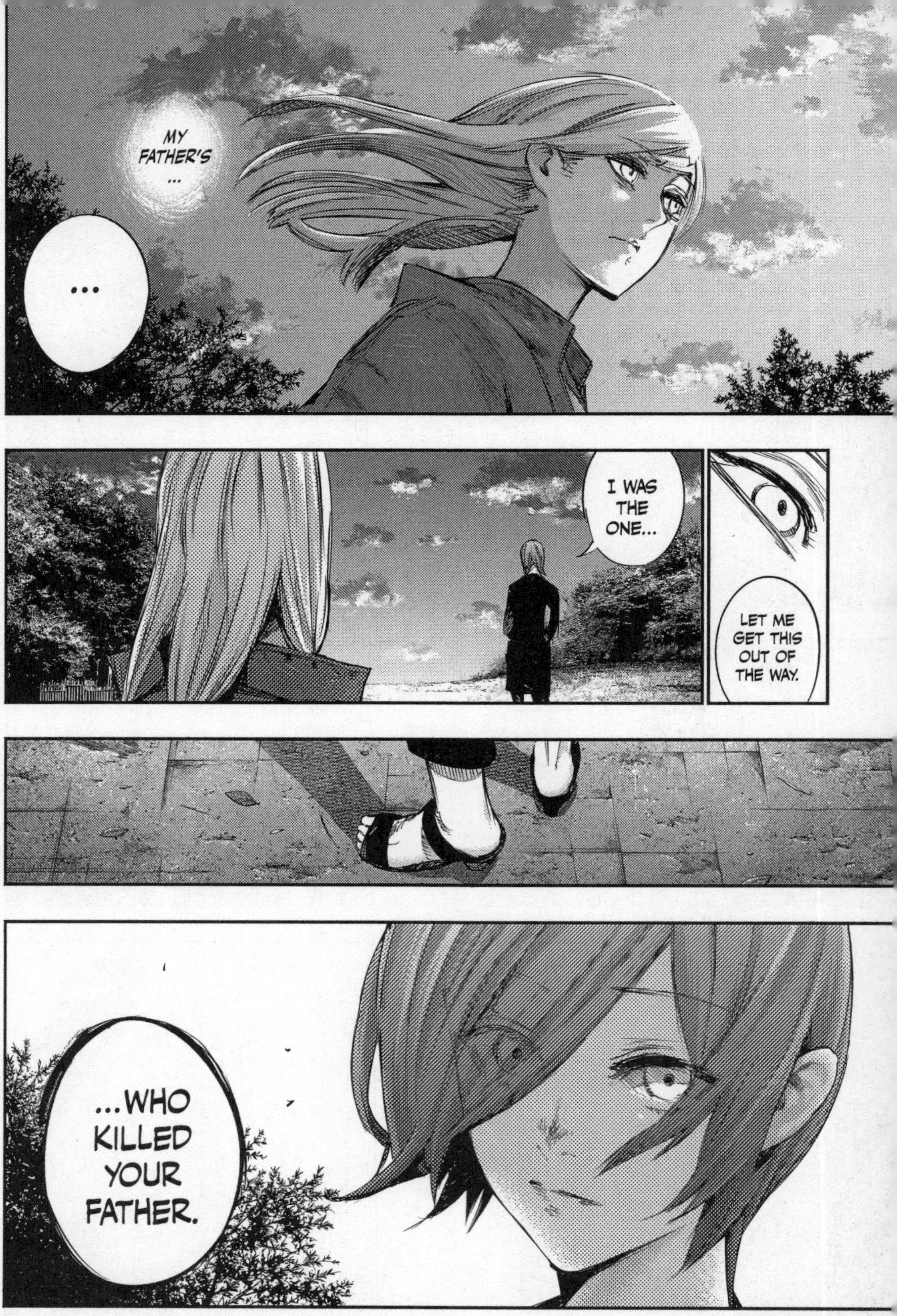
MY FATHER'S ...
...
LET ME GET THIS OUT OF THE WAY.
I WAS THE ONE...
...WHO KILLED YOUR FATHER.

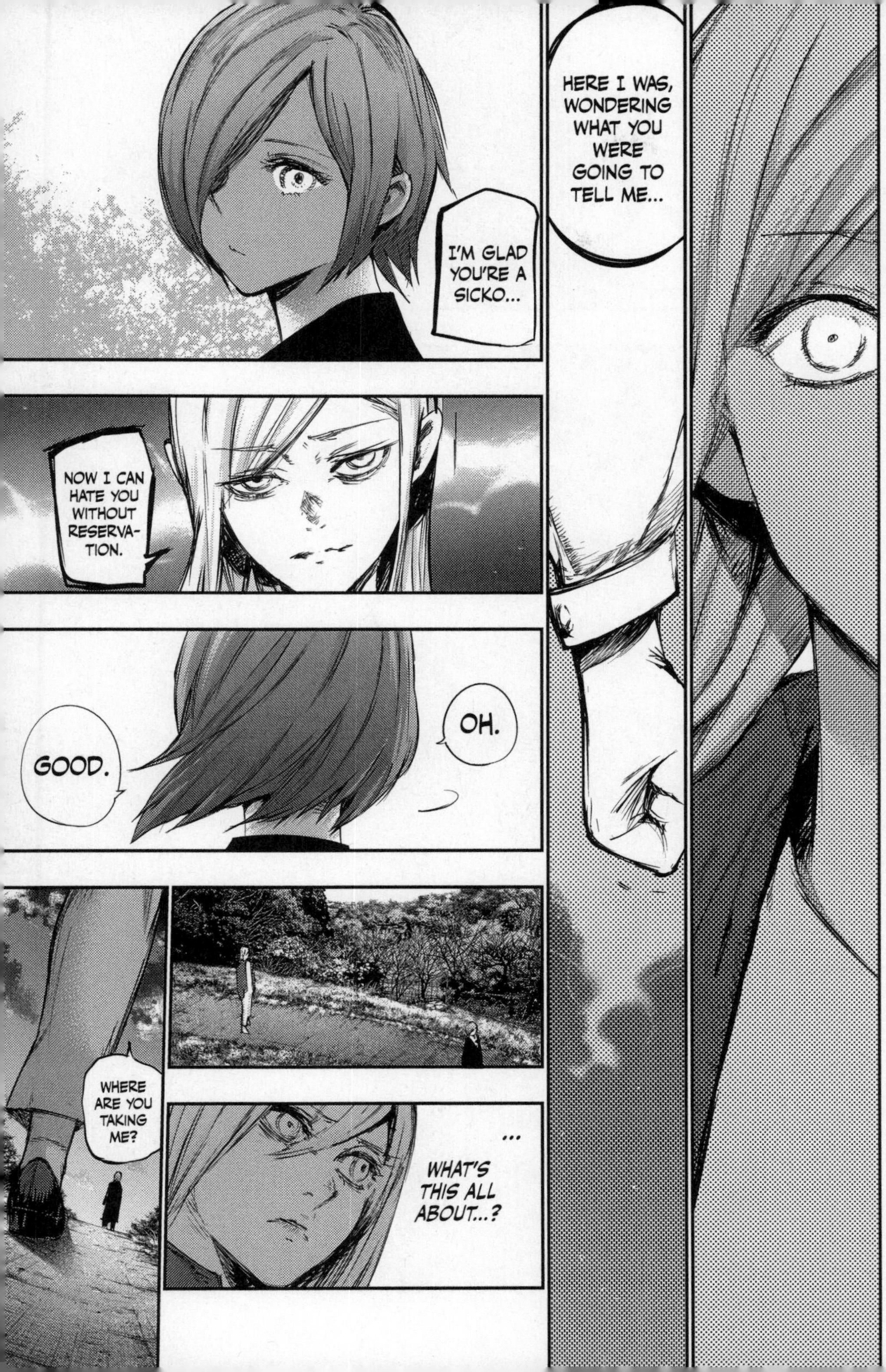
HERE I WAS, WONDERING WHAT YOU WERE GOING TO TELL ME...
I'M GLAD YOU'RE A SICKO...
NOW I CAN HATE YOU WITHOUT RESERVATION.
OH.
GOOD.
...
WHAT'S THIS ALL ABOUT...?
WHERE ARE YOU TAKING ME?

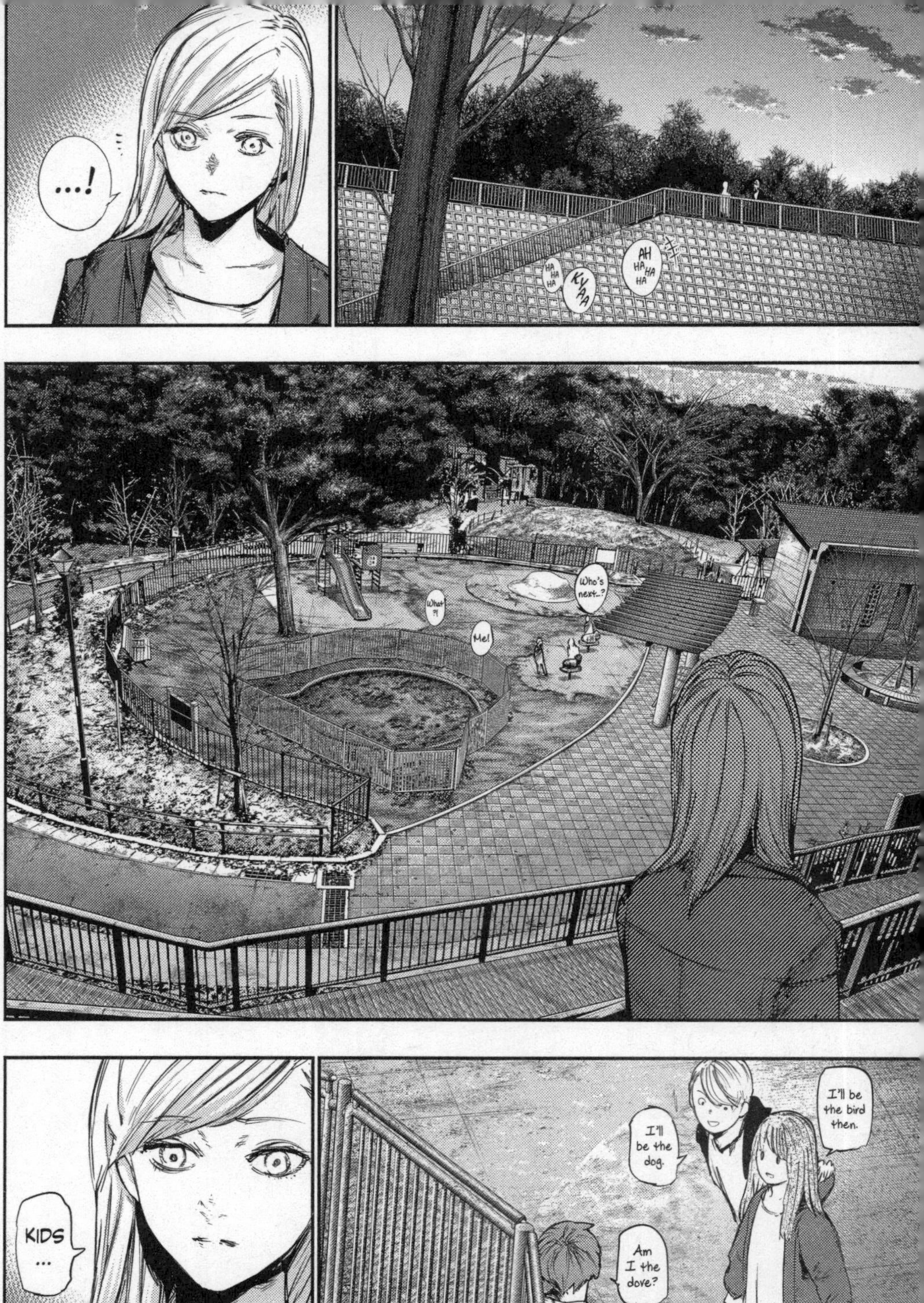
AH HA HA HA
KYAA
HA HA HA
...!
Who's next...?
Me!
What ?!
I'll be the bird then.
I'll be the dog.
Am I the dove?
KIDS ...

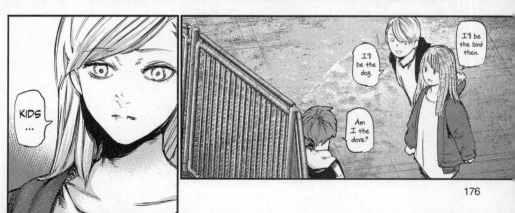

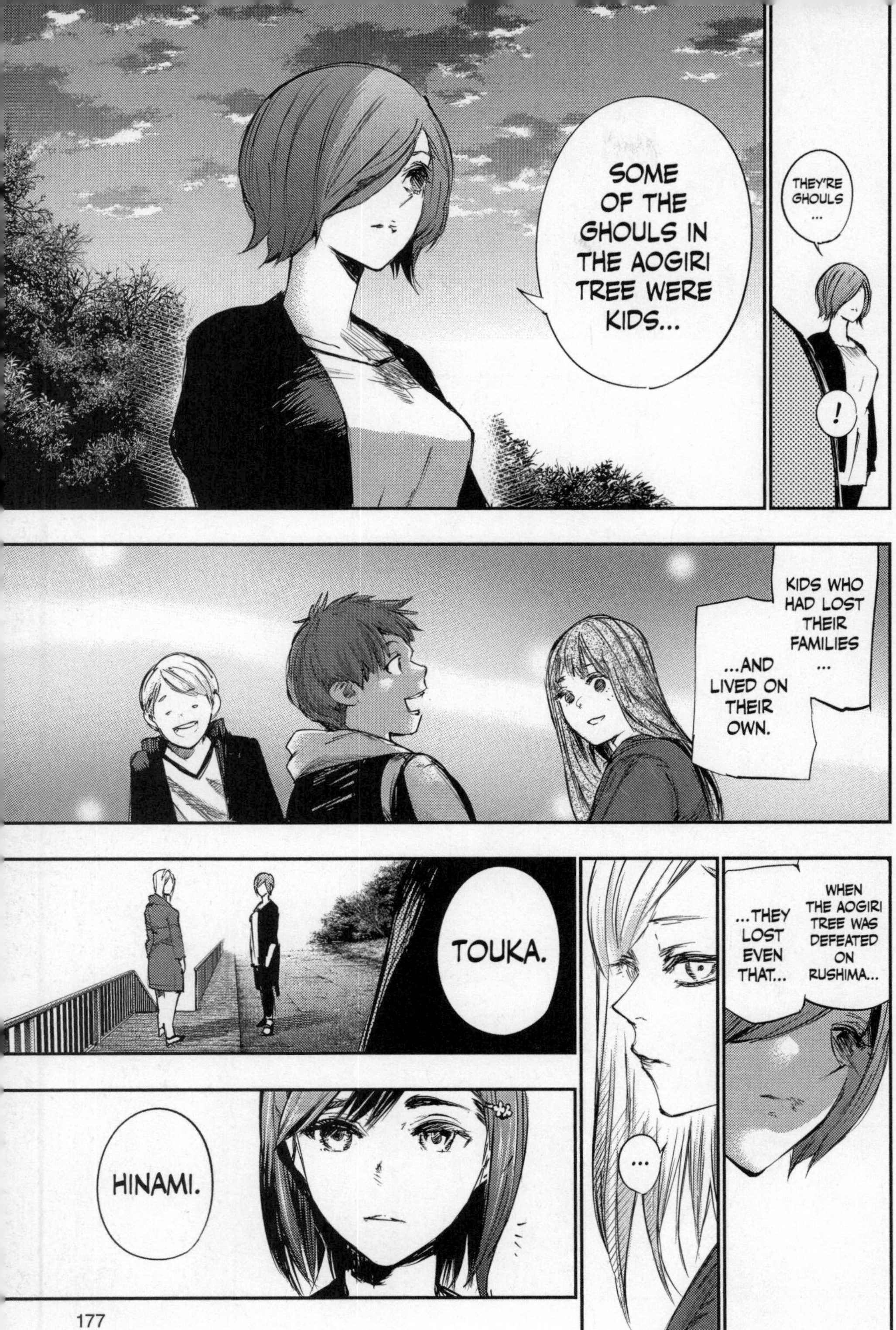
THEY'RE GHOULS ...
!
SOME OF THE GHOULS IN THE AOGIRI TREE WERE KIDS...
KIDS WHO HAD LOST THEIR FAMILIES ...
...AND LIVED ON THEIR OWN.
WHEN THE AOGIRI TREE WAS DEFEATED ON RUSHIMA...
...THEY LOST EVEN THAT...
...
TOUKA.
HINAMI.

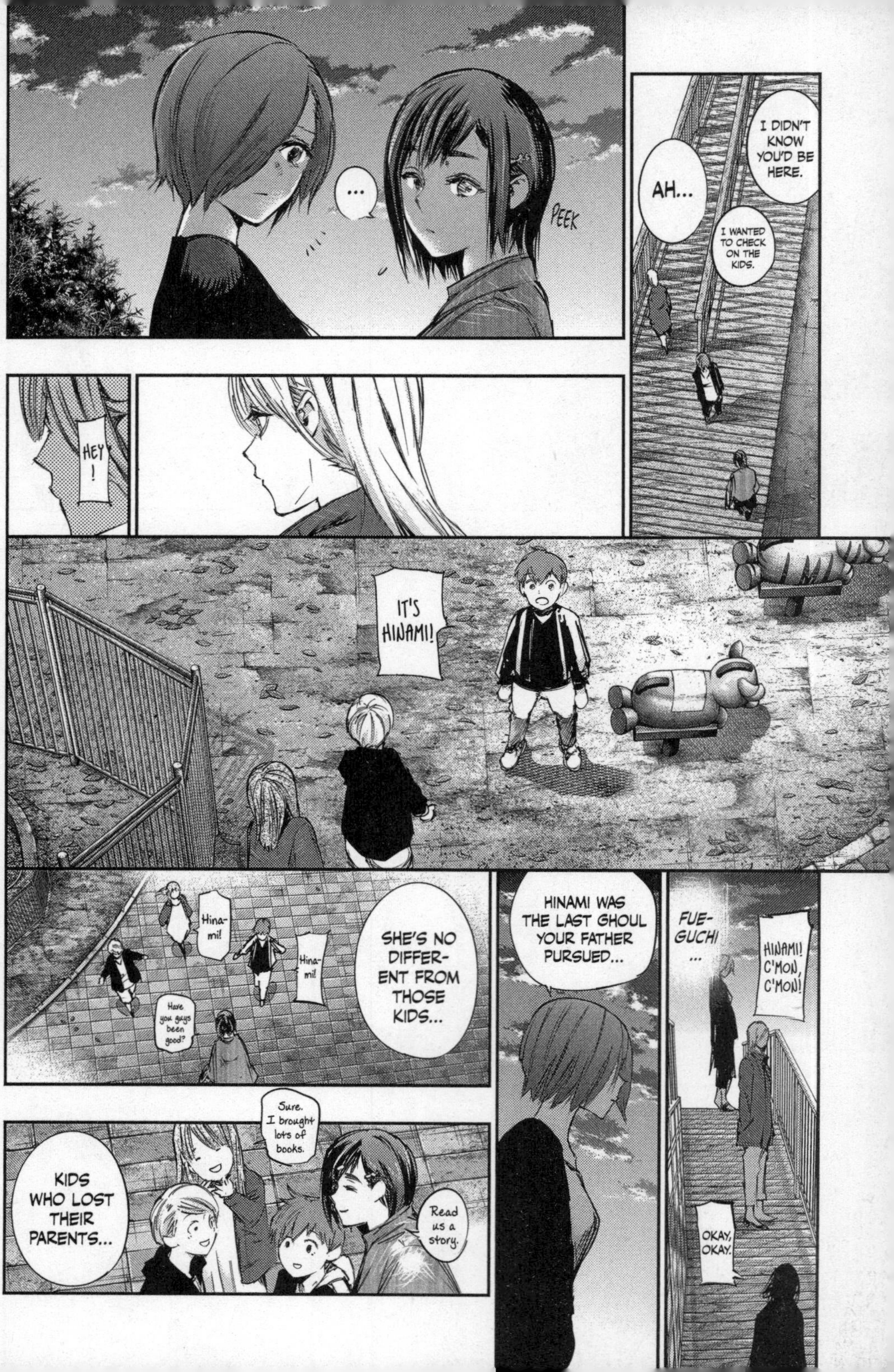
I DIDN'T KNOW YOU'D BE HERE.
AH...
I WANTED TO CHECK ON THE KIDS.
PEEK
...
HEY!
IT'S HINAMI!
HINAMI! C'MON, C'MON!
FUEGUCHI...
OKAY, OKAY.
HINAMI WAS THE LAST GHOUL YOUR FATHER PURSUED...
SHE'S NO DIFFERENT FROM THOSE KIDS...
Hina-mi!
Hina-mi!
Have you guys been good?
Sure. I brought lots of books.
Read us a story.
KIDS WHO LOST THEIR PARENTS...

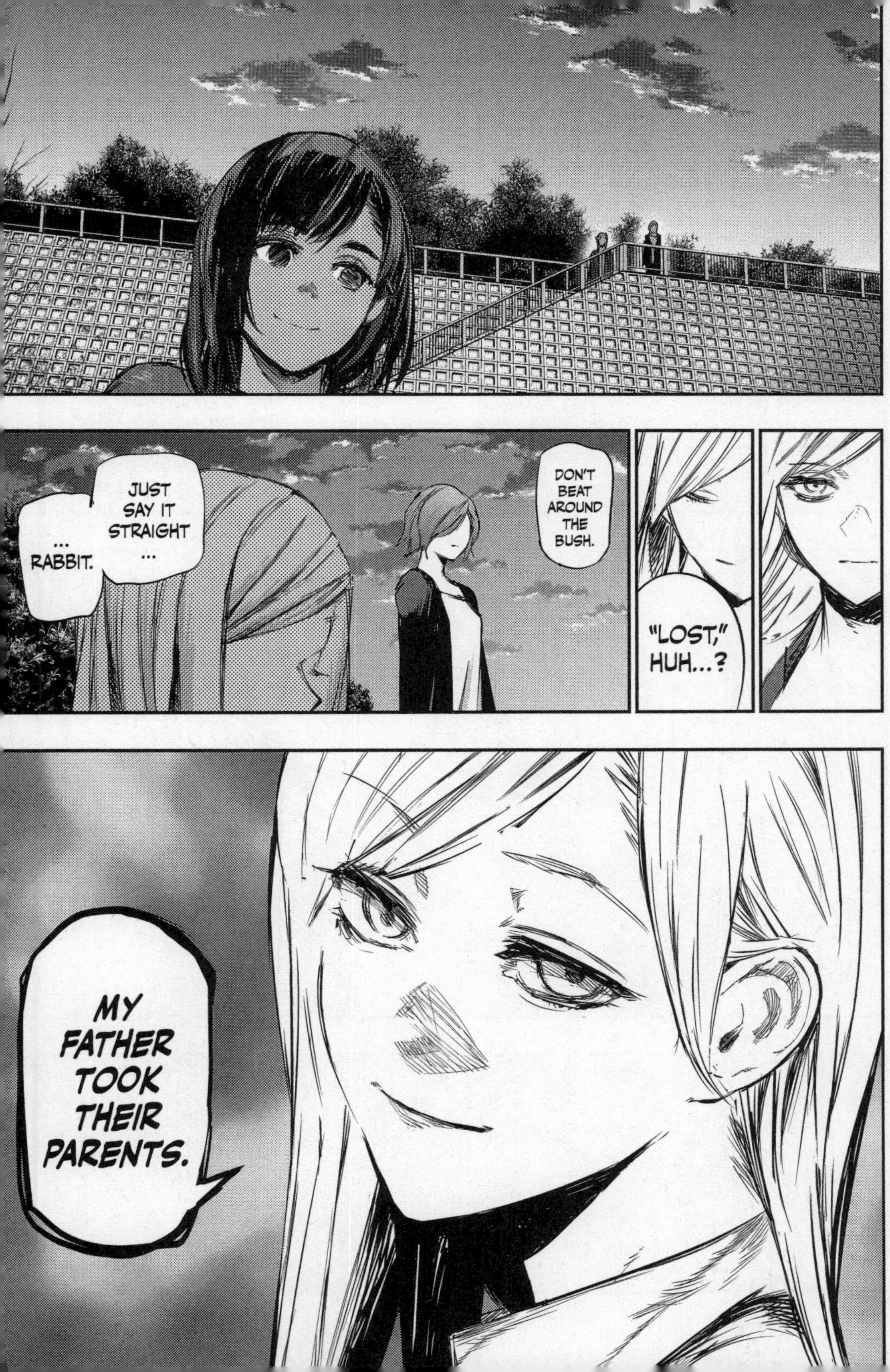
"LOST," HUH...?
DON'T BEAT AROUND THE BUSH.
JUST SAY IT STRAIGHT...
...RABBIT.
MY FATHER TOOK THEIR PARENTS.

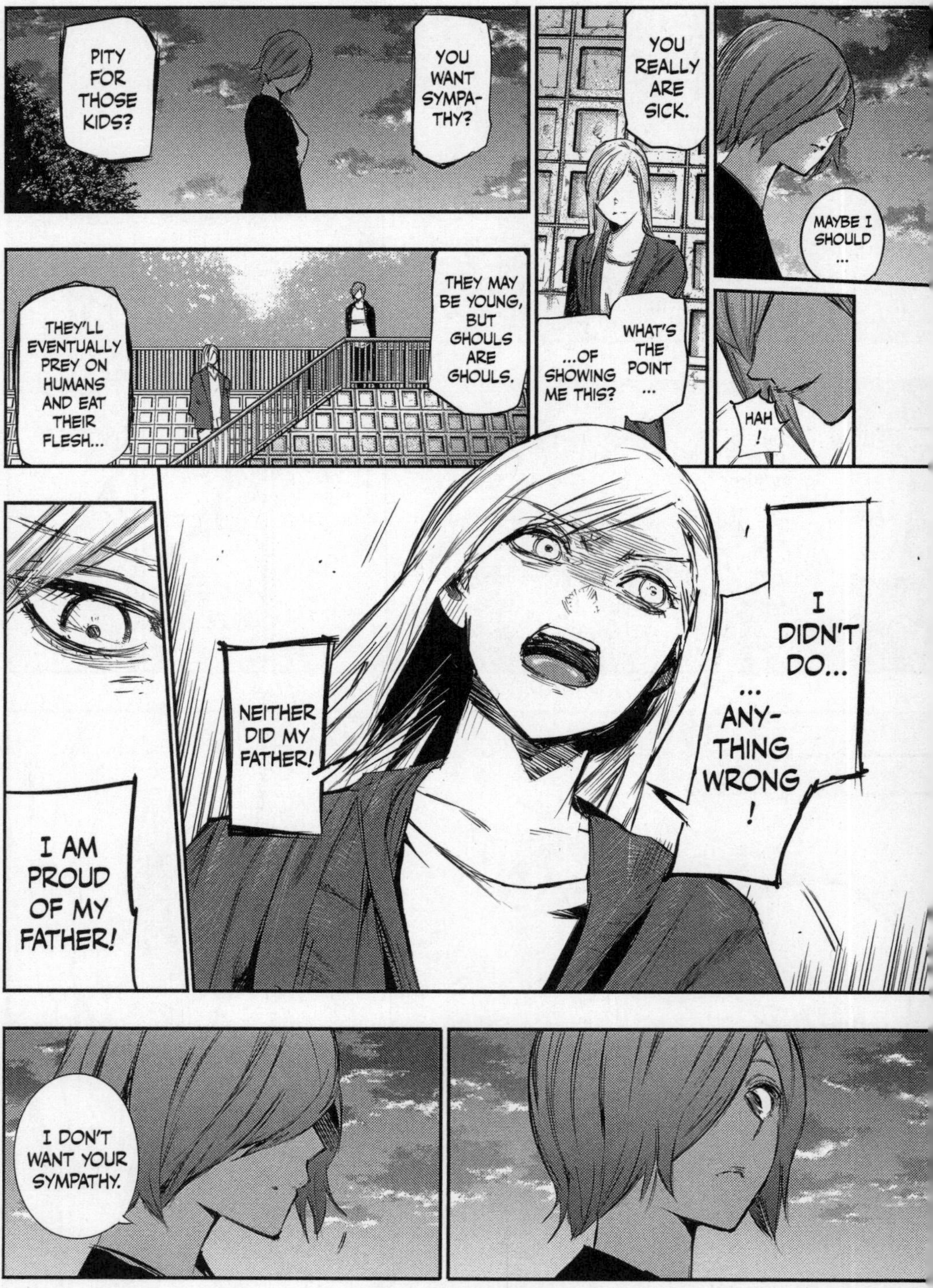

MAYBE I SHOULD ...
YOU REALLY ARE SICK.
WHAT'S THE POINT ...
...OF SHOWING ME THIS?
YOU WANT SYMPA-THY?
PITY FOR THOSE KIDS?
THEY MAY BE YOUNG, BUT GHOULS ARE GHOULS.
THEY'LL EVENTUALLY PREY ON HUMANS AND EAT THEIR FLESH...
HAH!
I DIDN'T DO...
... ANY-THING WRONG!
NEITHER DID MY FATHER!
I AM PROUD OF MY FATHER!
I DON'T WANT YOUR SYMPATHY.

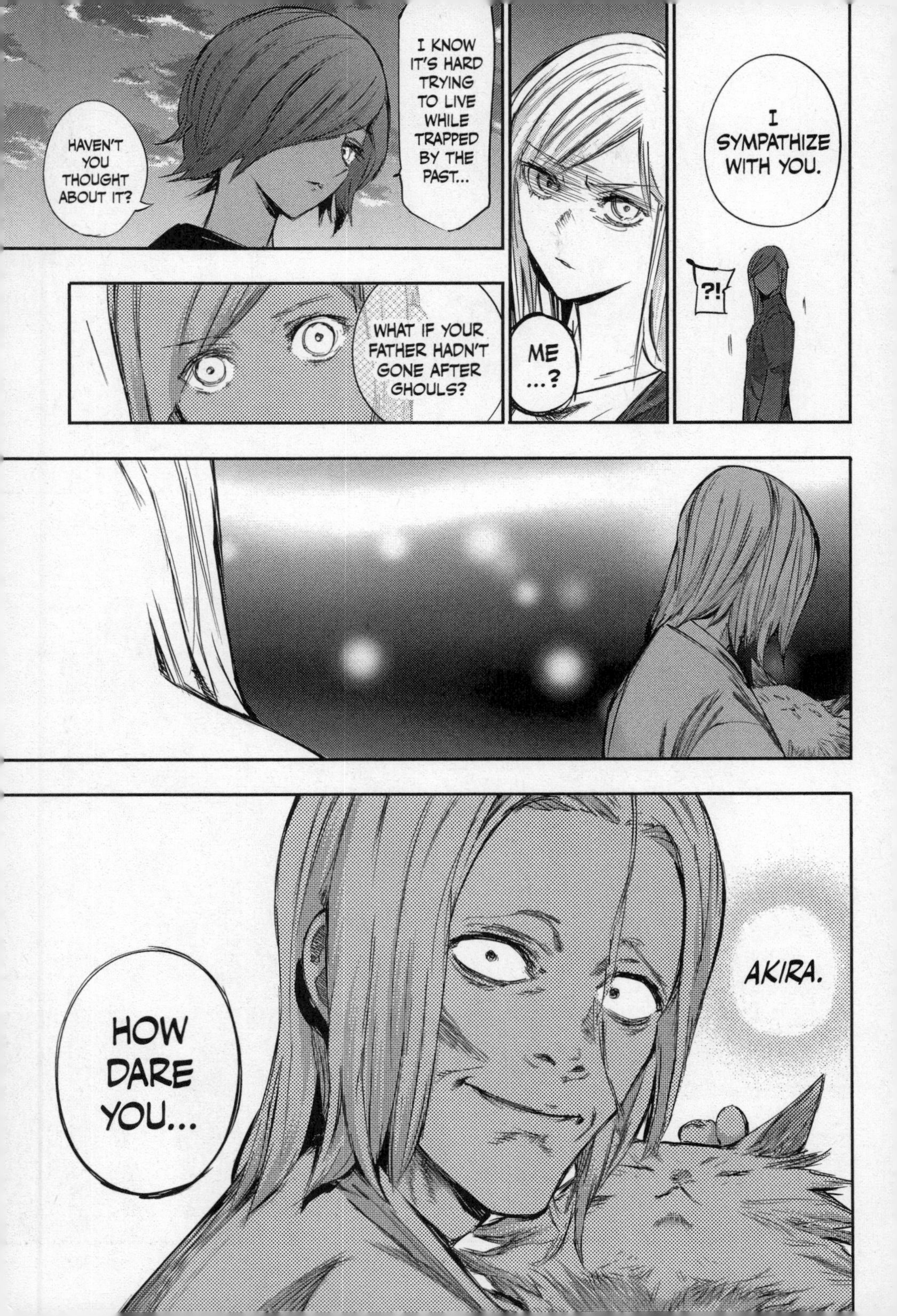
I SYMPATHIZE WITH YOU.
?!
ME ...?
I KNOW IT'S HARD TRYING TO LIVE WHILE TRAPPED BY THE PAST...
HAVEN'T YOU THOUGHT ABOUT IT?
WHAT IF YOUR FATHER HADN'T GONE AFTER GHOULS?
AKIRA.
HOW DARE YOU...

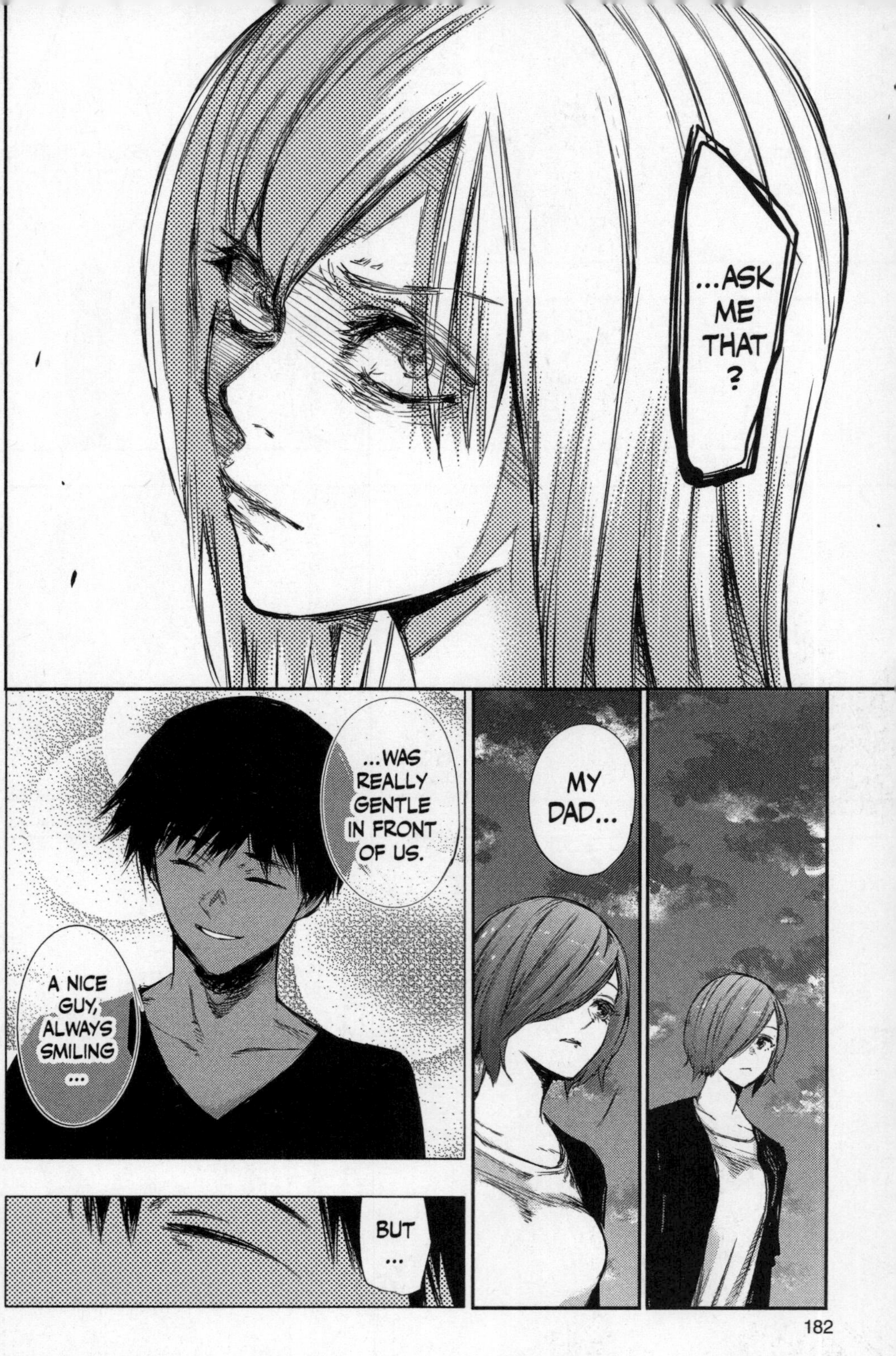
...ASK ME THAT?
MY DAD...
...WAS REALLY GENTLE IN FRONT OF US.
A NICE GUY, ALWAYS SMILING...
BUT...

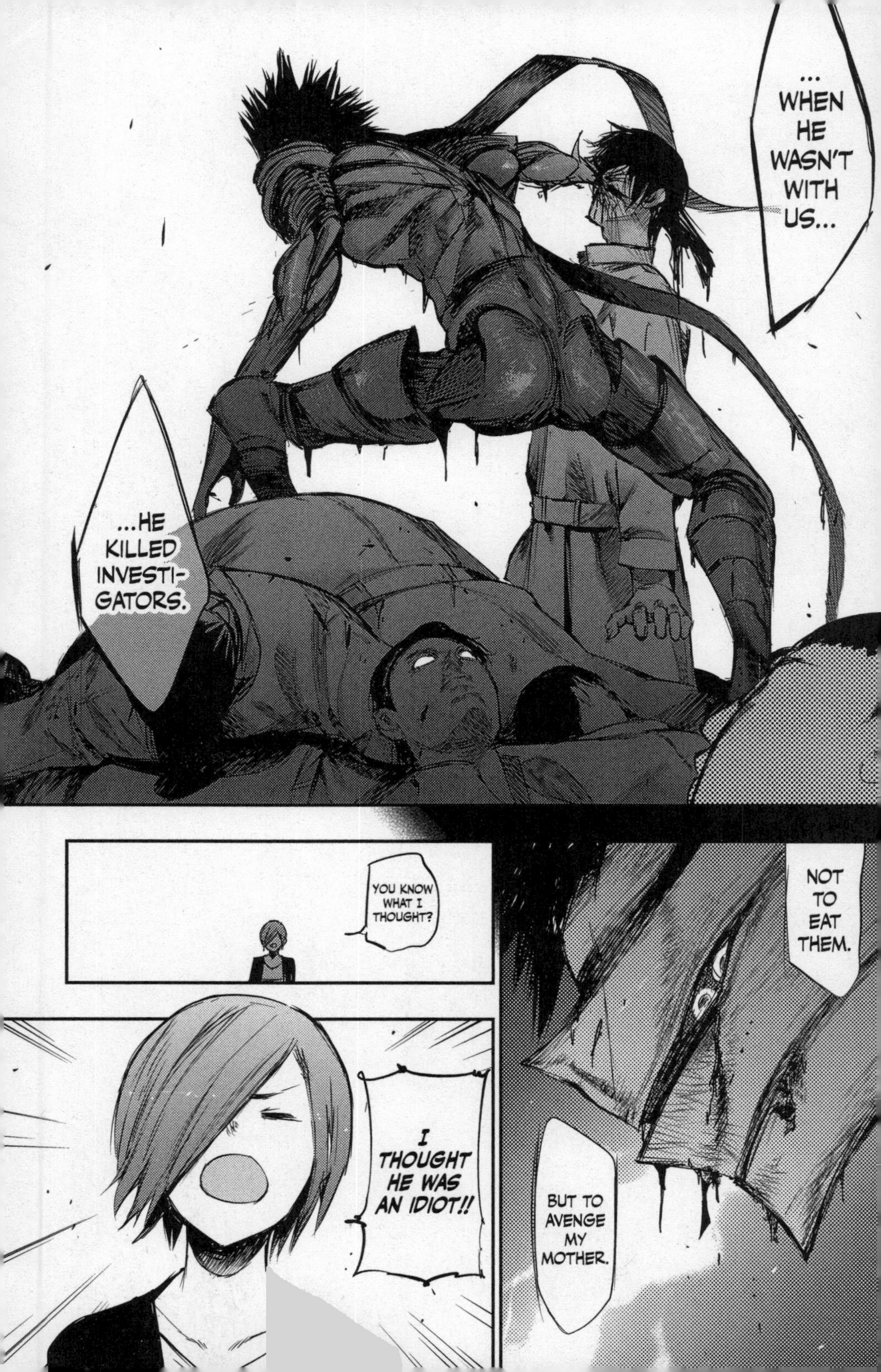
...WHEN HE WASN'T WITH US...
...HE KILLED INVESTI-GATORS.
NOT TO EAT THEM.
BUT TO AVENGE MY MOTHER.
YOU KNOW WHAT I THOUGHT?
I THOUGHT HE WAS AN IDIOT!!

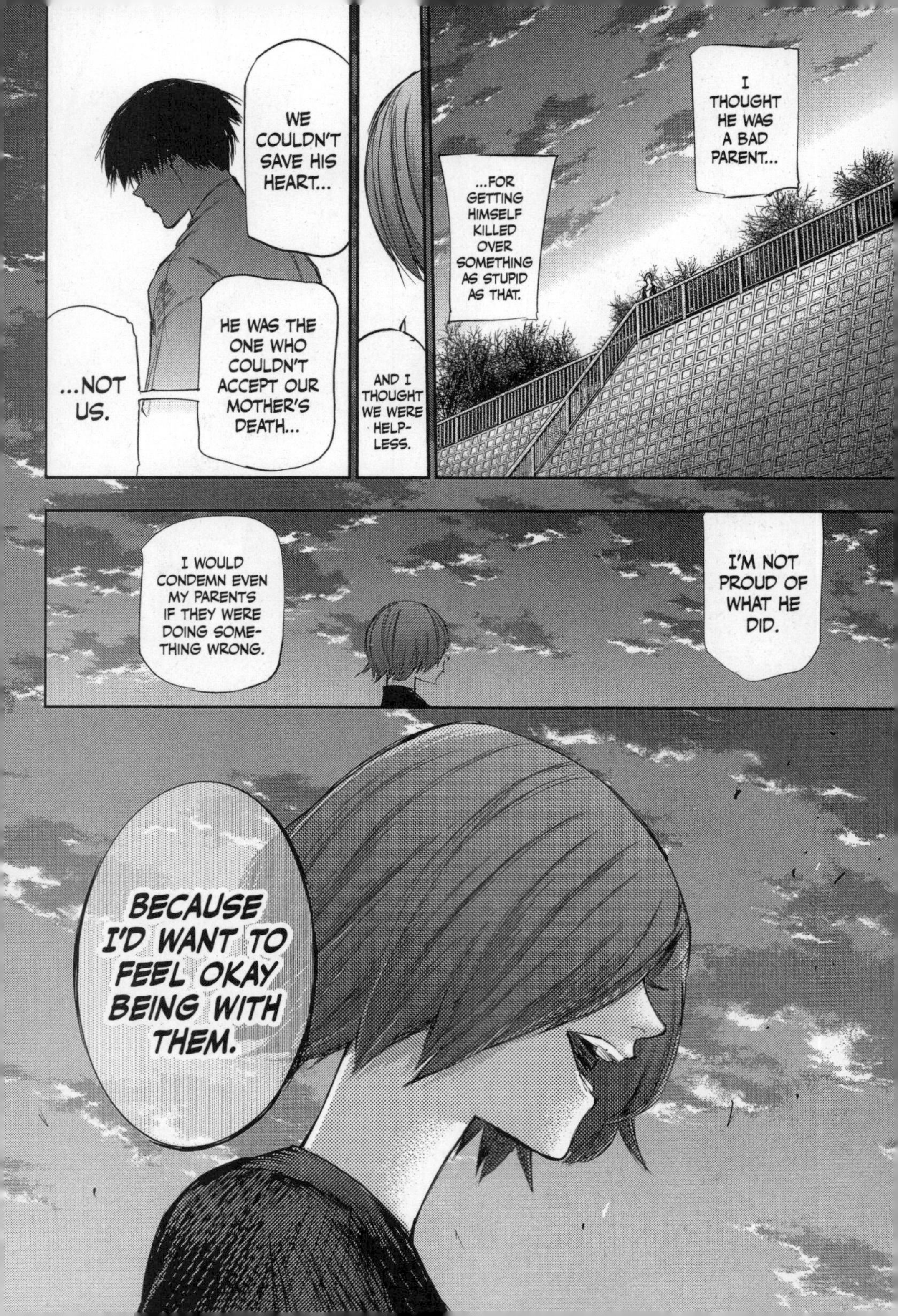
I THOUGHT HE WAS A BAD PARENT...
...FOR GETTING HIMSELF KILLED OVER SOMETHING AS STUPID AS THAT.
AND I THOUGHT WE WERE HELPLESS.
WE COULDN'T SAVE HIS HEART...
HE WAS THE ONE WHO COULDN'T ACCEPT OUR MOTHER'S DEATH...
...NOT US.
I'M NOT PROUD OF WHAT HE DID.
I WOULD CONDEMN EVEN MY PARENTS IF THEY WERE DOING SOMETHING WRONG.
BECAUSE I'D WANT TO FEEL OKAY BEING WITH THEM.

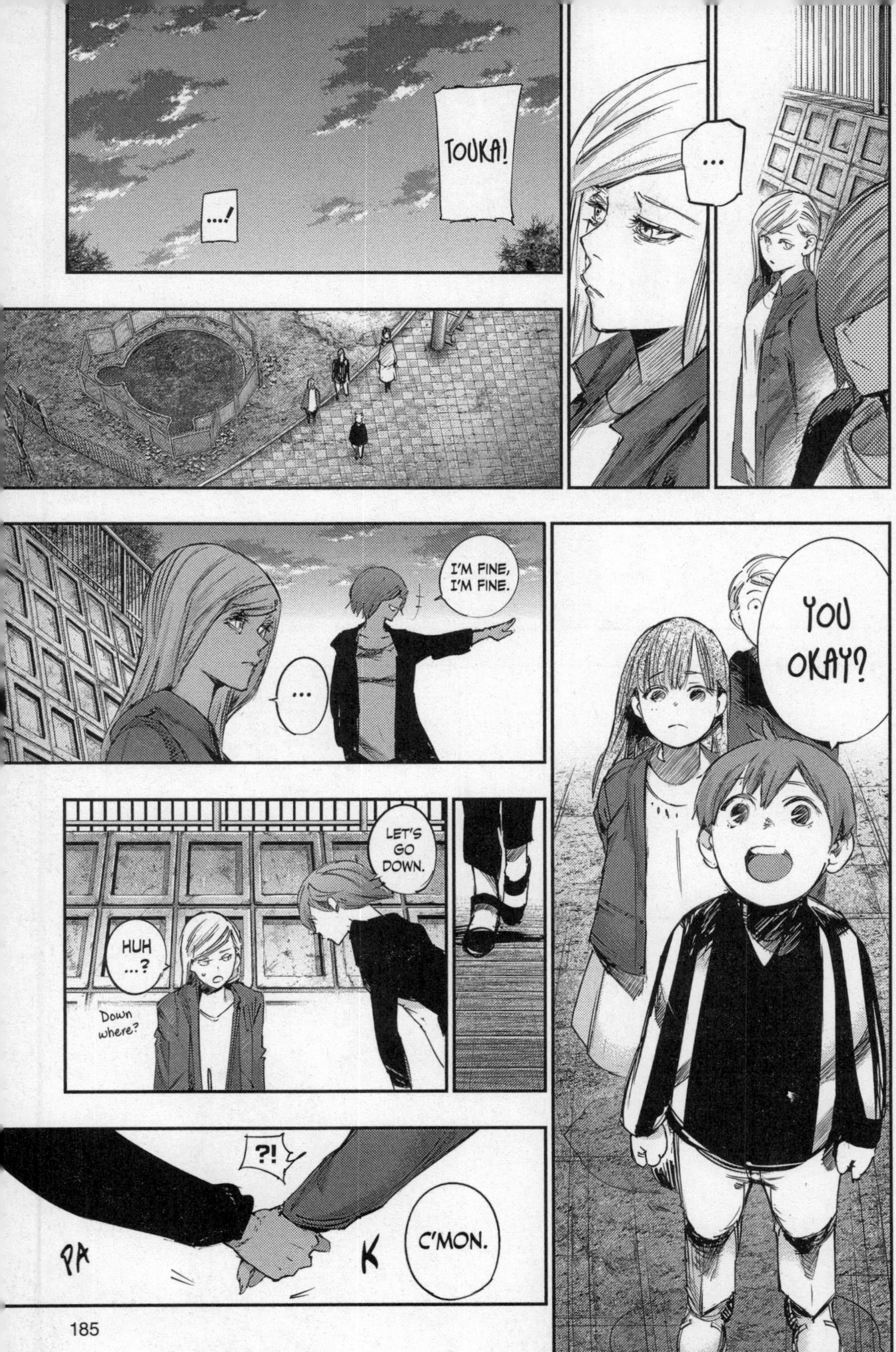
...
TOUKA!
...!
YOU OKAY?
I'M FINE, I'M FINE.
...
LET'S GO DOWN.
HUH ...?
Down where?
?!
C'MON.
PA
K

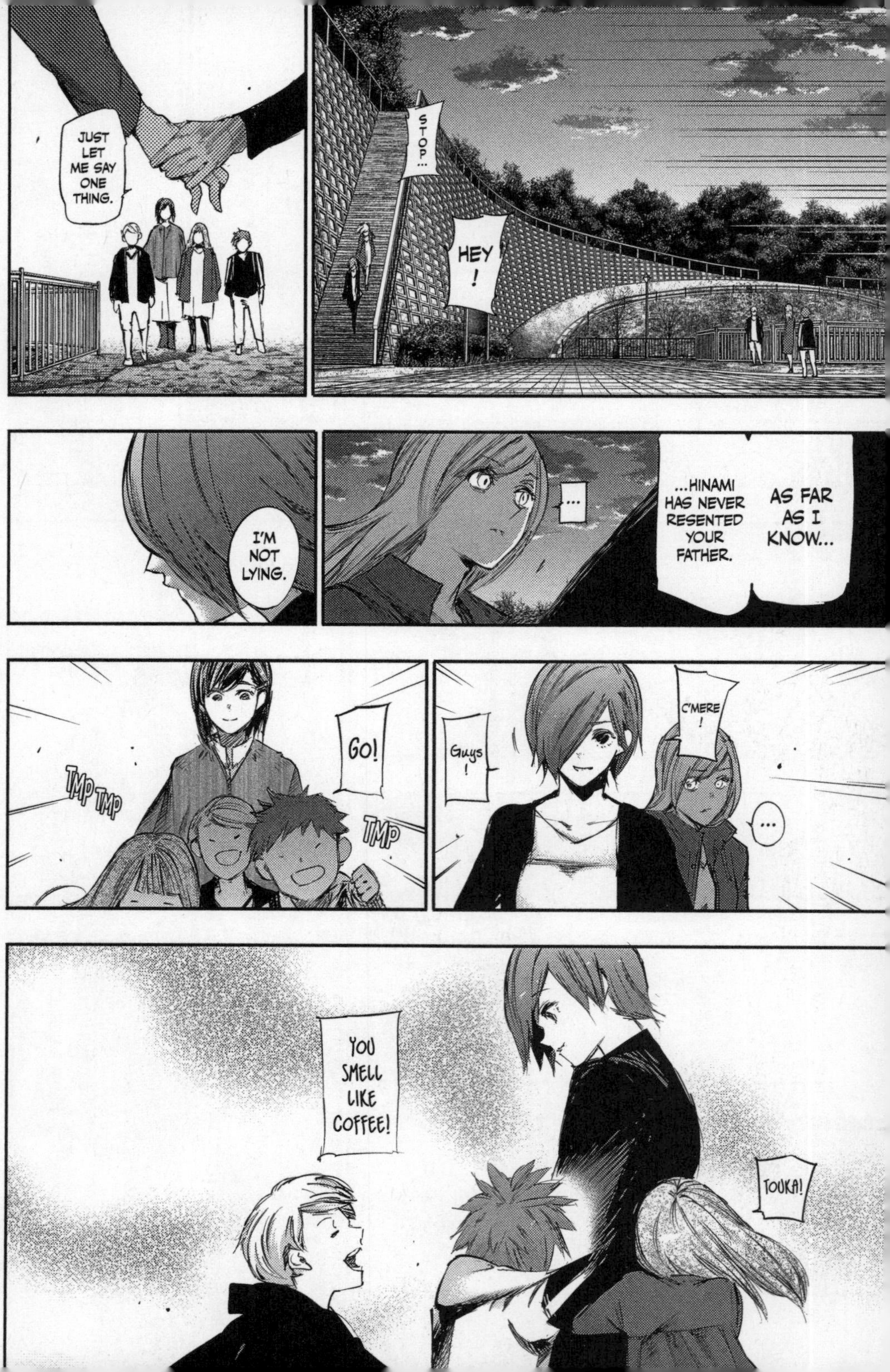
STOP...
HEY!
JUST LET ME SAY ONE THING.
AS FAR AS I KNOW...
...HINAMI HAS NEVER RESENTED YOUR FATHER.
...
I'M NOT LYING.
C'MERE!
Guys!
...
GO!
TMP TMP
TMP
TOUKA!
YOU SMELL LIKE COFFEE!

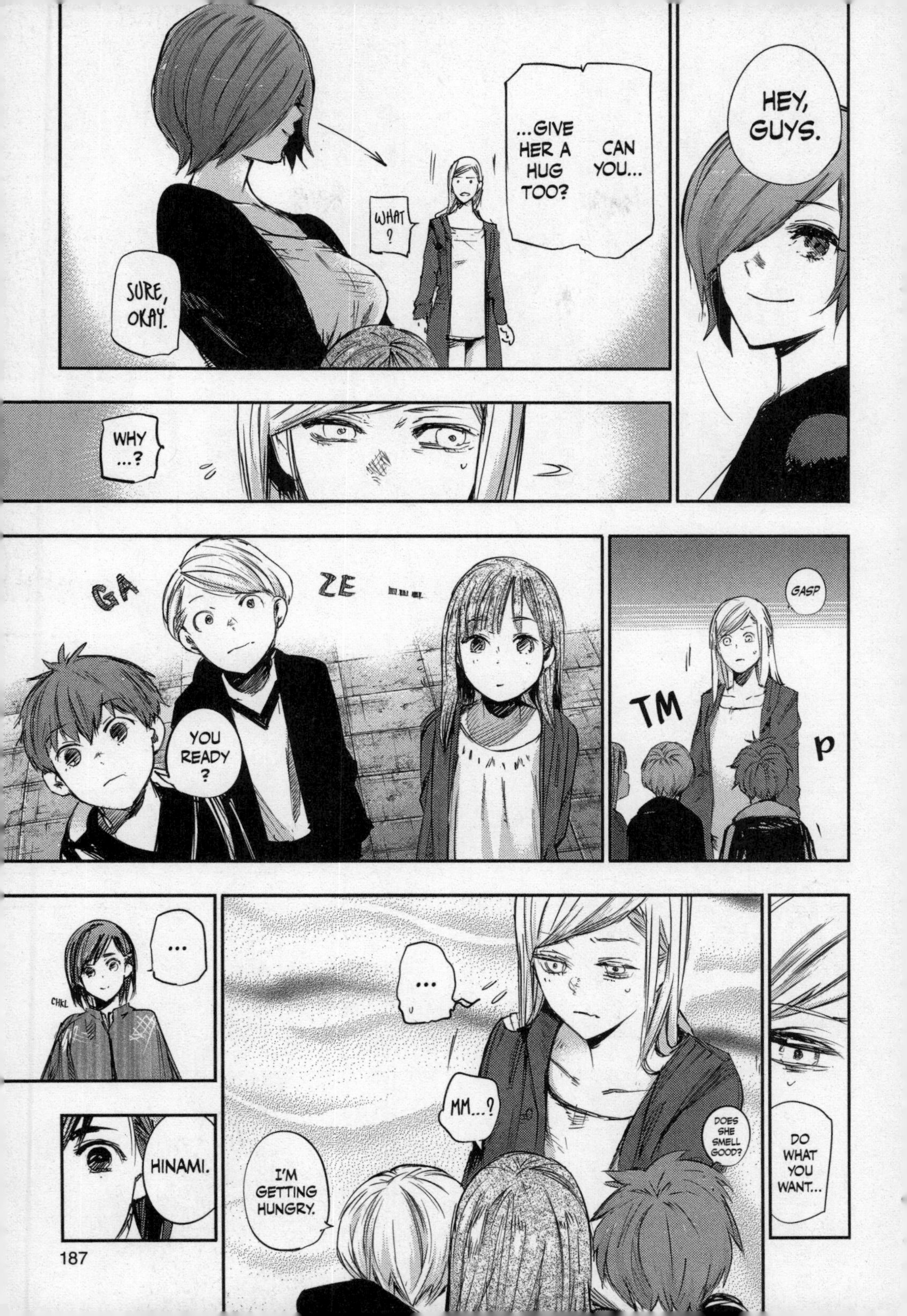
HEY, GUYS.
CAN YOU...
...GIVE HER A HUG TOO?
WHAT?
SURE, OKAY.
WHY...?
GASP
TMP
GA ZE
YOU READY?
DO WHAT YOU WANT...
...
MM...?
DOES SHE SMELL GOOD?
I'M GETTING HUNGRY.
...
CHKL
HINAMI.

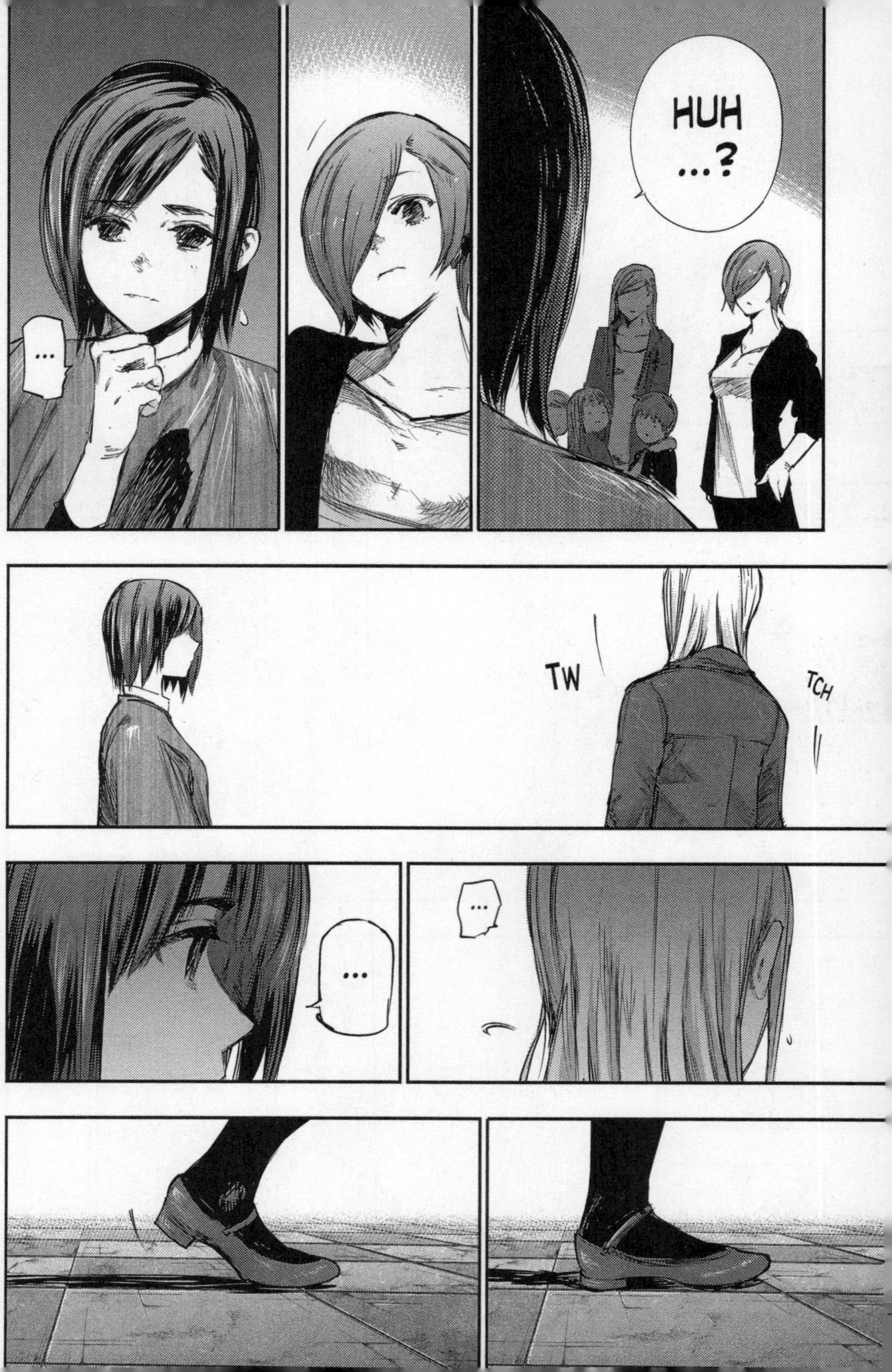
HUH ...?
...
TWTCH
...
...

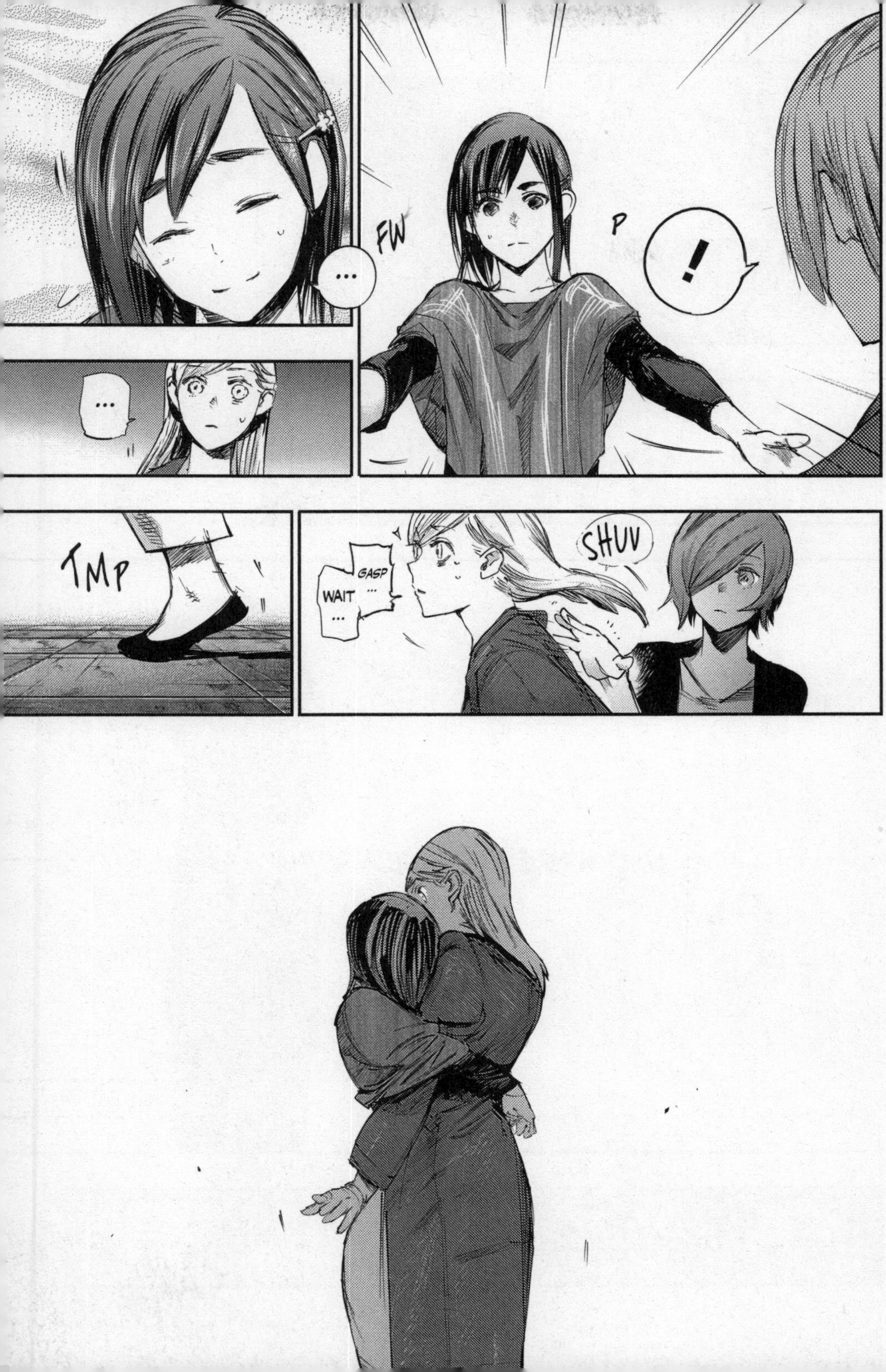
P
!
FW
...
...
SHUV
GASP ...
WAIT ...
TMP

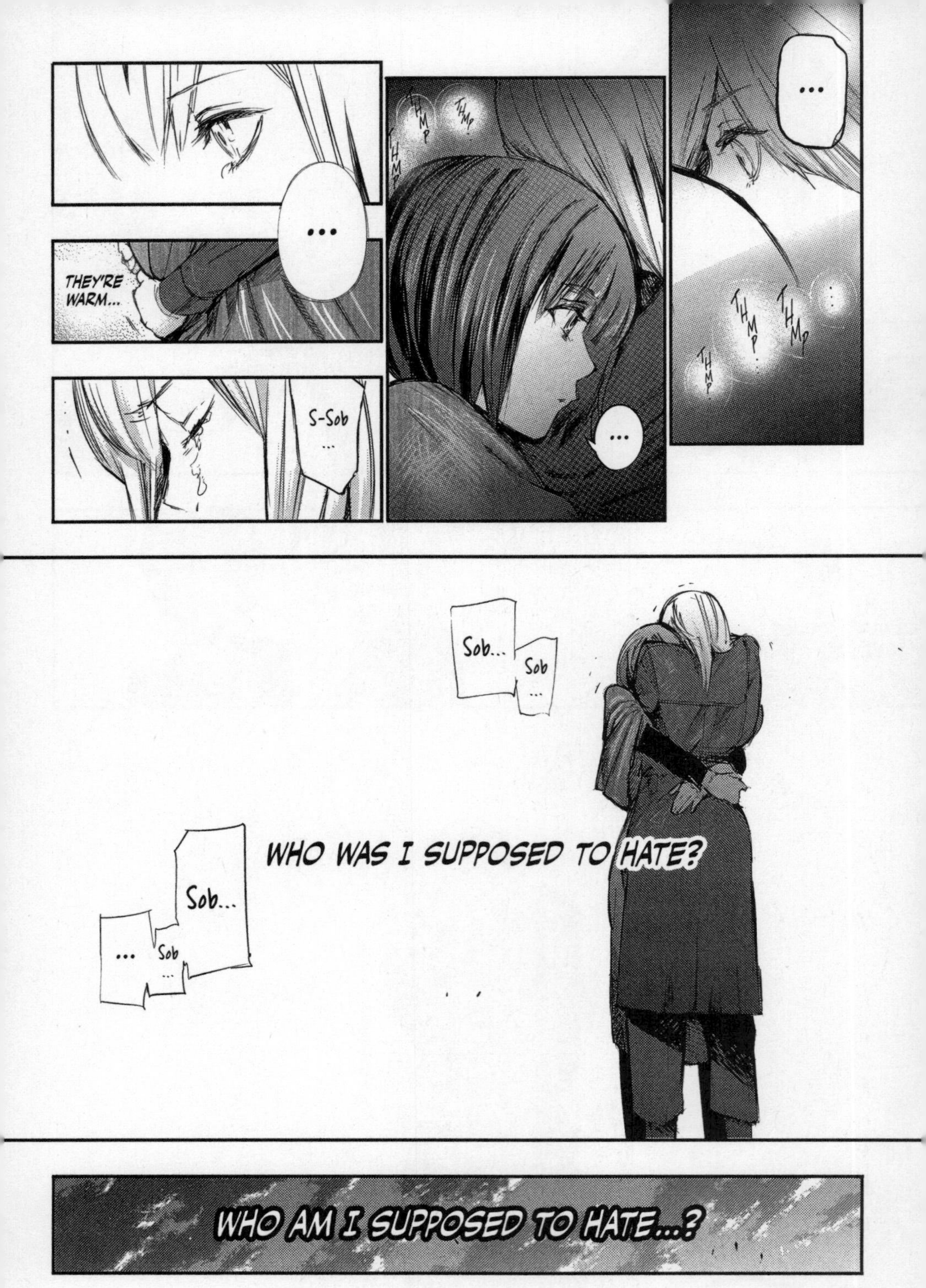
...
THMP
THMP
THMP
THMP
THMP
THMP
...
...
THEY'RE WARM...
S-Sob ...
Sob...
Sob ...
WHO WAS I SUPPOSED TO HATE?
Sob...
... Sob ...
WHO AM I SUPPOSED TO HATE...?

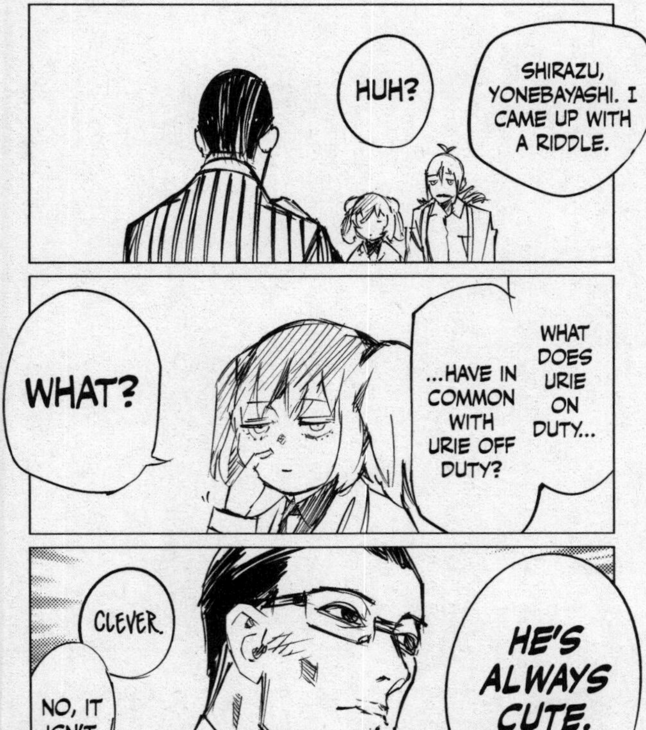
SHIRAZU, YONEBAYASHI. I CAME UP WITH A RIDDLE.
HUH?
WHAT DOES URIE ON DUTY...
...HAVE IN COMMON WITH URIE OFF DUTY?
WHAT?
HE'S ALWAYS CUTE.
CLEVER.
NO, IT ISN'T.

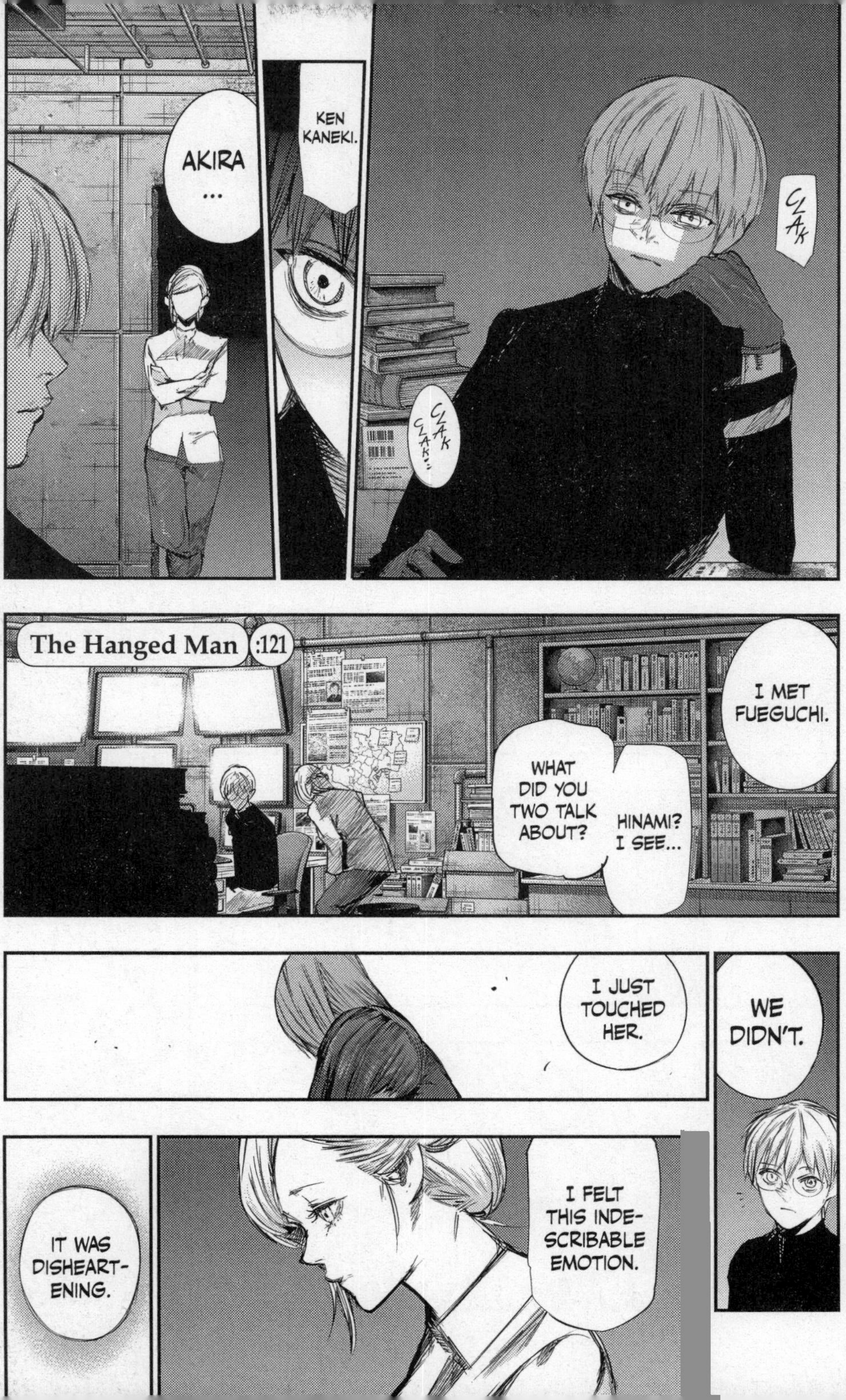
CLAK
CLAK CLAK...
KEN KANEKI.
AKIRA ...
The Hanged Man :121
I MET FUEGUCHI.
HINAMI? I SEE...
WHAT DID YOU TWO TALK ABOUT?
WE DIDN'T.
I JUST TOUCHED HER.
I FELT THIS INDE-SCRIBABLE EMOTION.
IT WAS DISHEART-ENING.

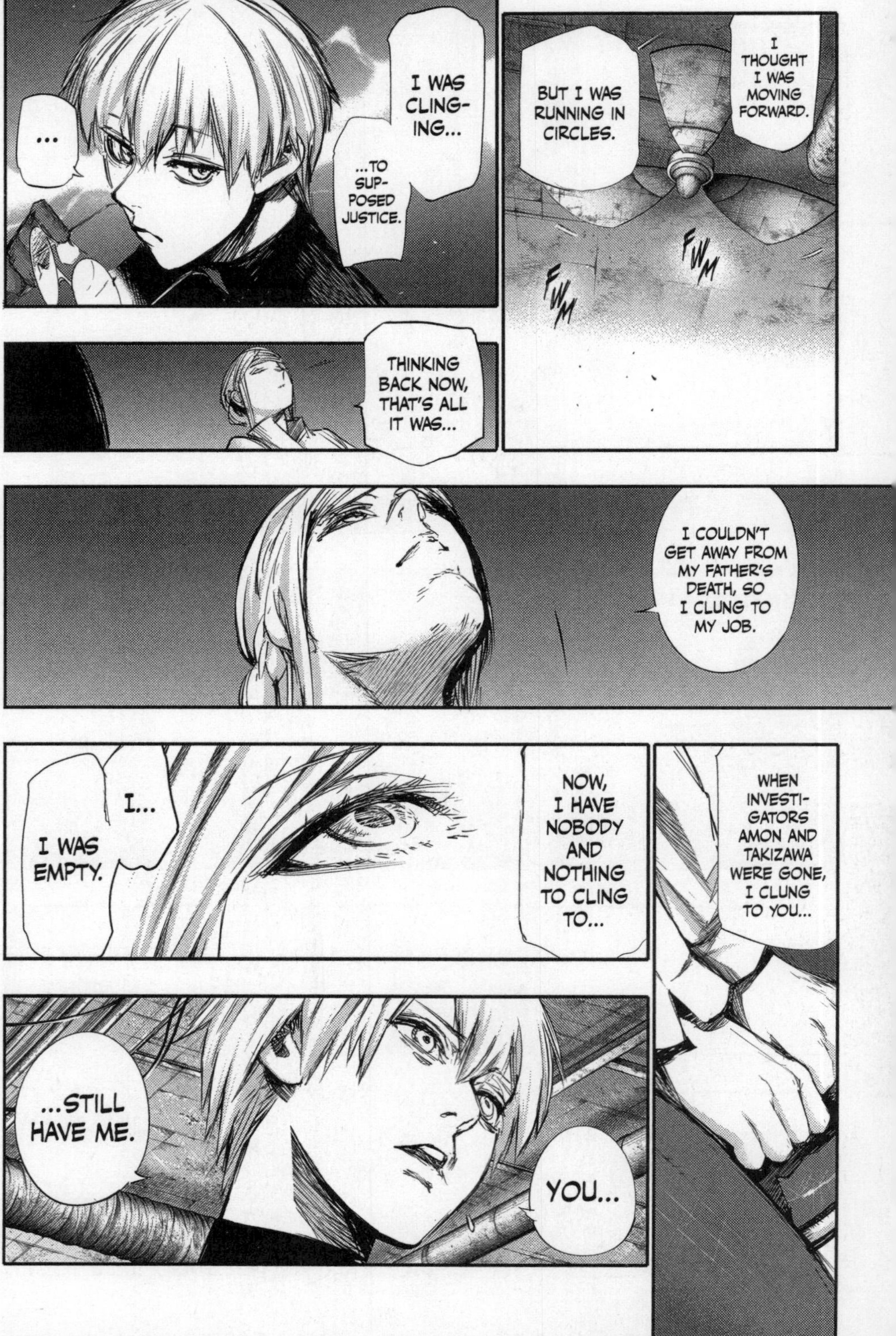
I THOUGHT I WAS MOVING FORWARD.
BUT I WAS RUNNING IN CIRCLES.
FWM
FWM
I WAS CLING-ING...
...TO SUP-POSED JUSTICE.
...
THINKING BACK NOW, THAT'S ALL IT WAS...
I COULDN'T GET AWAY FROM MY FATHER'S DEATH, SO I CLUNG TO MY JOB.
WHEN INVESTI-GATORS AMON AND TAKIZAWA WERE GONE, I CLUNG TO YOU...
NOW, I HAVE NOBODY AND NOTHING TO CLING TO...
I...
I WAS EMPTY.
YOU...
...STILL HAVE ME.

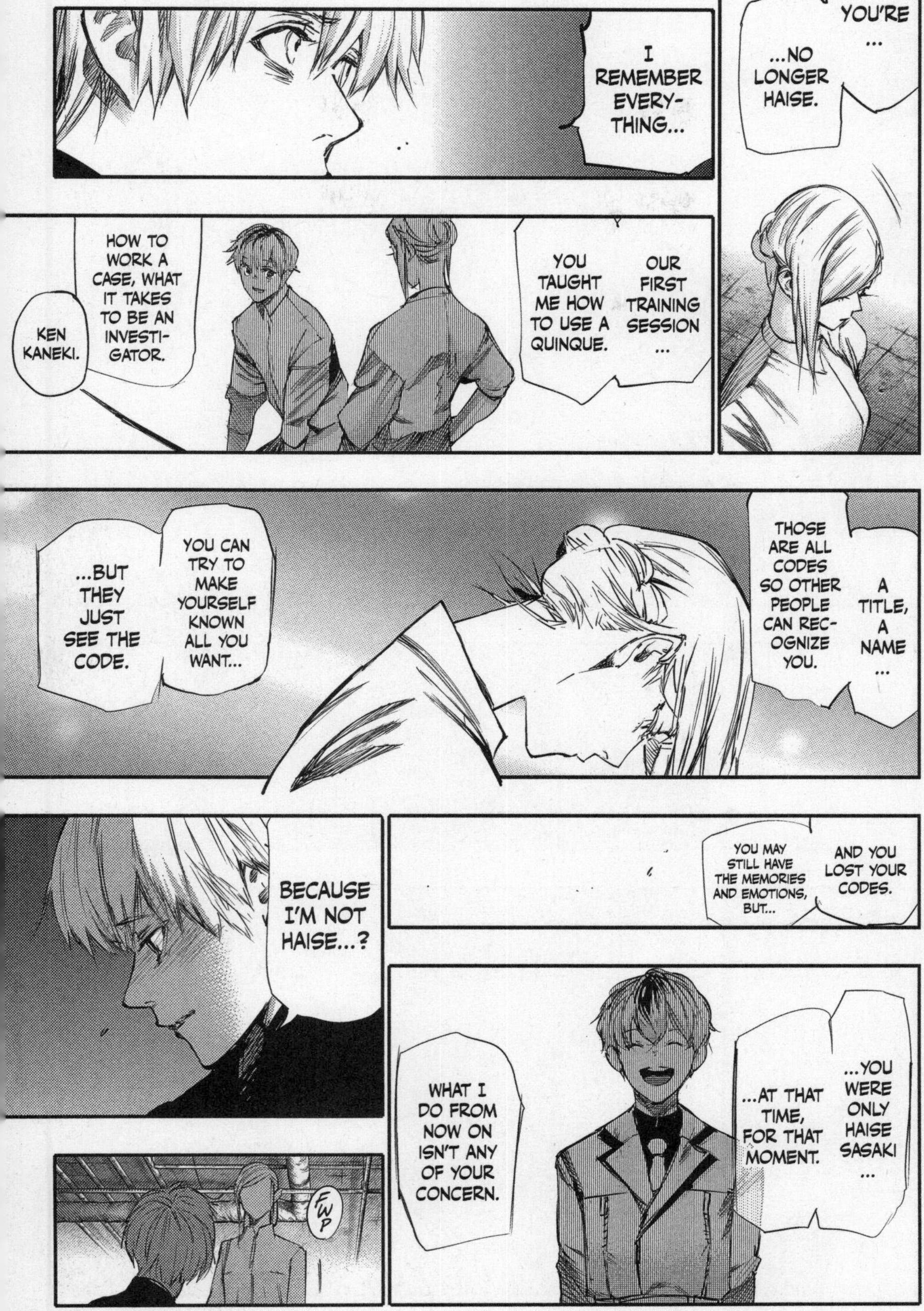
YOU'RE ...
...NO LONGER HAISE.
I REMEMBER EVERY-THING...
OUR FIRST TRAINING SESSION ...
YOU TAUGHT ME HOW TO USE A QUINQUE.
HOW TO WORK A CASE, WHAT IT TAKES TO BE AN INVESTI-GATOR.
KEN KANEKI.
A TITLE, A NAME ...
THOSE ARE ALL CODES SO OTHER PEOPLE CAN REC-OGNIZE YOU.
YOU CAN TRY TO MAKE YOURSELF KNOWN ALL YOU WANT...
...BUT THEY JUST SEE THE CODE.
AND YOU LOST YOUR CODES.
YOU MAY STILL HAVE THE MEMORIES AND EMOTIONS, BUT...
BECAUSE I'M NOT HAISE...?
...YOU WERE ONLY HAISE SASAKI ...
...AT THAT TIME, FOR THAT MOMENT.
WHAT I DO FROM NOW ON ISN'T ANY OF YOUR CONCERN.
FWP

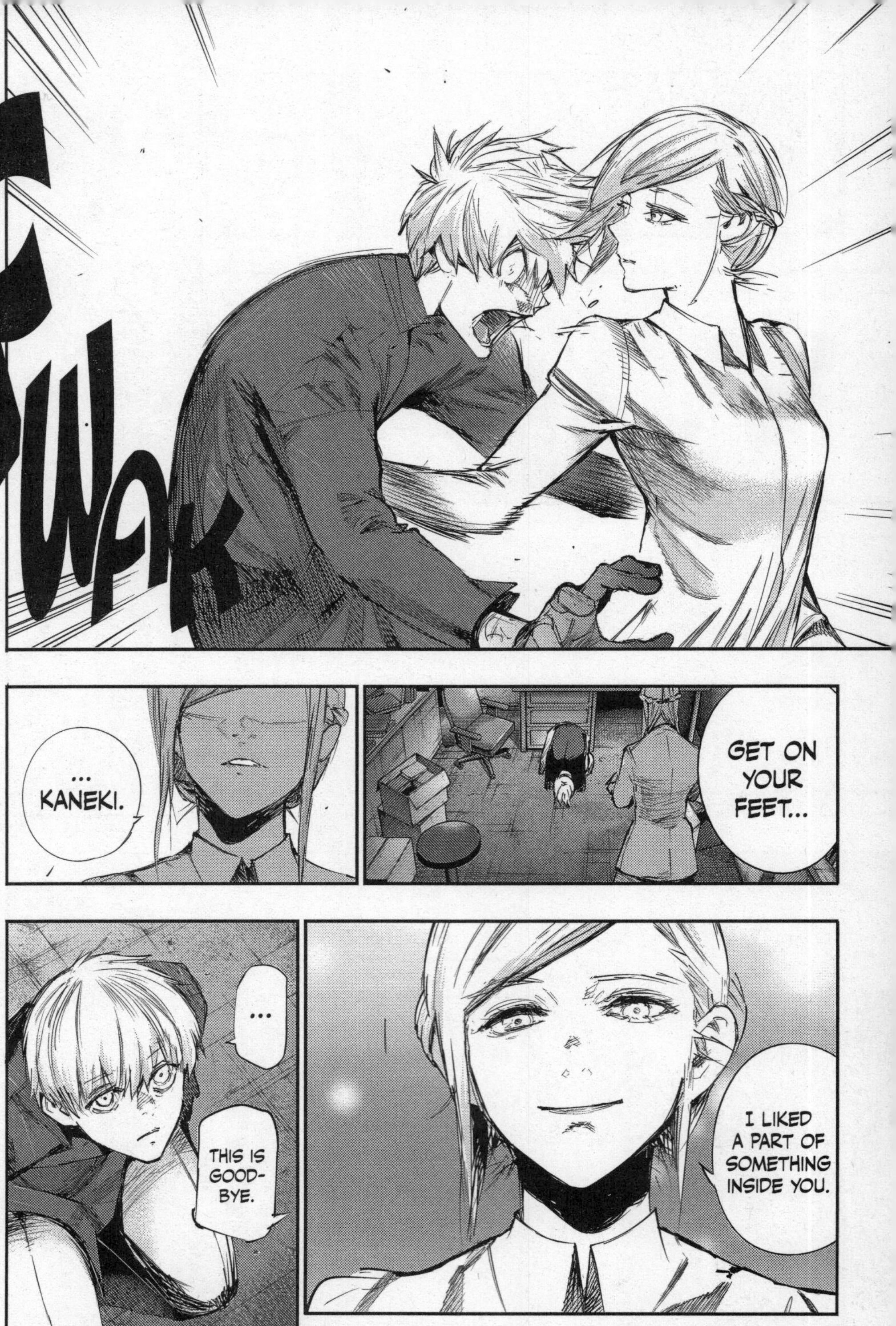
FWAK
GET ON YOUR FEET...
... KANEKI.
I LIKED A PART OF SOMETHING INSIDE YOU.
...
THIS IS GOOD-BYE.

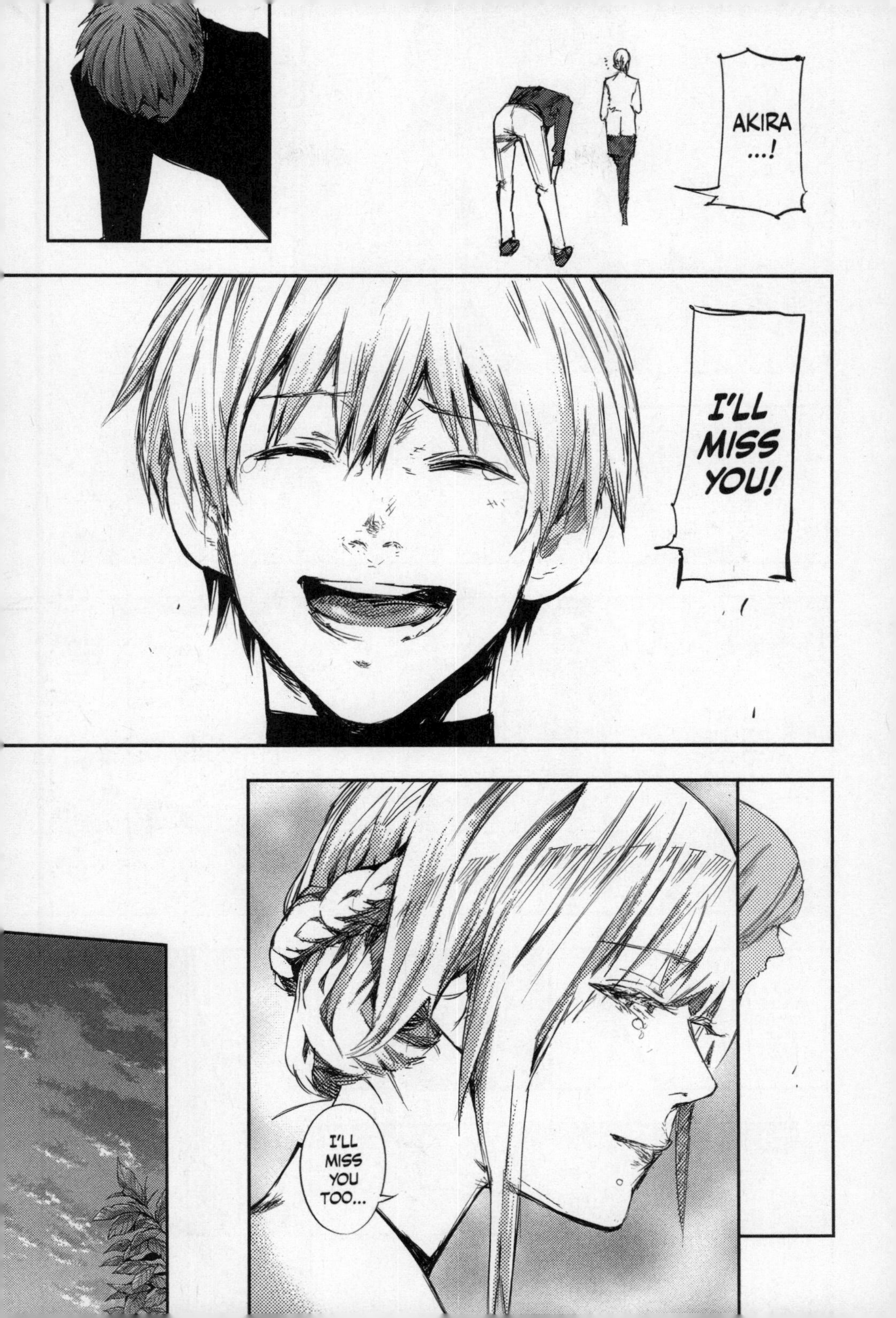
AKIRA ...!
I'LL MISS YOU!
I'LL MISS YOU TOO...

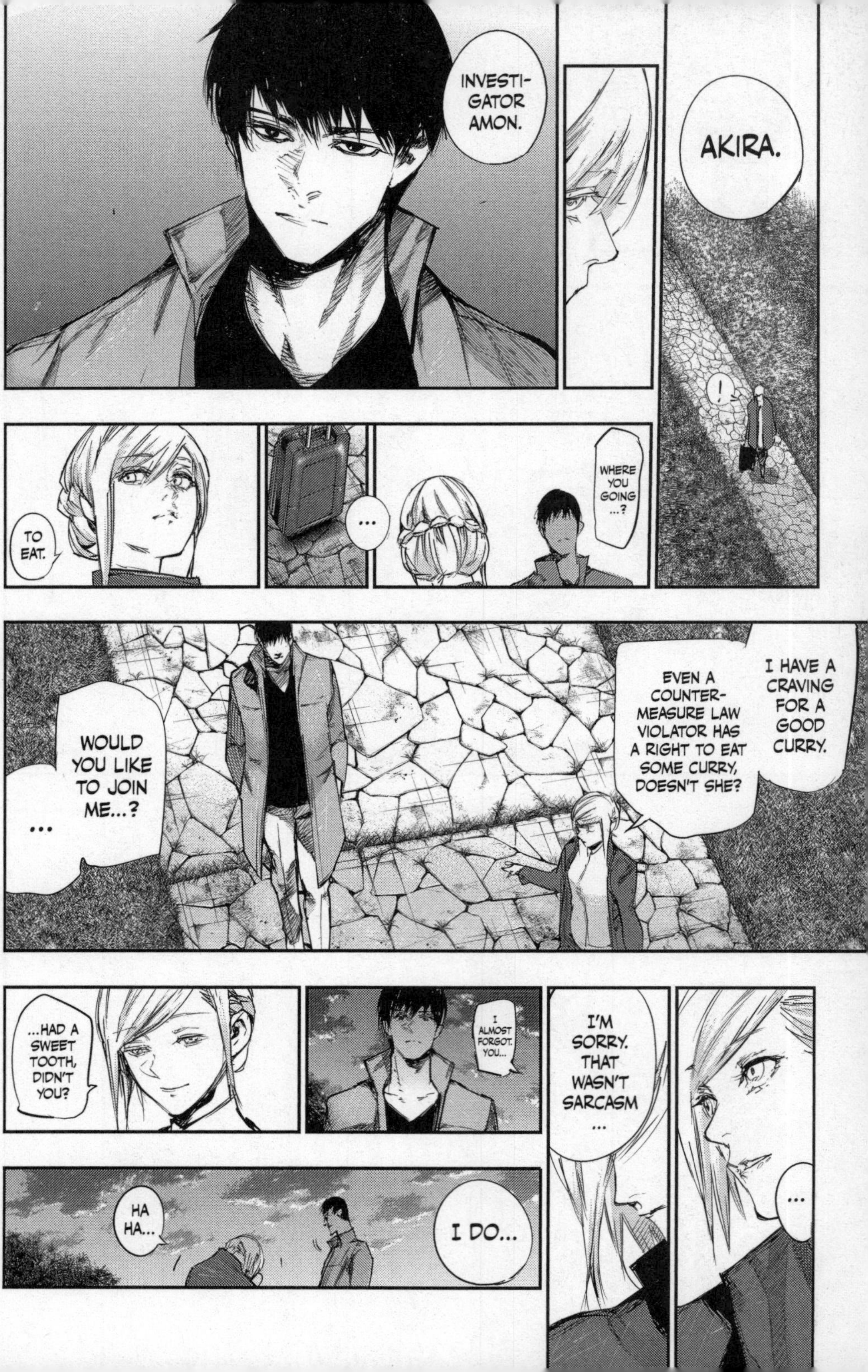
AKIRA.
!
INVESTI-GATOR AMON.
WHERE YOU GOING ...?
...
TO EAT.
I HAVE A CRAVING FOR A GOOD CURRY.
EVEN A COUNTER-MEASURE LAW VIOLATOR HAS A RIGHT TO EAT SOME CURRY, DOESN'T SHE?
WOULD YOU LIKE TO JOIN ME...?
...
...
I'M SORRY. THAT WASN'T SARCASM ...
I ALMOST FORGOT. YOU...
...HAD A SWEET TOOTH, DIDN'T YOU?
I DO...
HA HA...

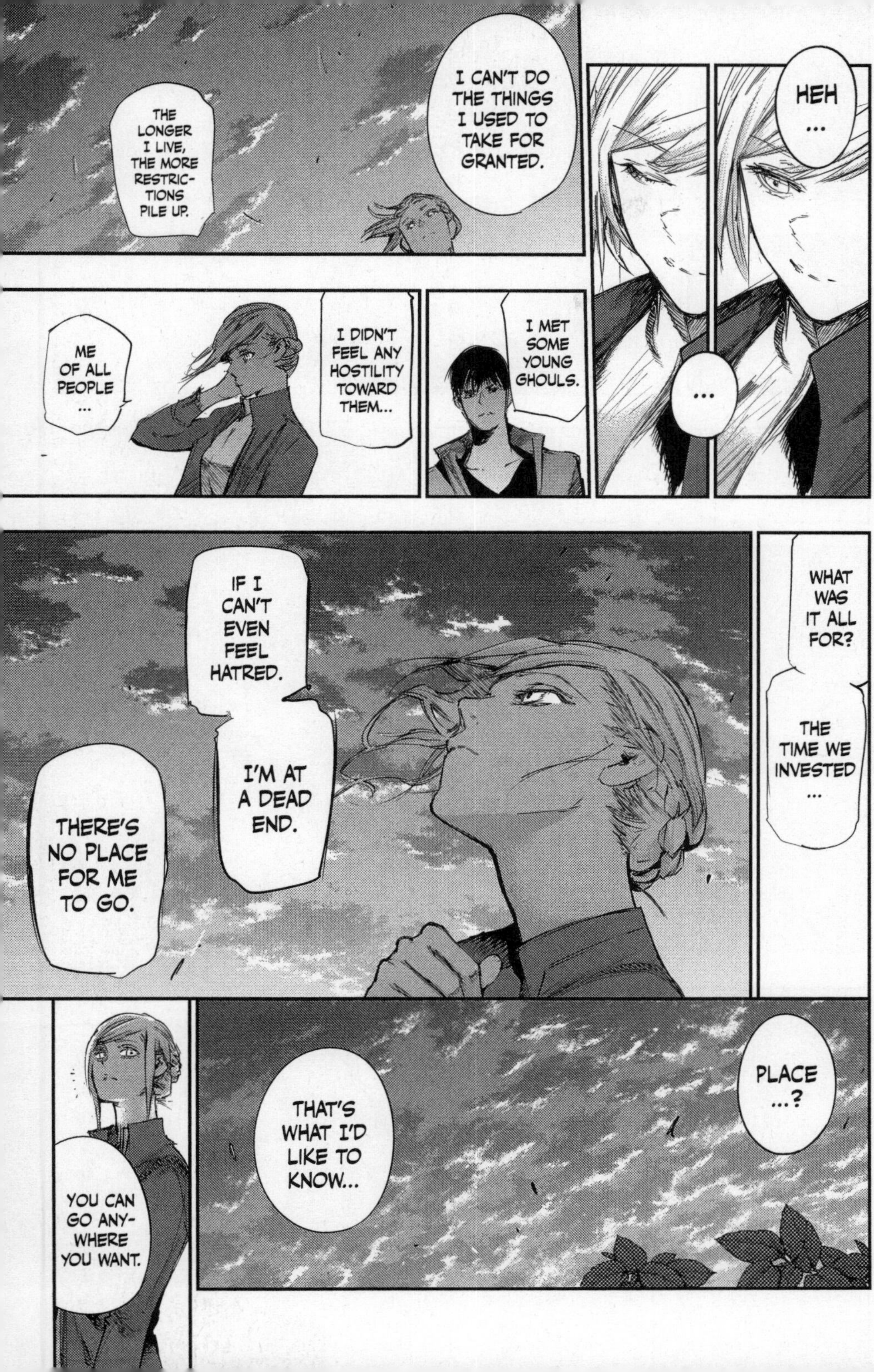
HEH ...
...
I CAN'T DO THE THINGS I USED TO TAKE FOR GRANTED.
THE LONGER I LIVE, THE MORE RESTRIC- TIONS PILE UP.
I MET SOME YOUNG GHOULS.
I DIDN'T FEEL ANY HOSTILITY TOWARD THEM...
ME OF ALL PEOPLE ...
WHAT WAS IT ALL FOR?
THE TIME WE INVESTED ...
IF I CAN'T EVEN FEEL HATRED.
I'M AT A DEAD END.
THERE'S NO PLACE FOR ME TO GO.
PLACE ...?
THAT'S WHAT I'D LIKE TO KNOW...
YOU CAN GO ANY- WHERE YOU WANT.

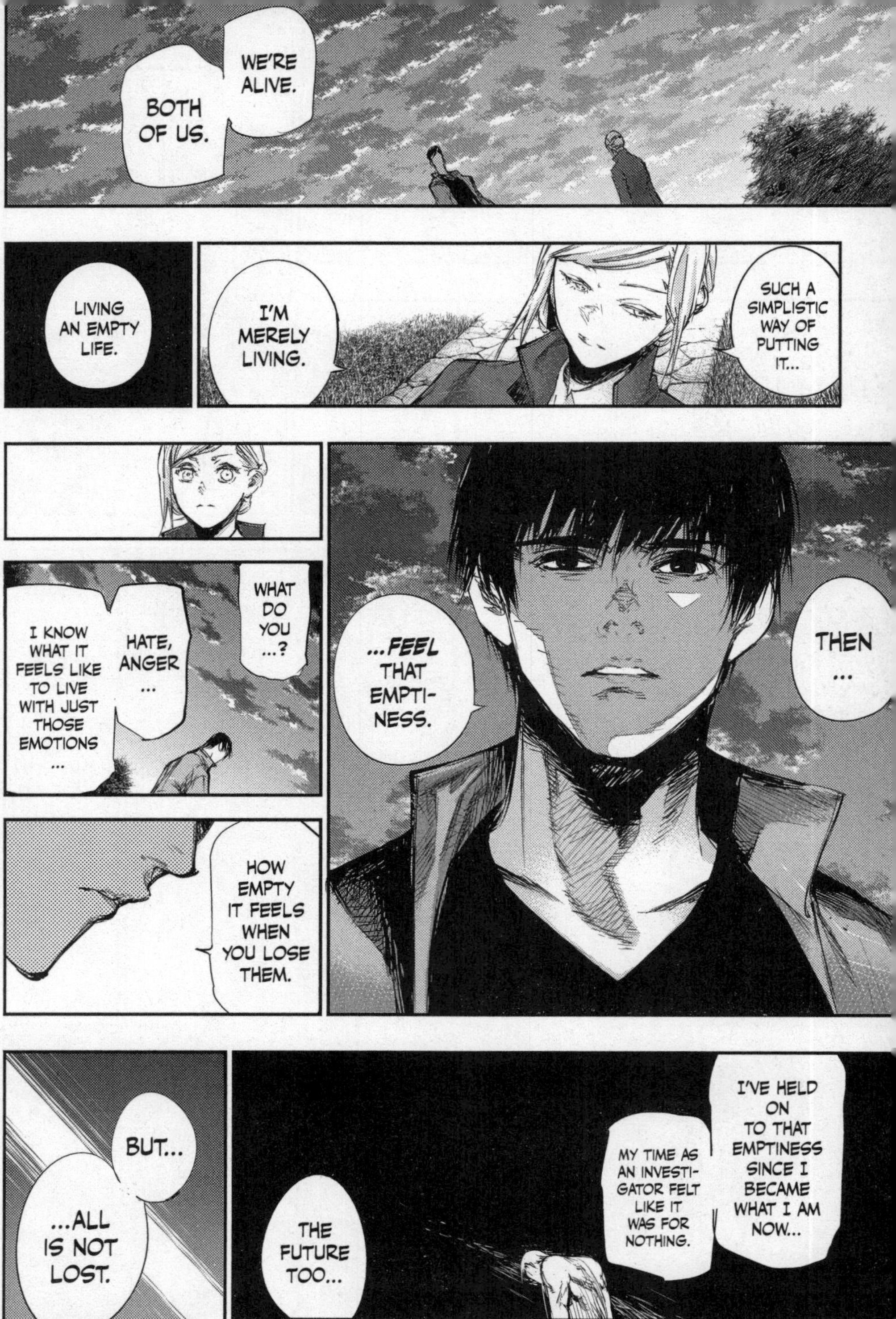
WE'RE ALIVE.
BOTH OF US.
SUCH A SIMPLISTIC WAY OF PUTTING IT...
I'M MERELY LIVING.
LIVING AN EMPTY LIFE.
THEN ...
...FEEL THAT EMPTINESS.
WHAT DO YOU ...?
HATE, ANGER ...
I KNOW WHAT IT FEELS LIKE TO LIVE WITH JUST THOSE EMOTIONS ...
HOW EMPTY IT FEELS WHEN YOU LOSE THEM.
I'VE HELD ON TO THAT EMPTINESS SINCE I BECAME WHAT I AM NOW...
MY TIME AS AN INVESTIGATOR FELT LIKE IT WAS FOR NOTHING.
THE FUTURE TOO...
BUT...
...ALL IS NOT LOST.

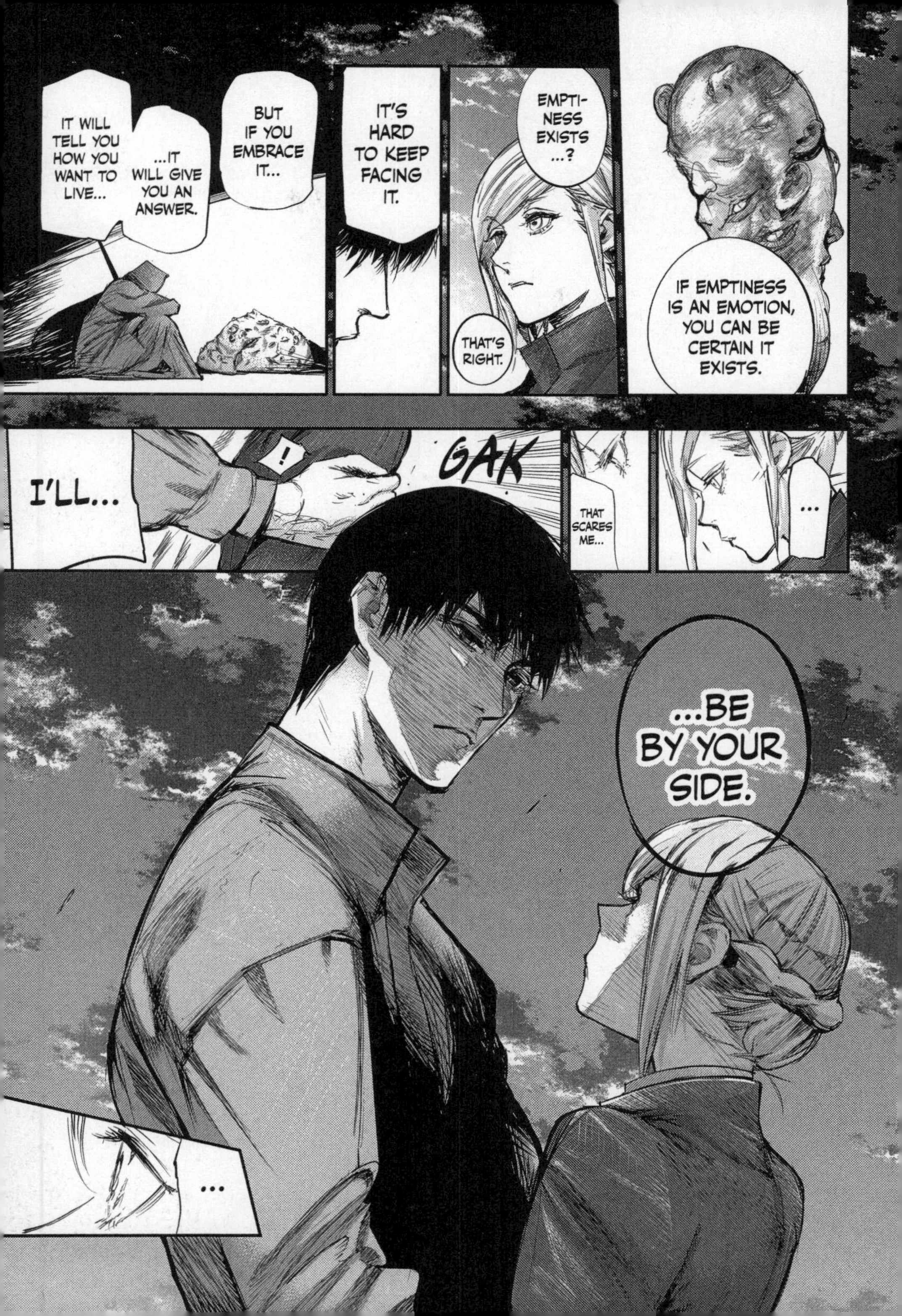
IF EMPTINESS IS AN EMOTION, YOU CAN BE CERTAIN IT EXISTS.
EMPTINESS EXISTS ...?
THAT'S RIGHT.
IT'S HARD TO KEEP FACING IT.
BUT IF YOU EMBRACE IT...
...IT WILL GIVE YOU AN ANSWER.
IT WILL TELL YOU HOW YOU WANT TO LIVE...
...
THAT SCARES ME...
GAK
!
I'LL...
...BE BY YOUR SIDE.
...

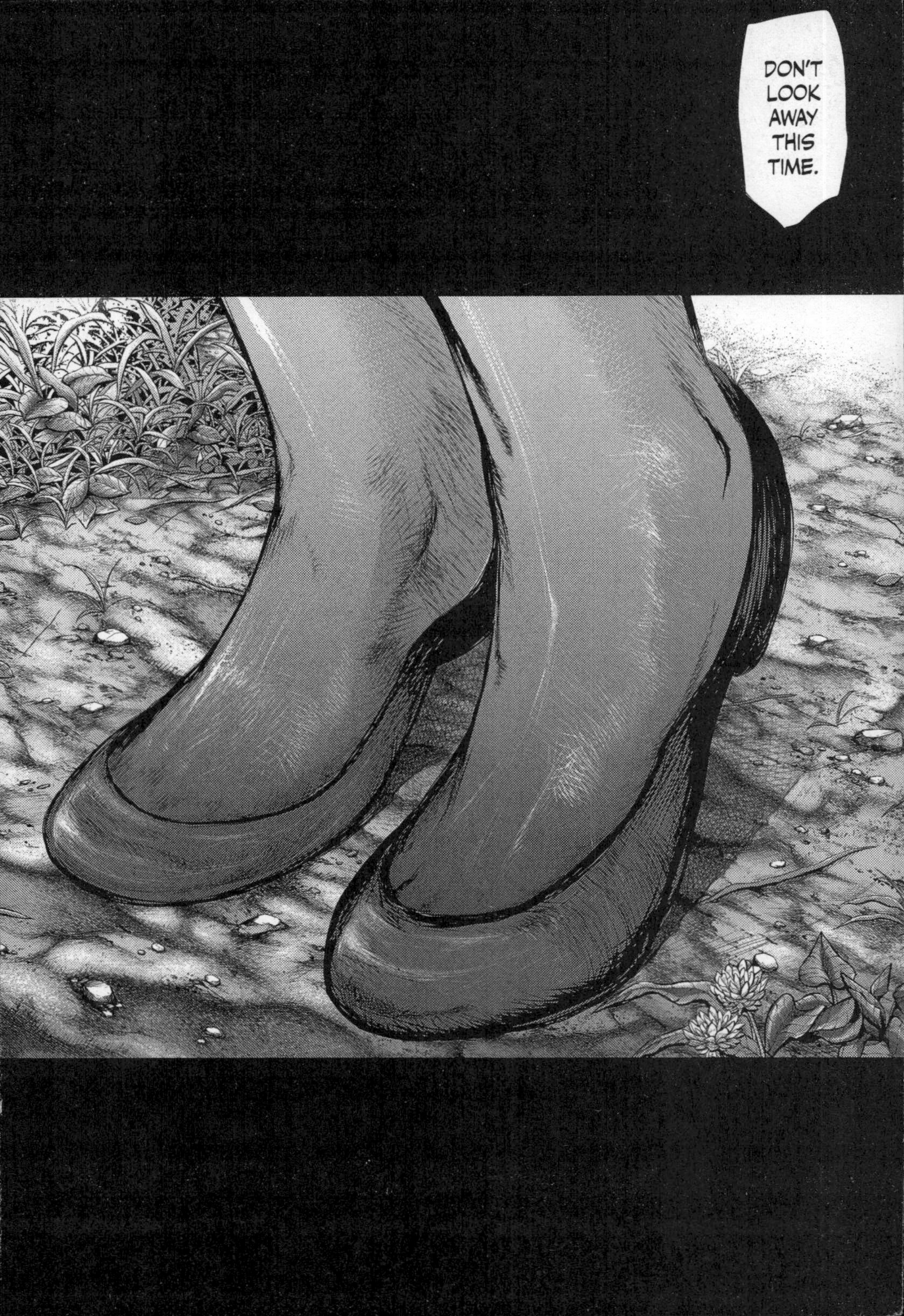
DON'T LOOK AWAY THIS TIME.

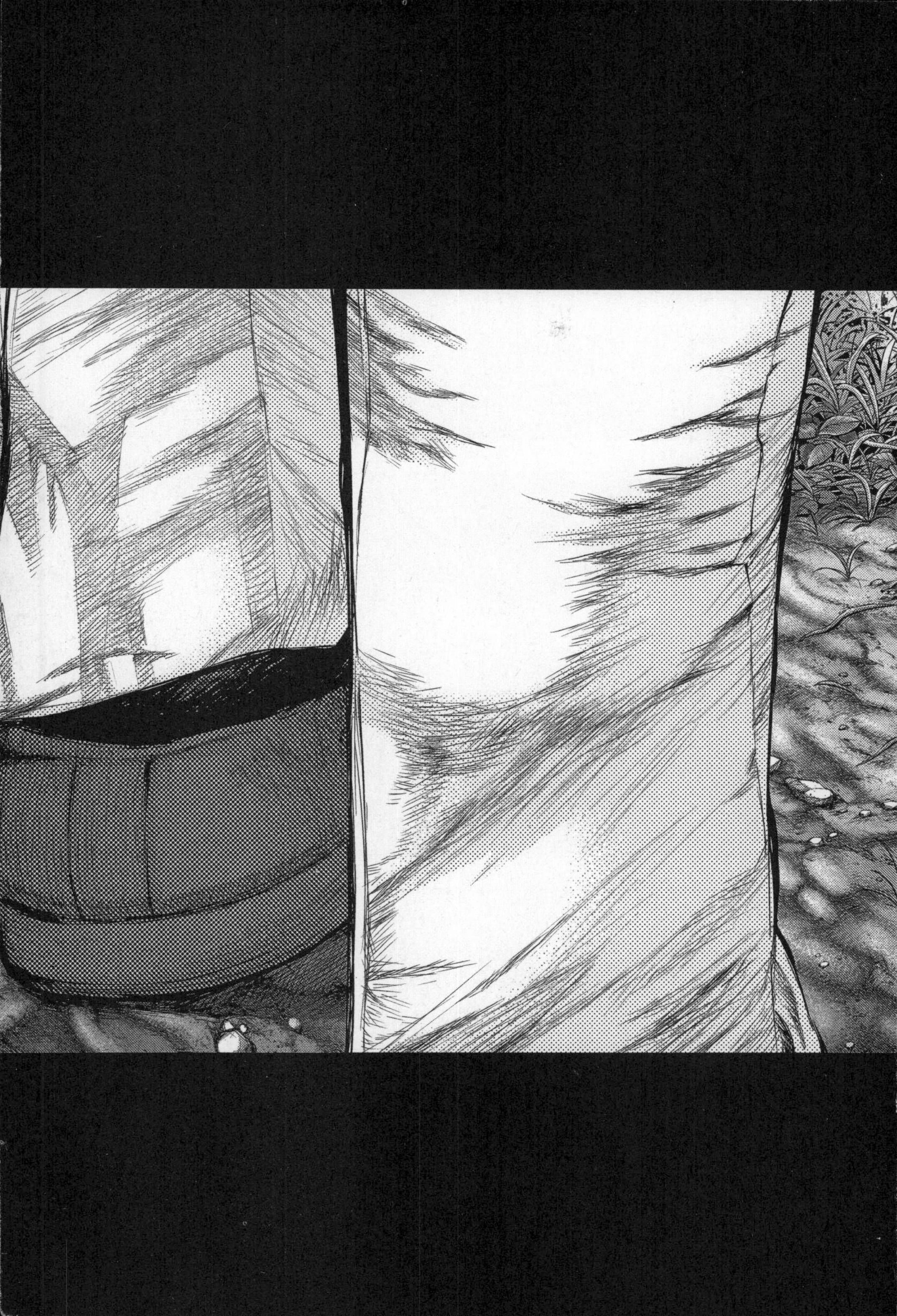

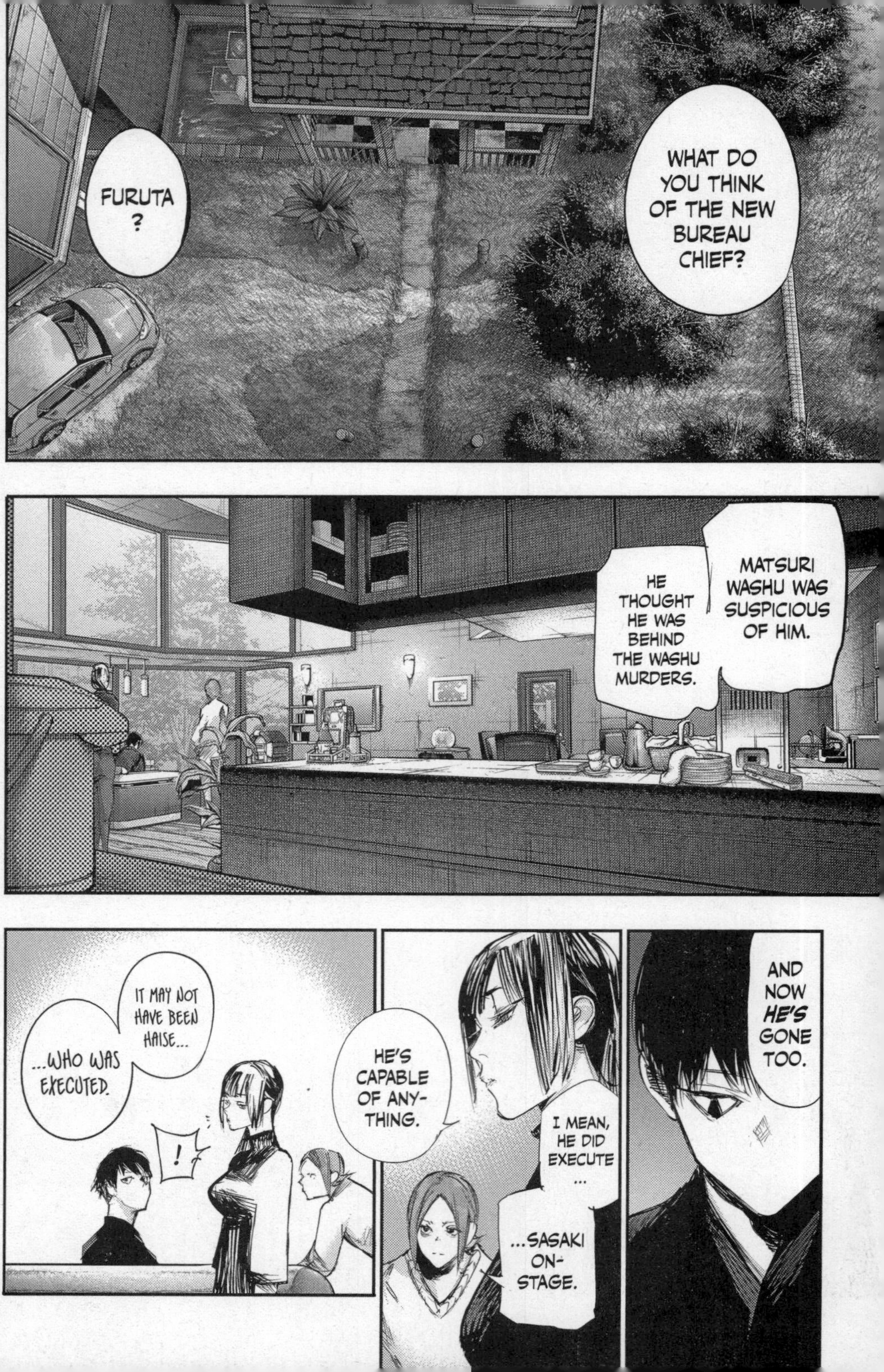
WHAT DO YOU THINK OF THE NEW BUREAU CHIEF?
FURUTA?
MATSURI WASHU WAS SUSPICIOUS OF HIM.
HE THOUGHT HE WAS BEHIND THE WASHU MURDERS.
AND NOW *HE'S* GONE TOO.
HE'S CAPABLE OF ANY-THING.
I MEAN, HE DID EXECUTE ...
...SASAKI ON-STAGE.
IT MAY NOT HAVE BEEN HAISE...
...WHO WAS EXECUTED.
!

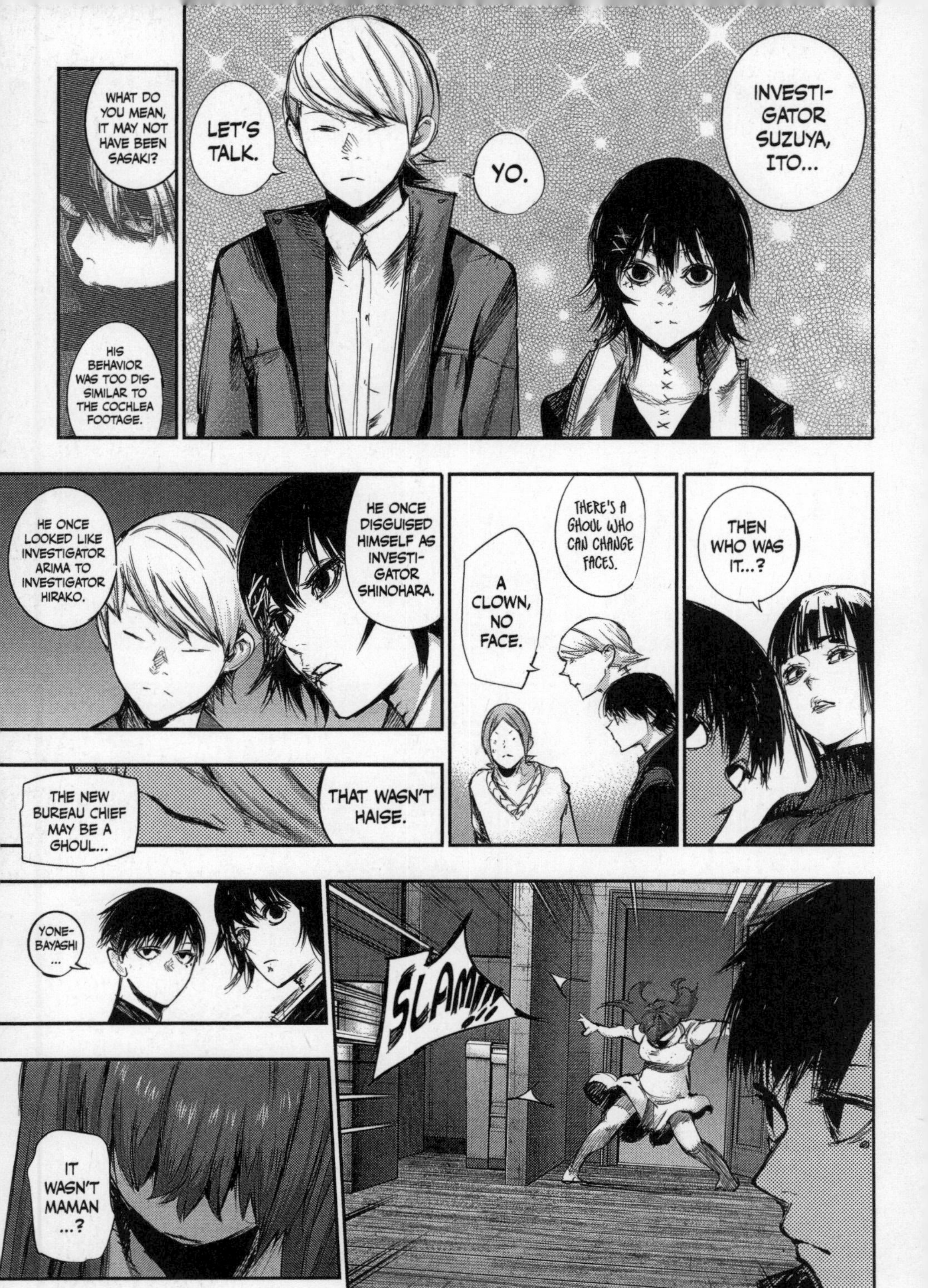
INVESTIGATOR SUZUYA, ITO...
YO.
LET'S TALK.
WHAT DO YOU MEAN, IT MAY NOT HAVE BEEN SASAKI?
HIS BEHAVIOR WAS TOO DISSIMILAR TO THE COCHLEA FOOTAGE.
THEN WHO WAS IT...?
THERE'S A GHOUL WHO CAN CHANGE FACES.
A CLOWN, NO FACE.
HE ONCE DISGUISED HIMSELF AS INVESTIGATOR SHINOHARA.
HE ONCE LOOKED LIKE INVESTIGATOR ARIMA TO INVESTIGATOR HIRAKO.
THAT WASN'T HAISE.
THE NEW BUREAU CHIEF MAY BE A GHOUL...
SLAM!!
YONEBAYASHI...
IT WASN'T MAMAN...?

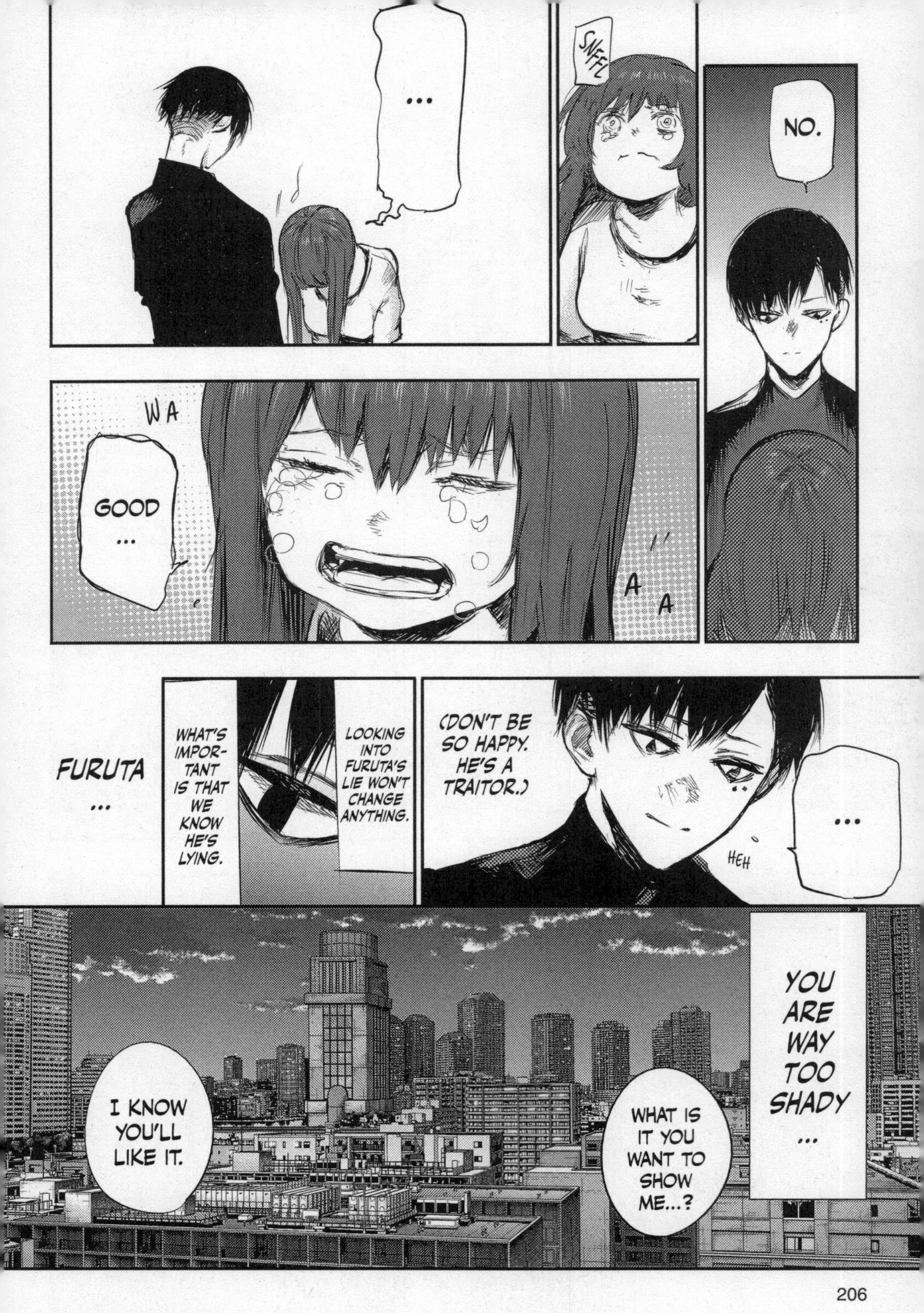
NO.
SNFFL
...
WA
GOOD ...
A A
(DON'T BE SO HAPPY. HE'S A TRAITOR.)
...
HEH
LOOKING INTO FURUTA'S LIE WON'T CHANGE ANYTHING.
WHAT'S IMPOR-TANT IS THAT WE KNOW HE'S LYING.
FURUTA ...
YOU ARE WAY TOO SHADY ...
WHAT IS IT YOU WANT TO SHOW ME...?
I KNOW YOU'LL LIKE IT.

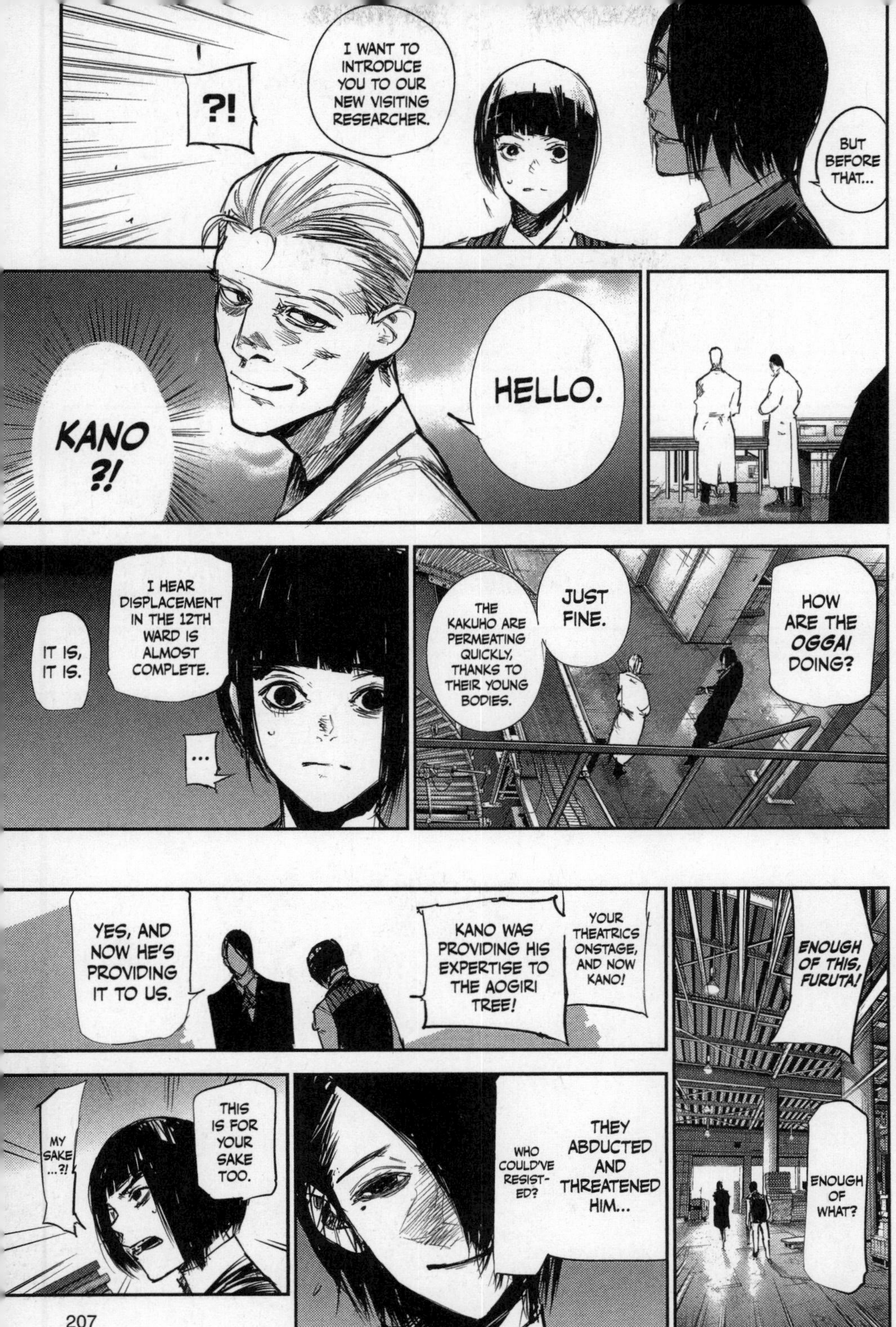
BUT BEFORE THAT...
I WANT TO INTRODUCE YOU TO OUR NEW VISITING RESEARCHER.
?!
HELLO.
KANO ?!
HOW ARE THE *OGGAI* DOING?
JUST FINE.
THE KAKUHO ARE PERMEATING QUICKLY, THANKS TO THEIR YOUNG BODIES.
I HEAR DISPLACEMENT IN THE 12TH WARD IS ALMOST COMPLETE.
IT IS, IT IS.
...
ENOUGH OF THIS, FURUTA!
ENOUGH OF WHAT?
YOUR THEATRICS ONSTAGE, AND NOW KANO!
KANO WAS PROVIDING HIS EXPERTISE TO THE AOGIRI TREE!
YES, AND NOW HE'S PROVIDING IT TO US.
THEY ABDUCTED AND THREATENED HIM...
WHO COULD'VE RESIST-ED?
THIS IS FOR YOUR SAKE TOO.
MY SAKE ...?!

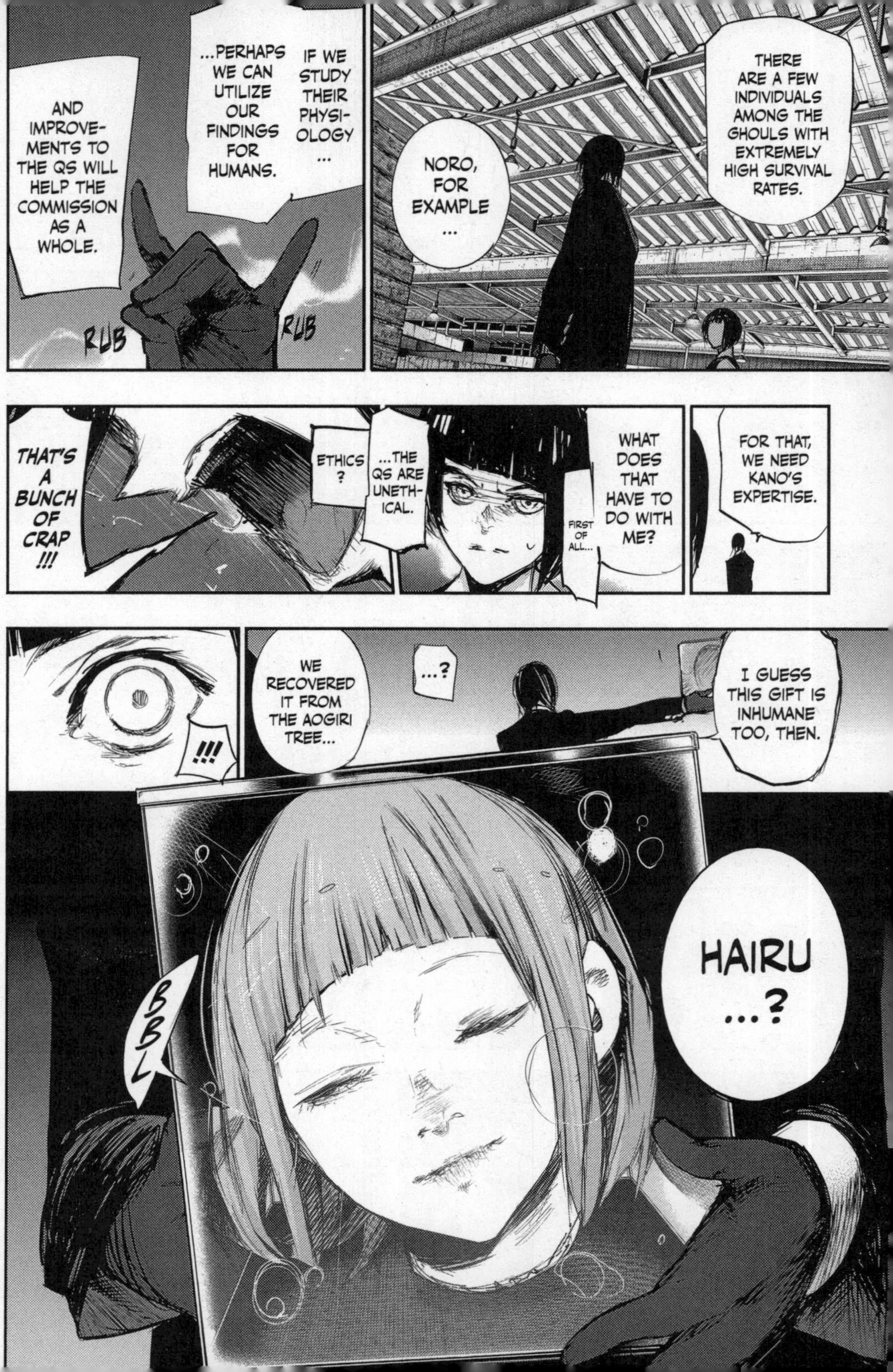
THERE ARE A FEW INDIVIDUALS AMONG THE GHOULS WITH EXTREMELY HIGH SURVIVAL RATES.
NORO, FOR EXAMPLE...
IF WE STUDY THEIR PHYSIOLOGY...
...PERHAPS WE CAN UTILIZE OUR FINDINGS FOR HUMANS.
AND IMPROVEMENTS TO THE QS WILL HELP THE COMMISSION AS A WHOLE.
RUB
RUB
FOR THAT, WE NEED KANO'S EXPERTISE.
WHAT DOES THAT HAVE TO DO WITH ME?
FIRST OF ALL...
...THE QS ARE UNETHICAL.
ETHICS?
THAT'S A BUNCH OF CRAP!!!
I GUESS THIS GIFT IS INHUMANE TOO, THEN.
...?
WE RECOVERED IT FROM THE AOGIRI TREE...
!!!
HAIRU...?
BBL

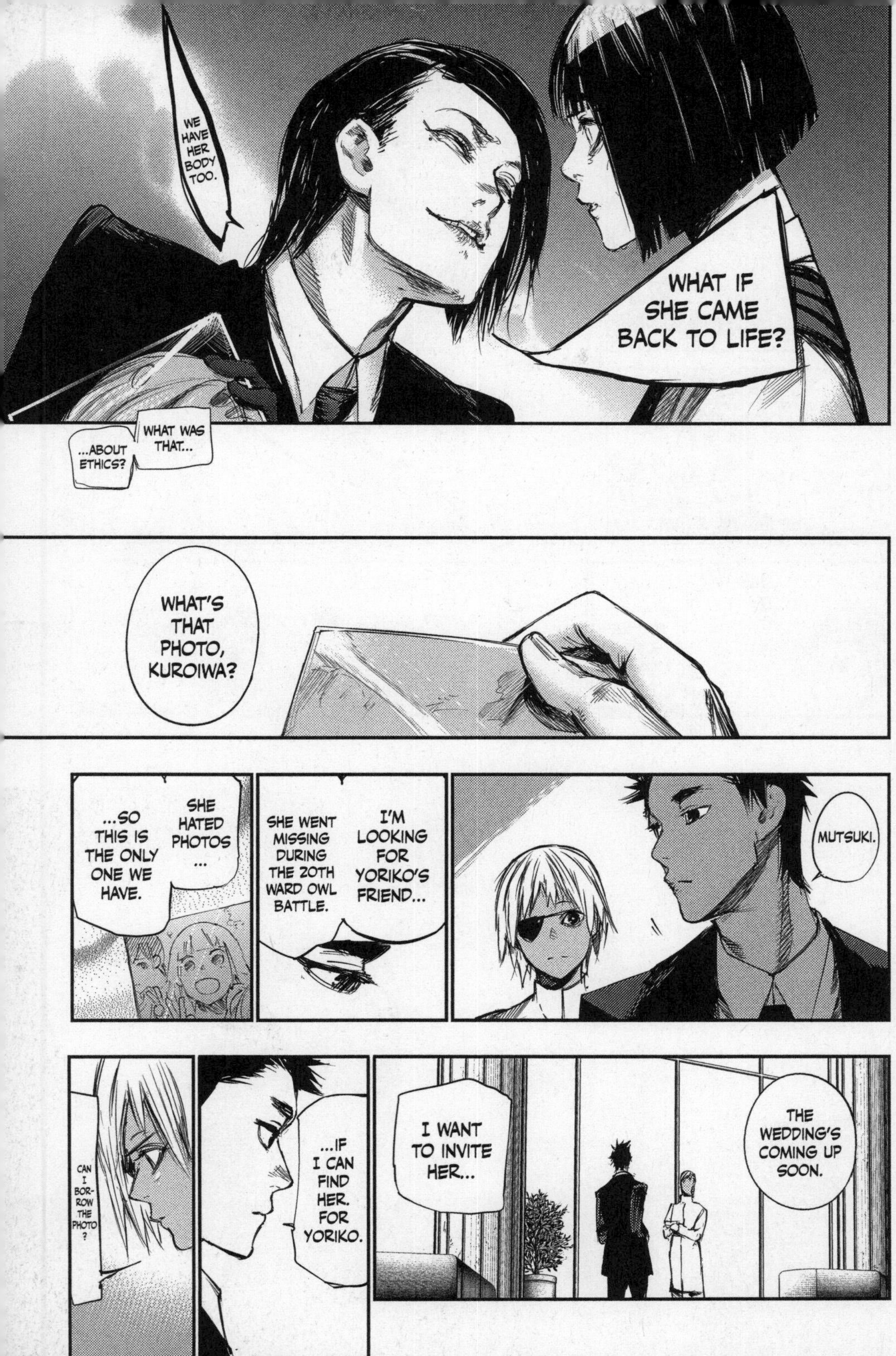
WHAT IF SHE CAME BACK TO LIFE?
WE HAVE HER BODY TOO.
WHAT WAS THAT...
...ABOUT ETHICS?
WHAT'S THAT PHOTO, KUROIWA?
MUTSUKI.
I'M LOOKING FOR YORIKO'S FRIEND...
SHE WENT MISSING DURING THE 20TH WARD OWL BATTLE.
SHE HATED PHOTOS...
...SO THIS IS THE ONLY ONE WE HAVE.
THE WEDDING'S COMING UP SOON.
I WANT TO INVITE HER...
...IF I CAN FIND HER. FOR YORIKO.
CAN I BORROW THE PHOTO?

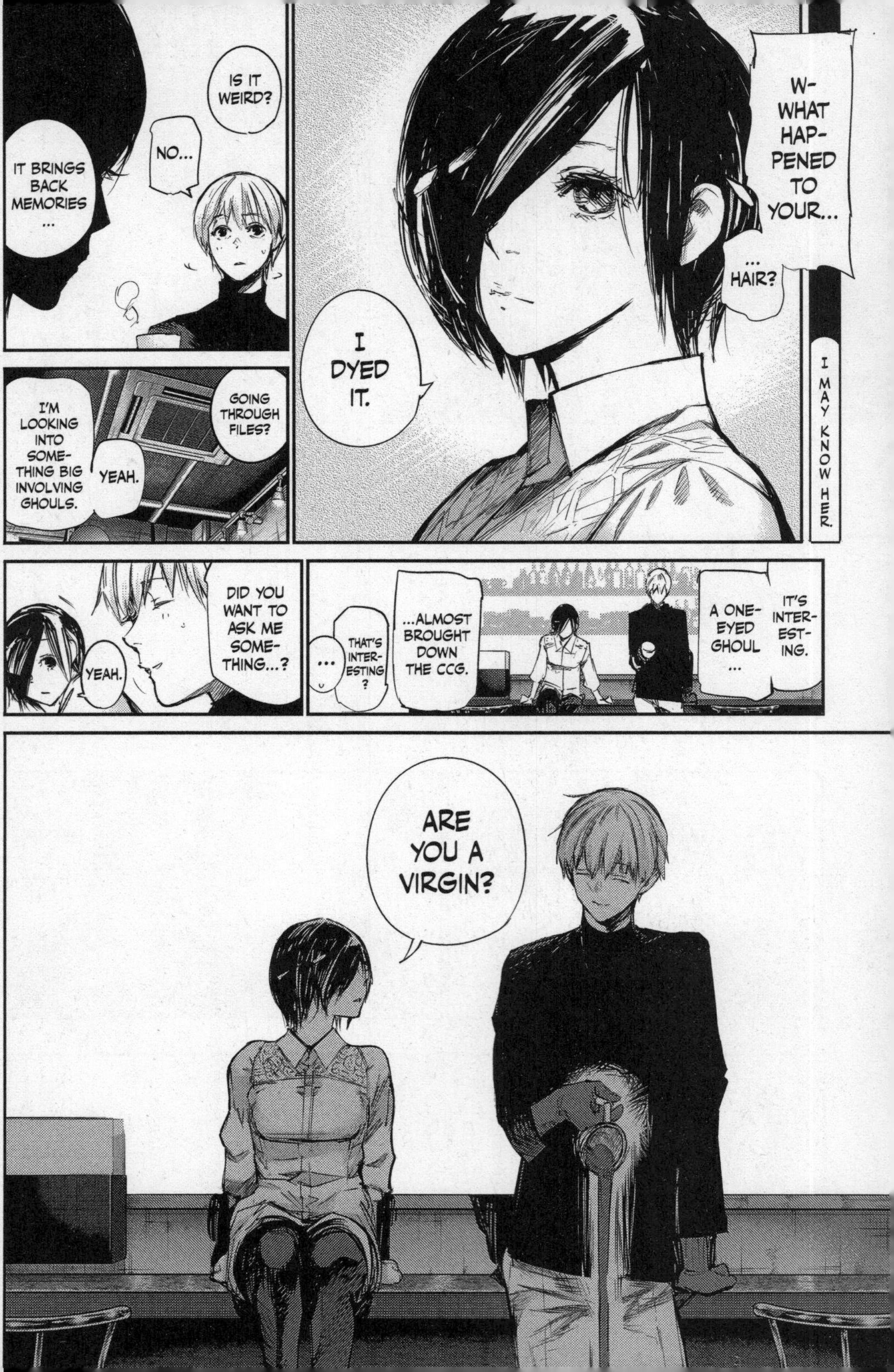
W-WHAT HAPPENED TO YOUR...
...HAIR?
I MAY KNOW HER.
I DYED IT.
IS IT WEIRD?
NO...
IT BRINGS BACK MEMORIES...
GOING THROUGH FILES?
YEAH.
I'M LOOKING INTO SOMETHING BIG INVOLVING GHOULS.
IT'S INTERESTING.
A ONE-EYED GHOUL...
...ALMOST BROUGHT DOWN THE CCG.
THAT'S INTERESTING?
...
DID YOU WANT TO ASK ME SOMETHING...?
YEAH.
ARE YOU A VIRGIN?

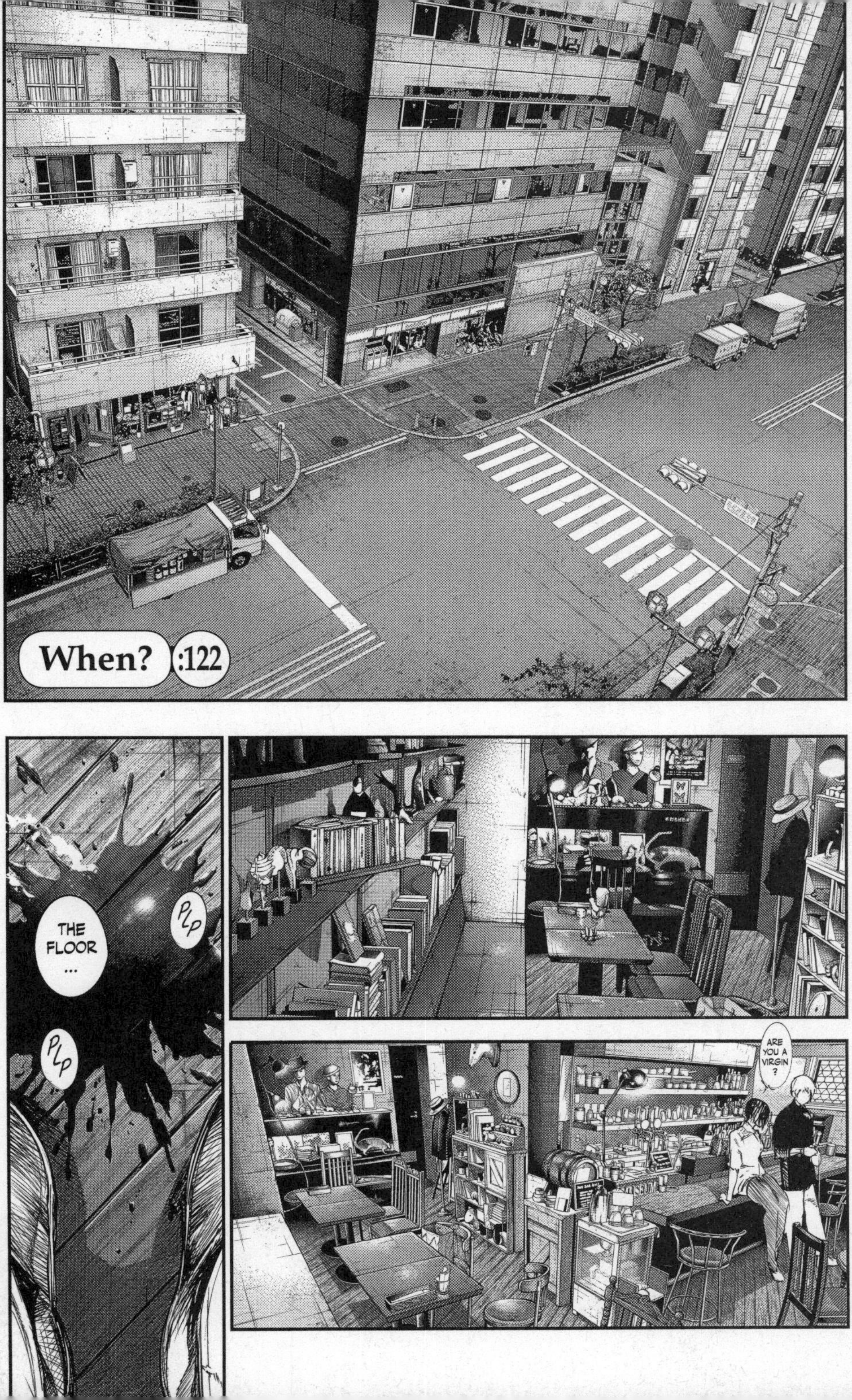
When? :122
ARE YOU A VIRGIN?
THE FLOOR ...
PLP
PLP

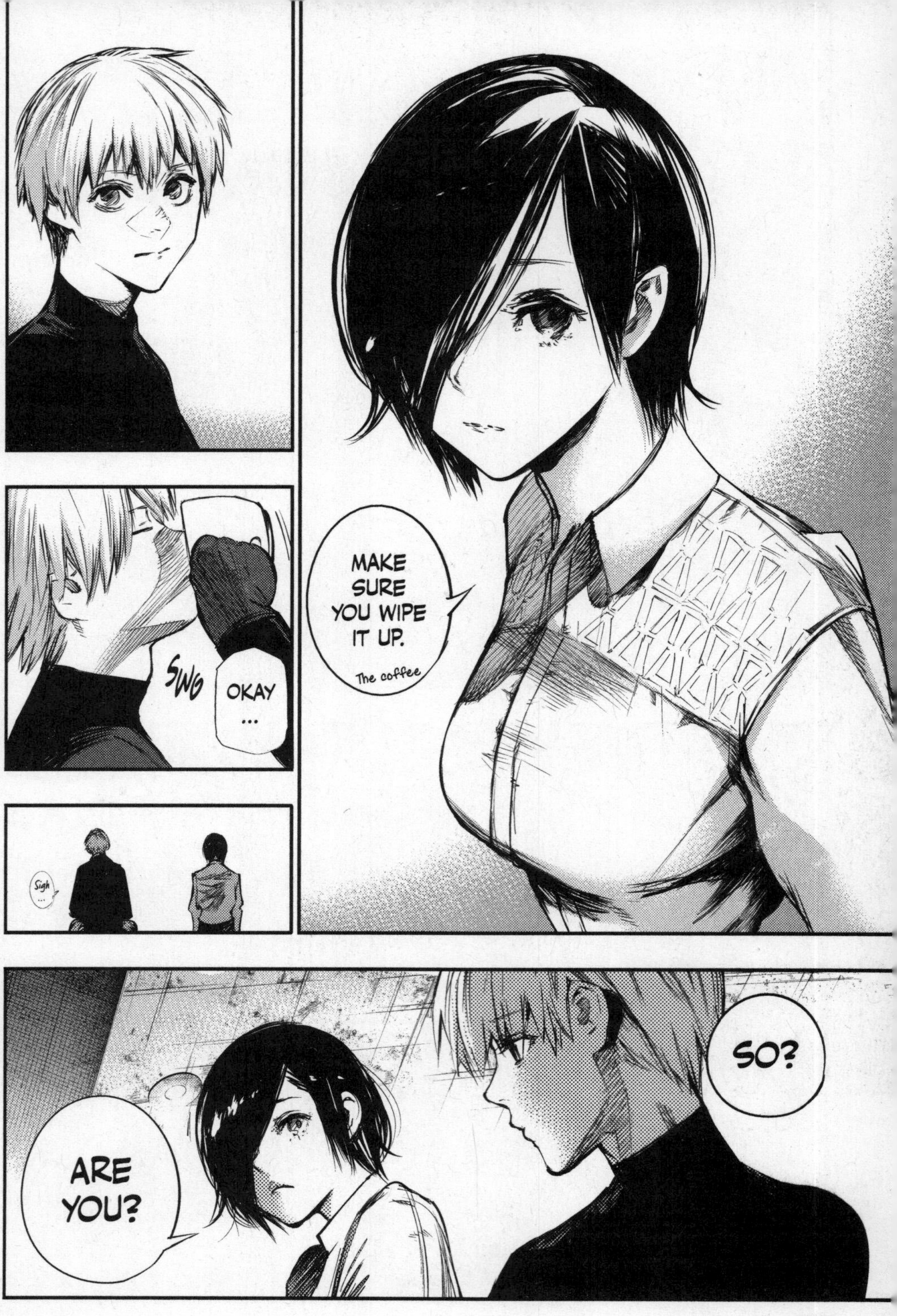
MAKE SURE YOU WIPE IT UP.
The coffee
SWG
OKAY ...
Sigh ...
SO?
ARE YOU?

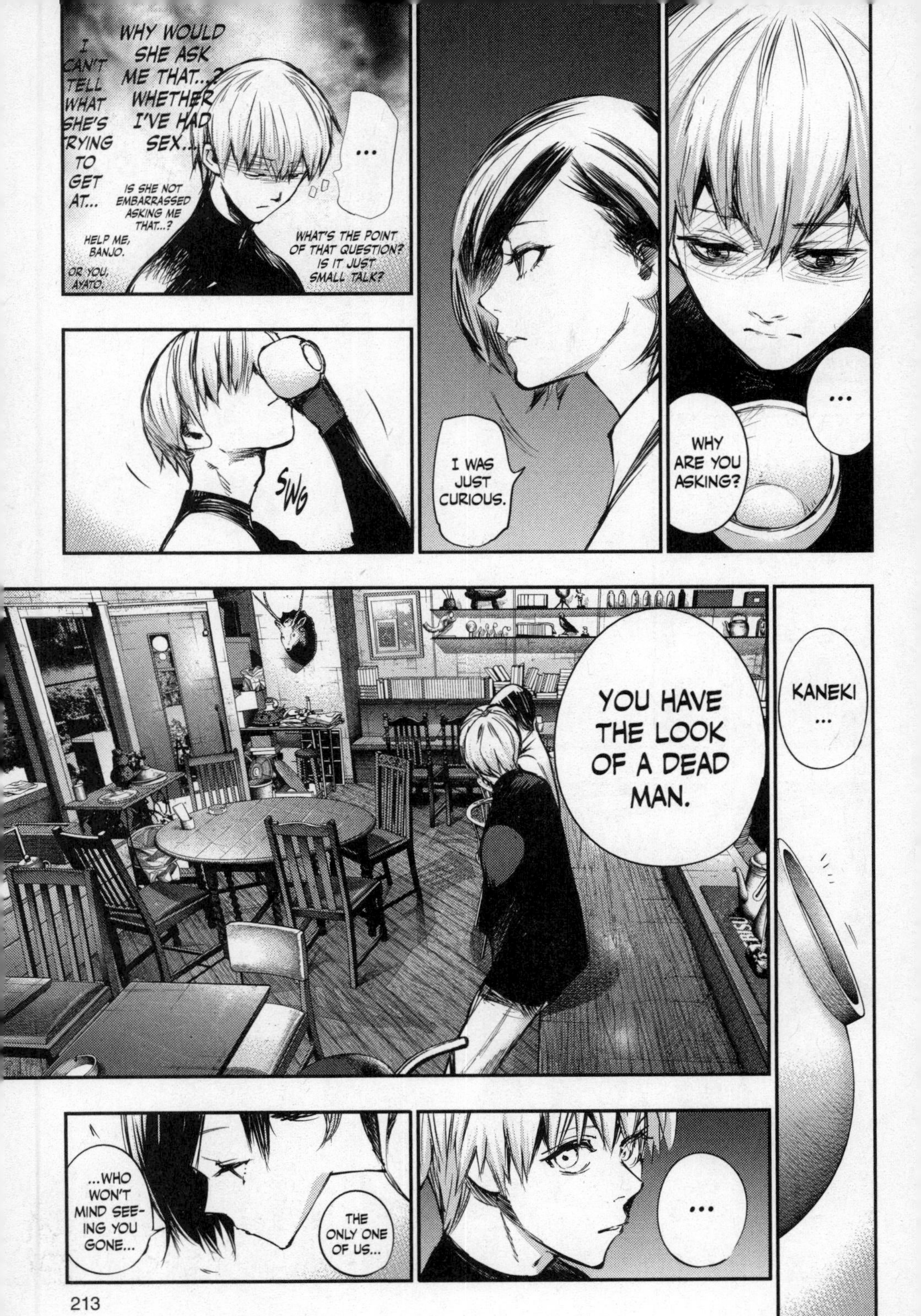
...
WHY ARE YOU ASKING?
I WAS JUST CURIOUS.
...
WHY WOULD SHE ASK ME THAT...? WHETHER I'VE HAD SEX...
I CAN'T TELL WHAT SHE'S TRYING TO GET AT...
WHAT'S THE POINT OF THAT QUESTION? IS IT JUST SMALL TALK?
IS SHE NOT EMBARRASSED ASKING ME THAT...?
HELP ME, BANJO.
OR YOU, AYATO.
SING
KANEKI ...
YOU HAVE THE LOOK OF A DEAD MAN.
...
THE ONLY ONE OF US...
...WHO WON'T MIND SEEING YOU GONE...

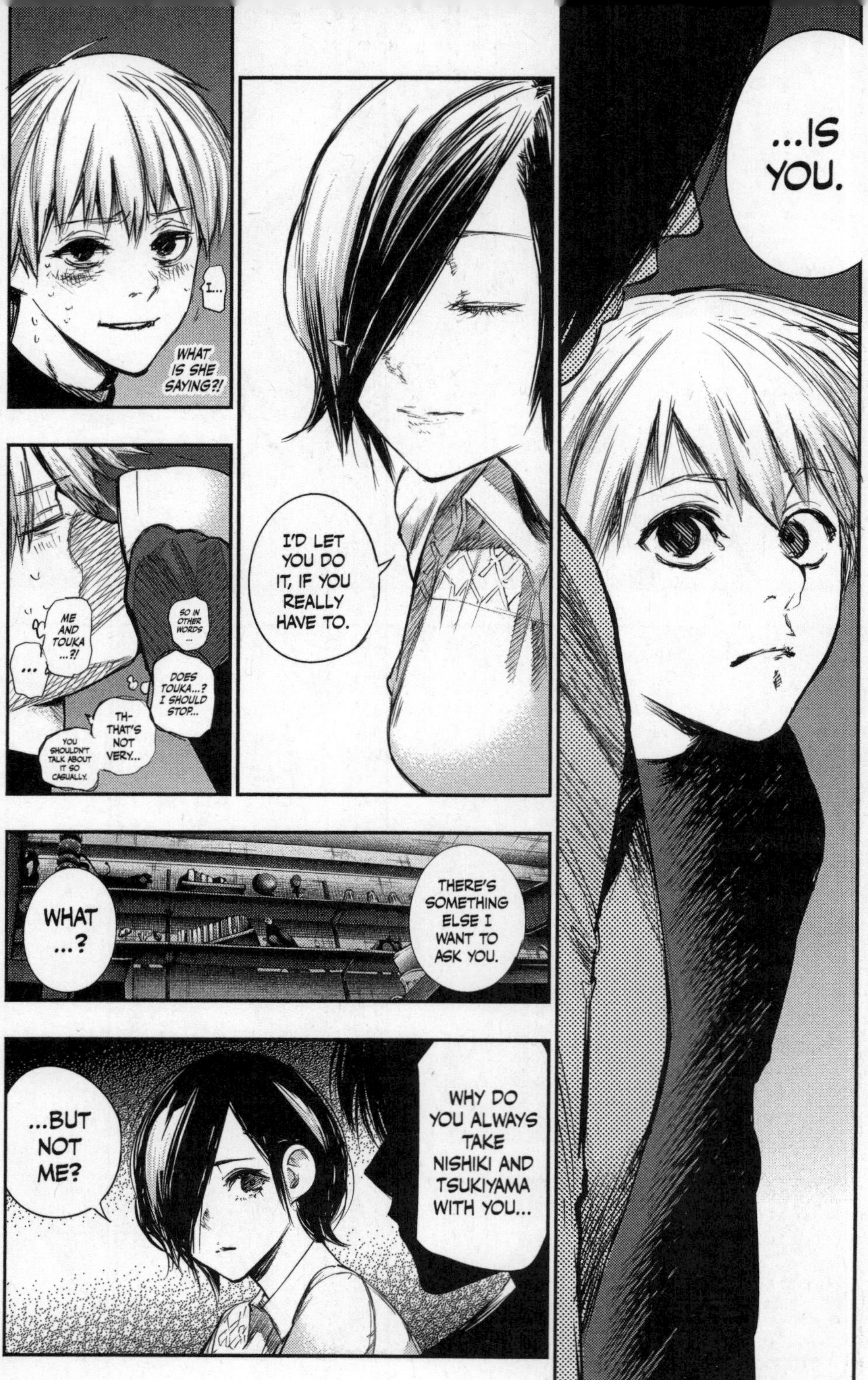
...IS YOU.
I'D LET YOU DO IT, IF YOU REALLY HAVE TO.
I...
WHAT IS SHE SAYING?!
SO IN OTHER WORDS...
ME AND TOUKA...?!
...
DOES TOUKA...? I SHOULD STOP...
TH-THAT'S NOT VERY...
YOU SHOULDN'T TALK ABOUT IT SO CASUALLY.
THERE'S SOMETHING ELSE I WANT TO ASK YOU.
WHAT...?
WHY DO YOU ALWAYS TAKE NISHIKI AND TSUKIYAMA WITH YOU...
...BUT NOT ME?

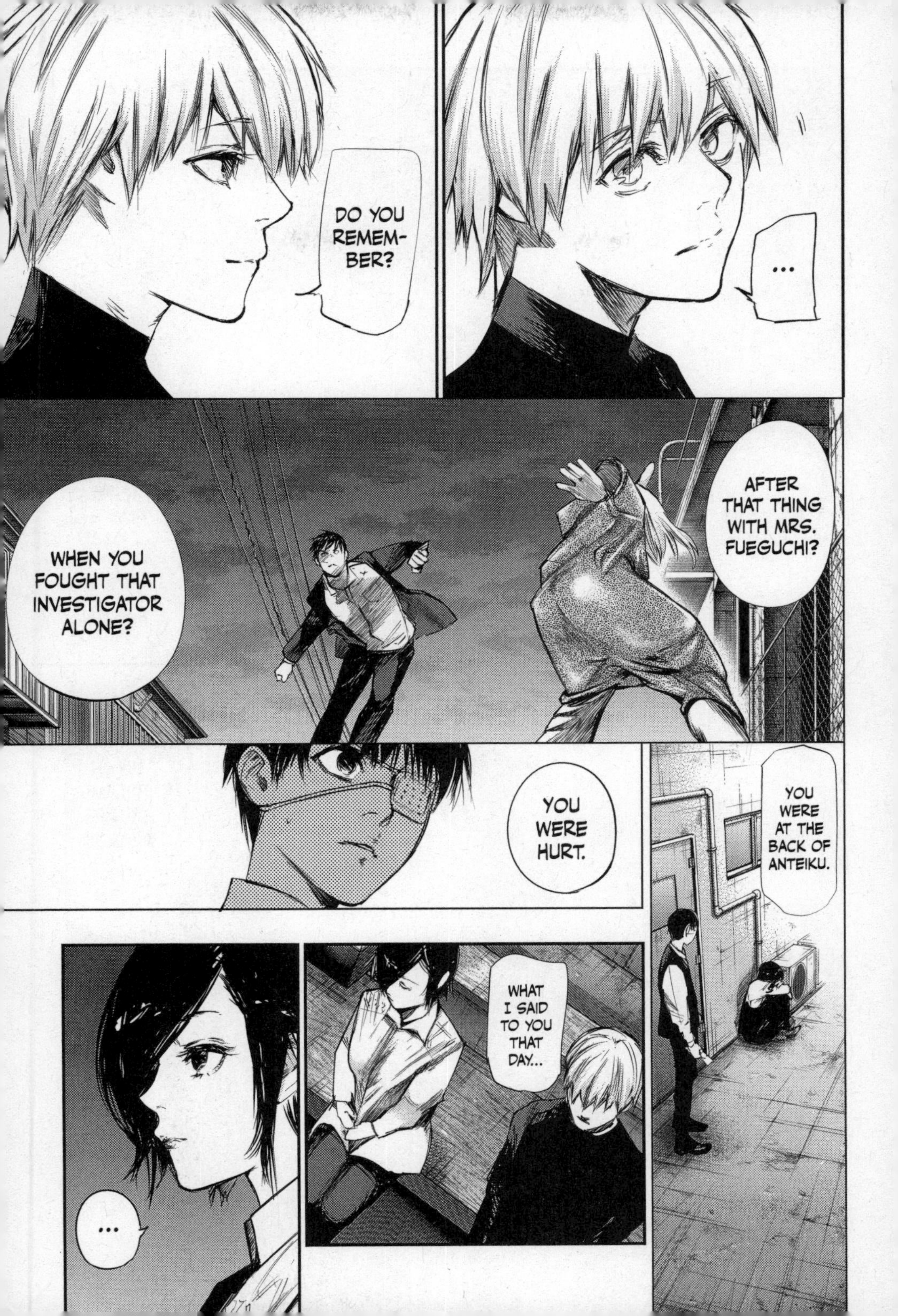
...
DO YOU REMEMBER?
AFTER THAT THING WITH MRS. FUEGUCHI?
WHEN YOU FOUGHT THAT INVESTIGATOR ALONE?
YOU WERE AT THE BACK OF ANTEIKU.
YOU WERE HURT.
WHAT I SAID TO YOU THAT DAY...
...

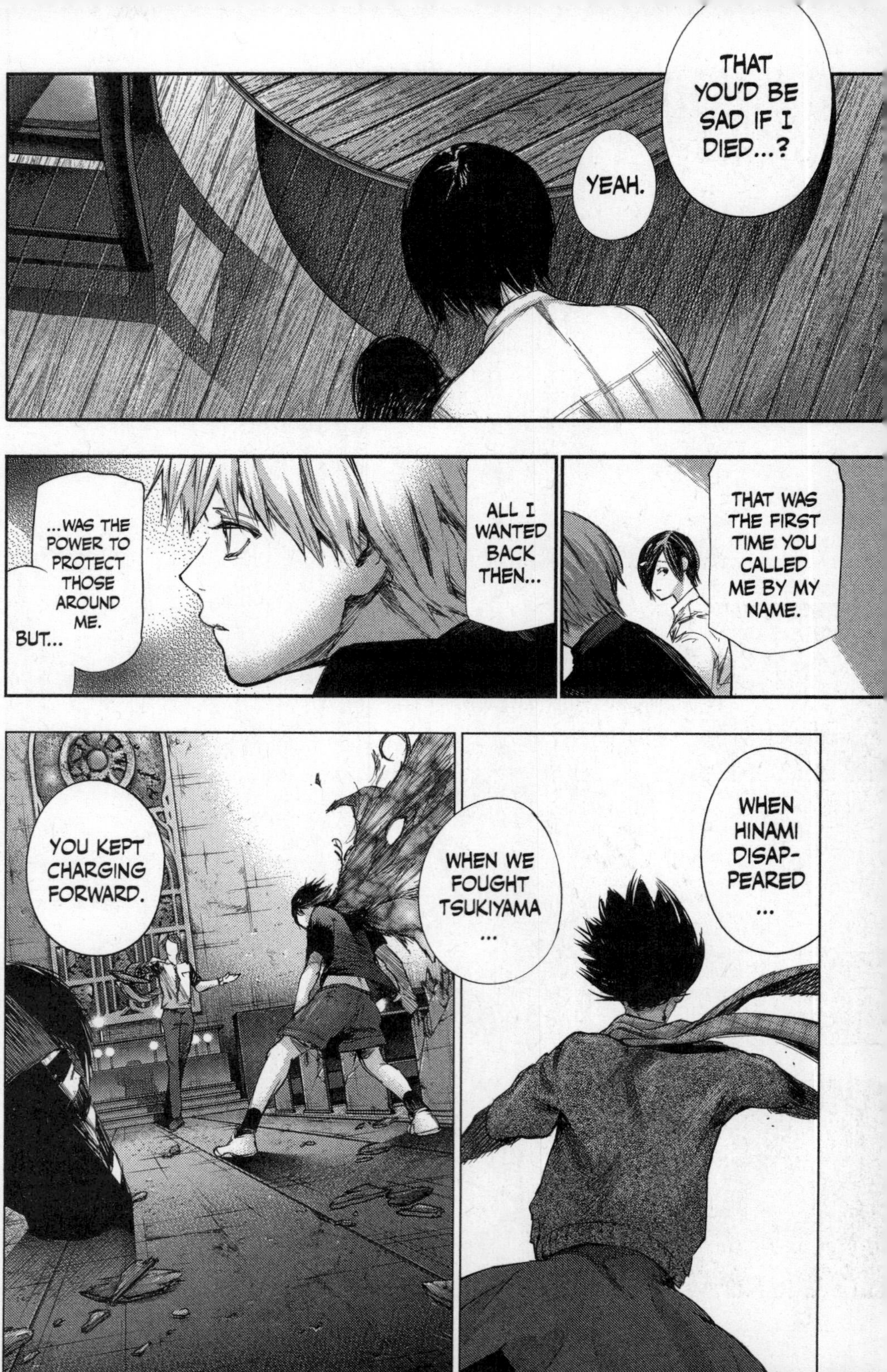
THAT YOU'D BE SAD IF I DIED...?
YEAH.
THAT WAS THE FIRST TIME YOU CALLED ME BY MY NAME.
ALL I WANTED BACK THEN...
...WAS THE POWER TO PROTECT THOSE AROUND ME.
BUT...
WHEN HINAMI DISAP-PEARED...
WHEN WE FOUGHT TSUKIYAMA...
YOU KEPT CHARGING FORWARD.

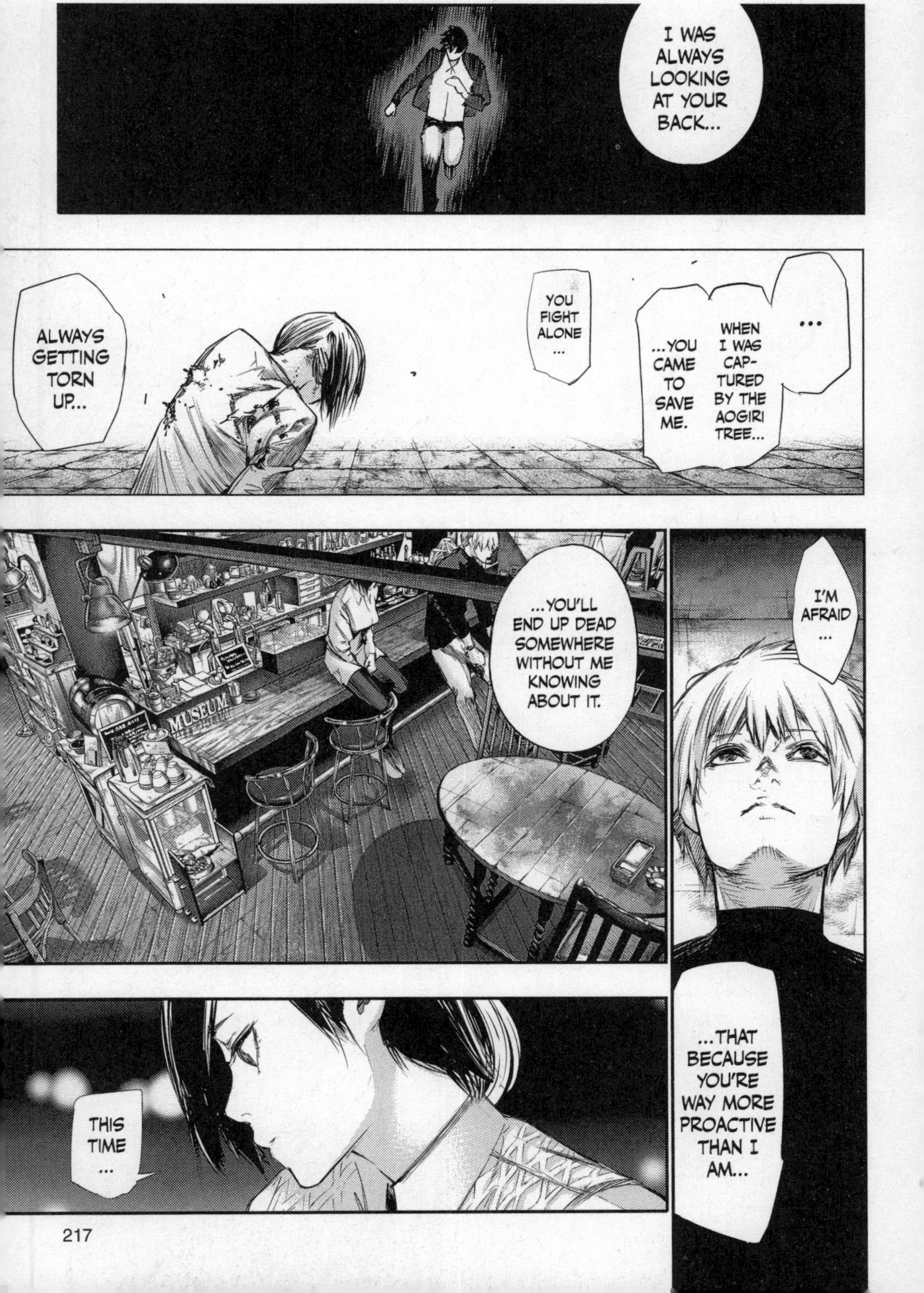
I WAS ALWAYS LOOKING AT YOUR BACK...
...
WHEN I WAS CAP-TURED BY THE AOGIRI TREE...
...YOU CAME TO SAVE ME.
YOU FIGHT ALONE ...
ALWAYS GETTING TORN UP...
I'M AFRAID ...
...THAT BECAUSE YOU'RE WAY MORE PROACTIVE THAN I AM...
...YOU'LL END UP DEAD SOMEWHERE WITHOUT ME KNOWING ABOUT IT.
MUSEUM
THIS TIME ...

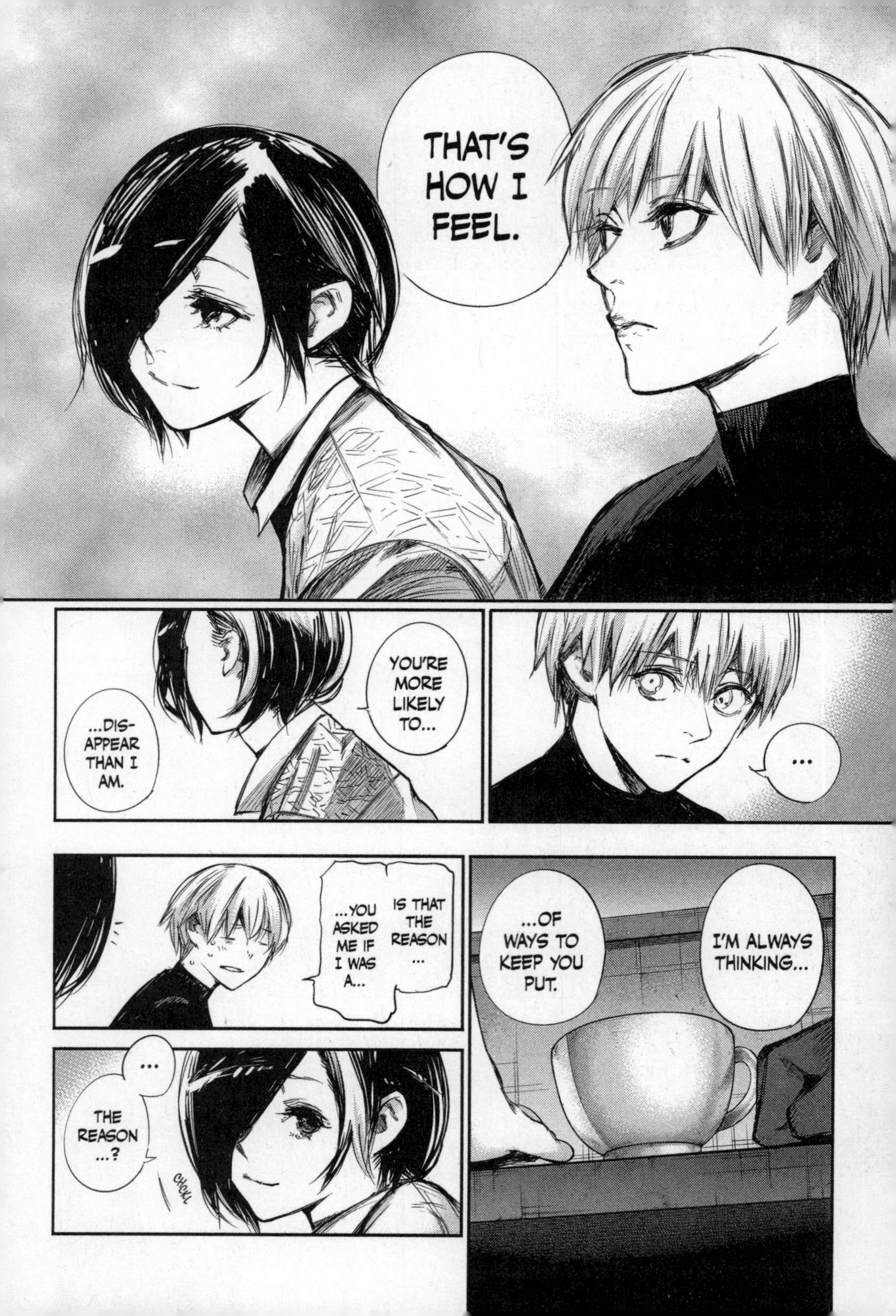
THAT'S HOW I FEEL.
...
YOU'RE MORE LIKELY TO...
...DIS-APPEAR THAN I AM.
I'M ALWAYS THINKING...
...OF WAYS TO KEEP YOU PUT.
IS THAT THE REASON ...
...YOU ASKED ME IF I WAS A...
...
THE REASON ...?
CHCKL

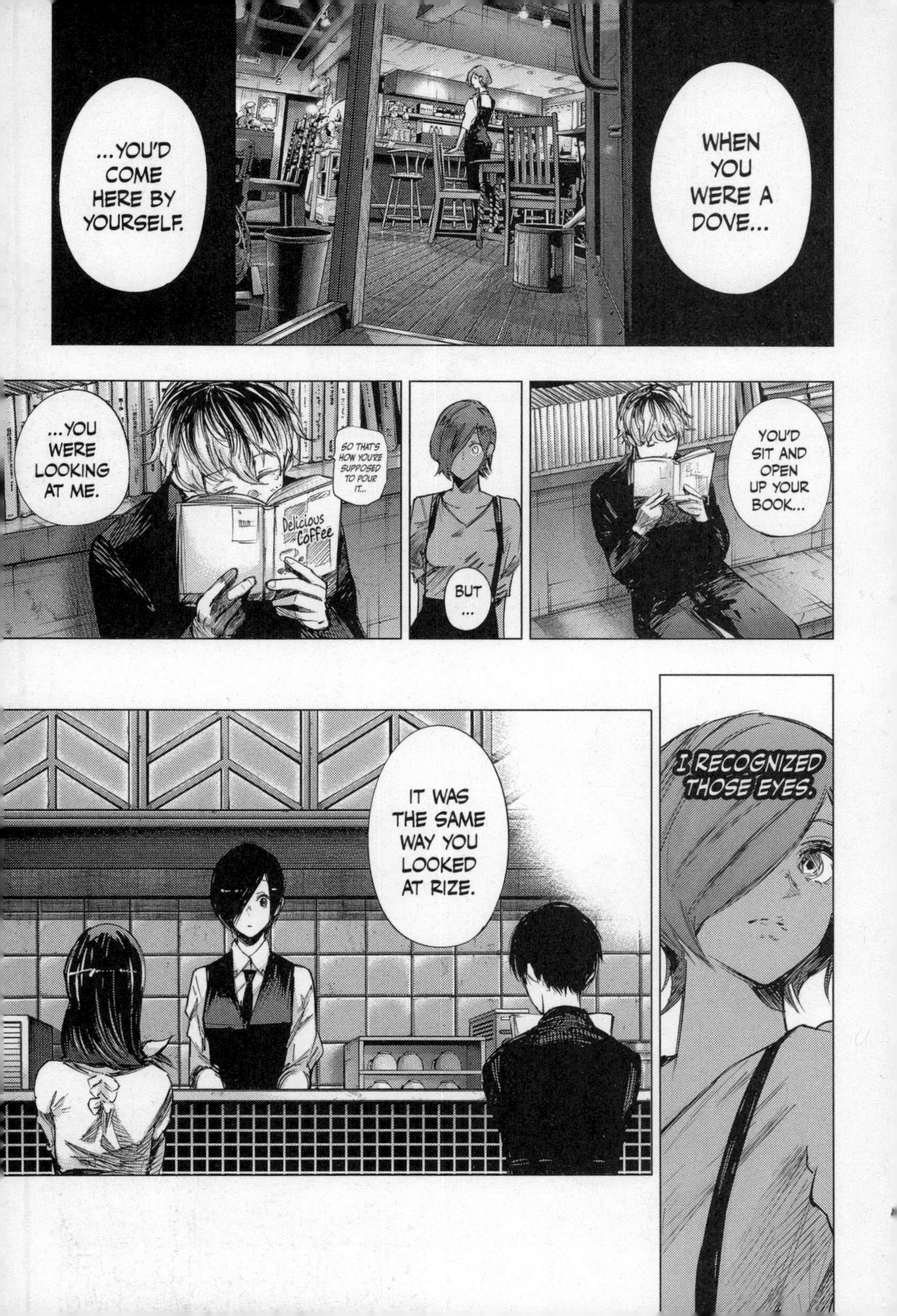
WHEN YOU WERE A DOVE...
...YOU'D COME HERE BY YOURSELF.
YOU'D SIT AND OPEN UP YOUR BOOK...
BUT ...
...YOU WERE LOOKING AT ME.
SO THAT'S HOW YOU'RE SUPPOSED TO POUR IT...
Delicious Coffee
I RECOGNIZED THOSE EYES.
IT WAS THE SAME WAY YOU LOOKED AT RIZE.

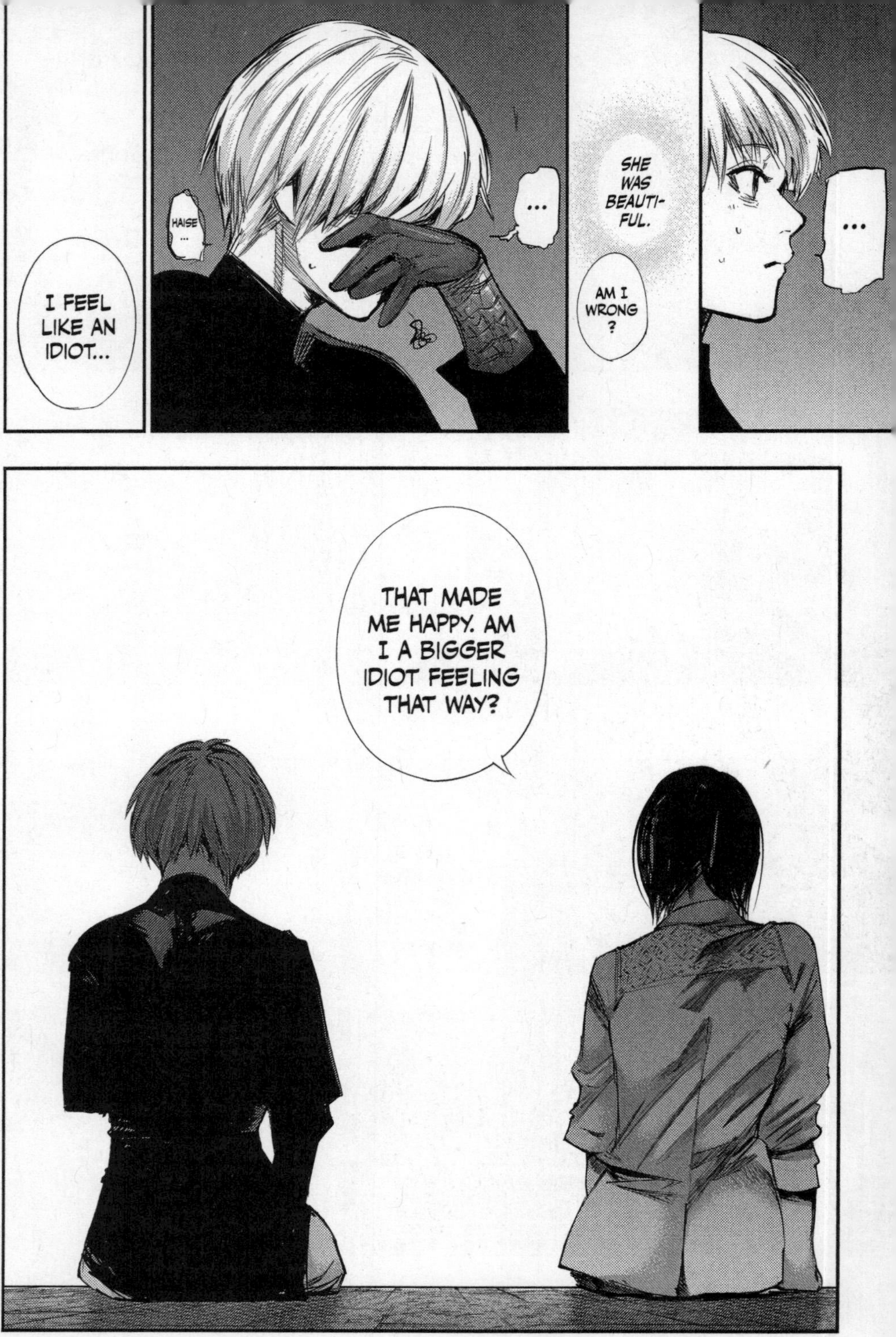
...
SHE WAS BEAUTIFUL.
AM I WRONG?
...
HAISE ...
I FEEL LIKE AN IDIOT...
THAT MADE ME HAPPY. AM I A BIGGER IDIOT FEELING THAT WAY?

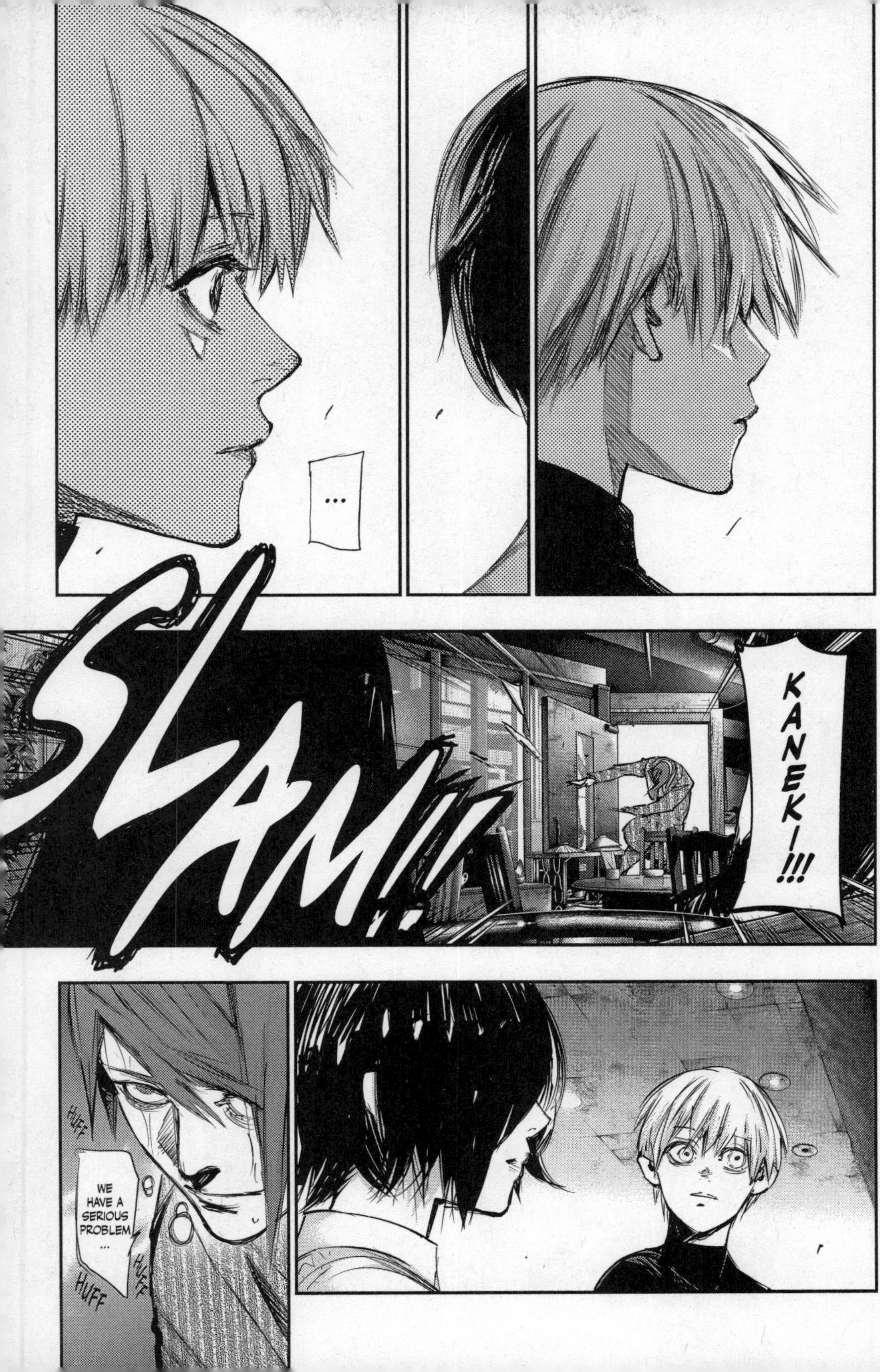
...
KANEKI!!!
SLAM!!
HUFF
WE HAVE A SERIOUS PROBLEM...
HUFF
HUFF

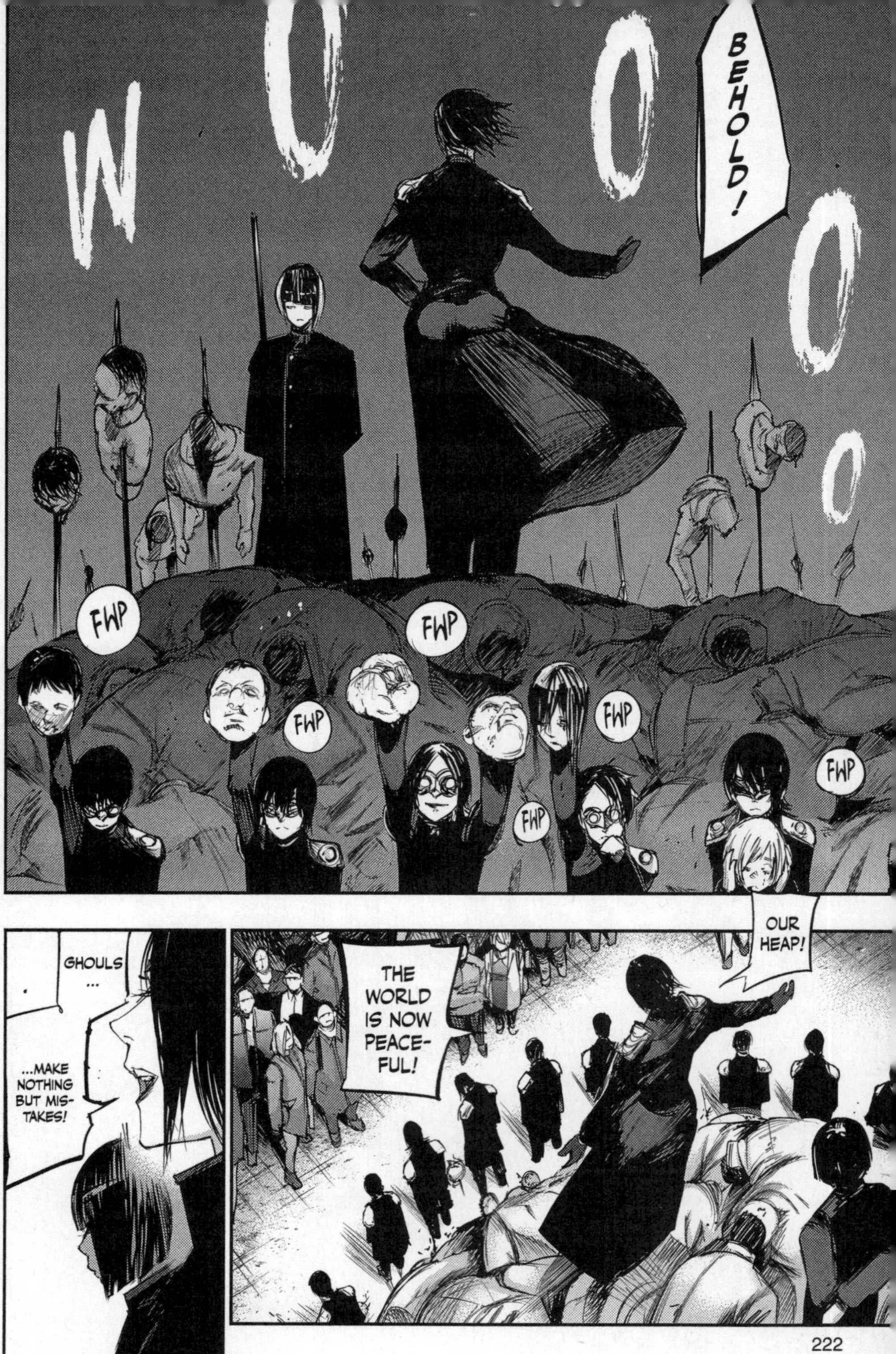
BEHOLD!
WOOOOOOO
FWP
FWP
FWP
FWP
FWP
FWP
OUR HEAP!
THE WORLD IS NOW PEACE-FUL!
GHOULS...
...MAKE NOTHING BUT MIS-TAKES!

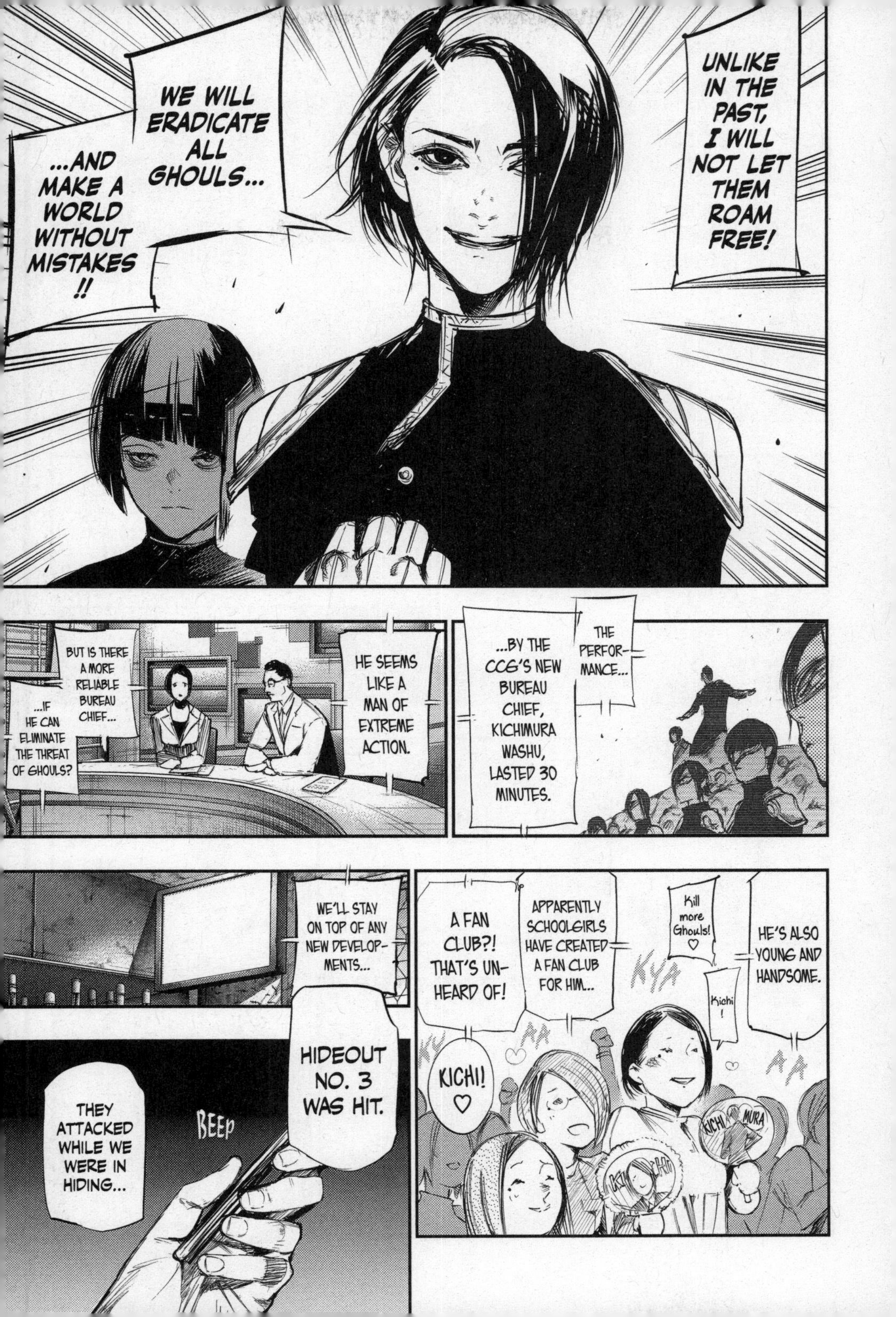
UNLIKE IN THE PAST, I WILL NOT LET THEM ROAM FREE!
WE WILL ERADICATE ALL GHOULS...
...AND MAKE A WORLD WITHOUT MISTAKES !!
THE PERFORMANCE...
...BY THE CCG'S NEW BUREAU CHIEF, KICHIMURA WASHU, LASTED 30 MINUTES.
HE SEEMS LIKE A MAN OF EXTREME ACTION.
BUT IS THERE A MORE RELIABLE BUREAU CHIEF...
...IF HE CAN ELIMINATE THE THREAT OF GHOULS?
HE'S ALSO YOUNG AND HANDSOME.
Kill more Ghouls! ♡
KYA
Kichi!
APPARENTLY SCHOOLGIRLS HAVE CREATED A FAN CLUB FOR HIM...
A FAN CLUB?! THAT'S UNHEARD OF!
AA
KICHI! ♡
KICHI MURA
WE'LL STAY ON TOP OF ANY NEW DEVELOPMENTS...
HIDEOUT NO. 3 WAS HIT.
BEEP
THEY ATTACKED WHILE WE WERE IN HIDING...

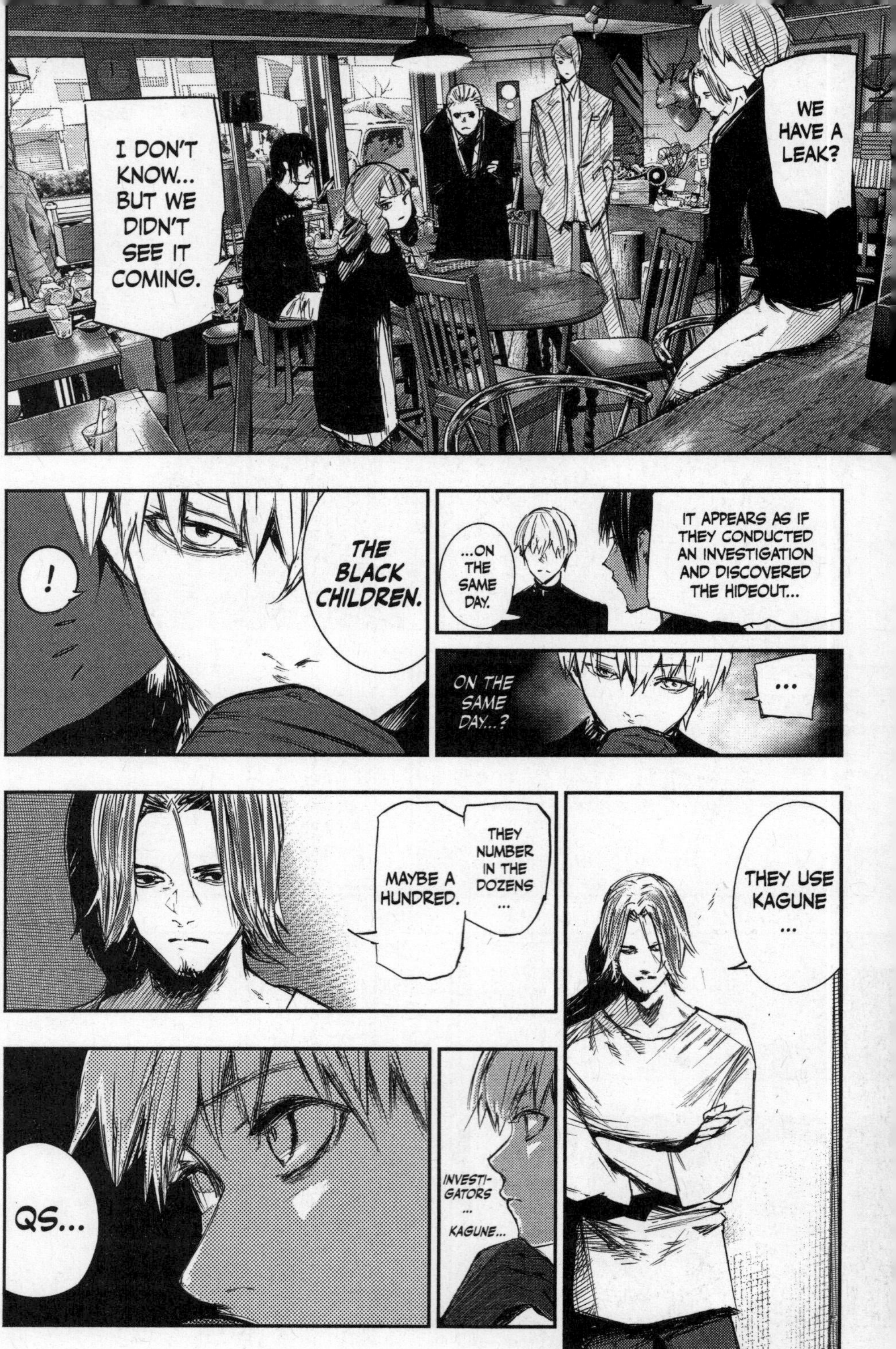
WE HAVE A LEAK?
I DON'T KNOW... BUT WE DIDN'T SEE IT COMING.
IT APPEARS AS IF THEY CONDUCTED AN INVESTIGATION AND DISCOVERED THE HIDEOUT...
...ON THE SAME DAY.
...
ON THE SAME DAY...?
THE BLACK CHILDREN.
!
THEY USE KAGUNE ...
THEY NUMBER IN THE DOZENS ...
MAYBE A HUNDRED.
INVESTI-GATORS ... KAGUNE...
QS...

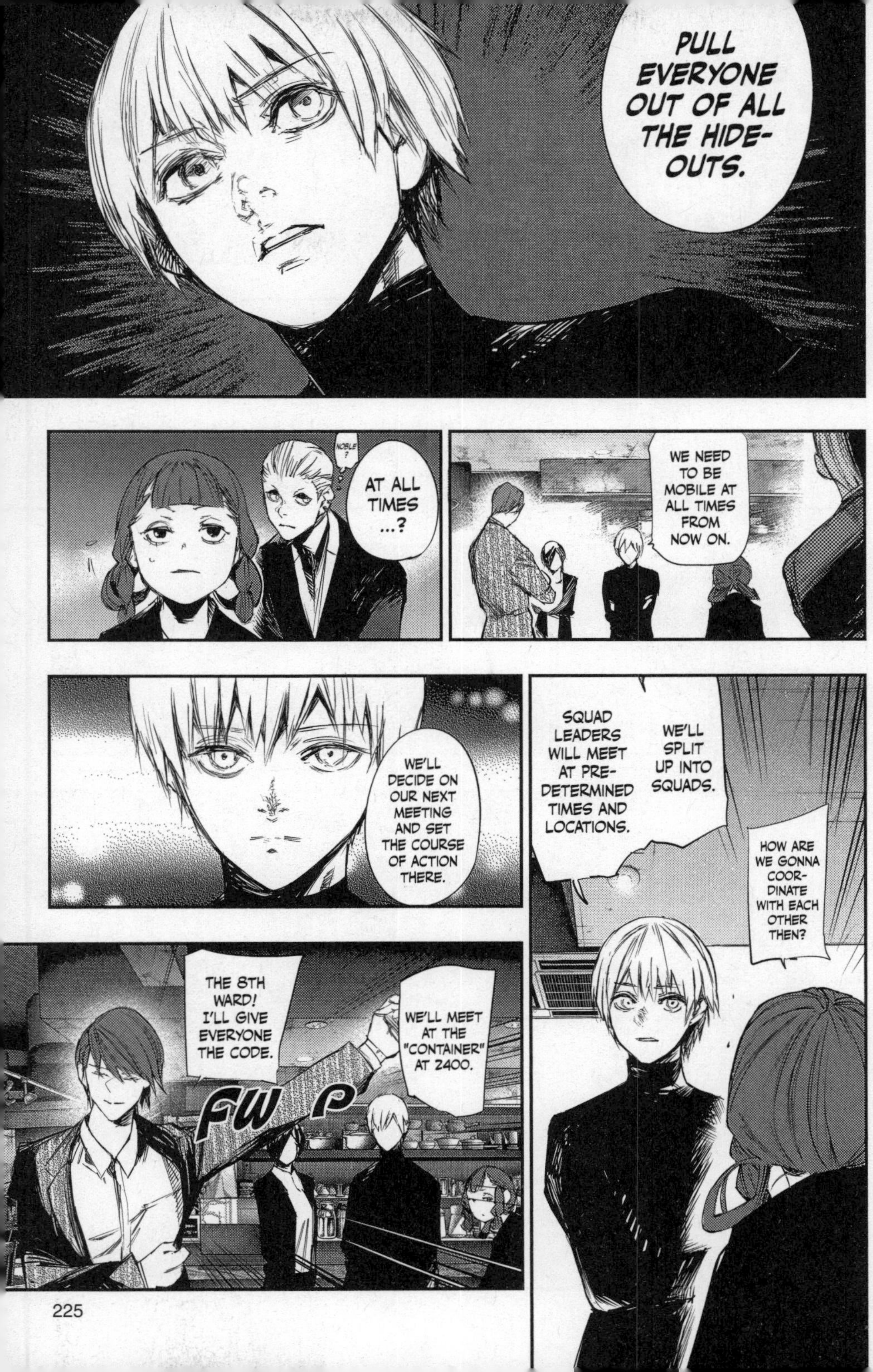
PULL EVERYONE OUT OF ALL THE HIDE-OUTS.
WE NEED TO BE MOBILE AT ALL TIMES FROM NOW ON.
AT ALL TIMES ...?
NOBLE ?
WE'LL SPLIT UP INTO SQUADS.
SQUAD LEADERS WILL MEET AT PRE-DETERMINED TIMES AND LOCATIONS.
HOW ARE WE GONNA COORDINATE WITH EACH OTHER THEN?
WE'LL DECIDE ON OUR NEXT MEETING AND SET THE COURSE OF ACTION THERE.
WE'LL MEET AT THE "CONTAINER" AT 2400.
THE 8TH WARD! I'LL GIVE EVERYONE THE CODE.
FWP

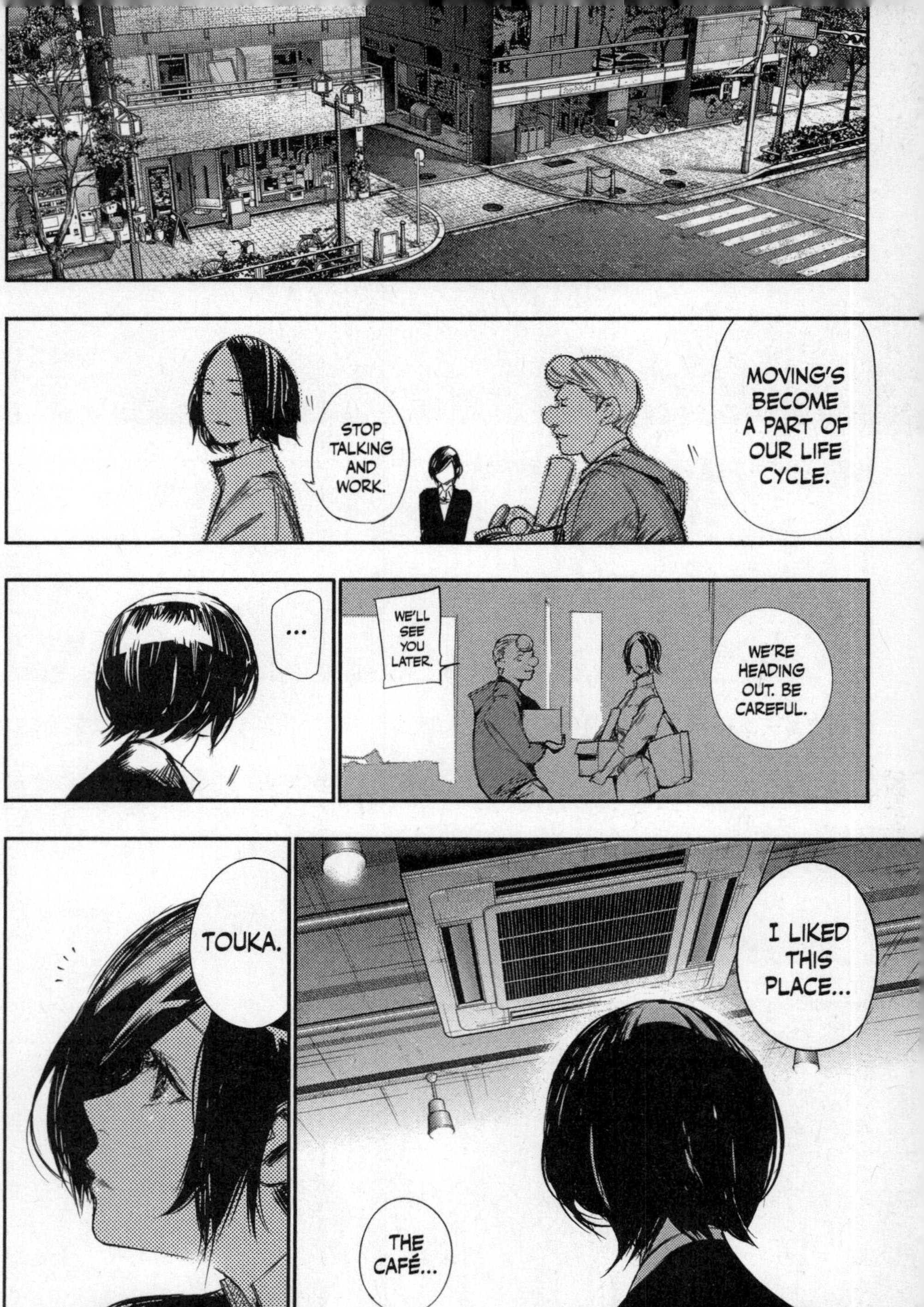
MOVING'S BECOME A PART OF OUR LIFE CYCLE.
STOP TALKING AND WORK.
WE'RE HEADING OUT. BE CAREFUL.
WE'LL SEE YOU LATER.
...
I LIKED THIS PLACE...
THE CAFÉ...
TOUKA.

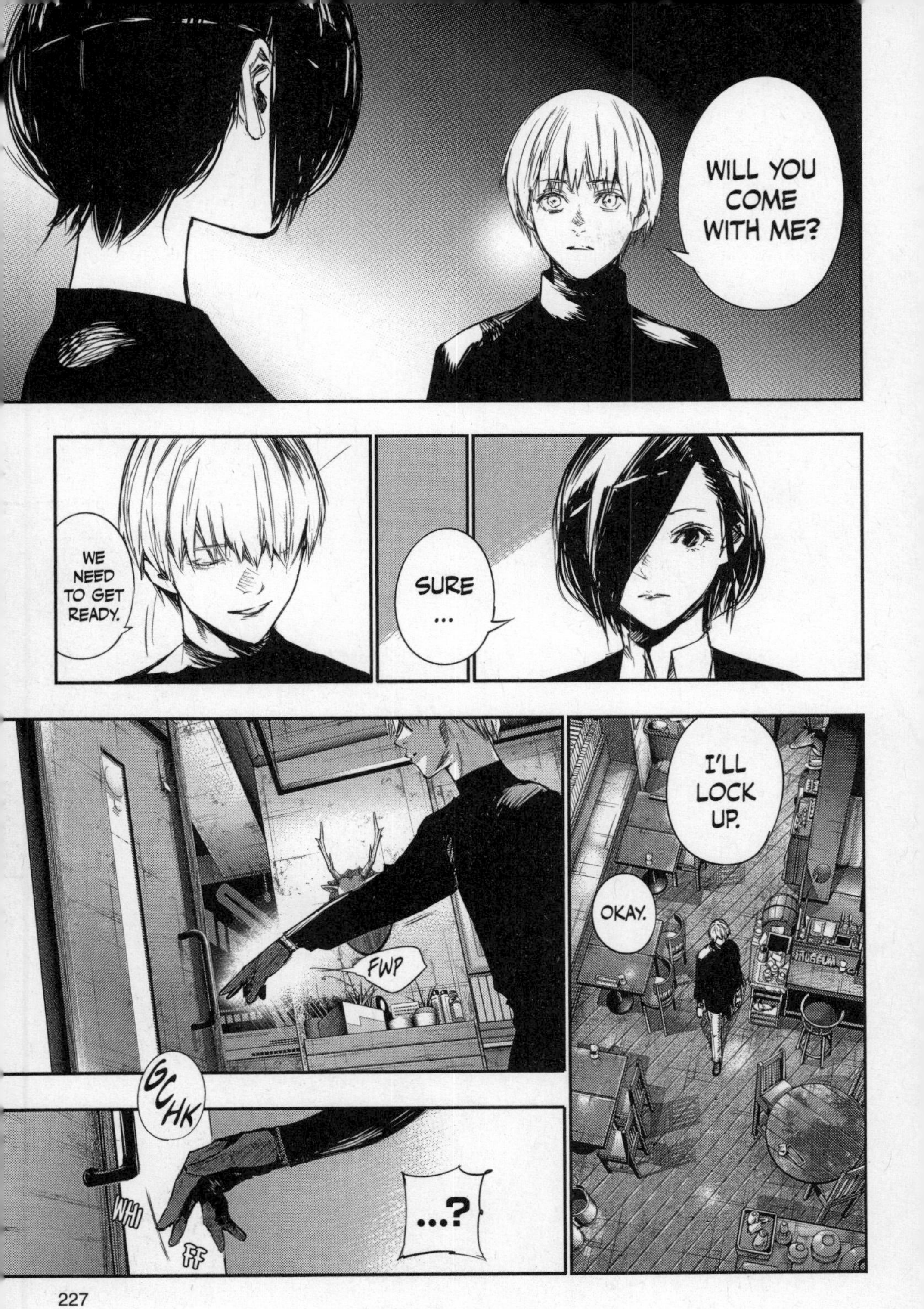
WILL YOU COME WITH ME?
SURE ...
WE NEED TO GET READY.
I'LL LOCK UP.
OKAY.
FWP
GCHK
WHIFF
...?

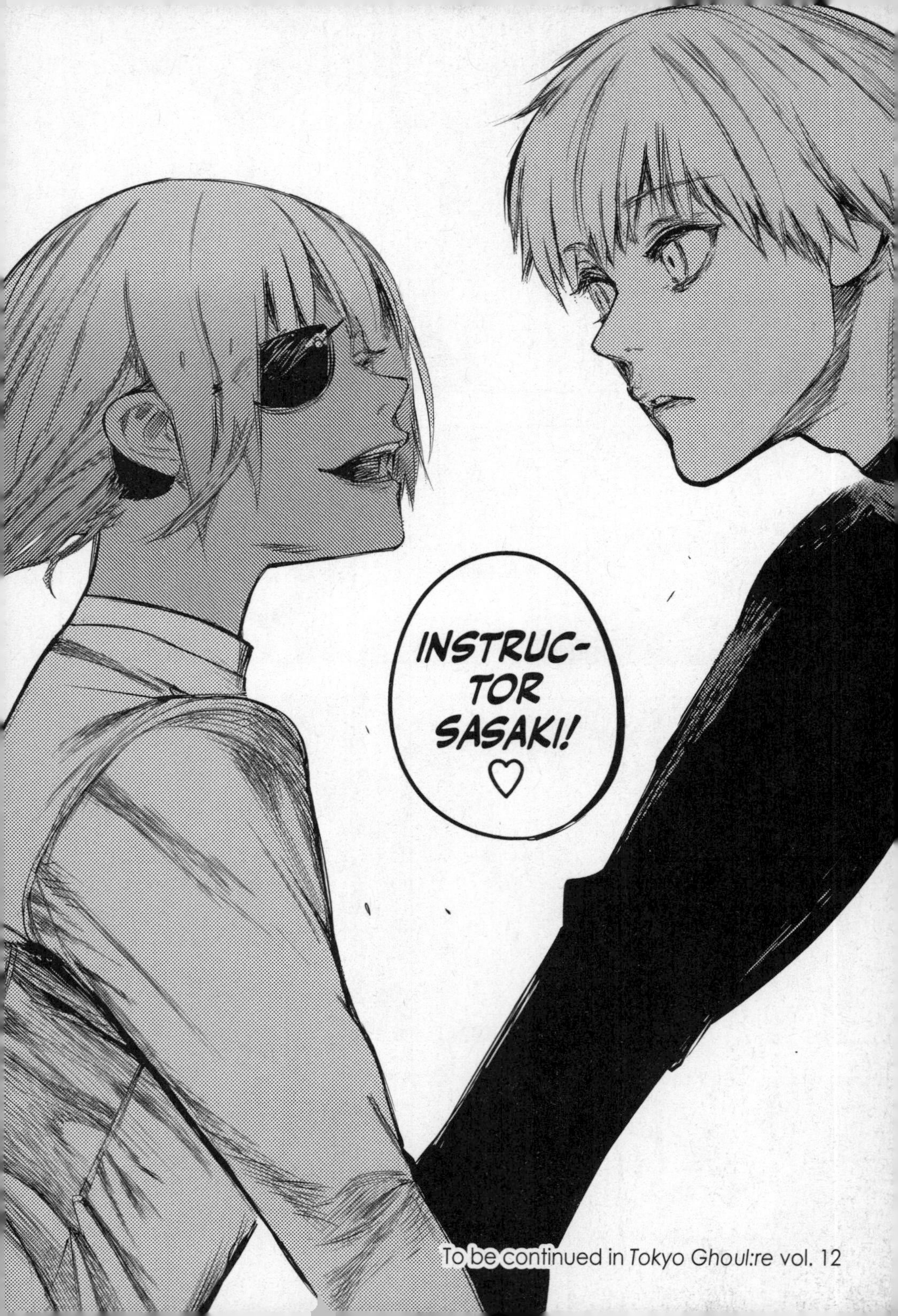
INSTRUC-TOR SASAKI! ♡

To be continued in *Tokyo Ghoul:re* vol. 12

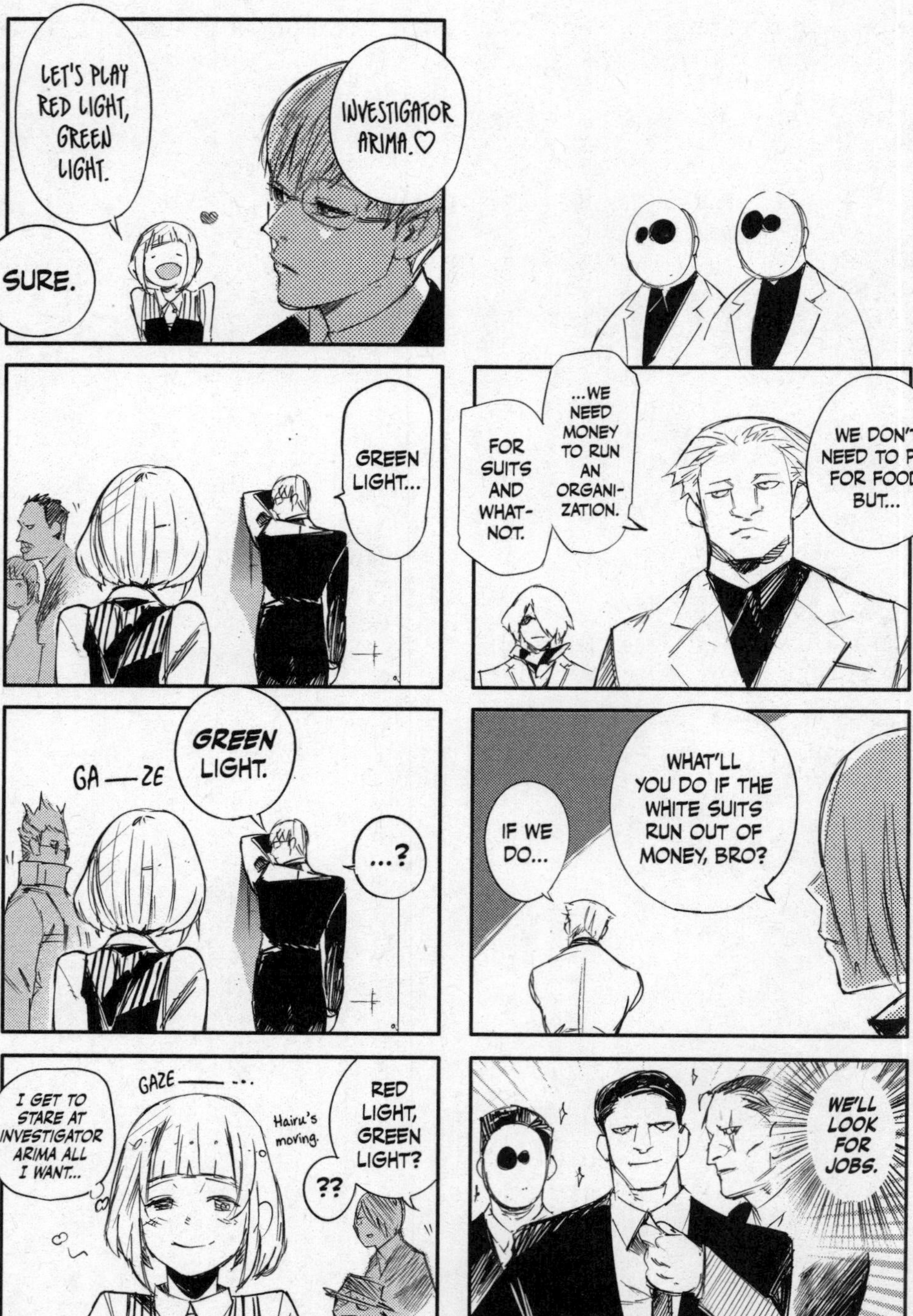
INVESTIGATOR ARIMA.♡
LET'S PLAY RED LIGHT, GREEN LIGHT.
SURE.
WE DON'T NEED TO PAY FOR FOOD, BUT...
...WE NEED MONEY TO RUN AN ORGANI-ZATION.
FOR SUITS AND WHAT-NOT.
GREEN LIGHT...
WHAT'LL YOU DO IF THE WHITE SUITS RUN OUT OF MONEY, BRO?
IF WE DO...
GREEN LIGHT.
GA—ZE
...?
WE'LL LOOK FOR JOBS.
RED LIGHT, GREEN LIGHT?
Hairu's moving.
??
GAZE——...
I GET TO STARE AT INVESTIGATOR ARIMA ALL I WANT...

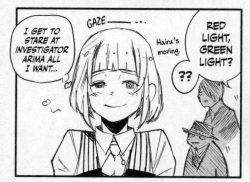

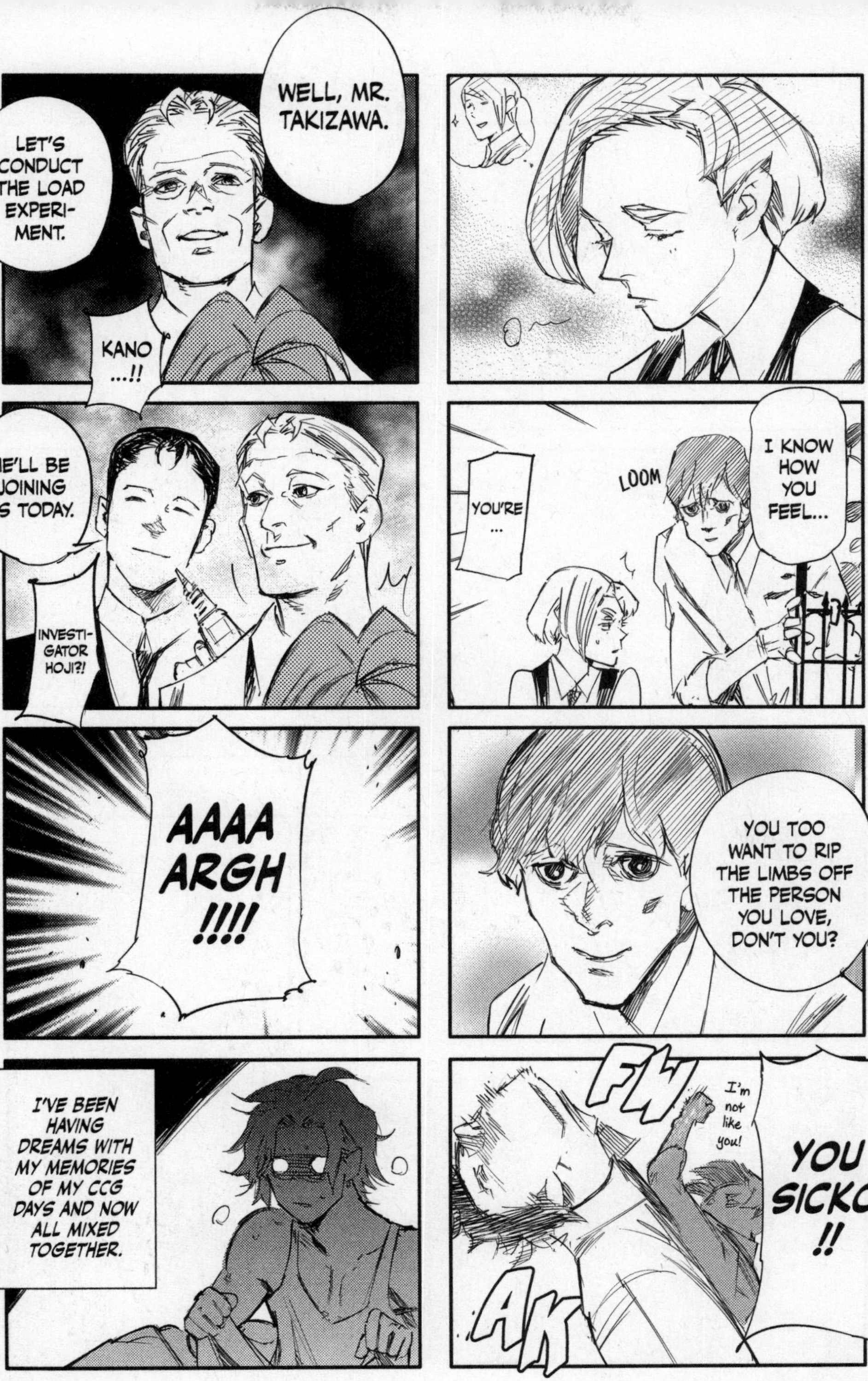
WELL, MR. TAKIZAWA.
LET'S CONDUCT THE LOAD EXPERIMENT.
KANO ...!!
I KNOW HOW YOU FEEL...
LOOM
YOU'RE ...
HE'LL BE JOINING US TODAY.
INVESTIGATOR HOJI?!
YOU TOO WANT TO RIP THE LIMBS OFF THE PERSON YOU LOVE, DON'T YOU?
AAAA ARGH !!!!
FW
I'm not like you!
YOU SICKO !!
AK
I'VE BEEN HAVING DREAMS WITH MY MEMORIES OF MY CCG DAYS AND NOW ALL MIXED TOGETHER.

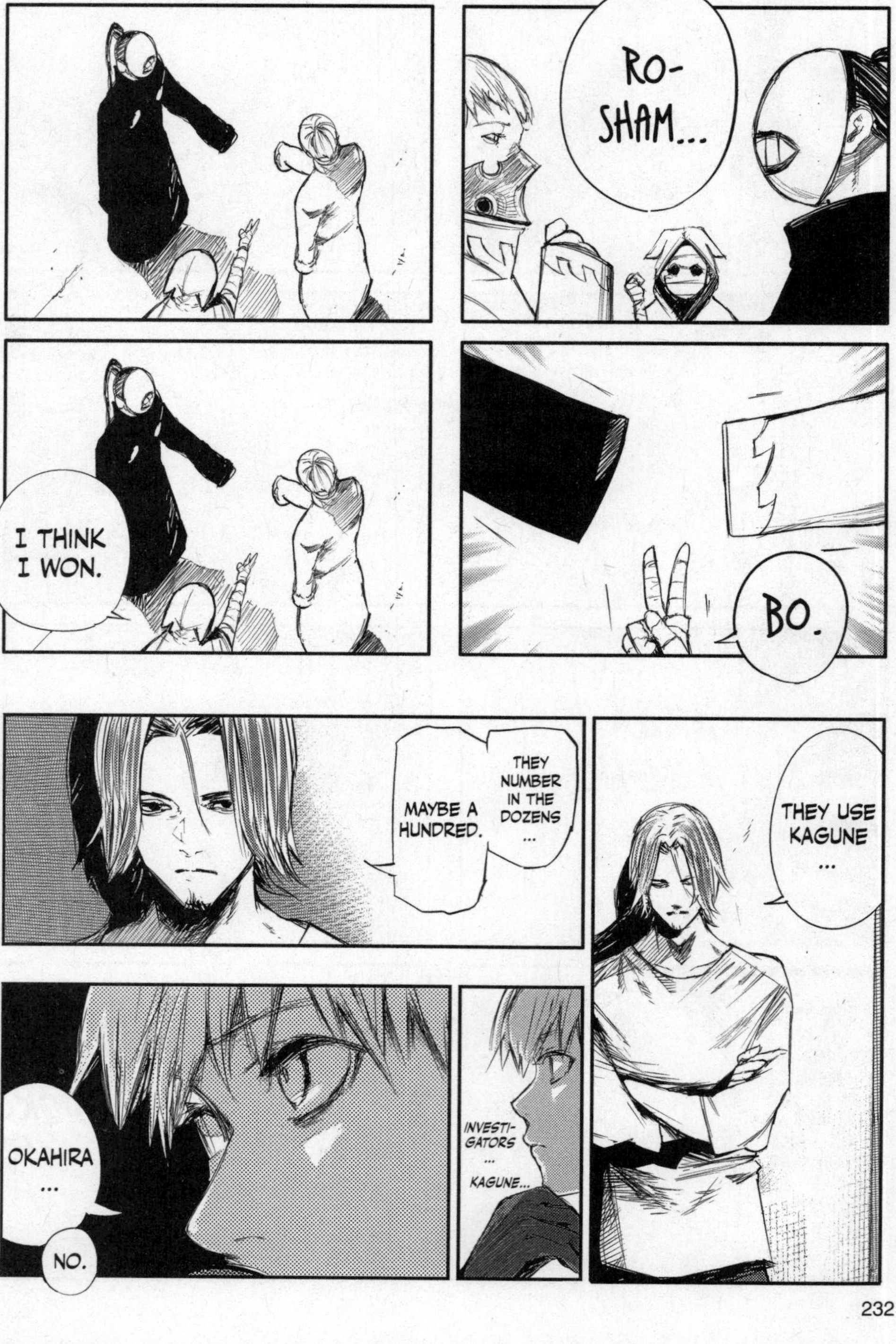
RO-SHAM...
BO.
I THINK I WON.
THEY USE KAGUNE ...
THEY NUMBER IN THE DOZENS ...
MAYBE A HUNDRED.
INVESTI-GATORS ... KAGUNE...
OKAHIRA ...
NO.

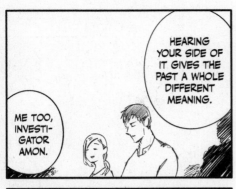

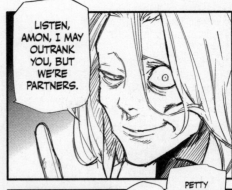

LISTEN, AMON, I MAY OUTRANK YOU, BUT WE'RE PARTNERS.
HEARING YOUR SIDE OF IT GIVES THE PAST A WHOLE DIFFERENT MEANING.
ME TOO, INVESTIGATOR AMON.
PETTY MODESTY WILL AFFECT OUR INVESTIGATION.
FEEL FREE TO VOICE YOUR OPINIONS.
I'M GLAD.
EVERY TIME I LEARN SOMETHING NEW ABOUT MY FATHER...
...IT'S LIKE HE'S ALIVE AGAIN.
... ...
OKAY ...
SEEING HIS GOOFY SIDE REALLY MADE THINGS EASIER.
OH, THAT.
Heh heh
HE SAID YOU HAD THE FUNNIEST EXPRESSION.
TELL ME MORE STORIES ABOUT KUREO MADO.
I HAVE ALL THE TIME IN THE WORLD...
Staff: Hashimoto
Kiyotaka Aihara
Niina
Ippo Yaguchi
Akikuni Nakao
Nomaguchi
Abe
Comic Design: Hideaki Shimada (L.S.D.)
Magazine Design: Miyuki Takaoka (POCKET)
Photography: Wataru Tanaka
Editor: Junpei Matsuo
Volume 12 will be on sale August 2019!

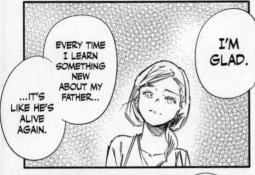

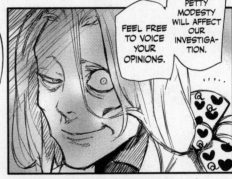

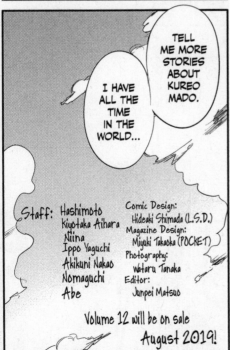

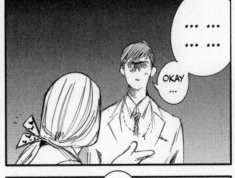

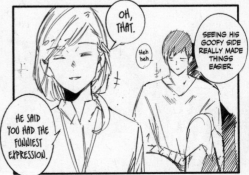

● Hajime
ハジメ

- Age: 11 • Blood type: AB • Height/weight: 155cm/52kg
- Leader of the Oggai A Squad.
- Trained at the CCG's protective institution after his parents were killed by Ghouls. Underwent Kano's Qs procedure when it was discovered that he was a suitable candidate.

SUI ISHIDA is the author of the immensely popular *Tokyo Ghoul* and several *Tokyo Ghoul* one-shots, including one that won second place in the *Weekly Young Jump* 113th Grand Prix award in 2010. *Tokyo Ghoul:re* is the sequel to *Tokyo Ghoul*.

TOKYO GHOUL:re

VOLUME 11
VIZ SIGNATURE EDITION

Story and art by
SUI ISHIDA

First published in Japan in 2014 by SHUEISHA Inc., Tokyo.
English translation rights arranged by SHUEISHA Inc.

Translation Joe Yamazaki
Touch-Up Art & Lettering Vanessa Satone
Design Shawn Carrico
Editor Pancha Diaz

Printed in the U.S.A.

Published by VIZ Media, LLC
P.O. Box 77010
San Francisco, CA 94107

10 9 8 7 6 5 4 3 2 1
First printing, June 2019

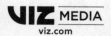

VIZ MEDIA
viz.com

VIZ SIGNATURE
vizsignature.com

ratings.viz.com
RATED T+ OLDER TEEN

PARENTAL ADVISORY
TOKYO GHOUL: RE is rated T+ for Older Teen and is recommended for ages 16 and up. This volume contains violence, gore and sexual situations.

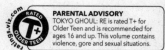

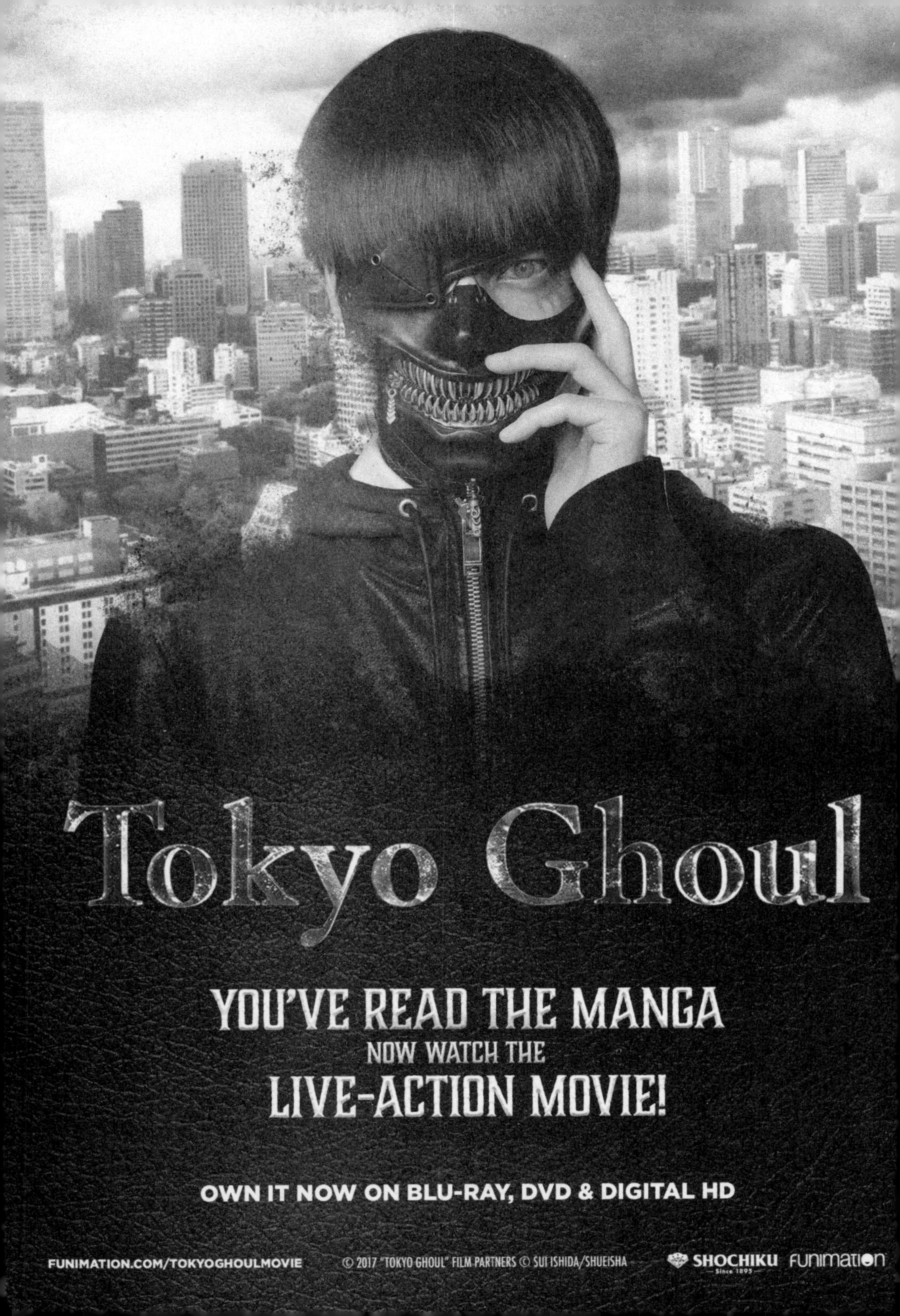
Tokyo Ghoul
YOU'VE READ THE MANGA
NOW WATCH THE
LIVE-ACTION MOVIE!
OWN IT NOW ON BLU-RAY, DVD & DIGITAL HD
FUNIMATION.COM/TOKYOGHOULMOVIE
© 2017 "TOKYO GHOUL" FILM PARTNERS © SUI ISHIDA/SHUEISHA
SHOCHIKU
Since 1895
funimation

TOKYO GHOUL

COMPLETE BOX SET

STORY AND ART BY SUI ISHIDA

KEN KANEKI is an ordinary college student until a violent encounter turns him into the first half-human, half-Ghoul hybrid. Trapped between two worlds, he must survive Ghoul turf wars, learn more about Ghoul society and master his new powers.

Box set collects all fourteen volumes of the original *Tokyo Ghoul* series. Includes an exclusive double-sided poster.

COLLECT THE COMPLETE SERIES

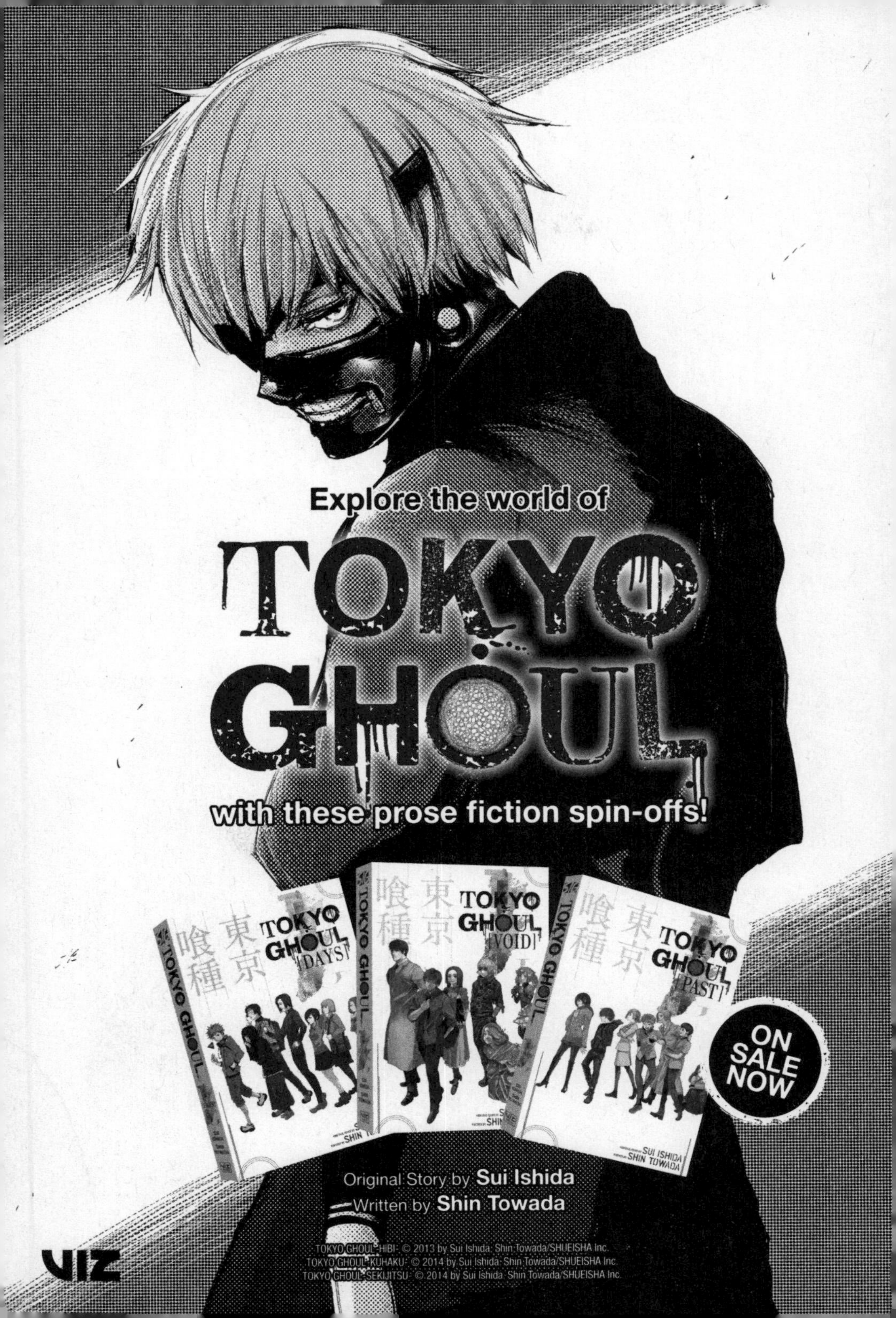

Explore the world of
TOKYO GHOUL
with these prose fiction spin-offs!
東京喰種
TOKYO GHOUL
[DAYS]
東京喰種
TOKYO GHOUL
[VOID]
東京喰種
TOKYO GHOUL
[PAST]
SUI ISHIDA
SHIN TOWADA
ON SALE NOW
Original Story by Sui Ishida
Written by Shin Towada
VIZ
TOKYO GHOUL -HIBI- © 2013 by Sui Ishida, Shin Towada/SHUEISHA Inc.
TOKYO GHOUL -KUHAKU- © 2014 by Sui Ishida, Shin Towada/SHUEISHA Inc.
TOKYO GHOUL -SEKIJITSU- © 2014 by Sui Ishida, Shin Towada/SHUEISHA Inc.

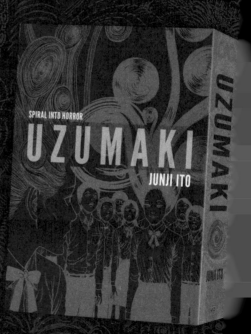

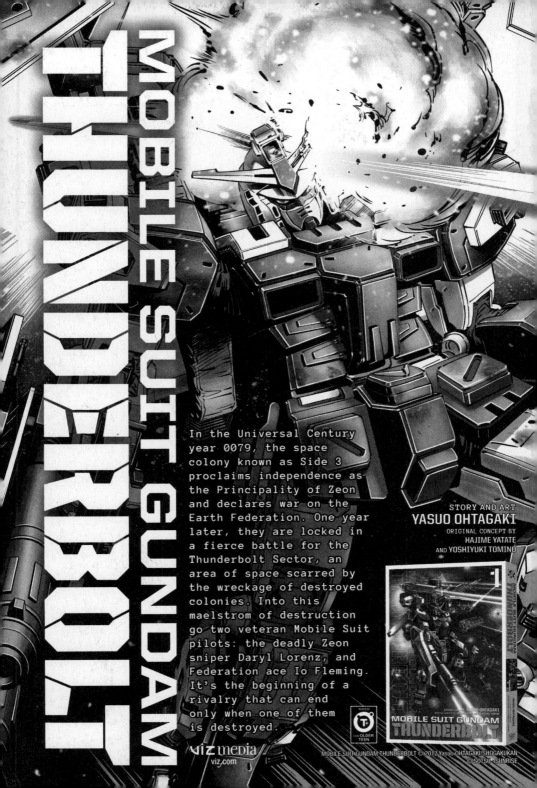

MOBILE SUIT GUNDAM THUNDERBOLT

In the Universal Century year 0079, the space colony known as Side 3 proclaims independence as the Principality of Zeon and declares war on the Earth Federation. One year later, they are locked in a fierce battle for the Thunderbolt Sector, an area of space scarred by the wreckage of destroyed colonies. Into this maelstrom of destruction go two veteran Mobile Suit pilots: the deadly Zeon sniper Daryl Lorenz, and Federation ace Io Fleming. It's the beginning of a rivalry that can end only when one of them is destroyed.

STORY AND ART
YASUO OHTAGAKI
ORIGINAL CONCEPT BY
HAJIME YATATE
AND YOSHIYUKI TOMINO

1
MOBILE SUIT GUNDAM THUNDERBOLT
YASUO OHTAGAKI
MOBILE SUIT GUNDAM
THUNDERBOLT

RATED T+ FOR OLDER TEEN

viz media
viz.com

TOKYO GHOUL:re

This is the last page.
TOKYO GHOUL:re reads right to left.